October 4–5, 2014
Honolulu, HI, USA

I0034589

**Association for Computing Machinery**

*Advancing Computing as a Science & Profession*

# SUI'14
## Proceedings of the 2nd ACM Symposium on
## Spatial User Interaction

*Sponsored by:*
## ACM SIGCHI & ACM SIGGRAPH

*Supported by:*
## Microsoft Research and Interaction Design Foundation

**Association for
Computing Machinery**

*Advancing Computing as a Science & Profession*

**The Association for Computing Machinery**
2 Penn Plaza, Suite 701
New York, New York 10121-0701

**ISBN:** 978-1-4503-2820-3 (Digital)

**ISBN:** 978-1-4503-3371-9 (Print)

Additional copies may be ordered prepaid from:

**ACM Order Department**
PO Box 30777
New York, NY 10087-0777, USA

Phone: 1-800-342-6626 (USA and Canada)
+1-212-626-0500 (Global)
Fax: +1-212-944-1318
E-mail: acmhelp@acm.org
Hours of Operation: 8:30 am – 4:30 pm ET

Printed in the USA

# SUI 2014 Chairs' Welcome

It is our great pleasure to welcome you to the second ACM Symposium on Spatial User Interaction - SUI'14. This event focuses on the user interface challenges that appear when users interact in the space where the flat, two-dimensional, digital world meets the volumetric, physical, three-dimensional (3D) space we live in. This considers both spatial input as well as output, with an emphasis on the issues around the interaction between humans and systems. The goal of the symposium is to provide an intensive exchange between academic and industrial researchers working in the area of SUI and to foster discussions among participants. The SUI symposium was held October 4–5, 2014, in Honolulu, USA.

The call for papers attracted 62 submissions from Asia, Europe, Australia, and North and South America in all areas of Spatial User Interaction research. The international program committee consisting of 19 experts in the topic areas and the three program chairs handled the highly competitive and selective review process. Every submission received at least four detailed reviews, two from members of the international program committee and two or more from external reviewers. The reviewing process was double-blind, where only the program chairs as well as the program committee member, who was assigned to each paper to identify external reviewers, knew the identity of the authors. In the end, the program committee accepted overall 18 (11 long papers plus 7 short papers) out of 62 submissions, which corresponds to an acceptance rate of 29% in total. Additionally, 25 posters complement the program and appear in the proceedings. Furthermore, several demos were presented at the symposium. The topics range from spatial interaction techniques, gestures, vision in 3D space, spatial applications, to interaction with multi-touch technologies and spatial interaction in augmented reality. We hope that these proceedings will serve as a valuable reference for Spatial User Interaction researchers and developers.

Putting together the content for SUI'14 was a team effort. We first thank the authors for providing the content of the program. Special thanks go to the members of the international program committee, who successfully dealt with the reviewing load. We also thank the external reviewers.

Gerd Bruder and Rob Teather handled the posters, Jason Leigh and Hideki Koike the demonstrations. We thank our social and web chair Florian Daiber, our awards chairs Bruce Thomas and Patrick Baudisch, our publication chairs Kyle Johnsen and Scott Kuhl, and Tobias Isenberg, Mark Hancock, Kiyoshi Kiyokawa for being SUI 2014 publicity chairs. The local organization team, led by the general chair, deserves many thanks for organizing the event. James Stewart from PCS assisted by providing and maintaining the reviewing system. Lisa Tolles from ACM and Sheridan Communications helped greatly to create the proceedings. Our company and universities, Microsoft Research, the University of Hamburg, York University and the University of Southern California and colleagues supported us in this endeavor. Finally, we thank the sponsoring organizations, the ACM Special Interest Groups on Graphics and Human-Computer Interaction (SIGGRAPH, SIGCHI) for co-sponsoring this event.

We hope that you will find our program interesting, and that SUI'14 will inspire you to discuss and share ideas with other researchers and practitioners from institutions around the world.

**Andy Wilson**
*SUI'14 General Chair*

**Frank Steinicke, Evan Suma, Wolfgang Stuerzlinger**
*SUI'14 Program Chairs*

# Table of Contents

## Session: Spatial Pointing and Touching

## Keynote Address

## Poster Session

# SUI 2014 Symposium Organization

**General Chair:** Andy Wilson *(Microsoft Research, USA)*

**Program Chairs:** Frank Steinicke *(University of Hamburg, Germany)*
Evan Suma *(University of Southern California, USA)*
Wolfgang Stuerzlinger *(York University, Canada)*

**Poster Chairs:** Rob Teather *(McMaster University, Canada)*
Gerd Bruder *(University of Hamburg, Germany)*

**Demo Chairs:** Jason Leigh *(University of Hawaii, USA)*
Hideki Koike *(Tokyo Institute of Technology, Japan)*

**Publication Chairs:** Kyle Johnsen *(University of Georgia, USA)*
Scott Kuhl *(Michigan Tech, USA)*

**Web & Social Media Chair:** Florian Daiber *(DFKI, Germany)*

**Publicity Chairs:** Mark Hancock *(University of Waterloo, Canada)*
Tobias Isenberg *(INRIA, France)*
Kiyoshi Kiyokawa *(Osaka University, Japan)*

**Award Chairs:** Bruce Thomas *(University of South Australia, Australia)*
Patrick Baudisch *(Hasso-Plattner-Institut, Germany)*

**Program Committee:** Ferran Argelaguet Sanz *(INRIA, France)*
Gerd Bruder *(University of Hamburg, Germany)*
Bruno De Araujo *(INRIA Nord Lille, France)*
Steven K. Feiner *(Columbia University, USA)*
Martin Hachet *(INRIA at Bordeaux, France)*
Victoria Interrante *(University of Minnesota, USA)*
Manfred Lau *(Lancaster University, UK)*
Joseph LaViola *(University of Central Florida, USA)*
Christian Sandor *(Nara Institute of Science and Technology, Japan)*
Rob Teather *(McMaster University, Canada)*
Kazuki Takashima *(Tohoku University, Japan)*
Daniel Keefe *(University of Minnesota, USA)*
Tobias Isenberg *(INRIA-Saclay, France)*
Scott Kuhl *(Michigan Technological University, USA)*
Tobias Höllerer *(University of California, Santa Barbara, USA)*
Andreas Butz *(University of Munich, Germany)*
Robert W. Lindeman *(Worcester Polytechnic Institute, USA)*
Matt Adcock *(CSIRO, Australia)*
Petra Isenberg *(INRIA-Saclay, France)*

**Additional reviewers:**

Andujar, Carlos
Anslow, Craig
Ardouin, Jerome
Arif, Ahmed
Avellino, Ignacio
Azuma, Ronald
Barentzen, J. Andreas
Badam, Sriram Karthik
Bae, Seok-Hyung
Balakrishnan, Ravin
Billinghurst, Mark
Boring, Sebastian
Bousseau, Adrien
Bowden, Richard
Buchanan, Sarah
Buschek, Daniel
Cauchard, Jessica
Cernea, Daniel
Chen, Xiang 'Anthony'
Chen, Xilin
Cheng, Kelvin
Chong, Ming Ki
Couture, Nadine
Dünser, Andreas
Dachselt, Raimund
Davoudi, Anahita
Dey, Arindam
Dingle, Brent
Duval, Thierry
Echtler, Florian
Ens, Barrett
Ferwerda, Bruce
Gauglitz, Steffen
Giesler, Alexander
Grossman, Tovi
Gunn, Chris
Guo, Rongkai
Hancock, Mark
Hayashi, Eiji
Henzen, Christin
Hilliges, Otmar
Huang, Weidong
Huang, Yingdan
Humayoun, Shah Rukh
Jacob, Robert

Jankowski, Jacek
Jeon, Myounghoon
Jerald, Jason
Jorge, Joaquim
Jota, Ricardo
Kalwar, Santosh
Kane, Bridget
Kara, Levent Burak
Kato, Hirokazu
Katzakis, Nicholas
Kim, Jeeeun
Kin, Kenrick
Kirkham, Reuben
Kiyokawa, Kiyoshi
Knudsen, Soren
Kohli, Luv
Kopper, Regis
Korsakov, Fedor
Kotranza, Aaron
Kratz, Sven
Krichenbauer, Max
Kunz, Benjamin
Lau, Rynson
LeVan, Samantha
Lindlbauer, David
Lischke, Lars
Liu, Li
Livingston, Mark
Lopez-Gulliver, Roberto
Lu, Zhihan
Luebke, Arno
Marzo, Asier
Merienne, Frederic
Mittal, Manas
Mohler, Betty
Moscovich, Tomer
Moser, Kenny
Nguyen, Huyen
Nuernberger, Benjamin
Özacar, Kasim
Orbay, Günay
Ortega, Michael
Ortega, Michael
Peck, Tabitha
Poor, G Michael

**Additional reviewers**
**(continued):**

| | |
|---|---|
| Pusch, Andreas | Tang, Anthony |
| Raynal, Mathieu | Thomas, Bruce |
| Reuter, Patrick | Valkov, Dimitar |
| Roudaut, Anne | Veas, Eduardo |
| Sakamoto, Daisuke | Verma, Ansh |
| Samavati, Faramarz | Vi, Chi |
| Sanders, Betsy | Wacharamanotham, Chat |
| Sato, Tomokazu | Waegel, Ky |
| Scerbo, Siroberto | Wagner, Julie |
| Schaub, Florian | Walker, James |
| Schemali, Leila | Wartell, Zachary |
| Schroeder, David | Weir, Peter |
| Seo, Stela | Welch, Greg |
| Shizuki, Buntarou | Whitton, Mary |
| Simeone, Adalberto | Willemsen, Pete |
| Singer, Leif | Winkler, Christian |
| Singh, Karan | Wozniak, Pawel |
| Smith, Ross | Wobbrock, Jacob |
| Steed, Anthony | Xie, Xianshi |
| Steinicke, Frank | Yamamoto, Goshiro |
| Taketomi, Takafumi | Young, James |
| Takouachet, Nawel | Yuichiro, Fujimoto |
| | Zhou, Ming |

# The Coming Age of Computer Graphics and the Evolution of Language

**Ken Perlin**

New York University, Media Research Lab

715 Broadway, NY, NY

## ABSTRACT

Sometime in the coming years — whether through ubiquitous projection, AR glasses, smart contact lenses, retinal implants or some technology as yet unknown — we will live in an *eccescopic* world, where everything we see around us will be augmented by computer graphics, including our own appearance. In a sense, we are just now starting to enter the Age of Computer Graphics.

As children are born into this brave new world, what will their experience be? Face to face communication, both in-person and over great distances, will become visually enhanced, and any tangible object can become an interface to digital information [1]. Hand gestures will be able to produce visual artifacts.

After these things come to pass, how will future generations of children evolve natural language itself [2]? How might they think and speak differently about the world around them? What will life in such a world be like for those who are native born to it?

We will present some possibilities, and some suggestions for empirical ways to explore those possibilities now — without needing to wait for those smart contact lenses.

## Author Keywords
Augmented reality; eccescopy; language; gesture

## ACM Classification Keywords
H.5.1 Multimedia Information Systems: Artificial, augmented, and virtual realities; H.5.2 User Interfaces (D.2.2, H.1.2, I.3.6): Interaction styles (e.g., commands, menus, forms, direct manipulation); H.5.3 Group and Organization Interfaces: Computer-supported cooperative work

## BIO
Ken Perlin, a professor in the Department of Computer Science at New York University, directs the NYU Games For Learning Institute, and is a participating faculty member in the NYU Media and Games Network (MAGNET). He was also founding director of the Media Research Laboratory and director of the NYU Center for Advanced Technology. His research interests include graphics, animation, augmented and mixed reality, user interfaces, science education and multimedia. He received an Academy Award for Technical Achievement from the Academy of Motion Picture Arts and Sciences for his noise and turbulence procedural texturing techniques, which are widely used in feature films and television, as well as the 2008 ACM/SIGGRAPH Computer Graphics Achievement Award, the TrapCode award for achievement in computer graphics research, the NYC Mayor's award for excellence in Science and Technology, the Sokol award for outstanding Science faculty at NYU, and a Presidential Young Investigator Award from the National Science Foundation. He has served on the program committee of the AAAS, was general chair of the UIST2010 conference, and has been a featured artist at the Whitney Museum of American Art.

Dr. Perlin received his Ph.D. in Computer Science from New York University, and a B.A. in theoretical mathematics from Harvard University. Before working at NYU he was Head of Software Development at R/GREENBERG Associates in New York, NY. Prior to that he was the System Architect for computer generated animation at Mathematical Applications Group, Inc (MAGI).

[1] Ishii, H., and Tangible Media Group, "Tangible Bits: Towards Seamless Interface between People, Bits, and Atoms," NTT Publishing Co., Ltd., Tokyo, Japan, June 2000 (ISBN4-7571-0053-3)

[2] Senghas, A., and M. Coppola 2001 "Children creating language: How Nicaraguan Sign Language acquired a spatial grammar" *Psychological Science*, **12, 4**: 323-328.

*SUI'14*, October 4–5, 2014, Honolulu, HI, USA.
ACM 978-1-4503-2820-3/14/10.
http://dx.doi.org/10.1145/2659766.2661116

# Ethereal Planes: A Design Framework for 2D Information Spaces in 3D Mixed Reality Environments

**Barrett Ens**
University of Manitoba
Winnipeg, Canada
bens@cs.umanitoba.ca

**Juan David Hincapié-Ramos**
University of Manitoba
Winnipeg, Canada
jdhr@cs.umanitoba.ca

**Pourang Irani**
University of Manitoba
Winnipeg, Canada
irani@cs.umanitoba.ca

## ABSTRACT

Information spaces are virtual workspaces that help us manage information by mapping it to the physical environment. This widely influential concept has been interpreted in a variety of forms, often in conjunction with mixed reality. We present Ethereal Planes, a design framework that ties together many existing variations of 2D information spaces. Ethereal Planes is aimed at assisting the design of user interfaces for next-generation technologies such as head-worn displays. From an extensive literature review, we encapsulated the common attributes of existing novel designs in seven design dimensions. Mapping the reviewed designs to the framework dimensions reveals a set of common usage patterns. We discuss how the Ethereal Planes framework can be methodically applied to help inspire new designs. We provide a concrete example of the framework's utility during the design of the Personal Cockpit, a window management system for head-worn displays.

## Author Keywords

Information spaces; mixed reality; design framework; head-worn displays; spatial user interfaces

## ACM Classification Keywords

H.5.2 **Information Interfaces and Presentation]**: User Interfaces – Theory and methods

## INTRODUCTION

The recent proliferation of low-cost yet robust display and sensing technologies is opening the door to new paradigms for everyday computing. Displays and sensors are quickly becoming small and lightweight enough for wearable applications while approaching benchmarks in latency and fidelity that make them practical. Similar to the shift from mouse and keyboard toward the more intuitive paradigm of direct touchscreen manipulation, we now foresee the widespread adoption of spatial interaction and mixed reality for everyday information management in platforms such as head-worn displays (Figure 1). Yet these platforms are still in their relative infancy and there is a lack of

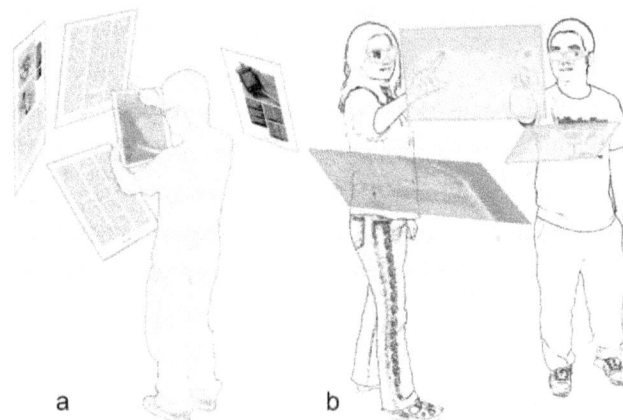

**Figure 1. Our design framework, Ethereal Planes, facilitates the classification and comparison of designs that use 2D information spaces in 3D mixed reality environments. Analysis techniques can inspire the construction of new designs. Informed decision-making is an important step toward advanced productivity features for multitasking (a), analytic reasoning and co-located collaboration (b).**

methodological tools to support the design of everyday applications.

In this paper we aim to assist the design process by collecting and organizing concepts introduced and explored in previous research endeavors. Based on a systematic literature review, we present a design framework we call Ethereal Planes. Ethereal Planes describes the design space of planar (2D) interfaces in 3D mixed reality environments. We focus on 2D designs because they are familiar [30,36], intuitive [23], and have advantages in efficiency, speed, precision and reduction of clutter [15,16,52]. While there are many instances where 3D interfaces will prove useful, 2D interfaces are currently ubiquitous both within and beyond the realm of computing interfaces and will remain suitable for a wide range of uses, particularly those involving information simplification or abstraction (e.g. text, floor plans, control panels).

Ethereal Planes employs the concept of information spaces [24] in assisting the design of advanced and productive interfaces. Information spaces support intuitive computing interaction by mapping information to real world space, allowing us to look beyond the boundaries of the computing device and perceive information where it belongs – in the surrounding environment. Information spaces have been implemented in diverse platforms including spatially-aware handheld devices, personal projectors [12,67] , tabletops [59] and digital paper [58]. Ethereal Planes is primarily aimed at supporting interface design on head-worn displays (HWDs) [6,22], which due to their wearable nature are always-available and hands-free, in a way not possible with previous technologies. Ethereal Planes is intended for interaction designers of mixed-reality HWDs applications.

Ethereal Planes was derived from a systematic literature review of information spaces with 2D instantiations. We encapsulate the recurring design themes into seven design dimensions. By analyzing common design choices from existing implementations we identified common design patterns. Further, we discuss several analysis techniques (e.g. tweaking, combining) that can help inspire new designs, and discuss our own use of the framework in the design of a system called the Personal Cockpit [3].

## BACKGROUND

Our goal in defining Ethereal Planes is to support the design of user interfaces for emerging HWD technologies. However, we look beyond the individual technical challenges of these novel technologies towards a framework to encourage the development of everyday user interfaces for everyday applications. We encourage new and useful designs by providing a unifying foundation for the description and categorization of tools needed for manipulating spatially distributed information. In this section we introduce the concepts of design frameworks and mixed-reality technologies.

### Design Frameworks

Design frameworks are conceptual tools created to help designers conceptualize the nuances of particular technologies and formalize the creative process. Design frameworks have an established history in interface design, and have shown their value in providing terminology to categorize ideas [50] and organize complex concepts into logical hierarchies [46]. Design frameworks often accompany either the introduction of a previously unexplored concept (e.g. Graspable User Interface [25]) or the exploration of existing work in a new light (e.g. Ambient Information Systems [49], Availability Sharing Systems [35], and Ephemeral User Interfaces [20]).

Several frameworks related to spatial and mixed reality interactions have previously been developed for immersive virtual environments. For example, Bowman and Hodges 8 describe a framework outlining techniques for virtual navigation. Poupyrev et al. [48] present a taxonomy of virtual object manipulation techniques. Mine et al. [44] introduce a framework to leverage proprioception to assist interaction with virtual objects. Also, a well-known survey by Hinckley et al. [36] discusses many general issues relevant to spatial user interaction. In contrast to these previous frameworks, Ethereal Planes specifically addresses interface design for 2D, mixed reality information spaces and draws from work developed for a wide variety of mixed reality platforms.

In creating Ethereal Planes we used techniques also applied to HWD interface design by Robinett [54] and similar to those formalized in Zwicky's General Morphological Analysis [53]. This method treats a set of defined taxonomical terms as a set of orthogonal *dimensions* in a geometric *design space*. The resulting theoretical matrix provides a structure for objective classification and comparison. The methodical filling-in of this structure helps to categorize existing concepts, differentiate ideas, and identify unexplored terrain. In summary, there are three basic steps in the development and usage of our design framework, which we follow through the course of this paper:

1. Review of existing designs to distill a set of characteristic dimensions
2. Categorization of existing designs among these dimensions to identify both gaps and common usages
3. Generation of new designs through an analytic process of combining and altering design choices

Along these steps, our Ethereal Planes framework fulfills several purposes: The distillation from existing literature of a set of general but widely encompassing design dimensions provides a taxonomy for designers, researchers, teachers and students to express their creations. The dimensional organization also helps the understanding of existing designs by providing a means to categorize them; by contrasting and comparing these, designers gain insight into general patterns and identify gaps in the dimensional framework where designs do not yet exist. Designers can then use this information to assist with the creation of new designs, either by applying the strengths of existing patterns to the correct contexts or thorough experimentation, by altering one or more dimension and then imagining the resulting implications.

### Mixed Reality Technologies

Mixed reality, the combination of real and virtual objects, has its roots in the see-through HWD technology introduced by Sutherland [60]. Buxton and Fitzmaurice [11] identified three potential platforms for realizing information spaces: Caves, HWDs and handheld devices. These technologies, and more recently, projection, have since have since become staples of mixed reality. These methods cover the breadth of visual output platforms that surface in our literature review.

Each of these technologies has its advantages and limitations. Caves can produce high-fidelity immersive environments, but size and cost restricts them from common use. HWDs are recently available in lightweight form factors, both monocular [27] and stereoscopic [9,63]. The latter hold promise for mixed reality due to their capability for producing convincing 3D effects similar to those available in a Cave environment. Moreover, HWDs possess an advantage over Caves in their capability to produce different perspectives of the same object for multiple viewers 1. Handheld devices are now ubiquitous, making them a popular target platform, but only serve as a small window to virtual content (e.g. [68]). Projectors are also becoming popular with the advent of compact portable versions (e.g. [12,40]). Projectors are spatially less restrictive than handhelds, but require an external surface for projection.

We created the Ethereal Planes framework primarily for the design of next-generation HWD interfaces. The potential versatility and affordance for mobility of HWDs, along with support of integrated sensors [47,56] for sophisticated user input (e.g. mid-air gestures), makes these devices a promising future ubiquitous mixed-reality platform.

## ETHEREAL PLANES FRAMEWORK
The foundation of our Ethereal Planes design framework is an organizational taxonomy for classifying designs that incorporate virtual 2D workspaces.

### Research Method
The taxonomy was the product of an extensive review of literature related to information spaces, and spatial interaction. Within this body of work, we found a subset of designs that embody the concept of Ethereal Planes. We began with a thorough archive search for papers exploring spatial user interfaces that occupy real world space, extending or existing fully beyond the limits of a conventional display screen. We focused on designs involving planar information spaces thus excluded designs that do not explicitly discuss 2D workspaces, for example those that involve navigating 3D workspaces through a 2D display. We also excluded papers that do not introduce distinct differences from previous designs, for example the use of an existing design in a new context or focus on the technology for implementing a known design. To begin, we manually sifted through the previous 5 years' proceedings of CHI, UIST, ISWC and VRST. We also conducted a tree search of references and citations of the initial papers we identified and of seminal papers on spatial interaction frameworks (e.g. [8,36,44,48]). The final list, containing 34 papers, is not intended to be exhaustive, however represents a diverse selection of designs from which we draw. (A complete list of all 34 designs in our survey, along with their dimensional classifications, may be found on our project page: http://hci.cs.umanitoba.ca/projects-and-research/details/personal-cockpit-spatial-user-interface)

From the papers in our literature review, we distilled a set of design dimension using a bottom up approach resembling open coding. We began with [18] candidate dimensions that fit the concepts found in the reviewed literature, then iteratively reduced these into a set small enough to manage in a concise framework, yet containing enough dimensions to make it useful. We eliminated dimensions, for example, that expressed concepts that we deemed relatively insubstantial (e.g. fidelity), that were later incorporated into other dimensions (e.g. spatial reference frame) or that were substantial enough that treatment in our current framework would be superficial

| Group | Dimension | Values | | |
|---|---|---|---|---|
| *Reference Frame* | *Perspective* | egocentric | | exocentric |
| | *Movability* | movable | | fixed |
| *Spatial Manipulation* | *Proximity* | far | near | on-body |
| | *Input mode* | direct | | indirect |
| | *Tangibility* | tangible | | intangible |
| *Spatial Composition* | *Visibility* | high | intermediate | low |
| | *Discretization* | continuous | | discrete |

**Table 1. Seven dimension of our design framework, their three groups and their potential values.**

(e.g. co-located collaboration). Several important concepts that deserve further consideration are listed in a later section (Framework Extensions). This process resulted in seven design dimensions, listed in Table 1. We further organized the dimensions into three groups based on the strongest dependencies between them. This grouping is used to organize several resulting design recommendations.

### Design Space Dimensions
*Perspective* denotes the conceptual viewpoint of the observer. To delineate this dimension, we borrow the terminology of *egocentric* and *exocentric* reference frames, used in early virtual reality literature [65] and later included in a taxonomy for virtual object manipulation by Poupyrev et al. [48]. The exocentric perspective the viewer is an outside observer, whereas the egocentric perspective is immersive. These terms correspond to the sub-divisions of world- and body-based coordinate systems used in other taxonomies, such as that of Cockburn et al. [16]. Feiner et al. [22] expanded these to three possible reference frames for virtual windows, view-fixed, surround-fixed or object-fixed. Billinghurst [6] similarly refers to head-, body- or world-stabilized information displays. Hinckley et al. [36] use the terms relative and absolute gesture to denote motions in body- and world-centric space, respectively. In our framework, *egocentric* reference frames denote 'first person' (body-centric) reference points, such as the head or body, whereas *Exocentric* frames are set relative to any object or other real-world (world-centric) reference point.

*Movability* denotes whether workspaces are *movable* or *fixed* with respect to a given frame of reference. Fixed workspaces are indefinitely locked in place to their respective coordinate systems. Movable ones can be relocated in relation to their egocentric or exocentric reference point. In most contexts, we consider a hand-fixed information space as *movable* because it can be moved to different coordinate points within the reference fame, whether body- or world-centric. A mobile device display, for example, can be often relocated with respect to the user's head or body, thus does not usually qualify as *fixed*.

4

*Proximity* describes the distance relationship between an information space and its user. We use a set of regions drawn from neuropsychology [21,34] also used by Chen et al. [14]: *on-body* (coincides with pericutaneous space, on the body surface), *near* (peripersonal space, within arm's reach) and *far* (extrapersonal space, beyond arm's reach). The majority of implementations we examined involve interaction within arm's reach, often by direct input (e.g. [12]) or with a handheld device (e.g. [68]). Some systems allow interaction with distant objects, particularly those for immersive virtual worlds or for outdoor use (e.g. Augmented Viewport [37]). Other researchers have explored the human body as an interface (e.g. [32]).

*Input mode* falls coarsely into two camps, *indirect* and *direct*. Indirect input includes cursors, ray-casting and variations of these methods. Direct input includes input using direct touch by hand, fingertip or stylus as well as virtual 'touch' with intangible surfaces (e.g. [13,29]).

*Tangibility* defines whether an information space is mapped to a surface that can be touched. Our frame work classifies implementations as either *tangible* or *intangible*. Tangible interfaces often leverage surfaces in the nearby environment, such as a wall (e.g. [12]) or device screen (e.g. [68]) and benefit from haptic feedback. *Intangible* designs typically make use of 'in-air' gestures (e.g. [29]) for user input.

*Visibility* describes the amount of visual representation available in an interface and also determines the degree to which spatial memory relies upon proprioception. Our framework uses three levels of visibility, *high*, *intermediate* and *low*. *High* visibility means that the information space is

| Input mode | direct | | indirect |
|---|---|---|---|
| **Tangibility** | tangible | intangible | |
| on-body | Skinput [32], OmniTouch [31] | | |
| near | Peephole displays [68], Cao et al. [12] | Touching the void [13], Imaginary interfaces [29] | Sidesight [10], Windows on the world [22] |
| far | | | Virtual shelves [41], Augmented Viewports [37] |

**Table 2. Example combinations between proximity, input mode and tangibility categories of *Spatial Manipulation*.**

largely or fully visible. *Intermediate* visibility means some type of viewing constraint is present, for instance if only a small section of the workspace may be seen at one time (e.g. [68]). *Low* visibility implies that information management relies very little or not at all on visual feedback (e.g. [29]).

*Discretization* specifies whether an information space is *continuous* or composed of *discrete* units. The majority of designs in our survey use *continuous* space. Examples of *discrete* mappings are the body-centric browser tab mappings described by Chen et al. [14] and the bins Wang et al. [64] placed around a mobile device for sorting photos.

**Dimensional Interdependencies**

While the dimensions of a design space are ideally orthogonal, dependencies between dimensions are rarely entirely absent. As a case in point, some choices in the Ethereal Planes dimensions will have implications for others. We clustered the dimensions by their closest dependencies into groups we call *Reference Frame*, *Spatial Manipulation* and *Spatial Composition* (Table 1). Here we discuss some of the tradeoffs between design choices within each of the three groups.

*Reference Frame – Perspective* and *movability* together encompass the concept of a spatial reference frame. Combinations of these two dimensions are summarized in Figure 2. Different reference frames are better suitable for different types of applications. In a mobile scenario, an *egocentric* perspective is more useful, since it will move along with a user on-the-go. In collaborative scenarios, *exocentric* space is more appropriate, since users will benefit from a shared, world-based reference frame, as is the case with a real-world, wall-fixed whiteboard. *Exocentric* frames are also useful for situating information spaces in the contexts where they are most practical [24]. However, in free space interactions, Hinckley et al. [36] note that *egocentric* coordinate systems are easier for users to comprehend and manipulate than *exocentric* frames.

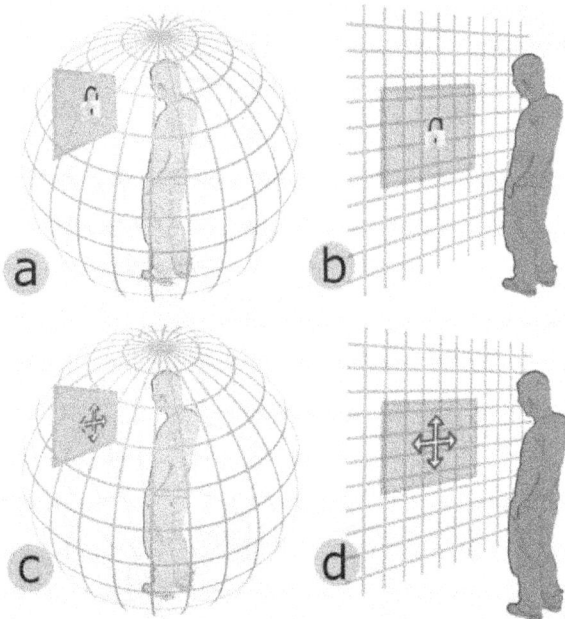

**Figure 2. Four general *Reference Frames* for Ethereal Planes: (a) fixed-egocentric, (b) fixed-exocentric, (c) movable-egocentric and (d) movable-exocentric.**

*Fixed* information spaces are useful in situations where spatial memorability is important, for example in the placement of application shortcuts [41]. Once learned, objects in *fixed* spaces can also be recalled with the aid of proprioception [30,41,68]. *Movable* workspaces, conversely, are better for short-term memorability such as when the information contents are short-term, volatile or highly dynamic.

*Spatial Manipulation* – The three dimensions of *proximity*, *input mode* and *tangibility* are related to the manipulation of information spaces and of data and objects within them. Table 2 provides examples of relevant combinations between these dimensions. For various reasons, some combinations have no existing counterparts in our Ethereal Planes-related literature. With indirect input, for example, the concept of *tangibility* becomes less relevant, thus we do not include *tangibility* under the indirect column of the table. Conversely, it is difficult to imagine direct input with *far* proximity, thus no examples appear in our survey (although this does not mean that some conception of such a concept cannot be realized in future).

*Input mode* is dependent on *proximity*: whereas *indirect* input allows interaction with surfaces that are beyond reach, *direct* input is intuitive when the interface lies within reach. *Direct* input is practical with *on-body* surfaces since it leverages proprioception. Leveraging available surfaces, whether body or other, also assists motor precision [42].

*Tangibility* is influenced by the implementation technology. Projection-based interfaces are often *tangible*, since a projection surface is required. Stereoscopic displays (i.e. Caves, some HWDs) often use *intangible*, virtual surfaces, although information spaces are sometimes intentionally set to coincide with physical surfaces [61]. In free space, researchers have found that *indirect* input is faster, less fatiguing and more stable [2,36,62] than *direct* input. However, *direct* input is intuitive and can make use of expressive gestures, thus may be desirable even without the aid of a *tangible* surface. Our survey turned up many designs using *direct* input both with (e.g. [12,32]), and without (e.g. [13,29]) *tangible* surface contact.

*Spatial Composition* – Together, *visibility* and *discretization* contribute to the way information is organized spatially. One important factor related to these dimensions is spatial memory. Spatial memory is important in many of the interface designs considered in our survey, particularly when the information spaces are not confined within the boundaries of a typical display screen (e.g. [68]). Table 3 shows examples of different pairings between *visibility* and *discretization*. The majority of interfaces represent information visually, however some present little or no visual information. Spatial memory can be built either purely visually, or by muscle memory, although many designs leverage some combination of both (e.g. [32,68]). Designs with little or no visual feedback are more likely to rely highly on proprioception for object recall (e.g.

|  |  | **Discretization** | |
|  |  | *continuous* | *discrete* |
| *Visibility* | *low* | Imaginary interfaces [29] | Virutal shelves [41], Piles across space [64], mSpaces [17], body-centric browser tabs [14] |
|  | *intermediate* | Peephole displays [68] | Skinput [32], Chameleon [26] |
|  | *high* | Pen light [57], Mouse light [58] |  |

**Table 3. Example pairings between the visibility and discretization categories of *Spatial Composition*.**

[29,41]). *Discrete* spatial mappings are commonly used with interfaces with *intermediate* or *low* visibility. When little or none of the interface can be seen, designers can instead leverage spatial memory or proprioception, (e.g. Virtual Shelves [41]). In such cases, *discretization* is often leveraged to make recall manageable.

**FRAMEWORK APPLICATIONS**

We created our Ethereal Planes framework to guide our own research and also to assist future designers. Here we discuss how our framework can be used to categorize and compare existing designs as well as aid the creation of new designs.

**Categorizing Existing Designs**

A fundamental aspect of any framework is its descriptive capacity. To show how Ethereal Planes can be used to describe existing designs, we apply it to the works from our literature review. For each design, we assigned dimensional values and classified the results, which provides us with a methodical system to contrast and compare these different designs. We acknowledge that our framework does not provide an absolute partitioning in which designs fit cleanly into the dimensional values. Rather there are many cases where different values apply to multiple presented concepts or the chosen values are open to interpretation. However, the goal of our framework is not to provide a set of arbitrary sorting bins, but to make the designer aware of important design choices and help them weigh the potential benefits of these choices.

Several distinct categories of similar designs emerged from our analysis, each of which we describe in detail below. Although these five categories represent only a small geometric region of the full design space, we found that the majority of reviewed designs (30 of 34) are a very good fit to one of them. As with the assignment of dimensional values, these categories are not absolute, thus we include minor variations that fit closely to the overall character of the group. A few more diverse exceptions are discussed at the end of this section and in section.

*Peephole* – In the first and largest of our categories, we group concepts that build on the *spotlight* and *peephole* metaphors. These designs allow interaction through 'peephole windows' that are moved around the surface of a 2D workspace. Both are conceptually similar with their main difference being the technology used: Whereas *peephole* interaction implies the use of spatially aware mobile devices, the *spotlight* metaphor typically refers to projection-based environments. The common moniker of 'peephole' interaction was coined by Yee [68], but is a direct descendant of Fitzmaurice's Chameleon. The common theme motivating these designs is to expand the workspace beyond the limited boundaries. To prevent getting lost in a large, mostly invisible space, the workspace remains world-fixed while the device user navigates the content within. Whereas the original Chameleon 26 implementation used the *discretized* space of a spreadsheet application, most variations use *continuous* 2D space. Several other variations, not discussed here, explore 2D 'image-plane' representations of 3D space. Variations from our research include: Touch Projector [7], mSpaces [17], Chameleon [26], Pass-them-around [43], Peephole displays [68], dynamically defined information spaces [12], PenLight [57], MouseLight [58], Augmented Surfaces [51], PlayAywhere [66], Lightspace [67], Bonfire [39] and X-Large virtual workspaces [40].

*Floating* – This group contains various instantiations of virtual windows that appear to *float* in mid-air. A common goal of these designers is to import the familiar characteristics of ubiquitous 2D applications into an immersive environment. *Floating* windows have often been used to implement auxiliary input controls such as panels, dialog boxes and menus, in immersive virtual reality environments 18. Since mid-air displays are *intangible*, designers often use *indirect* input modes such as mice [22,37] or ray-casters [2]. Chan et al. [13] provide an interesting exploration of *direct* interaction with *intangible* displays. Other variations include: Windows on the World [22], Wearable Conferencing Space [6], Friction Surfaces [2] and Augmented Viewport [37]. Most of these implementations use *exocentric* information spaces, however some HWD implementations [6,22] provide the option of *egocentric* floating windows for mobile users.

*Off-Screen* – This category includes designs that allow *indirect* input in the 'off-screen' region that surrounds a device's periphery. As in the peephole concept, *off-screen* designers address the problem of limited screen space by extending the theoretical plane of a device's screen into surrounding space. However, these systems are easily portable, allowing the surrounding workspace to be conveniently repositioned. They also avoid occlusion with *indirect* input, and are useful for navigational operations such as panning and zooming. We generalize this category as *exocentric* because two of the included designs (SideSight [10] and Portico [4]) use a device placed on a surface. However, the third example (off-screen pan and zoom [38]) is *egocentric*, since it uses a handheld device.

*On-body* – Another convenient tangible surface is the human *body*, used by the designs in this category. In many instances, a hand or arm doubles as a convenient projection surface in lieu of a wall or table, and is a convenient, always-available place to store buttons or task shortcuts. Body parts have the primary benefit of assisting target acquisition with proprioception, as evidenced in Harrison et al.'s Skinput [32]. Variations on this theme include

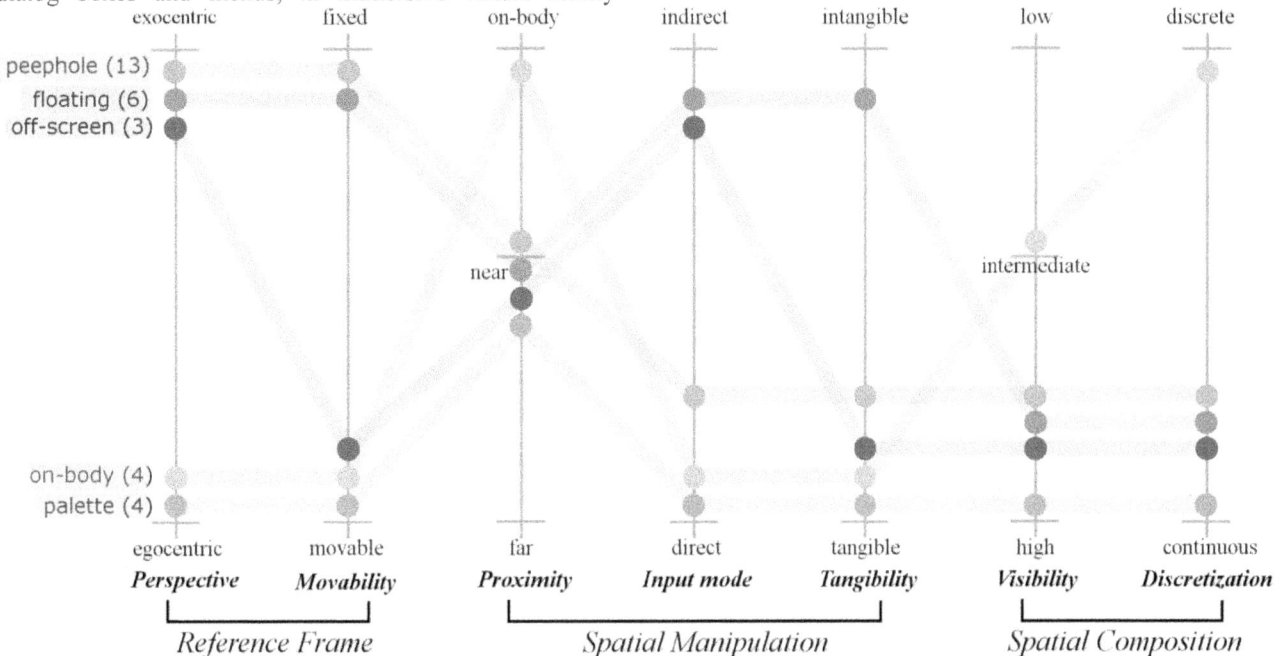

Figure 3. A parallel coordinates graph showing the main design categories found in our analysis of existing designs. Each category is plotted along the seven dimensions of the Ethereal Planes framework. (Best viewed in colour)

Imaginary Phone [30], OmniTouch [31] and Chen et al.'s Body-centric prototype [14].

*Palette* – These designs align the information space with a handheld *palette*, such a paddle or transparent sheet. This use of a handheld plane allows bimanual interaction, which can facilitate task performance [42]. Handheld tangible surfaces have commonly been used in immersive environments since *tangible* surfaces provide increased speed and control over *intangible* floating surfaces [42]. Variations include the Personal Interaction Panel [61] and various similar implementations [19,42,55].

In Figure 3 we provide a visual summary of the major design categories in a parallel coordinates graph. This graph shows the values of each category along the seven design dimensions. This figure fulfills several purposes: 1) It enables easy comparison between the patterns, revealing where they are similar and where they differ. 2) It shows clustering within the dimensions, including commonly occurring values (e.g. *near proximity - high visibility*) and commonly joined pairs (e.g. *exocentric-mixed - direct-tangible*). 3) Is makes clear areas of the design space that are under-utilized (e.g. *far proximity - intangible*).

For example, one particular design that defied easy classification is the Virtual Shelves implementation described by Li et al. [41]. With the Virtual Shelves interface, selectable objects, such as icons, are distributed in an *egocentric* sphere around the user. The user relies on spatial memory to make selections using a ray-casting metaphor, thus the objects are conceptually at a *far proximity*. This design combines some dimensional values not found in any of the main categories (Figure 4), such as an *egocentric-fixed* reference frame and *low visibility* with *discrete* space. The parallel coordinates visualization makes it easy to see that this design creates a unique pattern in the Ethereal Planes design space.

### Filling Gaps, Tweaking and Combining

Beyond classification and comparison of existing designs, one purpose of a framework is to inspire and guide new creations. To show the generative potential of Ethereal Planes, we discuss several analytic processes that can be undertaken with our framework. Based on the work of Robinett [54], we explore three primary operations that can be used to transform our prior set classifications into ideas for new designs, by identifying *gaps* in the matrix, by *'tweaking'* (altering) existing designs or by *combining* two or more of them.

The first way to think about new designs is *filling gaps*; to look for valid combinations that have not been tried. By Robinett's method, our framework dimensions can be viewed as a seven-dimensional matrix, where each cell is a different combination of chosen values. Theoretically, this matrix has 288 unique design patterns. This number seems remarkable, considering that we were able to classify a large number of designs into only a handful of patterns. What then is the explanation for this difference? One

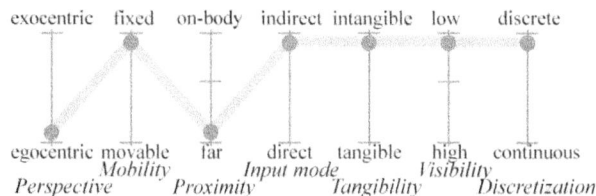

**Figure 4. The Virtual Shelves design of Li et al. [41] holds a unique position in the design space from the major categories we identified in Figure 3.**

primary reason is the number of interdependencies between the framework dimensions. Because the dimensions are not purely orthogonal, many of the possible combinations may be considered invalid. For instance, *direct* input with *far* information spaces seems impractical. However, the Ethereal Planes design space is still relatively unexplored and perceived dependencies may in fact be a result of attachment to prior paradigms. For instance, the most common reference frame types in the explored literature are *fixed-exocentric* and *movable-egocentric*, which correspond respectively to the most common types of real-world displays: desktop monitors and mobile devices. As designers gain more experience with mixed reality applications, some of the combinations that appear invalid may be explored with new and unconventional concepts. For example the *direct-far* combination mentioned above may be solved by the introduction a mechanism for controlling stretchable virtual limbs. On the other hand, *indirect-on-body* interaction might be found useful when looking at one's self in a mirror. In this manner, the Ethereal Planes framework is useful for plotting existing designs across the design dimensions, providing a methodical tool to help designers to identify new ground and inspire unique creations.

A second method for creating new designs is *tweaking*; rather than create a new combination from scratch, we can change one or two dimensions of existing patterns and imagine the resulting implications. In fact, one such example we identified in our literature review is the Imaginary Interfaces design of Gustafson et al. [29]. It is similar in nature to the *palette* category, however the user can 'draw' objects such as letters or mathematical functions with their fingertip on an intangible and invisible surface. This unusual design breaks the conventions of previous patterns by combining *low* visibility with a *continuous* workspace (Figure 5). Although only two dimensions are changed, the result introduces some significant design challenges, many of which are addressed in this novel work.

One other way to generate new ideas is to *combine* two or more existing patterns. An example of this type was also identified in our reviewed designs, in the AD-Binning implementation of Hasan et al. [33]. This interface extends the interaction plane of a mobile device screen into space around the device for making *discrete* item selections. This design has many dimensional values in common with

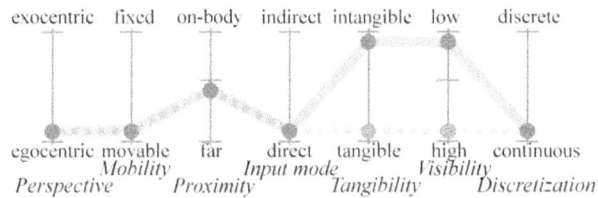

**Figure 5. The Imaginary Interfaces design of Gustafson et al. [29] (solid path) varies from the *palette* category (dashed path) only in the *tangibility* and *visibility* dimensions.**

palette category (*egocentric, movable, near proximity, direct input*), but also some in common with Virtual Shelves (*intangible, invisible, discrete* space). Combining these dimensions creates a new hybrid pattern, as seen in Figure 6. A similar fit to the framework was found in the Piles Across Space implementation of Wang et al. [64], which was designed for sorting photos into virtual piles around a desktop monitor. Designers of future interfaces can benefit from a design space that provides a conceptual workspace for trying new combinations.

One particular instance where combining existing designs can be useful is to support multiple interface 'modes' within a compound design. For example imagine a sketching application with read and write modes. Suppose a series of sketches are distributed in an egocentric sphere, floating around the user, which can be viewed using a mobile screen. When editing the sketches in write mode, the user uses the display as a *peephole*, since it provides a *tangible* surface to assist drawing in *continuous* space. To make drawing easier, the sketches are mapped to a single stationary (*exocentric*) plane, so the user doesn't need to change the device orientation. When viewing the sketches in read mode, however, the user can simply hold the device in one place and use her second hand as a pointer; the user knows the *discrete* location of each sketch in the *egocentric* sphere and whichever one she points to appears on the display. A single dimension can also act as a 'mode switch' within a single design. Imagine for instance an image browsing application. The user can have both a collaborative mode and a personal mode. To support sharing, the collaborative mode uses *exocentric* space, whereas the personal mode is placed in *egocentric* space.

### Example: Designing the Personal Cockpit
To provide a final example of our framework's utility, we discuss a case where the Ethereal Planes framework was

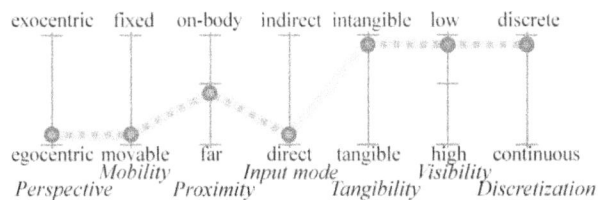

**Figure 6. The AD-Binning design of Hasan et al. [33] (solid path) shares some dimensional values with the *palette* category (orange) and others with the Virtual Shelves design (green).**

applied to an actual design. This case occurred during our work on the Personal Cockpit [3], a multi-display interface intended for use on HWDs (Figure 7). Here we briefly describe our implementation and walk through the seven design dimensions; along the way, we present our design choices, explain how they were influenced by the framework dimensions and provide some possible alternative choices for future implementations.

The Personal Cockpit is a spatial user interface for HWDs, intended for use with everyday mobile applications. Our design leverages free space around the user, allowing the user to partition content into multiple virtual windows that appear to float around the user's body. As an improvement over view-fixed windows available on current displays, our design allows faster task switching. We implemented the Personal Cockpit in a Cave environment, in which we emulated a HWD's limited field of view (FoV), and refined our design with several user studies. (For full details of the design, we refer readers to the referenced paper.)

*Reference frame:* The perspective of an information space is, to some extent, platform dependent. We have seen, for example, that designs leveraging the *peephole* metaphor use *exocentric* space to mitigate the limited display space of mobiles and projectors. An *exocentric* reference frame allows users to take advantage of proprioception for building spatial memory and helps to prevent them from getting lost in a large workspace.

With an ideal see-through HWD we would allow users to move virtual windows (2D information spaces) around freely in their environment. However, current devices require rendered content to fit within a limited FoV of about 40° or less (e.g. [63]). Since viewing content with this limitation is analogous to shining a projector's 'spotlight', we use *fixed* reference frames to maximize memorability. We allow the user to choose between *egocentric* and *exocentric* perspectives for different situations: *egocentric* windows are necessary for mobile use, whereas *exocentric* windows can be mapped to existing surfaces around the home or office to minimize occlusion and allow *tangible, direct* input. We nonetheless allow some *movable* exceptions to fixed windows: although windows will remain primarily fixed, users may want to periodically customize their arrangement, much as one

**Figure 7. The Personal Cockpit [3] is a user interface design for using everyday applications on head-worn displays.**

would rearrange icons on their mobile's home screen from time-to-time. For this purpose, we put handles on the windows, allowing them to be moved or resized using pinch gestures [45]. Also, users can move data objects from one window to another, or open a new window by dropping an application icon in mid-air.

*Spatial Manipulation:* We opted to explore *direct* input in our design to create an intuitive experience for users. Whereas some mechanism for *indirect* input makes sense with view-fixed displays (e.g. [27]), *direct* input is a good fit for the spatially-situated windows of the Personal Cockpit and may reinforce the user's sense or spatial awareness through proprioception. The use of *direct* input requires windows to be placed within arm's reach, in the *near* region. Unlike a peephole display, whose tangible surface aligns with the information space, the floating windows in our design are *intangible*. Because the lack of tangibility is known to present issues for direct input [13], we were required to mitigate these in our design. First, to provide depth feedback, we introduced a cursor that indicates whether a user's finger is in front of, intersecting, or behind a window. Second, the handles for moving or resizing windows are invisible by default, but change colour to indicate affordance for grasping when a hand is near (by turning green) and feedback when pinched (blue).

*Spatial Composition:* The information spaces in the Personal Cockpit are implemented as virtual windows, which are visible to the wearer of a HWD. Since these windows can be used to view rich application content, each window contains a *continuous* workspace. However, we also make the workspace *discrete* in a sense, since individual tasks are partitioned into different windows. Because the HWD's limited FoV allows only one window to be fully viewed at a time, our multi-window design has only *intermediate visibility,* however users will build up their spatial memory after repeated instances of switching between *fixed* windows. To reinforce visual spatial memory with proprioception, we place the body-fixed layout at a constant distance of 50 cm from the user's right shoulder. To make use of additional *egocentric* space around the user, the design could be expanded to include additional items placed fully out of normal viewing range. For example, a set of shortcut triggers could be placed at a region 90° to either side. Since the user will not often want to turn their head so far these items have a *low visibility*, supported by *discrete* space for easy recall.

## FRAMEWORK EXTENSIONS
We acknowledge that there are limitations to our Ethereal Planes framework which may make it seem incomplete in certain contexts. However, we view Ethereal Planes as a core template that can be modified to suit a designer's needs, rather than a final product that fits all circumstances. Here we briefly discuss several potential extensions of our framework. These extensions include ideas that we initially attempted to introduce into our list of framework dimensions, but warrant deeper consideration at a higher

level than is possible with the initial framework we introduce in this paper. Each of these topics requires several dimensions of its own that could constitute a separate layer of a more complete framework. In each case, these dimensions must be drawn from an additional body of literature and must be considered at a higher level than the basic interaction concepts of our initial framework.

*Multi-modal interaction:* Our input dimension takes into account only the paradigms of pointer selection and direct manipulation. This dimension could be expanded to include other input modes, particularly voice. The *visibility* dimension could similarly be expanded to consider non-visual output modes such as audio output. Such extensions would allow our framework to be extended to the design of interfaces for people with motor-skills or visual disabilities.

*Co-located Collaboration:* One of the applications of our framework is for collaborative scenarios. HWDs connected by network can be configured to allow multiple people to view the same virtual workspace from different perspectives [1]. Our framework could be extended by taking into consideration the large body of research on multi-surface environments. The modified framework should include aspects pertaining to the movement of content between surfaces and consideration of public vs private content [28].

*Beyond 2D Surfaces:* Our current framework focuses on 2D surfaces, although it could be extended to handle 3D objects. Such an extension should include additional dimensions to handle manipulation and viewing (grasping, rotation) of 3D objects. It should also include dimensions that take into account occlusion caused by the object's relative orientation or clutter from multiple objects.

## CONCLUSION
We presented our Ethereal Planes framework for describing existing and new designs that use 2D information spaces in 3D mixed reality environments. From a bottom-up review of existing designs, we inferred our framework's seven dimensions – *perspective, movability, proximity, input mode, tangibility, visibility* and *discretization*. We provided a description of each of these dimension. We demonstrated how our framework can be used to describe, contrast and compare existing designs by grouping these into five representative categories that emerged from our analysis. We also show how our framework can assist in the development of new systems through operations such as filling gaps, tweaking or combining existing designs and discuss the framework's application during our design of the Personal Cockpit [3]. We provide examples of potential extensions to our framework to accommodate the specific needs of future designers.

## ACKNOWLEDGMENTS
We acknowledge support from a NSERC Discovery Grant and a NSERC PGS scholarship for work on this project. We thank the anonymous reviewers for their helpful input.

**REFERENCES**

1. Agrawala, M., Beers, A.C., McDowall, I., Fröhlich, B., Bolas, M. and Hanrahan, P. The two-user responsive workbench: support for collaboration through individual views of shared space. *SIGGRAPH'97* (1997), 327-332.

2. Andujar, C. and Argelaguet, F. Friction surfaces: Scaled ray-casting manipulation for interacting with 2D GUIs. *Proc. EGVE '06*, Eurographics (2006), 101-108.

3. Ens, B., Finnigegan, R. and Irani, P. The Personal Cockpit: A spatial window layout for effective task switching on head-worn displays. *Proc. CHI '14*, ACM (2014), 3171-3180.

4. Avrahami, D., Wobbrock, J.O. and Izadi, S. Portico: Tangible interaction on and around a tablet. *Proc. UIST '11*, ACM (2011), 347-356.

5. Beaudonuin-Lafon, M. Instrumental interaction: An interaction model for designing post-WIMP user interfaces. *Proc. CHI '00*, ACM (2000), 446-453.

6. Billinghurst, M., Bowskill, J., Jessop, M. and Morphett, J. A wearable spatial conferencing space. Proc. ISWC '98, IEEE (1998), 76-83.

7. Boring, S., Baur, D., Butz, A. Gustafson, S. and Baudisch, P. Touch projector: Mobile interaction through video. *Proc. CHI '10*, ACM (2010), 2287-2296.

8. Bowman, D.A. and Hodges, L.F. Formalizing the design, evaluation and application of interaction techniques for immersive virtual environments. *Journal of Visual Languages and Computing 10* (1999), 37-53.

9. Brin, S. and Amirparviz, B. Laser alignment of binocular head mounted display. Patent No. 20130038510, Filed Aug. 9th, 2011, Iss. Feb. 14th, 2013.

10. Butler, A., Izadi, S., and Hodges, S. SideSight: multi- "touch" interaction around small devices. *Proc. UIST '08*, ACM (2008), 201-204.

11. Buxton, B. and Fitzmaurice, G. HMDs, Caves & Chameleon: A human-centric analysis of interaction in virtual space. *Computer Graphics 32*, 4 (1998), 69-74.

12. Cao, X. and Balakrishnan, R. Interacting with dynamically defined information spaces using a handheld projector and a pen. *Proc. UIST '06*, ACM (2006), 225-234.

13. Chan, L.W., Kao, H.S., Chen, M.Y., Lee, M.S., Hsu, J. and Hung, Y.P. Touching the void: Direct-touch interaction for intangible displays. *Proc. CHI '10*, ACM (2010), 2625-2634.

14. Chen, X.A., Marquardt, N., Tang, A., Boring, S. and Greenberg, S. Extending a mobile device's interaction space through body-centric interaction. *Proc. MobileHCI '12*, ACM (2012), 151-160.

15. Cockburn, A. and McKenzie, B. Evaluating the effectiveness of spatial memory in 2D and 3D physical and virtual environments. *CHI '02* (2002), 203-210.

16. Cockburn, A., Quinn, P., Gutwin, C., Ramos, G, and Looser, J. Air pointing: Design and evaluation of spatial target acquisition with and without visual feedback. *Int. Journal of Human-Computer Studies*. 69, 6, Academic Press (2011), 401-414.

17. Cuchard, J., Löchtefeld, M., Fraser, M., Krüger, A. and Subramanian, S. m+pSpaces: Virtual workspaces in the spatially-aware mobile environment. *Proc. MobileHCI '12*, ACM (2012), 171-180.

18. de Haan, G., Griffith, E.J., Koutek, M. and Post, F.H. Hybrid interfaces in VEs: Intent and interaction. *Proc. EGVE '06*, Eurographics (2006), 109-118.

19. de Haan, G., Koutek, M. and Post, F.H. Towards intuitive exploration tools for data visualization in VR. *Proc. VRST '02*, ACM (2002), 105-112.

20. Döring, T., Sylvester, A. and Schmidt, A. A design space for ephemeral user interfaces. *Proc.TEI '13*, ACM (2013), 75-82.

21. Elias, L.J. and Saucier, D.M. *Neuropsychology : clinical and experimental foundations.* Pearson (2006).

22. Feiner, S., MacIntyre, B., Haupt, M. and Solomon, E. Windows on the world: 2D windows for 3D augmented reality. *Proc. UIST '93*, ACM (1993), 145-155.

23. Fisher, S.S., McGreevy, M., Humphries, J. and Robinett, W. Virtual environment display system. *Proc. I3D '86*, ACM (1986), 77-87.

24. Fitzmaurice, G.W. Situated information spaces and spatially aware computers. *Communications of the ACM 36, 7*, ACM (1993), 39-49.

25. Fitzmaurice, G.W., Ishii, H. and Buxton, W. Bricks: Laying the foundations for graspable user interfaces. *Proc. CHI '95*, ACM (1995), 442-449.

26. Fitzmaurice, G.W., Zhai, S. and Chignell, M.H. Virtual reality for palmtop computers. *Proc. TOIS '93*, ACM (1993), 197-218.

27. Google Glass. http://www.google.com/glass/start/

28. Greenberg, S., Boyle, M., and Laberge, J. PDAs and shared public displays: Making personal information public, and public information personal. *Personal Technologies* 3, 1 (1999), 54-64.

29. Gustafson, S., Bierwirth, D. and Baudisch, P. Imaginary interfaces: Spatial interaction with empty hands and without visual feedback. *Proc. UIST '10*, ACM (2010), 2-12.

30. Gustafson, S., Holz, C. and Baudisch, P. Imaginary phone: Learning imaginary interfaces by transferring spatial memory from a familiar device. *Proc. UIST '11*, ACM (2011), 283-292.

31. Harrison, C., Benko, H., and Wilson, A. D. OmniTouch: Wearable multitouch interaction everywhere. *Proc. UIST '11*, ACM (2011), 441-450.

32. Harrison, C., Tan, Desney and Morris, D. Skinput: Appropriating the body as an input surface. *Proc. CHI '10*, ACM (2010), 453-462.

33. Hasan, K., Ahlström, D. and Irani, P. AD-Binning: Leveraging around device space for storing, browsing

and retrieving mobile device content. *Proc. CHI '13*, ACM (2013), 899-908.

34. Holmes, N.P. and Spence, C. The body schema and multisensory representation(s) of peripersonal space. *Cognitive Processing 5*, 2 (2004), 94–105.

35. Hincapié-Ramos, J.D., Voida S. and Mark, G. A design space analysis of availability-sharing systems. *Proc. UIST '11*, ACM (2011), 85-95.

36. Hinckley, K., Pausch, R., Goble, J.C. and Kassell, N.F. A survey of design issues in spatial input. *Proc. UIST '94*, ACM (1994), 213-222.

37. Hoang, T.N. and Thomas, B.H. Augmented viewport: An action at a distance technique for outdoor AR using distant and zoom lens cameras. *ISWC '10* (2010), 1-4.

38. Jones, B., Sodhi, R., Forsyth, D., Bailey, B. and Maciocci, G. Around device interaction for multiscale navigation. *Proc. MobileHCI '12*, ACM (2012), 83-92.

39. Kane, S.K., Avrahami, D., Wobbrock, J.O., Harrison, B., Rea, A.D., Philipose, M. and LaMarca, A. Bonfire: A nomadic system for hybrid laptop-tabletop interaction. *Proc. UIST '09*, ACM (2009), 129-138.

40. Kaufmann, B. and Hitz, M. X-large virtual workspaces for projector phones through peephole interaction. *Proc. MM '12*, ACM (2012), 1279-1280.

41. Li, F.C.Y., Dearman, D. and Truong, K.N. Virtual shelves: Interactions with orientation aware devices. *Proc. UIST '09*, ACM (2009), 125-128.

42. Lindeman, R.W., Sibert, J.L. and Hahn, J.K. Towards usable VR: An empirical study of user interfaces for immersive virtual environments. *CHI '99* (1999), 64-71.

43. Lucero, A. Holopainen, J. and Jokela, T. Pass-them-around: Collaborative use of mobile phones for photo sharing. *Proc. CHI '11*, ACM (2011), 1787-1796.

44. Mine, M.R., Brooks, F.P. and Sequin, C. Moving objects in space: Exploiting proprioception in virtual-environment interaction. *SIGGRAPH '97* (1997), 19-26.

45. Piekarski, W. and Thomas, B.H. Tinmith-Metro: New outdoor techniques for creating city models with an augmented reality wearable computer. *Proc. ISWC '01*, IEEE (2001), 31-38.

46. Plaisant, C., Carr, D. and Shneiderman, B. Image-browser taxonomy and guidelines for designers. *Software 12*, 2 (Mar. 1995), 21-32.

47. PMDTechnologies. http://www.pmdtec.com

48. Poupyrev, I., Weghorst, S., Billinghurst, M. and Ichikawa, T. Egocentric object manipulation in virtual environments: Empirical evaluation of interaction techniques. *Comp. Graphics Forum 17*, 3 (1998), 41-52.

49. Pousman, Z. and Stasko, J. A taxonomy of ambient information systems: Four patterns of design. *Proc. AVI '06*, ACM (2006), 67-74.

50. Price, B.A., Baecker, R.M. and Small, I.S. A principled taxonomy of software visualization. *Journal of Visual Languages & Computing 4*, 3 (Sept. 1993), 211-266.

51. Rekimoto, J. and Saitoh, M. Augmented surfaces: A spatially continuous work space for hybrid computing environments. *Proc. CHI '99*, ACM (1999), 378-385.

52. Ren, G. and O'Neill, E. 3D selection with freehand gesture. *Comp. and Graphics 37*, 3 (2013), 101-120.

53. Ritchey. T. Fritz Zwicky, 'Morphologie' and policy analysis. Paper presented at *16th EURO Conference on Operational Analysis,* Brussels (1998).

54. Robinett, W. Synthetic experience: A taxonomy, survey of earlier thought, and speculations on the future. Technical report. University of North Carolina (1992).

55. Schmalstieg, D, Encarnação, L.M. and Szalavári, Z. Using transparent props for interaction with the virtual table. *Proc. I3D '99*, ACM (1999), 147-153.

56. SoftKinetic. http://www.softkinetic.com

57. Song, H., Grossman, T., Fitzmaurice, G., Guimbretiere, F., Khan, A., Attar, R. and Kurtenbach, G. PenLight: combining a mobile projector and a digital pen for dynamic visual overlay. *Proc. CHI '09* (2009), 143-152.

58. Song, H. Guimbretiere, F., Grossman, T. and Fitzmaurice, G. MouseLight: Bimanual interactions on digital paper using pen and a spatially-aware mobile projector. *Proc. CHI '10,* ACM (2010), 2451-2460.

59. Spindler, M., Büschel, W. and Dachselt, R. Use your head: Tangible windows for 3D information spaces in a tabletop environment. *Proc. ITS '12* (2012), 245-254.

60. Sutherland, I.E. A head-mounted three dimensional display. *Proc. AFIPS '68*, ACM (1968), 757-764.

61. Szalavári, Z. and Gervautz, M. The personal interaction panel: A two-handed interface for augmented reality. *Computer Graphics Forum 16*, Eurographics (1997), 335-346.

62. Teather, R.J. and Stuerzlinger, W. Pointing at 3D targets in a stereo head-tracked virtual environment. *Proc. 3DUI '11*, IEEE (2011), 87-94.

63. Vuzix Corporation. http://www.vuzix.com.

64. Wang, Q., Hsieh, T and Paepcke, A. Piles across space: Breaking the real-estate barrier on small-display devices. *Int. J. Hum.-Comput. Stud. 67*, 4, Elsevier (2009), 349-365.

65. Wickens, C.D. and Baker, P. Cognitive issues in virtual reality. In *Virtual Environments and Advanced Interface Design*, Furness, T.A. and Barfield, W. (Eds.). Oxford (1995), 514-542.

66. Wilson, A.D. PlayAnywhere: A compact interactive tabletop projection-vision system. *Proc. UIST '05*, ACM (2005), 83-92.

67. Wilson, A.D. and Benko, H. Combining multiple depth cameras and projectors for interactions on, above and between surfaces. *Proc. UIST '10* (2010), 273-282.

68. Yee, K. Peephole Displays: Pen interaction on spatially aware handheld computers. *Proc. CHI '03* (2003), 1-8.

# Combining Multi-touch Input and Device Movement for 3D Manipulations in Mobile Augmented Reality Environments

**Asier Marzo**
Public University of Navarre
Pamplona, Spain.
asier.marzo@unavarra.es

**Benoît Bossavit**
Public University of Navarre
Pamplona, Spain.
benoit.bossavit@unavarra.es

**Martin Hachet**
INRIA Bordeaux
Talence, France.
Martin.hachet@inria.fr

## ABSTRACT

Nowadays, handheld devices are capable of displaying augmented environments in which virtual content overlaps reality. To interact with these environments it is necessary to use a manipulation technique. The objective of a manipulation technique is to define how the input data modify the properties of the virtual objects. Current devices have multi-touch screens that can serve as input. Additionally, the position and rotation of the device can also be used as input creating both an opportunity and a design challenge. In this paper we compared three manipulation techniques which namely employ multi-touch, device position and a combination of both. A user evaluation on a docking task revealed that combining multi-touch and device movement yields the best task completion time and efficiency. Nevertheless, using only the device movement and orientation is more intuitive and performs worse only in large rotations.

## Author Keywords

Mobile Augmented Reality; manipulation; multi-touch.

## ACM Classification Keywords

H.5.1. Information interfaces and presentation: Artificial, augmented, and virtual realities.

## INTRODUCTION

Mobile Augmented Reality (MAR) is a visualization technique which superimposes virtual content over the real environment on a mobile device. Currently, it has reached a mature state as it is supported by most handheld devices and numerous MAR apps are available. This was made possible by the advances in mobile technologies as well as by the progresses in computer vision and graphics techniques. Nonetheless, the way of interacting with these augmented environments is to some point still unclear and thus constitutes a bottleneck for the appearance of highly interactive MAR applications.

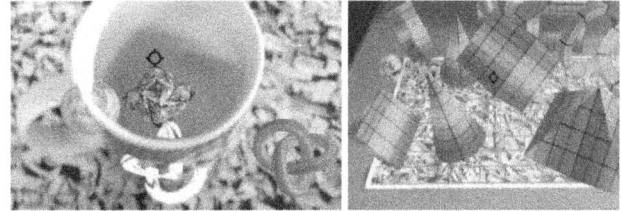

**Figure 1. Manipulating virtual objects in a MAR environment. Left) Virtual objects positioned around a real object. Right) Positioning obstacles in a space game.**

To interact with a virtual environment, one of the most important tasks is the manipulation of virtual objects. For example, in MAR the task of manipulation is required as soon as the user needs to position and orientate 3D virtual objects in the real environment, as illustrated on Figure 1.

At this time, mobile devices offer multi-touch screens as a standard input. Additionally, in MAR applications, the position and orientation of the device in the real world can be known. Therefore, the challenge is to determine which of these input modalities are better suited for MAR 3D manipulation and if it is beneficial to combine them.

## RELATED WORK

In this study, we are focused on manipulation techniques that can be implemented in normal handheld devices and that may achieve efficient interactions. Therefore, we excluded input modalities such as finger or hand tracking as they are not stable on current mobile devices. Similarly, although some studies have used additional devices in combination with the phone, we preferred to concentrate on the input space offered by a standard mobile.

The first study using a mainstream mobile device to manipulate virtual objects in MAR employed different input modalities to separately translate or rotate an object [4]. According to the authors, the best strategy was to map the physical translations of the device to the virtual object translations, and to use the keypads to rotate the object. In later studies keypad, tilt and finger tracking were compared as an input method to complement device movement [5]. Despite finger tracking being promising, keypad input for rotations outperformed the rest of the methods. Multi-touch screens were not tested as they were not widespread yet.

More recently, a user study compared the performance of touch gestures and finger tracking [1]. The former input modality could be used while pointing with the device to the virtual object (free-touch) or in a freeze-touch mode. The freeze-touch mode consists in manipulating the object from the point of view of a selected still frame; thus it is not necessary to point to the object during the process. Finger tracking performed two times worse in terms of task completion time (TCT) and accuracy; freeze-touch was slightly better than free-touch but not significantly. The techniques described above were designed to manipulate only 2DOF and none of them employed the device movement alone or in combination with other techniques.

A current study aimed at comparing touch modality with device movement [8]. They concluded that moving the device was better than using the touch screen for translating or rotating virtual objects. Nonetheless, the employed techniques used only one-hand interactions and no hybrid approach was tested.

In a previous preliminary study we observed that combining multi-touch and device movement could be beneficial [6]. In this paper, we analyse more thoroughly the usage of each modality and also report qualitative feedback.

## INTERACTION TECHNIQUES
Three interaction techniques to manipulate virtual objects in MAR environments are described in this section.

### Multi-touch
Various multi-touch techniques have been developed to manipulate objects with 6DOF [3][7]. However, most of them do not adapt well to small handheld devices. For instance, with small screens, it is difficult to use more than two fingers simultaneously. Similarly, although widgets are a current trend in manipulations for touchscreens [2], they are not adequate for small screens due to cluttering issues and fat finger problems. We conducted a pilot study with 6 subjects to determine which technique was better suited for 6DOF manipulations on handheld devices. This led us to propose a variation of the DS3 technique [7].

The resulting manipulation technique uses one finger to move the object along a plane parallel to the device that pass through the object. The interaction with two fingers serves various purposes. Firstly, the distance between the two fingers modifies the position across the line that joins the object and the device; therefore, a zoom gesture will bring the object closer and a pinch gesture will move it away (Z-Dist). Secondly, the angle variation of the vector that joins the two fingers is transferred to the rotation of the object across the view axis (Z-Rot). Lastly, the displacement of the middle point between the two fingers controls an Arcball rotation [9]. This last part of the technique differs from the original DS3 technique that uses a constraint solver. This solver tries to preserve contact points between the fingers and the object, which is not appropriate on small screens. To maximize the interaction surface, the Arcball rotation of this technique employs the entire screen as the virtual ball, instead of using only the object.

### Device Position and Rotation
The most straightforward approach to manipulate a virtual object with the device is to transfer the translation and rotation applied to the device (input) to the translation and rotation of the object (output). This technique may work for translations. Nonetheless, orienting the device to rotate the object may be problematic, as the user will lose sight of the manipulated object in the screen.

Previous approaches [4][5][8] employed the grasping technique in which the position and orientation of the object remain constant relatively to the device. In the pilot study, this technique appeared as the most suitable one for manipulating virtual objects using only device movements. It keeps the object inside the virtual field of view and the metaphor of grasping the objects helps the users to understand how the objects will behave. The users can clutch the manipulation by touching or not the screen.

### Hybrid
This third approach mixes multi-touch screen input and device movements. Previous work [4] suggests that for object translation, using the device movement is the most efficient way; and that for rotation, using the keypad is the best option. We took into account these suggestions by combining the grasping technique for translation with a touch control for rotation. The most used technique to perform general rotations is Arcball [9]. Therefore, since one-finger touch input is not dedicated to translations anymore, it is used to perform Arcball rotations in view space. The Hybrid technique also supports the use of two fingers to supplement the Arcball rotation (Z-Rot and Z-Dist gestures).

### USER STUDY
We conducted a user study to compare the three modalities associated with the interaction techniques described above. The study involved 12 people (2 female and 10 male). Participants' age ranged from 24 to 40 (M=27.3, SD=8.9). Participants had medium experience with 3D and three users were left-handed. The experiment was performed using a $3^{rd}$ generation iPod. The software ran under iOS 6, was developed using C++ and used Vuforia SDK for the tracking. The participants were seated in front of a table that reached below their chests. A paper marker is needed to achieve the tracking. It was printed on a 49x34 cm paper sheet and was placed on the table.

The task to perform was a 3D docking similar to Zhai's et al. [10]. Participants were asked to manipulate a bright chair (cursor) in order to overlap it with a static dark chair (target). The target chair was always static, located at the centre of the scene, whereas the cursor was located at different positions and orientations according to the trial. The experiment was divided into 4 blocks of 5 trials each. The order of the trials was: *Only translation, Small Simple Rotation, Small Complex Rotation (x2)* and *Large Complex Rotation.* All the trials implied translations.

Small angles ranged from 30 to 60 degrees and large ones from 110 to 180 degrees. *Simple rotations* implied rotations around one of the primary axes whereas *complex* ones were performed around a random axis. The distance between the target and the cursor varied from 7 to 15 centimetres. The size of the chairs was 4x4x6 cm. The error tolerance was 1 cm for translation and 12 degrees for rotation. If a participant could not complete the trial in 40 seconds, the trial ended in failure. Selection methods for the objects were removed from the evaluation and the cursor object was always preselected.

Each participant spent approximately 40 minutes for completing the entire experiment. For each condition, the participant had a short training during few minutes. Then, they performed the docking task. Finally, they filled in the NASA TLX questionnaire and a custom questionnaire. The order of the modalities was determined according to a Latin Square. The transformations of the chairs were randomly generated but they were the same for each participant. The timer was stopped when the marker needed to track the device was not visible. This tracking method is a current limitation that will be overcome in the future. For similar reasons, subjects were not allowed to manipulate the marker.

To summarize, the experiment consisted of: 12 participants x 3 techniques x 4 blocks x 5 trials = 720 docking tasks.

## RESULTS

Data were analyzed using RM-ANOVA to detect significant effects of technique; T-pair tests with Bonferroni adjustment were used as post-hoc tests. Greenhouse-Geisser correction was applied when sphericity was violated. Only completed tasks were included in the analysis. Success rate was close to 100% across all participants and techniques.

### Task Completion Time

Task Completion Time (TCT) represents the average time measured in seconds that the participants needed to complete each trial. TCT split by type of trial and technique is shown on Figure 2, left.

### Inefficiency

Inefficiency is the ratio between the length of the real path and the length of the optimal path [10]. Inefficiency is shown on Figure 2, right.

### Device Movement and Position

Device movement and speed were measured. They are shown averaged per trial on Figure 3. All the values are reported using the OpenGL coordinate system.

### Multi-touch Gestures

We examined the percentage of time that a certain number of fingers were used to interact (Figure 4, left). Specific gestures usage is shown on Figure 4, right. Move and Z-Dist gestures are expressed in the displacement of fingers relatively to the height of the screen (5.5cm). Z-Rot and Arcball are reported in the amount of radians that were applied. All the data are averaged per trial.

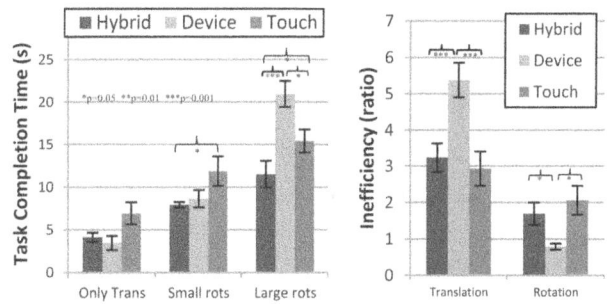

**Figure 2. Left) task completion time grouped by technique and type of trial. Error bars represent standard deviation. Right) Inefficiency in translation and rotation.**

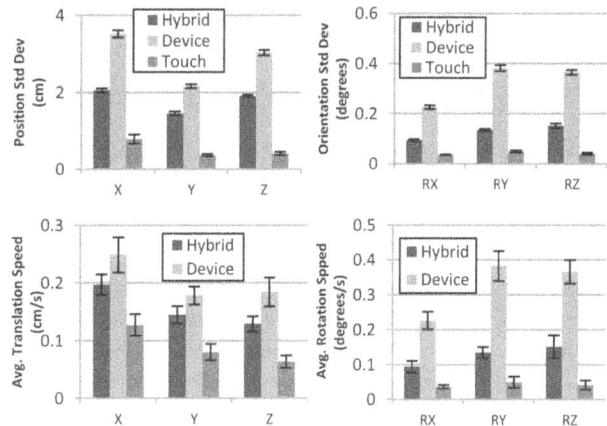

**Figure 3. Top) Standard dev. in position (left) and in rotation (right). Bottom) Speed for position (left) and rotation (right).**

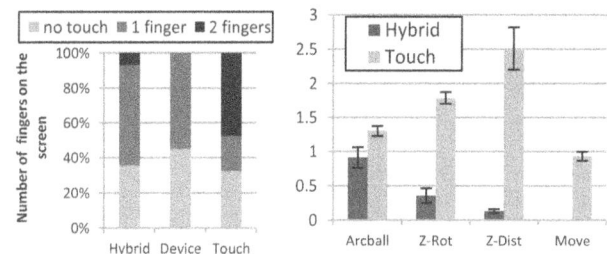

**Figure 4. Left) percentage of time spent with a certain number of fingers on the screen. Right) specific gestures usage.**

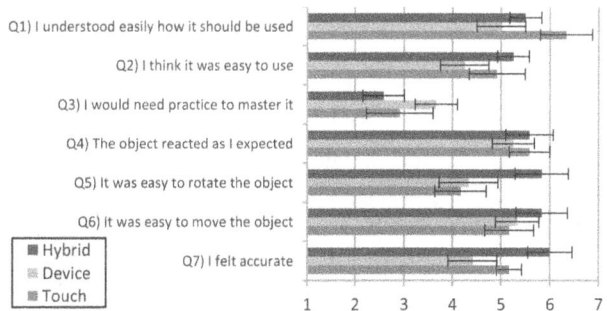

**Figure 5. Subjective Custom Questionnaire.**

15

**Subjective Ratings**

The score of the NASA TLX ranges from 0 (low cognitive load) to 100 (high cognitive load). In our case, this test showed a score of 25.23 (SD=18.41) for *Hybrid*, 31.25 (SD=20.89) for *Device* and 40.05 (SD=19.59) for *Touch*. The results of the custom questionnaire are shown on Figure 5.

**DISCUSSION**

In average, *Hybrid* had the lowest TCT. For *only translation*, *Hybrid* and *Device* had similar TCT as they both use the grasping technique; *Touch* was the worst but not significantly. For small rotations, *Hybrid* and *Device* performed similarly because the users always employed the device in *Hybrid*. *Touch* performed significantly worse than the other techniques. It seems that for small rotations using the device is better than using multi-touch gestures. For large rotations, *Hybrid* was the best. *Device* was the worst in large rotations as the object had to be rotated using successive manoeuvres. This fact is reflected in the high inefficiency that *Device* had in translation because while rotating the object it was also translated purposelessly. The other two techniques were more efficient in translation but *Device* was the most efficient in rotation.

The amount of movement in position and rotation of the device is always in the order *Device>Hybrid>Touch*. In position, there is more movement on the X axis and less in the Y axis. The *Hybrid* technique reduces the amount of position movement significantly but not for the Y axis since it is the only way of moving the object up. For *Touch*, position movement was low for all the axes but not for X. This could be caused by the users' necessity of adopting different points of view. In rotation, movement was smaller for X in *Device* probably because it was hard to point upwards without losing the target chair or the marker. *Hybrid* mitigates this problem as the finger can be used to rotate around the X axis. Furthermore, *Hybrid* reduces the amount of rotation in all the axes. Speeds follow the same pattern as the amount of movement.

Users spent a similar percentage of time without touching the screen in all techniques. In *Touch*, the amount of time with one and two fingers is proportional to the DOF that can be controlled with them. The *Hybrid* technique used the Arcball gesture slightly less than *Touch*, possibly because the device was used for the remaining rotation. The Z-Dist gesture in *Touch* is unusually high; we assume that this is caused by small involuntary changes of the distance between the two fingers when the user is performing other two-finger gestures (Arcball or Z-Rot).

NASA TLX showed a tendency of *Touch* inducing the highest cognitive load and *Hybrid* the lowest one. In the custom questionnaire, preference was *Hybrid >Device>Touch*; however, it was easier to move (Q6) and rotate (Q5) with *Touch* than with *Device*. *Device* appeared as the most intuitive (Q1) and *Hybrid* as the most accurate (Q7). Nonetheless, results were not significant.

A previous study [8] stated that *Device* was better than *Touch*. Differently, our study reveals that they are similar for translation; *Device* is better for small rotations and *Touch* for large ones. This difference could be due to the solely use of one-hand techniques. Another study [1] revealed that freeze-touch is better for DOF-constrained manipulations. For constrained manipulations, it could be enough to use *Touch* or *Device*. However, none of these studies evaluated a hybrid approach.

**CONCLUSION**

Three techniques to manipulate virtual objects with 6 DOF have been compared in a MAR environment. Our user study suggests that combining device movement with multi-touch input offers the overall best results. Nonetheless, using only the device performs worse exclusively on large rotations. Using only the device is interesting as it appeared intuitive and removes the necessity of doing touch gestures on the screen.

**REFERENCES**

1. Bai, H., Lee, G. A. and Billinghurst, M. Freeze view touch and finger gesture based interaction methods for handheld augmented reality interfaces. IVCNZ. ACM (2012).

2. Cohé, A., Dècle, F. and Hachet, M. tBox: a 3d transformation widget designed for touch-screens. CHI. ACM (2011).

3. Hancock, M., Carpendale, S. and Cockburn, A. Shallow-depth 3d interaction: design and evaluation of one-, two- and three-touch techniques. CHI. ACM (2007).

4. Henrysson, A., Billinghurst, M. and Ollila, M. Virtual object manipulation using a mobile phone. ICAT. ACM (2005).

5. Henrysson, A., Marshall, J. and Billinghurst, M. Experiments in 3D interaction for mobile phone AR. GRAPHITE. ACM (2007).

6. Marzo A., Bossavit B. and Hachet M. [Poster] Combining Multi-touch and Device Movement in Mobile Augmented Reality Manipulations. ISMAR. IEEE 2014.

7. Martinet, A., Casiez, G. and Grisoni, L. Integrality and separability of multitouch interaction techniques in 3D manipulation tasks. IEEE Transactions on Visualization and Computer Graphics, 18(3), 369-380. (2012).

8. Mossel, A., Venditti, B. and Kaufmann, H. 3DTouch and HOMER-S: intuitive manipulation techniques for one-handed handheld augmented reality. Virtual Reality International Conference: Laval Virtual. ACM (2013).

9. Shoemake, K. ARCBALL: a user interface for specifying three-dimensional orientation using a mouse. Graphics Interface (Vol. 92, pp. 151-156). (1992).

10. Zhai, S. and Milgram, P. Quantifying coordination in multiple DOF movement and its application to evaluating 6 DOF input devices. CHI. ACM (1998).

# HOBS: Head Orientation-Based Selection in Physical Spaces

**Ben Zhang†, Yu-Hsiang Chen†, Claire Tuna†, Achal Dave†,**
**Yang Li‡, Edward Lee†, Björn Hartmann†**
†: UC Berkeley EECS & CITRIS Invention Lab       ‡: Google Research
{benzh,clairetuna,achal,eal,bjoern}@berkeley.edu, sean.yhc@gmail.com, yangli@acm.org

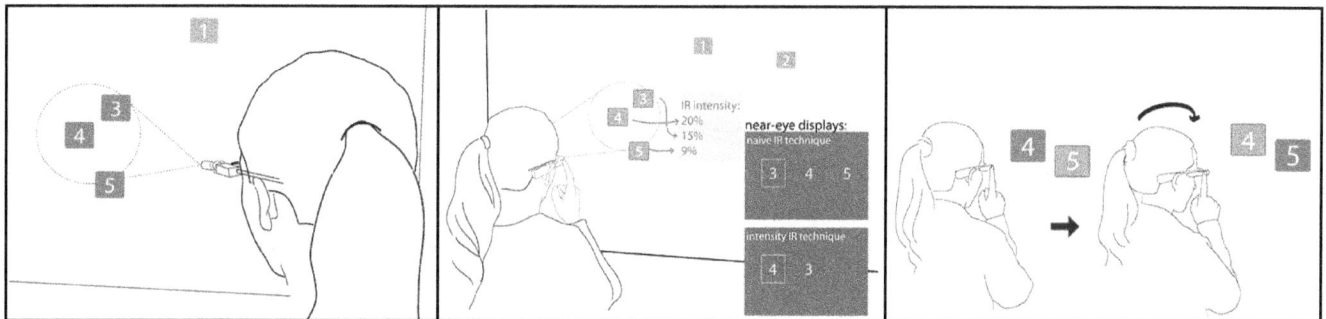

Figure 1. *Left*: Our head orientation-based selection techniques use an IR emitter – multiple targets may fall within its illumination area. *Center*: We offer two list-based refinement techniques – *Naive IR* uses alphabetical ordering; *Intensity IR* orders targets by IR intensity. *Right*: Using *Head-motion Refinement* technique, users can refine their selection through head orientation refinement in a quasi-mode when they hold the touchpad.

## ABSTRACT

Emerging head-worn computing devices can enable interactions with smart objects in physical spaces. We present the iterative design and evaluation of HOBS – a Head Orientation-Based Selection technique for interacting with these devices at a distance. We augment a commercial wearable device, Google Glass, with an infrared (IR) emitter to select targets equipped with IR receivers. Our first design shows that a naive IR implementation can outperform list selection, but has poor performance when refinement between multiple targets is needed. A second design uses IR intensity measurement at targets to improve refinement. To address the lack of natural mapping of on-screen target lists to spatial target location, our third design infers a spatial data structure of the targets enabling a natural head-motion based disambiguation. Finally, we demonstrate a universal remote control application using HOBS and report qualitative user impressions.

## Author Keywords

Wearable Computing; Spatial Interaction; Selection; Glass

## ACM Classification Keywords

H.5.2. Information Interfaces and Presentation (e.g. HCI): Interaction styles

*SUI '14*, Oct 04-05 2014, Honolulu, HI, USA
ACM 978-1-4503-2820-3/14/10.
http://dx.doi.org/10.1145/2659766.2659773

## INTRODUCTION

The number of smart objects in our environment with embedded computation and communication has grown rapidly. These objects are all potential targets for interaction. To initiate *spatial interactions*, a user needs to first acquire the target object – a fundamental task that has been extensively studied in graphical user interfaces, but not yet well-explored in *physical spaces*.

Today, companies like Samsung and Whirlpool are making smart appliances with companion applications that use smartphones as *universal remote controls*. With these applications, the user can select a device from a list in order to control it with a device-specific user interface. However, this method faces *naming* issues (i.e. "what do we name the lamp on the left?") and *scaling* issues as the number of controlled devices increases. These solutions also present a necessarily flawed mapping from the positions of the appliances in the rich, 3-dimensional world to their place in a 1D or 2D list presented on the screen. Past research has used direct aiming at target devices in space with phones to overcome these problems [2, 14]. Such techniques have a few drawbacks: the aiming device first has to be retrieved; the user's hands have to be free for operation; and the user's visual attention is split between looking down at a screen and out at targets in the world.

Emerging head-worn computing devices do not require retrieval since the devices are already worn; they may enable hands-free or uni-manual interactions; and they offer near-eye or see-through displays to present information in the wearer's field of view. We thus investigate how such computing devices may be used for the selection and control of devices in physical spaces. Head-worn devices can naturally exploit the user's head orientation, an important (but imprecise) indicator of the user's *locus of attention* [18]. It suggests the general direction, but not the particular point of focus. We draw an analogy to assistive area cursors and adapt area cursor techniques [7, 26, 5] for physical selection. Such techniques employ a two-step selection process: a *coarse* selection of an area of interest, followed by a *refinement* to select a target within that area.

In this paper, we describe the iterative development and evaluation of HOBS, an area-selection technique that can be readily implemented with small hardware changes to emerging head-worn devices. We augment Google Glass[1] to enable infrared (IR) communication between Glass and target appliances. We contribute and evaluate new methods for addressing selection ambiguity in this context. In all our techniques, the emitted IR beam provides an initial *coarse* selection area (illustrated in Figure 1 *left*). To *refine* selection when multiple targets have received IR signals, we describe and evaluate three techniques:

Our *Naive IR* technique shows an alphabetically ordered disambiguation list on the near-eye display (Figure 1 center). A study with 14 participants finds that target acquisition with naive IR targeting is preferred by users and is faster than pure list selection without IR, but refinement is still time consuming.

Our *Intensity IR* technique improves refinement as target objects compare IR received signal strength (RSS). This value allows the system to eliminate some peripheral targets and to re-order the refinement interface's list by their intensity values. For example, in Figure 1 of *Intensity IR* technique, device 5 is eliminated first and the list is re-ordered based on the intensity readings. A second study with 10 participants shows that *Intensity IR* successfully reduces both the probability of needing to do refinement as well as the time spent in list navigation when compared to *Naive IR*.

Our final *Head-motion Refinement* addresses the lack of a natural mapping when users select a target in the refinement step using their device's touchpad — the axes of motion do not map directly to the spatial layout of target devices in a room. We first learn the relative spatial structure of the targets using Glass' orientation sensors. Users can then perform head movements to change selections to spatially adjacent targets (see the right of Figure 1). For example, nodding down to select the target below current selection, or tilting right to select the next target on the right. We present preliminary feedback from participants on this technique.

We also demonstrate an example application of our technique used as a remote control of smart appliances such as lighting and TV sets: a user looks at the appliance he wishes to control and confirms selection by tapping. An appliance-specific user interface is then shown on the user's near-eye display for further interactions.

---

[1]http://www.google.com/glass/start/

## BACKGROUND AND RELATED WORK

Our approach is related to head- and eye-controlled interfaces, area cursors, pointing in physical spaces and computer vision-based selections.

### Head and Gaze Input

Head movement has long been used for virtual camera control in VR applications [15] and as an assistive input technology for cursor control of desktop applications [16]. However, it is notable that human neck muscles have a lower bandwidth than other muscle groups, e.g., the wrist [4]. Prior work often focused on head orientation for controlling graphical interfaces; in contrast, we apply this modality to selection in physical spaces.

Gaze can also be used to control graphical user interfaces [9]. While there are wearable gaze trackers [3], turning information about a concrete point in space where a user is looking into a selection requires a map with known target locations. Our system works through point-to-point IR communication and does not require an *a priori* map or markers. Target objects in the environment can also be equipped with individual cameras that watch the user [22, 23]. Such an approach can enable similar benefits as our approach, but is computationally more expensive and may not work at greater distances or angles, because it relies on finding the user's pupils in a camera image.

### Area Cursors

In 2D area cursors for GUIs, the activation area of the cursor is enlarged, which facilitates acquiring smaller targets [7]. We argue that head orientation pointing has analogous characteristics (limited pointing performance and accuracy). Area cursors are especially appropriate for individuals with motor control impairments or difficulties [26, 5]. Similar ideas have also been extended into 3D to provide selection with progressive refinement in 3D scenes [1]. All area and space cursors necessitate disambiguation when there are multiple targets and no clear winner. This paper describes the trade-offs between several disambiguation approaches.

### Pointing in Physical Spaces

Rukzio et al. [20] studied alternative methods for selecting devices in physical spaces and found that users strongly preferred either tapping target appliances with a mobile device or pointing at a distance to browsing a list. Several other approaches to spatial selection with handheld devices [2, 14, 25, 21, 8] or finger-worn devices [11] exist.

In some techniques, users select objects of interest with laser pointers; however, the laser dot's small target area makes it poorly matched to head orientation input. Other approaches rely on virtual room models in which a user's location is estimated using IMU-based orientation sensing [25, 10] – in contrast, our technique does not require a static map ahead of time. In the FreeMote system, [6] an IR camera in a handheld controller interprets readings from IR emitters on target appliances. In contrast, we explore a lower cost alternative, using only IR emitters and receivers. Our system tackles an unresolved issue of prior approaches – navigating an area dense with potential targets and resolving selection ambiguity.

Figure 2. Our Glass hardware: Google Glass augmented with a repositionable IR holder, and an additional microcontroller that communicates with Google Glass and controls IR emitter.

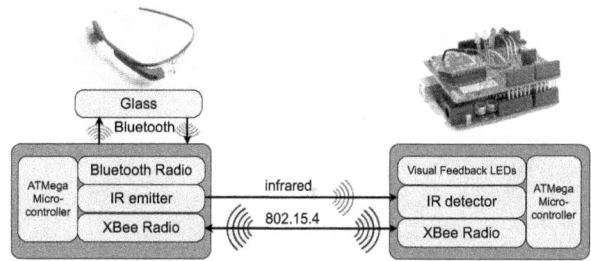

Figure 3. Our System architecture diagram. The selection is initiated through infrared but confirmed over 802.15.4.

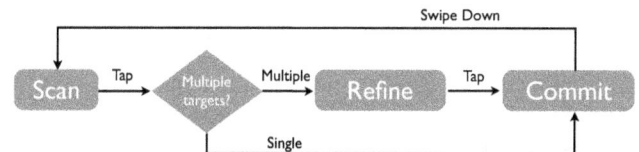

Figure 4. *scan* and *refine* – two main stages during the interaction with HOBS. For completeness, we have also added the final state of *commit*.

## Vision- and Projection-Based Target Selection

Many alternative solutions for detecting devices in contained spaces rely on computer-vision recognition of printed tags on devices. Unfortunately, these methods either impose significant constraints on the camera used for detection [12], require large or obtrusive tags [13], or are designed to work specifically at short distances [19]. Passive markers also cannot show visual feedback in the environment. Handheld projectors can both display a user interface in space and communicate control information optically, e.g., by encoding information temporally (using Gray codes in Picontrol [21] and RFIG Lamps [17]) or spatially (using QR codes in the infrared spectrum in SideBySide [24]). Our solution is similar in spirit but requires only small, low-cost IR emitters and detectors.

## IR FOR HEAD ORIENTATION-BASED TARGETING

In this section, we present our hardware platform (IR targeting) and interaction model (head orientation-based) that we will use throughout our iterative designs.

## Hardware

We hypothesize that infrared (IR) emitters are a good technology match for head orientation selection, since they emit light within a given angle, resulting in a cone in front of the emitter where the light is visible. IR LEDs with many different beam angles are commercially available. We augment Google Glass with a 940nm 5mm IR emitter with 10° beam angle (OSRAM SFH 4545). The emitter is controlled by an additional microcontroller which communicates with Google Glass through Bluetooth radio, since Glass does not directly support hardware modification (see Figure 2). Target devices use Vishay TSOP38238 IR receivers. Data is encoded using standard IR remote protocols at 38.0kHz.

IR signals are used for initial line-of-sight targeting; subsequently, we use bidirectional wireless communication to send information such as target IDs and signal strength from targets back to Glass. We have chosen the commercial off-the-shelf ZigBee implementation (XBee based on 802.15.4 radio) for this purpose (see Figure 3). This architecture was mostly chosen for reasons of expediency and we do not claim optimality for prototyping decisions. Future head-mounted devices could clearly integrate IR emitters; other wireless techniques (WiFi, Bluetooth) can also be used.

## Interaction Model

From the user's perspective, interaction with HOBS proceeds in two stages (Figure 4):

**Scan:** The user first scans the environment to locate the position of the target. During this stage, Glass constantly sends out IR signals, and targets offer immediate visual feedback when they receive a signal. The user confirms his desire to connect to a target by tapping on the Glass touchpad. Glass collects the responses from targets that have received IR reception through the backchannel of XBee. If there is only one single target in IR range, it is automatically selected. However, in a dense environment where multiple targets are within range, the user needs to refine his selection.

**Refine:** When disambiguation is needed, the user must make an explicit selection among the targets within their view range. We have designed multiple refinement mechanisms – all of which enable the user to select one from a subset of targets. The user confirms the current selection with a tap. Since the purpose of this stage is to disambiguate among potential targets, we will also use *disambiguation* to refer to this stage. Finally, a tap confirms a decision.

The overall target acquisition time thus depends on scan and refine times, the probability that refinement is needed, and the time to commit an action (tap):

$$t_{total} = t_{scan} + P(refine) * t_{refine} + t_{commit} \quad (1)$$

In the following sections, we describe our iterative design and evaluation process to minimize the overall target selection time.

## ITERATION 1: NAIVE IR

Our initial research question is: *Can IR-based targeting reduce the selection time compared to the case where only UI list navigation is used on a head-worn device?*

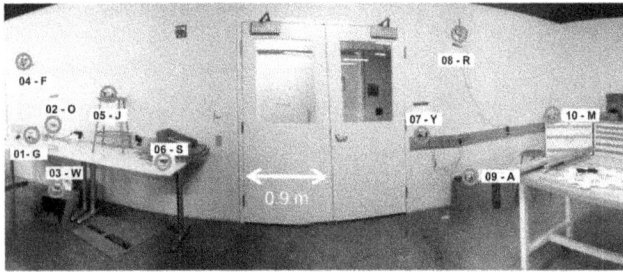

Figure 5. In the targeting study, participants were asked to find and select one of 10 targets in the lab environment.

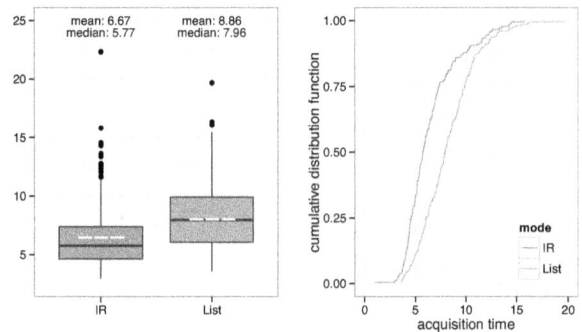

Figure 6. Boxplot of target acquisition time for *IR selection* and *list selection* is shown on the left. The center is the median value, and the mean value is shown using white dashed lines. The cumulative distributions are on the right.

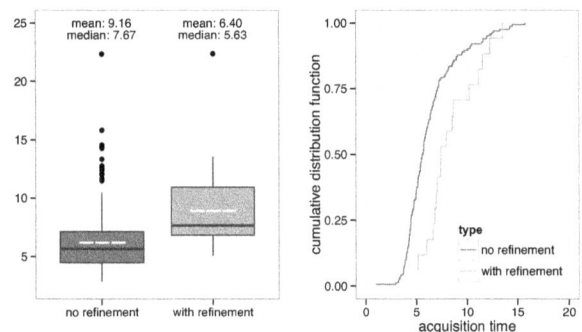

Figure 7. Boxplot and CDF of target acquisition time when refinement is needed or not in *IR selection*.

## Technique

In our first implementation, we use IR for scanning as described in the previous section. For the refinement stage, we simply show a list of the subset of targets that have received IR signals on the Glass display. Users swipe to select from that list and tap to confirm the intended target.

A natural point of comparison is an interface that does not use any head orientation information - it always shows a complete list of all targets. We implemented a list view where users swiped forward and backward on the Glass touchpad to navigate incrementally through the list. To quantify the benefit of using IR for the scanning step, we carried out a target acquisition study which compares the *Naive IR selection* and *list selection*.

## Method

We deployed 10 wireless nodes in an indoor environment (Figure 5), each with a number ID and a letter representing the name. For the study, we recruited 16 participants from our institution (9 males and 7 females) by email. Participants included undergraduate and graduate students, as well as university staff. Their educational backgrounds included Information Science (6), Engineering (4), Math and Science (4), Design (1), Others(1). 14 had never used Google Glass before, so we offered a tutorial before the experiment in order to introduce the device. Four participants wore prescription glasses, which makes Glass more cumbersome to use and adjust and may have affected their task performance. In this study, the IR LED was fixed and not repositionable as shown in Figure 2.

In the within-subject study, half of the participants performed *IR selection* first and the other half used *list selection* first. For each selection condition, we conducted 15 target selections by randomly choosing from all the targets. During the study, we measured the **target acquisition time** for each target selection. At the beginning of each acquisition, participants were asked to stand at a fixed position approximately 10-12 feet away from the nodes, looking down until a target is announced. Participants were allowed to physically move towards targets if they decided that this would help them with the task. After each task, they were asked to move back to the starting position. Afterwards, participants were asked to complete a survey of primarily open-ended questions about their experience.

## Results

Our results indicate that *IR selection* outperforms *list selection*. The average target acquisition time for *IR selection* is 6.67 seconds while *list selection* took 8.86 seconds (see Figure 6). A t-test shows a significant difference ($t(279) = -3.81, p < 0.001$).

To understand how scanning and refinement contribute to total selection time, we split the data from *IR selection* into two parts – trials that required refinement and ones that did not. It takes 6.40 seconds (on average) to complete a selection without any refinement, but 9.16 seconds with refinement, indicating that an additional 2.76 seconds are needed for disambiguation (see Figure 7). This difference is significant ($t(19) = -2.7827, p < 0.05$).Because many targets were spaced far apart, refinements were only necessary in 10% of total *IR selection* trials in this study.

To further generalize the results, in Figure 8, we show the acquisition time for each individual target in the *list selection* condition, ordered by their relative position in the list. Since with IR technique, the acquisition time is invariant from each target's order, we use solid lines to represent the average performance of *IR selection*. From this figure, we can see that once there are more than 6 targets, the average acquisition time will be larger than IR selection, even if disambiguation is needed.

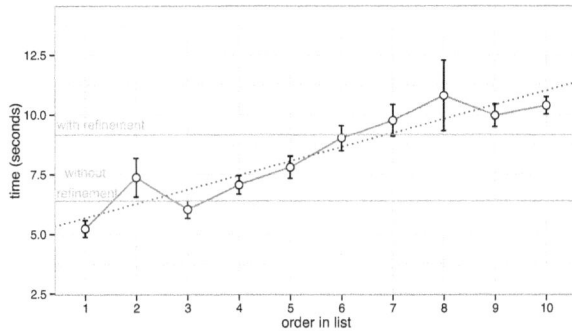

Figure 8. Times taken to select a device vs. its order in the *list selection*. The dotted line is a linear fit between the average time and target orders in the list. Two horizontal solid lines are the average target acquisition times in *Naive IR* when refinement is needed or not.

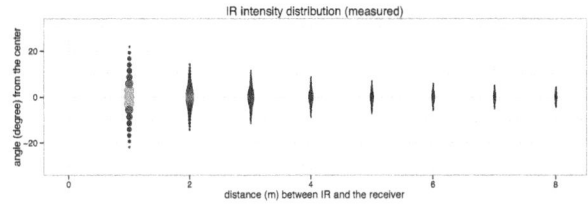

Figure 9. Empirical measurement of IR intensity at different positions. We measure the intensity on a horizontal plane at one-meter intervals from the IR emitter. On that plane, a sample is taken every 5 centimeters, and we stop when the intensity reading is around the level of ambient noise. To match our assumption about the relationship between angles and intensities, the vertical axis shows the relative degree of the angle rather than the distance to the center of the plane. The size and color brightness represent the intensity of the readings for visualization.

In the elicited qualitative feedback, 11 out of 16 participants preferred IR selection over list mode (3 preferred list, 2 were undecided). When asked: *"When you have multiple candidate targets within sight, which method for selecting between them did you use?"*, 81% chose *adjust head so that only one candidate is signaled*, 56% chose *tap (to enter refinement stage) and then choose between list*, and 25% chose *walk closer to the candidate for a better result* (multiple choices were allowed). While we observed more participants walking one or two steps during some tasks, this suggests that participants viewed their moving as a followed-through action of adjusting their heads instead of an intentional to walk closer to the targets.

While both interfaces were judged similarly on overall ease of connecting, IR selection was perceived to be more direct and pleasant. One user noted benefit of *IR selection "allowing users to focus on the targeted objects instead of the screen"*. One subject called it *"natural to interact with things just by looking at them"*. Another mentioned that *"it's really convenient that what I'm looking at is what I'm targeting"*.

In summary, *Naive IR* can outperform linear list selection, and most users prefer this head orientation-based targeting. From our quantitative result, however, we found that the refinement step detracts significantly from the efficiency of the technique.

### ITERATION 2: INTENSITY IR
Performance of the *Naive IR* technique will degrade as target density in an environment increases, as increased density will require refinement steps. We therefore ask a follow-up research question: *How might we improve selection time in a dense environment?*

### Technique
Previously we only used IR reception as a binary signal for identifying potential targets. We hypothesize that IR intensity at the receiver side can provide more information about the likelihood that a user intended to select a particular target. Received IR intensity falls off with distance between IR emitter and receiver as well as with the angle between the emitter

and receiver. To measure intensity, we add an IR light-to-voltage converter TSL267-LF by AMS-TAOS USA Inc.

We have empirically measured the intensity distribution at the receiver for this configuration in Figure 9. Our measurements confirm that angular difference has a large effect on the intensity readings, with rapid fall-off at increasing angles.

The intensity information is used in two ways:

1. When multiple targets have received IR signals and reported the intensity readings, we discard those whose intensities are significantly lower than the largest reading[2]. Therefore, when there is only one target within the line of sight, the IR intensity approach has the same behavior as the previous iteration - no disambiguation is needed. When the environment becomes more populated, the new design can filter some peripheral targets out, reducing $P(refine)$, the likelihood of entering the refinement stage.
2. When refinement is still needed, meaning that multiple targets have relatively close intensity values, the system sorts the disambiguation list according to the IR intensity, from strongest to weakest. We hypothesize that this will reduce $t_{refine}$ significantly by minimizing extra navigation steps, as the first list item will generally match the intended target.

### Method
To quantify the improvement in this design we performed a second study to compare the *Naive IR* and *Intensity IR* approaches. Because we were interested in discovering performance differences in denser environment, we re-positioned the 10 nodes and set them up in a smaller area (see Figure 10). We recruited 10 participants for this study. Each user performed 30 target acquisition tasks for each approach. As in our first within-subject study, half of them perform *Naive IR* first and the other half *Intensity IR* first.

### Results
*Intensity IR* reduces the number of trials in which refinement dialogs are needed from 225 of 300 in *Naive IR* to 167 of

---

[2]In our current implementation, we empirically set it to be half of the ADC resolution, which is frequently used as it indicates a 3dB loss in the signal strength.

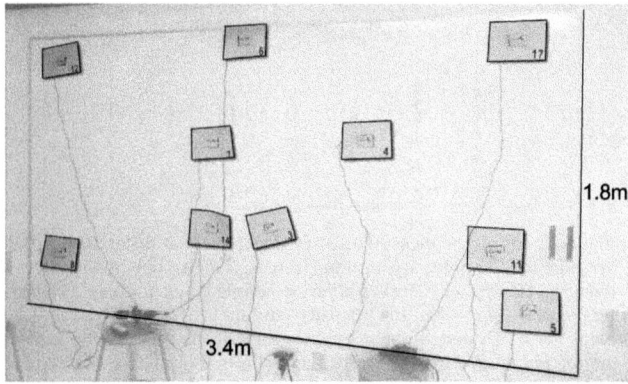

**Figure 10. The environment setup for our second study. In comparison to our first study, we have deliberately increased the target density.**

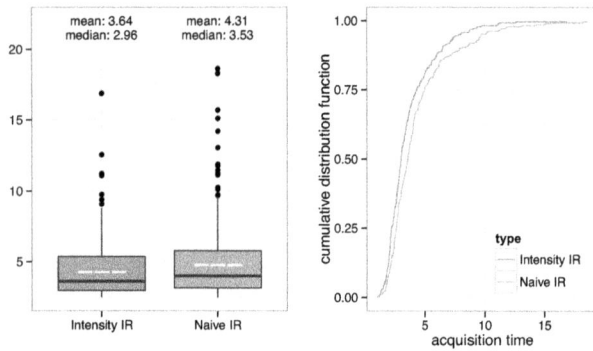

**Figure 11. Boxplot and CDF of the target acquisition time in *Naive IR* and *Intensity IR* conditions.**

300 trials. A Chi-square test shows this difference is significant ($\chi^2(1) = 24.755$, $p < 0.001$). This demonstrates that the new approach successfully reduces the probability that a disambiguation dialog is needed.

In the cases where disambiguation is inevitable, *Intensity IR* sorts the list based on the intensity reading, while *Naive IR* sorts alphabetically. *Intensity IR* reduces the fraction of refinement trails in which additional list navigation is necessary (i.e., the first, already selected element is incorrect). *Intensity IR* sorted the desired target as the first one in the list in 55% of cases (93 of 167). In comparison, for *Naive IR*, only 35% of trials sorted the desired target as the first one in the list (80 out of 225). A Chi-square test show that this difference is significant (with $\chi^2(1) = 15.758$, $p < 0.001$).

From Figure 11, we can see that the overall target acquisition time has decreased from 4.31 seconds for *Naive IR* to 3.64 second for *Intensity IR*. This difference is also significant ($t(555) = 3.2945$, $p = 0.001$).

One side effect that we have observed in this approach is that the *Intensity IR* sometimes eliminates the desired target during the *scanning* stage. Out of 300 trials, the target was accidentally eliminated in 13 (4.3%). This is higher than the error rate for *Naive IR* (5 out of 300, 1.6%). Even though the higher error rate increases the chance of multiple attempts in

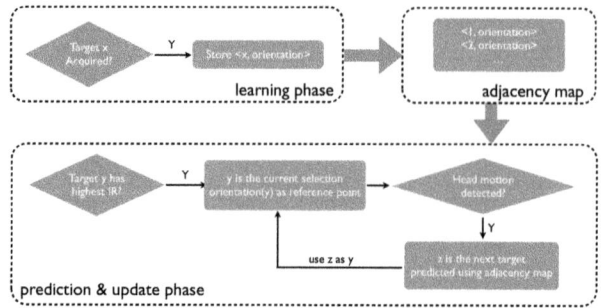

**Figure 12. Our third technique learned each target's absolute orientation and construct the adjacency map. During the *refinement* stage, the prediction is based on relative changes to a reference point.**

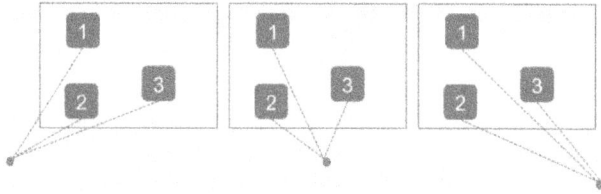

**Figure 13. This illustrates that the change of a user's absolution position doesn't change the relative relationship of physical targets.**

target selection, our analysis above illustrates that overall performance of *Intensity IR* is still better than *Naive IR*.

## ITERATION 3: HEAD MOTION REFINEMENT

Both *Naive IR* and *Intensity IR* rely on list navigation on the near-eye display for the refinement step. The list interface has a few clear shortcomings: navigation actions map poorly to real world results, and users must switch their focus back and forth between the physical scene and the near-eye display. These problems motivated us to design an approach that harnesses the head orientation during the *refinement* stage.

In our third iteration, we ask the research question – *can we build a system purely using head orientation and visual feedback from the environment for target selection?*

### Technique

We introduce a third technique that uses a combination of motion sensors and IR to learn the relative orientations of targets in a room and intelligently suggest targets during refinement (see Figure 12).

In the learning stage, as the user scans over targets in their normal use, the system attains the absolute orientation of each device from IR and motion sensors. From this information it can abstract out the relative positions of targets and construct an *adjacency map*. The absolute orientations in the map cannot be applied to all indoor environments, since the user's movements through the space could change the relationships between targets. However, with the constraint that the targets are spread around the periphery at similar distances, their relative orientations are stable (see Figure 13). This learning process can be transparent to the user and the map can be built without an explicit calibration phase.

After the map is created, the user can enter a quasi-mode for refinement by holding down on the touchpad. In this quasi-mode, a single selected device lights up at a time. When the user turns his head in the direction of another device, the selection (and indicator light) switches to that device. Therefore, the user can move between devices one at a time with slight head movements. This prediction is implemented by first calculating the user's direction of head motion, and searching through the adjacency map for the nearest device in that direction. To calculate the direction, we maintain a circular buffer of the last 10 sensor measurements, passed through a low pass filter. The direction is then calculated as the difference between the last sample and the first sample. We use a hysteresis method to avoid spurious selection changes — if the variance of the buffer is below a threshold, we assume no movement has occurred and do not select another device.

## Evaluation

We evaluated the head motion refinement method through an informal study and collected qualitative feedback from a subset of 4 users from the Iteration 2 study. In this evaluation, we asked users to cycle through multiple targets using the new quasi-mode.

The users had strong preferences for the new method of refinement. Our observations suggest that each trial became much easier than previous iterations. We conducted a survey to collect qualitative feedback after the experiment. On a scale from 1-7, 1 being the least mental effort and 7 being the most mental effort users rated the old technique 4.25 and the new technique 2 on average. All users indicated a preference for head movement to list navigation. One user referenced the issue of naming targets that the list necessitates, preferring the experience of *"matching visual cues rather than numbers"*. Another participant remarked that it *"just made more sense"* and was a *"more natural way for demonstrating intentionality"*. The users preferred the new mapping in relation to the whole environment: *"it leveraged the spatial sense that I already had just by using the system"*. They were also delighted to avoid list navigation, which they now called *"difficult"* and *"painful"*.

## APPLICATIONS

Head orientation targeting can enable a wide range of context-aware applications. We implement one particular demonstrative application: a universal smart appliance controller. Users select a smart device (e.g., light fixture, TV, or home appliance) with Glass — upon confirming the selection, an device-specific UI is shown on the user's near-eye display, and they can control the application (without having to continually look at it) through their device touchpad.

Our prototype, includes three smart devices: a lamp and a fan that could be switched on and off; and a smart TV with playback, volume and navigation controls (see Figure 14). The prototype used *Naive IR, as the small number of target devices made selection without disambiguation possible*. The appliances are switched with 120V AC relays. The smart TV is a 30" display connected to a laptop. User interfaces for each were pre-defined in our application.

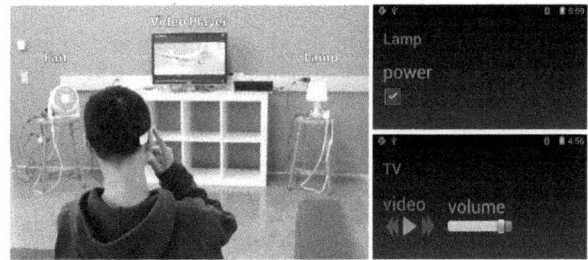

**Figure 14. In the smart home scenario, we have built three smart appliances for a user experience study. The interface supports both simple on/off appliances (lamp or fan) and multi-functional appliances (TV, for example).**

We set the devices up in a simulated living room environment and invited 14 users to step through a predefined set of tasks to control the appliances at a distance. The tasks included turning off a lamp, playing a movie and turning up the volume.

All participants successfully completed the list of tasks. They commented positively on the universal remote control functionality (e.g., *"I didn't have to search for different remote controllers for different appliances"*) and stated it was easy to target and connect to appliances, in line with the findings of the previous studies. Participants saw potential benefits of the device for families; one user remarked that he could imagine people using the system *"while keeping an eye on their children at the same time"*.

While our system enables users to select and control the example devices successfully, work remains in devising appropriate interfaces for complex devices. Users rated ease of use higher for the lamp and fan which had simple, discrete on/off actions, and lower for the TV control, which had more options. Multiple participants remarked that the difficulty was based on the affordances of Glass: *"most of the difficulty I had with Glass came from having to navigate the interface on the tiny screen with the touch pad"*. We leave addressing this fundamental usability challenge of wearable devices with near-eye displays to future work.

## DISCUSSION

The rapid development of sensing technologies has created many opportunities for new ways to interact with smart objects. In our exploration of the design space of HOBS, we carefully selected sensing techniques that are readily available and easy to deploy; and we added complexity to our system only when necessary.

### Interpretation of results

A primary goal of this paper was to provide an effective and efficient method for target selections in physical spaces. Targeting is a fundamental building block across many interaction tasks – it has a significant impact on user experiences collectively and can provide seamless interaction when designed well.

We formalized a *scan* and *refine* model of head orientation-based selection (Equation 1). We first introduced head orientation as an alternative to list selection and showed that *scanning* can outperform list selection. Our redesigns then focused on the case where refinement is needed. The two ways to reduce refinement time are 1) to reduce $P(refine)$, the probability that a manual refinement is necessary; and 2) to reduce $t_{refine}$, the time required to perform the refinement interaction itself. Using IR intensity readings addresses both these terms, as it can be used to both avoid showing refinement dialogs, and to optimize their display when they are needed.

Our final head orientation-based technique improves the nature of the mapping between items in the refinement dialog and the layout of targets in space. Informal testing suggests that users prefer using this spatial mapping.

### Limitations
Our system faces a few limitations. First, IR intensity measurements only work within the dynamic range of our sensor. Additional strong IR sources like direct sunlight may saturate the sensor and make discrimination impossible. Second, our adjacency map is built assuming stable relative target locations. If targets move, the map will have to be recalculated. This may be done incrementally during everyday interactions, but we have not yet tackled this challenge.

We also acknowledge several limitations of our study design: we have not yet systematically studied target density variation; our study was performed in a lab environment; and only measured first use. Future work should study how the technique applies in realistic settings over longer periods of time.

### CONCLUSION
In this paper, by presenting our iterative design process in head orientation-based targeting, we have learned that IR alone can help reduce the overall acquisition time by reducing the chances when we need to perform refinement. With IR intensity added, the targeting can work better in a relative dense environment. However, a more natural approach is to combine IR with head motion. Through our preliminary user studies, we learned that this is a more intuitive way of performing refinement in comparison to the menu-based selections. We leave a more comprehensive technical solution of using motion sensors and its evaluation as the future work.

### ACKNOWLEDGMENTS
This work was supported in part by the TerraSwarm Research Center, one of six centers supported by the STARnet phase of the Focus Center Research Program (FCRP) a Semiconductor Research Corporation program sponsored by MARCO and DARPA. Additional support was provided by a Sloan Foundation Fellowship and a Google Research Award.

### REFERENCES
1. Bacim, F., Kopper, R., and Bowman, D. A. Design and evaluation of 3d selection techniques based on progressive refinement. *International Journal of Human-Computer Studies 71*, 7 (2013), 785–802.

2. Beigl, M. Point & click-interaction in smart environments. In *Handheld and Ubiquitous Computing*, H.-W. Gellersen, Ed., no. 1707 in Lecture Notes in Computer Science. Springer Berlin Heidelberg, Jan. 1999, 311–313.

3. Bulling, A., Roggen, D., and Tröster, G. Wearable eog goggles: Seamless sensing and context-awareness in everyday environments. *Journal of Ambient Intelligence and Smart Environments 1*, 2 (2009), 157–171.

4. Card, S. K., Mackinlay, J. D., and Robertson, G. G. A morphological analysis of the design space of input devices. *ACM Trans. Inf. Syst. 9*, 2 (Apr. 1991), 99–122.

5. Findlater, L., Jansen, A., Shinohara, K., Dixon, M., Kamb, P., Rakita, J., and Wobbrock, J. O. Enhanced area cursors: reducing fine pointing demands for people with motor impairments. In *Proceedings of the 23nd annual ACM symposium on User interface software and technology*, ACM (2010), 153–162.

6. Hipp, M., Mahler, T. D., Spika, C., and Weber, M. Universal device access with freemote. In *Intelligent Environments* (2009), 311–318.

7. Kabbash, P., and Buxton, W. A. The prince technique: Fitts' law and selection using area cursors. In *Proceedings of the SIGCHI conference on Human factors in computing systems*, ACM Press/Addison-Wesley Publishing Co. (1995), 273–279.

8. Kemp, C. C., Anderson, C. D., Nguyen, H., Trevor, A. J., and Xu, Z. A point-and-click interface for the real world: laser designation of objects for mobile manipulation. In *Proceedings of the 3rd ACM/IEEE international conference on Human robot interaction*, HRI '08, ACM (New York, NY, USA, 2008), 241–248.

9. Kumar, M., Paepcke, A., and Winograd, T. Eyepoint: practical pointing and selection using gaze and keyboard. In *Proceedings of the SIGCHI conference on Human factors in computing systems*, ACM (2007), 421–430.

10. Lifton, J., Mittal, M., Lapinski, M., and Paradiso, J. A. Tricorder: A mobile sensor network browser. In *Proceedings of the ACM CHI 2007 Conference-Mobile Spatial Interaction Workshop* (2007).

11. Merrill, D., and Maes, P. Augmenting looking, pointing and reaching gestures to enhance the searching and browsing of physical objects. In *Pervasive Computing*. Springer, 2007, 1–18.

12. Mohan, A., Woo, G., Hiura, S., Smithwick, Q., and Raskar, R. Bokode: Imperceptible visual tags for camera based interaction from a distance. In *ACM SIGGRAPH 2009 Papers*, SIGGRAPH '09, ACM (New York, NY, USA, 2009), 98:1–98:8.

13. Moran, T. P., Saund, E., Van Melle, W., Gujar, A. U., Fishkin, K. P., and Harrison, B. L. Design and technology for collaborage: Collaborative collages of information on physical walls. In *Proceedings of ACM UIST*, ACM (New York, NY, USA, 1999), 197–206.

14. Patel, S. N., and Abowd, G. D. A 2-way laser-assisted selection scheme for handhelds in a physical environment. In *UbiComp 2003: Ubiquitous Computing*, Springer (2003), 200–207.

15. Pausch, R., Shackelford, M. A., and Proffitt, D. A user study comparing head-mounted and stationary displays. In *Virtual Reality, 1993. Proceedings., IEEE 1993 Symposium on Research Frontiers in* (1993), 41–45.

16. Radwin, R. G., Vanderheiden, G. C., and Lin, M.-L. A method for evaluating head-controlled computer input devices using fitts' law. *Human Factors: The Journal of the Human Factors and Ergonomics Society 32*, 4 (1990), 423–438.

17. Raskar, R., Beardsley, P., van Baar, J., Wang, Y., Dietz, P., Lee, J., Leigh, D., and Willwacher, T. RFIG lamps: interacting with a self-describing world via photosensing wireless tags and projectors. In *ACM SIGGRAPH 2004 Papers*, SIGGRAPH '04, ACM (New York, NY, USA, 2004), 406–415.

18. Raskin, J. *The Humane Interface: New Directions for Designing Interactive Systems*. ACM Press/Addison-Wesley Publishing Co., New York, NY, USA, 2000.

19. Rekimoto, J., and Ayatsuka, Y. Cybercode: Designing augmented reality environments with visual tags. In *Proceedings of DARE 2000 on Designing Augmented Reality Environments*, DARE '00, ACM (New York, NY, USA, 2000), 1–10.

20. Rukzio, E., Leichtenstern, K., Callaghan, V., Holleis, P., Schmidt, A., and Chin, J. An experimental comparison of physical mobile interaction techniques: Touching, pointing and scanning. In *UbiComp 2006: Ubiquitous Computing*. Springer, 2006, 87–104.

21. Schmidt, D., Molyneaux, D., and Cao, X. PICOntrol: using a handheld projector for direct control of physical devices through visible light. In *Proceedings of the 25th annual ACM symposium on User interface software and technology*, UIST '12, ACM (New York, NY, USA, 2012), 379–388.

22. Smith, B. A., Yin, Q., Feiner, S. K., and Nayar, S. K. Gaze locking: passive eye contact detection for human-object interaction. In *Proceedings of the 26th annual ACM symposium on User interface software and technology*, ACM (2013), 271–280.

23. Vertegaal, R., Mamuji, A., Sohn, C., and Cheng, D. Media eyepliances: using eye tracking for remote control focus selection of appliances. In *CHI'05 Extended Abstracts on Human Factors in Computing Systems*, ACM (2005), 1861–1864.

24. Willis, K. D., Poupyrev, I., Hudson, S. E., and Mahler, M. SideBySide: ad-hoc multi-user interaction with handheld projectors. In *Proceedings of the 24th annual ACM symposium on User interface software and technology*, UIST '11, ACM (New York, NY, USA, 2011), 431–440.

25. Wilson, A., and Shafer, S. XWand: UI for intelligent spaces. In *Proceedings of the SIGCHI Conference on Human Factors in Computing Systems*, CHI '03, ACM (New York, NY, USA, 2003), 545–552.

26. Worden, A., Walker, N., Bharat, K., and Hudson, S. Making computers easier for older adults to use: area cursors and sticky icons. In *Proceedings of the ACM SIGCHI Conference on Human factors in computing systems*, ACM (1997), 266–271.

# AnnoScape: Remote Collaborative Review Using Live Video Overlay in Shared 3D Virtual Workspace

Austin Lee*[1]    Hiroshi Chigira*[3]    Sheng Kai Tang[1]    Kojo Acquah[2]    Hiroshi Ishii[1]

[1]MIT Media Lab                    [2]MIT EECS                    [3]NTT Service Evolution Lab
Cambridge, MA 02139 USA        Cambridge, MA 02139              Yokosuka, Japan
{aslee, tonytang, ishii}@media.mit.edu    kacquah@mit.edu        chigira.hiroshi@lab.ntt.co.jp

## ABSTRACT

We introduce AnnoScape, a remote collaboration system that allows users to overlay live video of the physical desktop image on a shared 3D virtual workspace to support individual and collaborative review of 2D and 3D content using hand gestures and real ink. The AnnoScape system enables distributed users to visually navigate the shared 3D virtual workspace individually or jointly by moving tangible handles; simultaneously snap into a shared viewpoint and generate a live video overlay of freehand annotations from the desktop surface onto the system's virtual viewports which can be placed spatially in the 3D data space. Finally, we present results of our preliminary user study and discuss design issues and AnnoScape's potential to facilitate effective communication during remote 3D data reviews.

## Author Keywords

3D review; remote collaboration; hand-drawn annotation; video overlay.

## ACM Classification Keywords

H.5.2 [Information Interfaces and Presentation]: User Interfaces - Interaction styles.

## INTRODUCTION

When collaboratively reviewing visual content, leaving quick annotations and using natural hand gestures such as finger pointing, often helps participants communicate effectively [2]. However, in remote settings for reviewing shared contents, it is difficult for the participants to make use of physical workspace and take full advantage of traditional freehand sketching. This constraint pertains to reviewing both 2D and 3D content in most screen/desktop sharing programs [6, 19] or groupware [3, 4]. For example, in architectural practice, a common method for leaving annotations during a remote review of 3D information

includes importing renderings of digital snapshots on drawing software or printing paper plots from the 3D model [15]. In this paper, we aim to improve the remote collaborative review experience of 2D and 3D information by integrating the individual physical desktop with the virtual shared 3D workspace using spatial video overlay technique. Our system configuration enables sharing views of the digital 3D models and supports collaborative hand-drawn annotation in the virtual 3D space (Figure 1a-b). Providing a real-time shared view, tools for quick annotations on 3D digital information and a connection between the physical and the digital workspace has a great potential for remote collaboration between professionals in fields such as architectural/landscape design, planetary science or medical practice.

Figure 1. (a) AnnoScape prototype setup, (b) Shared 3D space.

## Contributions

We propose a new system design called AnnoScape that focuses on remote collaborative review of 3D digital data using a live video overlay of the physical desktop image on the viewports of the 3D scene. AnnoScape provides the capability to merge multiple work platforms into a shared virtual 3D workspace through spatial video overlay technique. This approach allows AnnoScape system to maintain the benefits of traditional sketching tools on the physical desktop workspace, which includes the tactility and familiarity provided by the basic desktop tools. Our contributions include:

- Application of video overlay techniques for 3D review, using hand-drawn annotations and materials on the physical desktop.

- Interaction techniques to support various work modes based on viewport configurations.

- A preliminary user study on the usage of physical artifacts and freehand annotations during the collaborative review of 3D information over a distance,

* The first two authors contributed equally to this work

to provide guiding principles for the future direction of 3D remote collaboration.

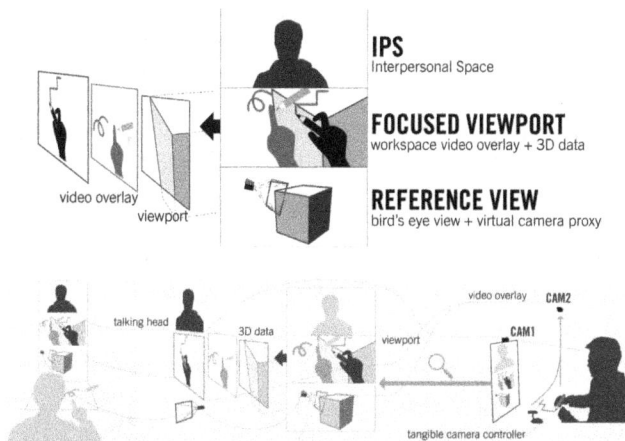

**Figure 2. AnnoScape interface consists of interpersonal space (IPS), focused viewport, and reference view (Top), AnnoScape interface flow and infrastructure (Bottom).**

## RELATED WORK

### Shared Surface Video Overlay Applications
Sharing live video of the physical workspace over distance has been explored mainly in reviewing 2D information [7, 8, 16] ClearBoard introduces the concept of seamlessly connecting remote drawing surfaces through a transparent surface. TeamWorkStation shows various workspace overlay techniques. IllumiShare [17] directly projects the remote collaborator's shared surface on the local workspace.

### 3D Review Using Tangible Controllers
Based on the concept of using physical artifacts as input devices [5], BUILD-IT demonstrates the use of brick-based navigation in a virtual camera in the 3D environment [14]. Other relevant projects using tangible controllers for 3d navigation include Augmented Surfaces [10] and DeskCube [12].

### Freehand Drawings in 3D Space
Virtual Notepad [9] and Boom Chameleon by Tsang et al. [13] utilize a spatially aware display to define the 2D plane for digital annotation. Second Surface is a tablet-based application that uses image-based AR recognition technology to enable participants to digitally annotate 2D content in user's real environment [18].

### The AnnoScape System
The key attribute of the AnnoScape system is providing tools for quick annotation that enhances the remote 3D review process. To reach this goal, our system design aims to integrate traditional freehand 2D annotations in the 3D space by combining the video overlay-based shared drawing techniques with virtual 3D viewport navigation system. The benefit of the spatial video overlay technique is that the system provides participants the freedom to utilize the individual desktop workspace. In our system, users can navigate in 3D and spatially arrange annotations in various

locations from multiple angles primarily by manipulating the virtual camera proxy that is synced to the Tangible Camera Controller. This approach allows the virtual camera proxy to capture natural hand movements of the remote participant. Also, the camera proxy provides video thumbnails of the participants' live annotation session (Figure 3b). The subtle awareness of the remote participant's activity enables the users to naturally monitor the focus of the partner's attention.

## DESIGN INTERACTIONS

### Hardware Setup and The Interaction Design
Each desktop station consists of a monitor and two webcams connected to a computer (Figure 3a). The prototype configuration includes one webcam (Video 1) facing the user to capture the talking head and another overhead mount video source to stream the information from the physical desktop (Video 2). We place a physical Tangible Camera Controller with markers attached on the desktop that can be detected by Video 2. The interface of the AnnoScape system consists of 1) Inter-Personal Space (IPS) for face-to-face conversations [8]; 2) focused viewport that can merge into a synced workspace; and 3) a reference view for navigation, which shows the location of the focused viewports in the 3D environment from a bird's-eye view (Figure 2) (Figure 4). In AnnoScape setup, we enable users to swap between canned 3D models by having them place paper print of the model with AR markers that trigger the 3D model to change and the scene to reset and clear out the annotations. In our demo, associated contents such as a time-lapse video of the building's construction site are placed in the parallel location where the video was actually taken. Users can snap their viewports onto the 2D content's location and review both 2D and 3D information.

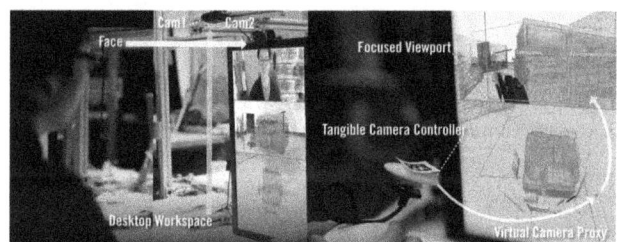

**Figure 3. (a) AnnoScape system hardware configuration, (b)Tangible Camera Controller for navigation.**

### Navigation
The Tangible Camera Controller enables remote participants to visually navigate the shared virtual 3D space individually or jointly and share viewports either asynchronously or in real time. When the collaborator's viewport is close to an existing annotation session, the scene snaps on top of the existing workspace. After navigating in 3D to a desired scene, participants can capture the focused viewport location by pressing the capture button. In our system, capturing the personal focused viewport means locking the scene into an area for annotation and individual virtual workspace. Once the

scene is locked, the overhead webcam simultaneously captures the physical individual desktop workspace, and the system overlays the extracted live video image onto the focused viewport. This allows users to place real-time annotation on the captured 3D scene from specific angles in the virtual space. When participants leave the workspace, the annotation is archived spatially in the virtual 3D space.

**Figure 4. Various annotation methods include physical ink, finger pointing, arbitrary objects and virtual camera proxy with live video stream of the individual workspace.**

## Annotation

In AnnoScape setup, we use dry erase markers on a horizontal white board for annotation (Figure 4). The system automatically extracts live image of the ink, hand, and physical object from the white foreground to provide legible information. Through background subtraction image processing [1], the pixels in the white area of the streaming image are set to be transparent. For example, hands in white gloves are invisible inside the virtual scene (Figure 4). Rarely, there were times when unwanted objects in the foreground would create markings after automatic background subtraction. We implemented a manual calibration feature using one click keyboard to achieve clean background subtraction.

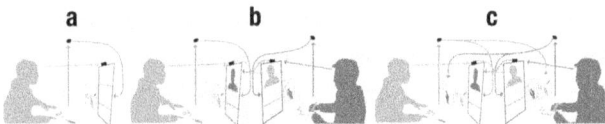

**Figure 5. (a)AnnoScape individual review mode, (b) AnnoScape loosely coupled collaboration mode, (c) AnnoScape tightly coupled collaboration mode.**

## Work Modes

In relation to how the viewports are tied to one another, the AnnoScape system presents the following three types of work modes (Figure 5):

### 1) Individual Review Mode

Individual Review mode is the asynchronous 3D review session done by an individual user. The user can spatially navigate in the virtual 3D workspace, capture viewports and place annotations on multiple 3D scenes. We also allow users to hide Interpersonal Space UI elements for better view (Figure 6a).

### 2) Loosely Coupled Real-time Collaboration Mode

The remote collaborators can both log into the system and synchronously work on separate parts of the shared 3D data. This is called Loosely Coupled Real-time Collaboration.

### 3) Tightly Coupled Real-time Collaboration Mode

When all users are logged into to the system, a user can join the remote collaborator's annotation session on the same 3D scene synchronously by navigating to the activated focused viewport location. The shared viewport generates a strict WYSIWIS platform [11] that is well suited for a real-time shared review. Each participant's viewport is synchronized in the Tightly Coupled Real-time Collaboration mode. In this mode, we allow users to switch the interface between the default interface and the custom interface for the mode, which is optimized for larger view of the shared workspace (Figure 6b).

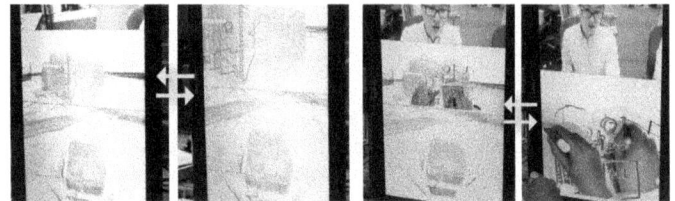

**Figure 6. (a)Custom individual review interface switch, (b) tightly coupled collaboration interface switch from the default interface.**

## PRELIMINARY USER STUDY

We recruited eight participants including three individuals with architectural and one with industrial design backgrounds. We grouped participants into pairs in random order and gave them tasks for each study, such as 1) navigation and capturing the Focused Viewport in the Individual Review Mode, 2) annotate information on the 3D model, 3) Communicate both with annotations and hand gestures, 4) Display of Physical Materials. All participants successfully performed the given tasks. We had the participants rate the fluidity of interaction and the ease or difficulty of completion for the tasks. A two-tailed paired t-test with a significance value of $p = 0.05$ was used for questions rated 1-7. A similar sign test was conducted for binary responses of preference questions. White gloves versus no white gloves test didn't result in any major differences. The responses when the material samples were used were significantly better than not using them.

## DISCUSSION AND FUTURE WORK

Based on the findings from the preliminary user study, we designed additional applications and features that could improve the AnnoScape system. Regarding the reference image for direct annotation, while options such as using overhead projection may have been a possibility; it also generated problems such as casting harsh shadows on the workspace during the annotation session. Later we learned the issue of indirectness could be drastically resolved by applying regular technical drawing tools such as a ruler to provide the reference point in the virtual scene. We included hidden features such as visually tilting or zooming the 3D view using keyboard input in current setup. We also implemented the preview mode, which allows users to transition to the archived annotation workspaces through smooth animation with simple keyboard input. As a separate application, we created tools for content-filtering options that can display captured images or associated contents with different alpha values. This was designed for scenarios with more than two users. The tool would help identify the contents based on the owners or the time in which it was created. We plan to evaluate the potential of these additional features further in future work. Although the primary driving idea of the AnnoScape is to make use of the live overlay of desktop in 3D space, we also saw great potential in a scalable multimodal system. As a proof of concept, we integrated the AnnoScape into a pair of tablet device. The mobile AnnoScape can possibly integrate a real-time live video feed from various physical locations into the 3D digital workspace. For example, the onsite construction can be streamed live inside the virtual 3D workspace in the parallel location using the camera from a tablet device. Achieving a seamless transition across a variety of work modes and enriching the representation of shared information are our long-term goals.

## REFERENCES

1. Ahmed M. Elgammal, David Harwood, and Larry S. Davis. 2000. Non-parametric Model for Background Subtraction. In *Proceedings of the 6th European Conference on Computer Vision-Part II (ECCV '00)*, David Vernon (Ed.).

2. Austin Seugmin Lee. 2013. Use of Live Video Overlay on 3D Data for Distributed Collaborative Review. M.S. thesis. Dept. of Architecture. Program of Media Arts and Sciences, Massachusetts Institute of Technology, Cambridge, MA, USA.

3. Autodesk Revit. Retrieved May, 2013, from: http://www.autodesk.com/products/autodesk-revit-family/overview

4. Digital Project, Gehry Technology. Retrieved May, 2013, from: http://www.gehrytechnologies.com/digital-project

5. George W. Fitzmaurice, Hiroshi Ishii, and William A. S. Buxton. 1995. Bricks: laying the foundations for graspable user interfaces. In *Proceedings of the SIGCHI Conference on Human Factors in Computing Systems* (CHI '95), Irvin R. Katz, Robert Mack, Linn Marks, Mary Beth Rosson, and Jakob Nielsen (Eds.).

6. Google Hangouts. Retrieved May, 2013, from: https://www.google.com/+/learnmore/hangouts/

7. H. Ishii. 1990. TeamWorkStation: towards a seamless shared workspace. In *Proceedings of the 1990 ACM conference on Computer-supported cooperative work* (CSCW '90).

8. Hiroshi Ishii and Minoru Kobayashi. 1992. ClearBoard: a seamless medium for shared drawing and conversation with eye contact. In *Proceedings of the SIGCHI Conference on Human Factors in Computing Systems* (CHI '92), Penny Bauersfeld, John Bennett, and Gene Lynch (Eds.).

9. I. Poupyrev, N. Tomokazu, and S. Weghorst. 1998. Virtual Notepad: Handwriting in Immersive VR. In *Proceedings of the Virtual Reality Annual International Symposium* (VRAIS '98).

10. Jun Rekimoto and Masanori Saitoh. 1999. Augmented surfaces: a spatially continuous work space for hybrid computing environments. In *Proceedings of the SIGCHI conference on Human Factors in Computing Systems* (CHI '99).

11. M. Stefik, D. G. Bobrow, G. Foster, S. Lanning, and D. Tatar. 1987. WYSIWIS revised: early experiences with multiuser interfaces. ACM Trans. Inf. Syst. 5, 2 (April 1987), 147-167. DOI=10.1145/27636.28056

12. Michael Glueck, Sean Anderson, and Azam Khan. 2010. DeskCube: using physical zones to select and control combinations of 3D navigation operations. In Proceedings of the 2010 Spring Simulation Multiconference (SpringSim '10). Society for Computer Simulation International, San Diego, CA, USA, Article 200 , 4 pages.

13. Michael Tsang, George W. Fitzmzurice, Gordon Kurtenbach, Azam Khan, and Bill Buxton. 2003. Boom chameleon: simultaneous capture of 3D viewpoint, voice and gesture annotations on a spatially-aware display. In *ACM SIGGRAPH 2003.*

14. Morten Fjeld, Fred Voorhorst, Martin Bichsel, Kristina Lauche, Matthias Rauterberg, and Helmut Krueger. 1999. Exploring Brick-Based Navigation and Composition in an Augmented Reality. In *Proceedings of the 1st international symposium on Handheld and Ubiquitous Computing* (HUC '99)

15. Moum, A. 2010. Design Team stories, Automation in Construction vol. 19 issue 5 August, 2010. p. 554-569.

16. Pierre Wellner. 1993. Interacting with paper on the DigitalDesk. Commun. *ACM 36, 7* (July 1993), 87-96.

17. Sasa Junuzovic, Kori Inkpen, Tom Blank, and Anoop Gupta. 2012. IllumiShare: sharing any surface. In *Proceedings of the 2012 ACM annual conference on Human Factors in Computing Systems* (CHI '12).

18. Shunichi Kasahara, Valentin Heun, Austin S. Lee, and Hiroshi Ishii. 2012. Second surface: multi-user spatial collaboration system based on augmented reality. In *SIGGRAPH Asia 2012 Emerging Technologies* (SA '12).

19. Timbuktu(software). Retrieved May, 2013, from:http://en.wikipedia.org/wiki/Timbuktu_(software)

# GestureAnalyzer: Visual Analytics for Pattern Analysis of Mid-Air Hand Gestures

Sujin Jang[1], Niklas Elmqvist[2], Karthik Ramani[1,2]

[1]School of Mechanical Engineering and [2]School of Electrical and Computer Engineering

Purdue University, West Lafayette, IN, USA

{jang64, elm, ramani}@purdue.edu

## ABSTRACT

Understanding the intent behind human gestures is a critical problem in the design of gestural interactions. A common method to observe and understand how users express gestures is to use elicitation studies. However, these studies require time-consuming analysis of user data to identify gesture patterns. Also, the analysis by humans cannot describe gestures in as detail as in data-based representations of motion features. In this paper, we present GestureAnalyzer, a system that supports exploratory analysis of gesture patterns by applying interactive clustering and visualization techniques to motion tracking data. GestureAnalyzer enables rapid categorization of similar gestures, and visual investigation of various geometric and kinematic properties of user gestures. We describe the system components, and then demonstrate its utility through a case study on mid-air hand gestures obtained from elicitation studies.

## Author Keywords

Gesture design; gesture pattern; visualization; motion tracking data; data mining.

## ACM Classification Keywords

H.5.2 Information Interfaces and Presentation: User Interfaces—*Evaluation/methodology, Graphical user interfaces (GUI)*

## INTRODUCTION

Natural human motion has been actively exploited in gestural interactions made possible by successful introduction of motion sensing technologies such as low-cost depth sensing cameras (e.g., Microsoft Kinect, Leap Motion) and hand-held motion sensors (e.g., Nintendo Wii). The fundamental problems in the design of gestural interactions are (1) accurate and efficient gesture recognition, and (2) natural and intuitive gesture vocabularies to control the system. To date, many research efforts have been targeted at the development of algorithms and tools for reliable gesture recognition [22]. In

contrast, relatively little research has focused on studying natural aspects of gesture behavior. Elicitation studies, such as Wizard-of-Oz [6] and Guessability studies [39], are useful to identify the most acceptable gesture patterns from candidate user groups, and to gain insights into the design of natural gestures. These study methods have been employed to generate user-defined gesture vocabularies in various interaction scenarios [13, 27, 30, 40].

However, the analysis of user gestures requires a certain amount of time and effort to generate a user-defined gesture vocabulary. The amount of effort increases when the number of users and gestures becomes larger. Also, elicitation studies are limited to constructing descriptive taxonomies of gestures, and cannot provide detailed characteristics of gestures which can be described by kinematic and geometric features of human motion. For example, natural aspects of gestures also can be described by position and velocity profile of gesturing hands, variations in the joint angles, or the most active/inactive body part in gesturing. The potential of such information, that can be generated from the human motion tracking data, has not been well understood in the design of gestural interactions. Moreover, there is no established guideline in the analysis of such high-dimensional, massive and complex data for the design of gestural interactions. So, a proper method to explore and communicate potential knowledge of the large data collections should be provided to the interaction designers.

Automated data analysis techniques such as data mining and pattern classification can be considered to identify subsets of data having similar properties from the massive and complex motion tracking data. However, such automated analysis methods cannot fully reflect the designer's perceptual definition of gesture similarity. The designer thus needs to integrate and insert their domain knowledge of human gestures into the results of such automated data analyses.

With these needs in mind, we propose GestureAnalyzer, a visual analytics system supporting categorization and characterization of various user gestures expressed in motion tracking data. We define *gesture data* as a sequence of human poses represented by motion tracking data. If a set of similar gesture data is frequently observed from different users, we identify the data set as a *gesture pattern*. To simplify and expedite the analysis procedure, GestureAnalyzer requires a specific data format where the user gestures are individually recorded and labeled with the corresponding elicitation task. Hierarchical clustering of gesture data is implemented to identify the most frequent and similar gesture patterns. The aggregation level of gesture data is dynamically adjustable, and different numbers of gesture clusters are generated. The hierarchical tree structure provides an overview of user gestures associated with a certain task. To support comparison of gesture data, we provide *animations* and *multiple-pose visualization* of motion trends. From these visualizations, the designer is able to compare similarity among the clustered gesture data. GestureAnalyzer also provides visualization of various features of gesture data such as variations in speed, joint angles, or distance between two joints. Through these visualizations, the designer can compare user gestures in various features, then characterize the gestures identifying the most informative features that uniquely define the gestures.

In this paper, we demonstrate GestureAnalyzer focusing on the analysis of user behavior in the design of mid-air hand gestures. We validate the utility of the system in supporting the categorization of various gestures expressed by users, and the exploration of various geometric and kinematic features of the user-defined gestures. In our analysis results, we describe how this approach can be beneficial and promising in the analysis of gesture patterns and detailed motion features. Also, we will explore how the analysis results can be used in the design of gestural interactions. The contributions of this paper include: (1) rapid categorization of user gestures leveraging an interactive hierarchical clustering method, (2) visual exploration of geometric and kinematic motion features of user gestures through interactive visualization, and (3) a visual analytics tool supporting data-driven analysis and precise communication of insights from human motion data.

## RELATED WORK
Our work closely relates to gesture elicitation studies, visual analysis of time-series data, and motion sensing data for interaction design. In this section, we briefly summarize prior research on these areas, and compare them to our approach.

### Eliciting Gestures from Users
To better understand user behavior and enhance the intuitiveness of interactions, elicited gestures from users have been commonly incorporated in the initial phase of gesture design. In practice, elicitation studies, such as Wizard-of-Oz and Guessability studies, have been performed to observe how users actually express their gestures in various interaction scenarios: surface computing [40], mobile interactions [30], action games for children [13], and mid-air/VR environments [27, 36]. Recently, Morris et al. [23] suggest modifications of the elicitation studies to enhance the quality of resulting gestures by reducing the effect of prior experience of users in eliciting biased gestures. In the analysis of such study results, researchers manually annotate and categorize user behavior to identify a common gesture pattern for a specific task. Basically, this analysis process is time-consuming when the number of subjects increases. Also, the researchers need to define criteria for the categorization of gestures. Some prior research has proposed taxonomies of human gestures (see Wobbrock et al. [40] for a review), but

the criteria could vary with context of interactions and demographics of users. In addition, it is challenging to formalize the criteria before the researchers understand the whole gesture patterns that occurred during the user study. In most previous work, the output gesture vocabulary is reported in a descriptive manner (e.g., illustrations) and does not convey detailed motion features (e.g., variations in joint angles).

In contrast, our approach allows rapid categorization of similar gestures by applying a data mining technique to motion tracking data. Also, visualization of various features of gestures enables the researchers to compare and identify detailed aspects of gestures across users and tasks.

### Visual Analytics for Temporal Data
The purpose of visual analytics is to integrate human insights and machine capabilities for improved knowledge discovery in the analysis process using interactive visualization techniques [14]. Specifically, the analysis of temporal data using such an interactive visualization approach is an important topic in various areas such as analysis of movement data, genome information, and financial data. Sensemaking based solely on the visualization techniques is insufficient for the analysis of multi-dimensional and complex time-series data. Thus, data analysis techniques such as temporal clustering (see Warren Liao [38] for a review) have been integrated with interactive visualization techniques.

In visual analytics, the density-based clustering algorithm, OPTICS [1], has been widely implemented to analyze complex and massive movement trajectories such as GPS-tracked position data [28], eye movements [26], and mouse trajectories [21]. Schreck et al. [33] propose a framework integrating interactive Self-Organizing Map (SOM) method with domain knowledge of analyst in the analysis of huge amounts of time-varying stock market data.

Hierarchical clustering methods also have been integrated with interactive visualization in many areas. Guo et al. [8] propose an interactive hierarchical clustering method enabling human-centered exploratory analysis of multivariate spatio-temporal data. Similarly, Seo and Shneiderman [34] present an interactive exploration tool for the visualization of hierarchical clustering results using dendrograms and color mosaic scatterplots. In both works, the analyst is able to control the aggregation and exploration level of clusters by changing clustering parameters. Wu et al. [42] employ the interactive clustering approach to hierarchical modeling of query interfaces for the analysis of Web data sources. Heinrich et al. [11] implement the interactive hierarchical clustering combining table-based data visualization in the analysis of massive genomic data. This approach allows the analyst to control the aggregation of rows and columns in the table.

Previous work on visual analysis of human motion tracking data are relatively few. MotionExplorer [3] is an interactive visual searching and retrieval tool for synthesis of human motion sequences. It provides an overview of sequential human poses in dendrograms and motion graphs. In these node-link models, each node represents a static human pose. This tool

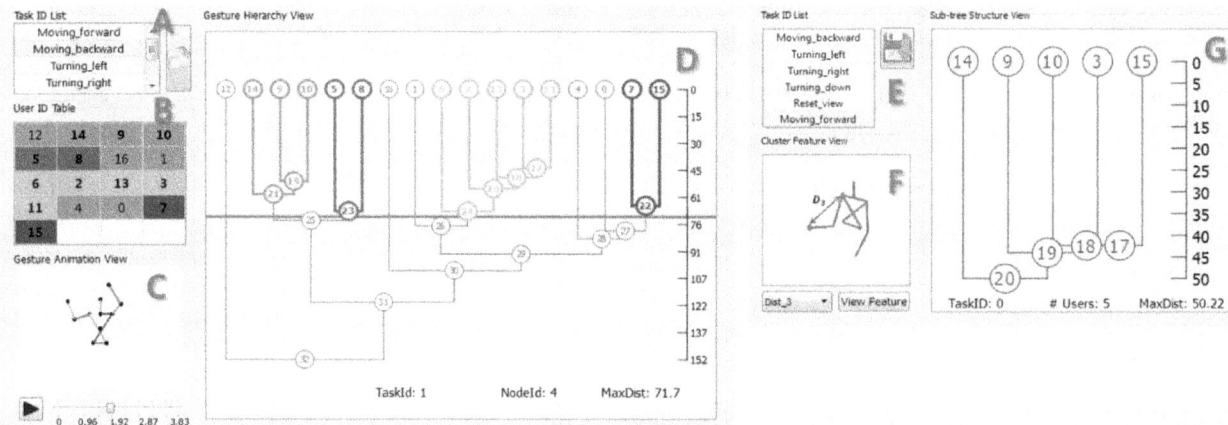

**Figure 1. The GestureAnalyzer interface. (A) is a list of tasks loaded from the database. (B) shows a table of user IDs. (C) shows the animation of user gestures. (D) is a panel that shows the interactive hierarchical clustering of gesture data. Information of currently selected task and cluster node are given at the bottom. (E) is a list of output clusters generated from the interactive hierarchical clustering. (F) provides a visual definition of gesture feature. (G) shows a tree diagram of gesture clusters.**

uses the Euclidean distance of raw joint coordinates to compute the similarity among human poses.

To provide an overview of motion clustering results, our approach adopts the interactive hierarchical clustering method. Since our data type is sequential human motion representing a trial of gesture, we choose to use individual tree nodes to represent a time-varying sequence of poses rather than a single human pose. Also, to better reflect the context of gestures in the analysis, our approach employs various pose similarity measures introduced by Chen et al. [5].

### Motion Data for Interaction Design
Various motion sensing data has been actively used in modern interaction scenarios as an input, *user gesture*, to the system: pen-based [12], fingers/hands [4, 35], and full-body motions [7, 18]. Much research also has been done in the development of gesture authoring tools. Exemplar [10] and MAGIC [2] enable designers to rapidly create sensor-based motion gestures by demonstration. Similarly, Kim et al. [16] introduced a demonstration driven gesture authoring tool, EventHurdle, for designing multi-touch or mid-air gestures. Proton++ [17] and Gesture Coder [20] are prototyping tools for multitouch gestures by demonstration. The main focus of these methods have been on the interpretation of human motion as an input to the system.

Few work has been done in the use of motion sensing data in the understanding of user behavior for the interaction design. Wang and Lai [37] use motion tracking data to investigate the frequency and similarity of gestures used in group brainstorming with different interaction modalities (face-to-face and computer-mediated). Schrammel et al. [32] discuss that interpretation of motion tracking data can be used in the understanding of user behavior such as pattern of pedestrian attention using body and head movements. Hansen [9] discusses the potential of body motion data as a material for interaction design, and argues that visualization of body movement is a necessary step for the exploration and generation of knowledge from the motion data.

Our work also exploits motion tracking data for the analysis and understanding of user behavior. However, to support and expedite the knowledge discovery from the motion tracking data, we propose a visual analytics approach integrating interactive clustering and visualization techniques. Specifically, in this paper, we focus on the use of motion tracking data to support analysis of gesture patterns.

## VISUAL ANALYTICS FOR GESTURE ELICITATION
Our goal is to study how to use visual analytics to support categorization and characterization of user-elicited gestures in motion tracking data. The benefit of applying visual analytics to this problem is that allows combining computational methods with the insights and intuition of a human analyst. Here, we discuss the design space for such a system.

### Data Model
We define our data model as high-dimensional motion tracking data labeled with user and task information. We require gesture data to have distinct starting and ending poses, since extracting meaningful gestures from continuous motion tracking data is outside the scope of the system.

### Analysis Tasks
The main activity in gesture elicitation studies is to categorize a large collection of recorded gesture data sets into a small set of similar gesture patterns. To support this analysis task, visual analytics software should provide an overview of the entire gesture data set as well as information about the relationship between individual gestures. This also requires the capacity to drill down into the data to see similarities, differences, and distances between gestures.

### Visualization
Visual representations of the input gesture data set should aid analysts to overview the high-dimensional motion tracking data. Furthermore, being able to play back an animation of an individual gesture data is a key aspect of the visualization.

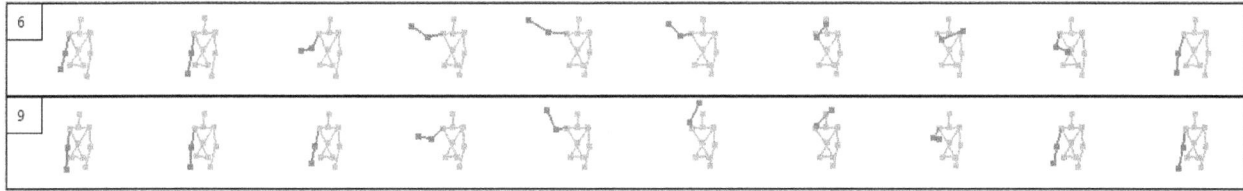

Figure 2. Multiple-pose visualizations. In this example, ten poses are extracted at regular intervals from the same gesture performed by two different users. Note that hands and elbows are detected as active joints, and indicated with red color. Corresponding user id is provided on upper-left corner.

## THE GESTUREANALYZER SYSTEM

Based on the design space of visual analytics for elicitation studies, we developed GestureAnalyzer (Figure 1) to support the analysis of gesture patterns. In this section, we describe the system components of GestureAnalyzer.

### Gesture Data and Feature Vectors

We define a gesture data as a sequence of human poses which are 3D positions of 11 body joints (hands, elbows, shoulders, head, neck, chest, and pelvis) as shown in Figure 1C. We obtain the human skeletal model using a Kinect camera. Khoshelham et al. [15] suggest the Kinect camera is reasonably accurate to represent indoor human activity, but there are occlusion and noise issues in human body tracking. In our gesture data recording, the users face the camera, and critical occlusion problems (i.e., lost tracking of multiple joints) therefore barely appear. To alleviate noise in the gesture data, we apply a Savitzky-Golay smoothing filter [31] to the motion tracking data. The position and orientation of body pose is normalize by shifting the chest position of each skeleton to the origin, and aligning the normal direction of the initial body pose to the camera direction.

In the early development stage, we noticed that Euclidean distance of raw joint coordinates does not provide sufficient gesture similarity. To address this issue, we adopt a geometry-based pose descriptors, proposed by Chen et al. [5]. Specifically, we use relative joint vector normalized to unit length. We extract the pairwise relative joint vector by extracting the difference between the position of joint $i$ and $j$: $p_{ij} = unit(p_i - p_j)$. Because frequent motion in mid-air hand gestures appears on hands, elbows, and shoulders, we define the feature vector, $X \in \mathbb{R}^{21}$ by 7 vectors consisting of relative position of hands and elbows, elbows and shoulders, hands and shoulders, and left and right hand. This selective feature vector is effective in eliminating irrelevant joint information, and reduces the size of feature vector decreasing computing time in similarity measure.

### Interface for Gesture Database Access

In the design of an interface for accessing to the gesture database, we consider a simple yet effective way to organize and represent the gesture data sets. Collected gesture data sets are readily available in the database on disk, and loaded to the system by selecting the corresponding task id in the *Task ID* list (Figure 1A). Then, a set of gesture data included in the selected task appears on *User ID* table (Figure 1B). Each gesture data is labeled with the corresponding user id. To provide an overview of similarity among user gestures, the *User ID*

table is organized according to the adjacency of gesture data in *Gesture Hierarchy* view (Figure 1D). By selecting a user id in the table, the corresponding gesture animation is played in the *Gesture Play-back* window (Figure 1C).

### Interactive Hierarchical Clustering

GestureAnalyzer uses a hierarchical clustering algorithm to aggregate similar gestures into several groups. A hierarchical tree structure of a given gesture data set is constructed using an agglomerative clustering algorithm. Inherently, human gestures could have infinite variations in motion. Even if one user performs the same gesture for several times, each trial could yield different lengths of gesture. To measure similarity among the variable length of gestures, we decide to use Dynamic time warping (DTW), a distance measure for variable lengths of time-series data, due to its computational efficiency and ease of implementation [24]. The agglomerative clustering algorithm starts from multiple root nodes representing individual gesture data, and merges them into a cluster node progressively until a single node is left. In the definition of distance between clusters, we use complete-linkage method representing maximum distance among cluster members. An example of the hierarchy tree is shown (Figure 1D). The root nodes are positioned at the very top, and labeled with the corresponding user id. The cluster nodes are numbered in a merging order.

The depth of nodes is defined by the maximum distance among associated cluster members. The distance is used as a *cut-off* value to define the depth level of tree structure. To adjust the cut-off value GestureAnalyzer provides a horizontal bar (horizontal red line in Figure 1D). The cut-off value can be read at the bottom of the tree diagram and the vertical scale. The maximum distance stands for the intra-cluster similarity of gesture clusters providing a measure of how cluster members are close to each other. Information of currently selected task and cluster node is given at the bottom of the tree diagram. By changing the cut-off value, different shape of gesture clusters are generated. The generated clusters are represented with different colors as shown in Figure 1D. This coloring scheme is also applied to the *User ID* table (Figure 1B). The colors and order of the cluster nodes are intended to aid rapid and accurate visual understanding of gesture data structure. The hierarchy tree provides a global overview of gesture data set, and indicates candidate gesture clusters having strong intra-cluster similarity and frequent occurrence in the data set. More detailed information on a gesture cluster can be queried through the functions described in the following sections.

## Visualization of Gesture Motion

The distance score given in the hierarchical tree view (Figure 1D) provides an immediate similarity measurement in the identification of frequent and concordant user gestures from a given data set. However, the output clusters do not necessarily reflect our perceptual model of gesture similarity. For example, we consider moving the right hand from *left to right* and *right to left* as different gestures, while the clustering algorithm would combine them into the same cluster. So, in the identification of gesture clusters, it is important to investigate what types of gestures are grouped together into a cluster, and how they are actually similar to each other. A key challenge in GestureAnalyzer is to provide an efficient yet effective way to compare the similarity among gesture data in the clusters.

To address this challenge, we provide two visualization methods to compare gesture data: animation and multiple-pose visualization. As shown in Figure 1C, we provide a window for gesture animation. By selecting a user id on the *User ID* table or in the tree diagram, the corresponding gesture data is animated in the window. Using animation of gestures makes it easy to understand motion trends and effective to compare small number of gestures. However, if the number of gesture data being compared increases, animating and replaying the entire gesture data become time-consuming. Due to limited capacity of human memory, some trends of gesture motion observed previously could be confused with new observations. Also, it is hard to judge where to start the investigation in the large data set.

Based on this observation, we provide a small-multiples visualization [29] of multiple gesture data, as a supplement to the gesture animation. As shown in Figure 2, several poses of gestures are extracted at regular intervals from the entire motion frames, and displayed from left-to-right. In Figure 2, ten frames of poses are extracted from *play next music* gesture performed by two different users.

As discussed by Ofli et al. [25], when users perform a gesture, they are not likely to move their entire body; instead there exists a set of joints that moves the most. In the multiple pose visualization, we highlight active joints having higher variance in motion than a certain threshold value. This aims to promote quick detection of active joint location, and reduce the overload of information in the multiple pose visualization.

## Generating User-defined Gesture Set

Once the analyst decides an output cluster from a task data set, he/she can save it to a database. The data set can now be compare with other gesture clusters generated from different task data. A complete cluster database consists of gesture clusters generated from each task data. The database stands for a user-defined gesture vocabulary.

In the representation of gesture clusters, we use a sub-tree structure extracted from the original hierarchical tree model rather than a representative gesture data (e.g., averaged gesture motion). This representation is intended to provide more detailed information of user-defined gestures including the internal structure and intra-cluster similarity of each gesture cluster. Figure 1G shows an example of an user-defined ges-

ture expressed in the sub-tree structure. Metadata of the user-defined gesture including motion tracking data, task id, the number of associated users, and maximum similarity score is provided along with the tree structure.

## Visualization of Gesture Features

Once a vocabulary of user-defined gestures is generated, GestureAnalyzer provides visualization of various geometric and kinematic features such as joint angles, distance between joints, speed, and relative joint positions to explore various aspects of gestures. This exploratory visualization aims to support rapid detection of the most static and dynamic gesture features across users and tasks.

## Saving Gesture Clusters to Database

As a result of the analysis, GestureAnalyzer generates (1) a set of sub-tree structures representing gesture clusters, (2) metadata of the gesture clusters including motion tracking data, task id, the number of associated users, and maximum distance among cluster members, and (3) the visual representation of various gesture features. This collection of data can be saved to the database on disk. Later, specific information can be queried from the database to compose a material for reporting results and findings from the analysis. Also, the database can be a good source in the design of user-informed gesture classifiers.

## CASE STUDY AND RESULTS

To demonstrate the utility of GestureAnalyzer, we conducted a case study on gesture data sets obtained from elicitation studies. Here, we briefly explain the procedure of the gesture elicitation studies, and discuss initial results from the analysis of the gesture data sets using GestureAnalyzer.

## Gesture Elicitation Studies

We conducted user elicited gesture studies for designing mid-air hand gestures. The studies and tasks were designed based on the procedure described in prior work [27, 36, 40].

*Tasks*

Our selection of gesture design tasks was intended to explore the design of mid-air hand gestures for the navigation in 3D space and the system control. In the elicitation studies, there were two gesture design scenarios: (1) camera view control in 3D space and (2) music player control. In the first session of study, the participants were asked to design mid-air

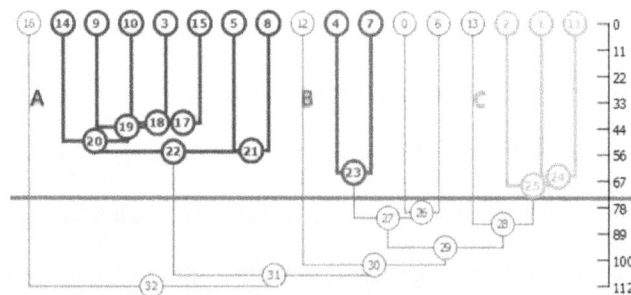

**Figure 3. Three gesture clusters, A, B, and C, are generated from the interactive hierarchical clustering.**

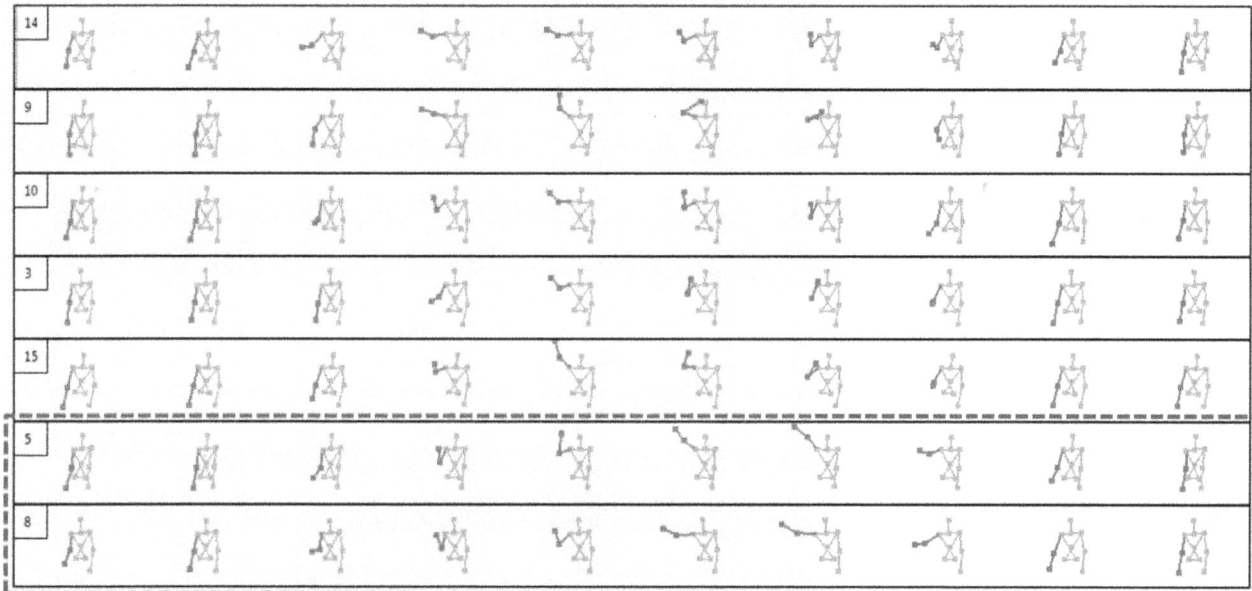

**Figure 4.** An overview of motion trends in the candidate gesture cluster for *camera moving forward* task. The gesture data within a red box (the gesture data labeled by 5 and 8) have different right hand motion from other gestures.

hand gestures to trigger seven different tasks for camera view control: camera moving forward/backward, turning left/right, turning up/down, and reset the camera view to the initial state (go back to the origin). In the design of gestures for the music player control, six tasks were given to the participants including start(pause)/stop music, previous/next track, and increase/decrease volume.

*Participants*
Seventeen participants were recruited for the study ranging in age from 21 to 31 years. All of them were male and university students. One of the participants was left-handed, and majority of the participants have used gesture-based interaction devices such as smart phones, tablet PCs, and gaming devices (Nintendo Wii and Xbox Kinect).

*Apparatus*
The gesture design space was physically defined as 3 x 3 x 5 m to ensure enough space for the participants. A Microsoft Kinect camera and OpenNI SDK was used to extract skeletal model of users. A laptop was connected to a large display equipment to indicate a referent of each task to the participants in the gesture design.

*Gesture Data Recording*
At the beginning of the study, the participants were briefly introduced to two study scenarios and the type of tasks to be performed. In the preliminary analysis of gesture data, it was noticed that the starting and ending pose of gestures significantly affect the similarity measure of gesture data, even if the intermediate gesture motions are quite similar. Based on this observation, we asked the participants to start and end gestures with natural standing pose. Also, since our current system aims to analyze the body motion tracking data, the participants were asked to use hands and arms rather than fingers in the gesture design.

In the first session of the study to design the camera view control gestures, a 3D model of building was presented in the large screen to show the effect of camera movements. Such an effect presenting the result of gesture is called a *referent*. For each task, an animation showing the referent was presented to the participants. No interface was presented in the design of music player control gestures. The referent was given to the participants while an experimenter controls the music player on computer. At each study session, the referent was presented in random order.

**Results**
In this section, we demonstrate GestureAnalyzer for the analysis of gesture data sets, and discuss the results. The first phase of analysis is to identify the most frequent and similar gesture patterns from the data sets. This demonstrates how the system supports generation of user-defined gesture vocabularies. Then, the system provides visualization of motion features of gesture groups. From this visual analysis, we are able to compare various features of gestures across the users and tasks. Through the comparison of gesture features, we can identify the most informative features of user-defined gestures.

*Categorization of User Expressed Gestures*
After importing a task data set into GestureAnalyzer, a hierarchical tree diagram is immediately presented in the *Gesture Hierarchy View* (Figure 1D). This view provides an overview of gesture data structure, and helps to identify candidate gesture clusters from the entire data set. In the rest of this section, we will explain the analysis procedure through an example task data set of the *camera moving forward*.

***Identifying candidate gesture cluster***: From the data set of *camera moving forward* task, three gesture clusters are generated by dragging the cut-off bar to around 72 value of max-

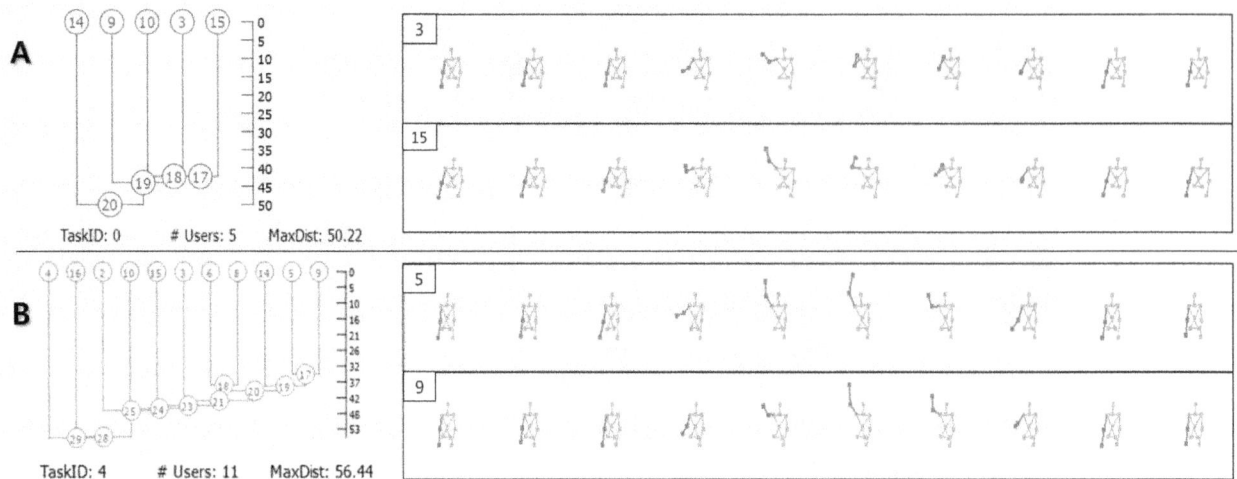

**Figure 5.** Gesture tree diagrams (left) and multiple-pose visualizations (right). The gesture cluster having the smallest MaxDist is presented in the multiple-pose visualizations. A: user-defined *camera moving forward* gesture. B: user-defined *increase volume* gesture.

imum similarity (Figure 3). From the tree diagram, we notice that the gesture cluster (A) includes larger number of gesture data at the root level than the other candidate clusters. So, the cluster (A) is selected as a candidate gesture group as a user-defined gesture for the imported task data.

*Visual investigation of candidate cluster*: Detailed investigation of the candidate cluster (A), in Figure 3, is performed through a combination of the sub-tree structure of cluster (A), the multiple-pose visualization, and the gesture animation. In the tree diagram, the order of node label reveals several cluster nodes where detailed investigation of gesture similarity would be required. For example, gesture data labeled by (5), (8) and (14) are merged into the cluster (A) at the last course of clustering with the highest distance value. This indicates that these gesture data could be outliers in the candidate cluster. An overview of motion trends in the candidate cluster is provided by the multiple-pose visualization in Figure 4. The multiple display reveals that the gesture data (5) and (8) show different movement of right arm. The animation of these data confirms that (5) and (8) gestures are moving right arm away from the body, and the other gestures show moving right arm close to the body. So, the outlier gesture data (5) and (8) should be removed from the candidate gesture cluster (A). We decide the output gesture cluster from the *camera moving forward* data set as the cluster node (20), and its corresponding sub-tree structure is shown in Figure 5A.

*Generating user-defined gestures*: Applying the analysis procedure to the entire task data sets, we were able to generate user-defined gestures represented by multiple poses and tree diagram. Multiple-poses visualizations and quality measures of the complete resulting gesture sets are provided in an appendix. Figure 5 shows examples of output tree diagrams representing the user-defined gestures for *camera moving forward* and *increase volume* tasks. The tree diagrams provide an overview of internal structure and similarity of gesture clusters. Metadata for each tree was stored in a gesture database on disk.

*Characterization of Gesture Vocabularies*

Once the user-defined gestures are extracted from the task data sets and stored in the database, geometric and kinematic features of each gesture are visualized in the gesture characterization phase. Figure 1F provides a visual definition of gesture features. We normalize the length of gesture data to 100 sec to aid comparison of different length of gestures. In this section, we use user-defined *increase volume* and *decrease volume* gestures to show how gesture features are used in the characterization of gestures.

*Comparison across users in the same task*: Figure 6 shows four features of user-defined *increase volume* gesture. From the feature visualization, we are able to notice that the joint angle of left elbow (A) and the distance between left hand and left shoulder (B) are static features, while the joint angle of right elbow (C) and the distance between hands (D) show relatively dynamic variations. Internal similarity of gesture features can be investigated from the feature visualization. Feature (D) shows more congruent shape of transition, while feature (C) has wide range of variations in the shape. So, we can consider feature (D) as a representative feature of *increase volume* gesture having similar behavior across users.

*Comparison across the tasks*: The feature visualization supports comparison of user-defined gestures across different tasks. For example, *increase volume* (Figure 6) and *decrease volume* gestures (Figure 7) show similar shape of gesture feature graphs for the right elbow joint angle and the distance between hands. However, two gestures have different trends in the timing of maximum and minimum point. The *decrease volume* gesture shows early occurrence of the maximum and minimum points. The designers would consider this finding in the design of gesture classifier by using these features.

## DISCUSSION AND LIMITATIONS

The utility of GestureAnalyzer is demonstrated in a case study where gesture data of 17 users are obtained from elicitation studies. Results from the case study provide a set of user-defined gestures represented by tree diagrams and mul-

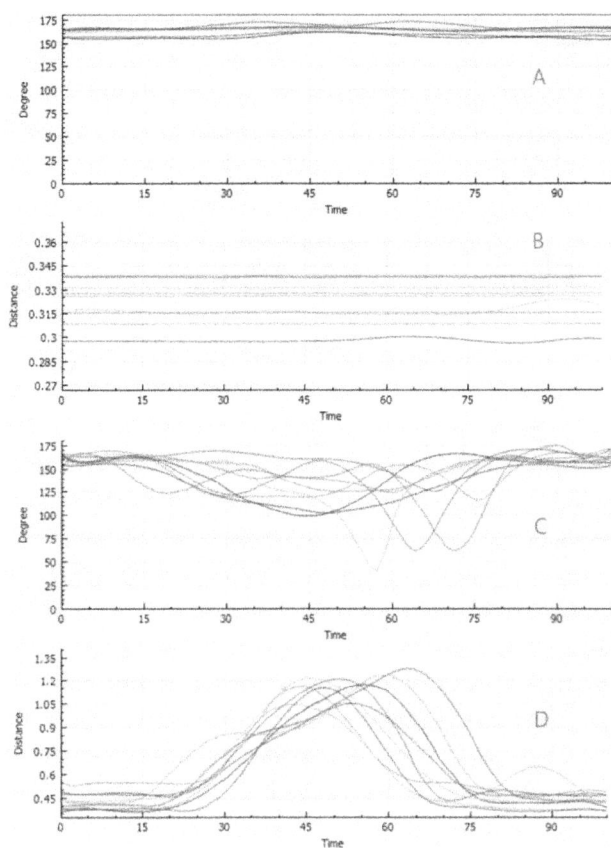

Figure 6. Visualization of geometric features of user-defined *increase volume* gestures of 17 users. Each user gesture is indicated with different color. (A: left elbow joint angle, B: distance between left hand and left shoulder, C: right elbow joint angle, D: distance between hands).

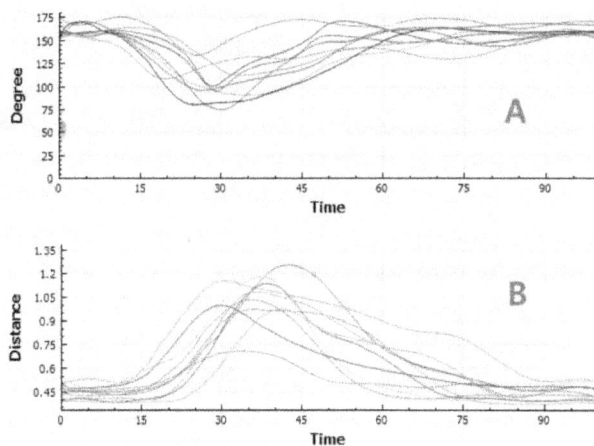

Figure 7. Visualization of geometric features of user-defined *decrease volume* gestures of 17 users. Each user gesture is indicated with different color. (A: right elbow joint angle, B: distance between two hands)

The findings and results generated from GestureAnalyzer can be used as supplementary materials in communicating discovered knowledge of user gestures. For example, detailed information of user behavior such as duration of static posture in a gesture pattern and intermediate motion between successive gestures can be further queried using the result data. Our system also can be used in usability research. Exploratory analysis of gesture patterns could be used in identifying usability problems that frequently occur in the gestural interactions. Then, these problems can be reported and communicated in detail using the data-driven analysis results. The analysis results also can be used in the design of gesture classifier reflecting user behavior.

There are some limitations in the current approach of GestureAnalyzer. In the multiple-pose visualization, reading the entire array of multiple-pose could take a long time when a large number of gesture data is displayed. Applying a color scheme to the multiple display to represent similar poses with the same color could be a strategy to alleviate the issue by enhancing the readability of pose connectivity. Alternatively, we could use the motion graph [19] in the visualization of gesture motions. Our approach is also limited to a specific gesture data format where the gestures start and end with a natural standing pose. To apply our system to broader contexts of interaction analysis, we should consider segmentation and annotation of the whole user study data composed of various natural human motions. We leave it to future work to integrate segmentation of motion data into GestureAnalyzer for detecting the starting and ending pose of the gestures. This extension of analytics capability could be useful in the analysis of natural human poses indicating gesture intent.

From our initial evaluation of GestureAnalyzer, we could imagine several possible extensions to other research areas. Especially, research area involving human behavior analysis could provide a number of interesting opportunities for extension of our research. In collaborative design, our approach could be used to analyze the relationship between natural human motions and collaborative design qualities. Our

tiple poses. Also, the visualization of gesture features reveals potential knowledge of gesture data such as static/dynamic feature behavior, unique characteristics of gestures, and internal similarity of gestures.

Our system enables rapid identification of frequent gesture patterns from a large data set without having prior knowledge of the data. An interactive hierarchical clustering plays a key role in the decision of output cluster structure. A combination of sub-tree diagram, multiple-pose display, and gesture animation aids to identify a candidate gesture cluster from the whole tree diagram. In our case study, a few mouse clicks was required to identify a frequent gesture pattern.

The gesture patterns are represented using tree structure along with metadata including the maximum distance among cluster members and the frequency of gesture patterns. The tree structure is useful to understand the relationship of cluster members such as how they are similar to each other and in what order they are clustered. The information of clustering order is helpful for detecting outliers in the interactive clustering process. The last clustered data has the highest potential to be an outlier of the cluster. GestureAnalyzer enables to generate such detailed information of the gestures that cannot be provided by traditional analysis.

approach also could support the analysis of learning process providing new insights from the motion tracing data. Worsley and Blikstein [41] discuss the possibility of hand gesture data in the analysis of expertness in object manipulation. While this work is limited to use only the cumulative displacement of two hands in the analysis, our approach could be used to explore human motion supported by interactive visualization and data processing techniques.

**CONCLUSION AND FUTURE WORK**

We have described the design and demonstration of Gesture-Analyzer, a visual analytics system supporting identification and characterization of gesture patterns from motion tracking data. We implemented an interactive hierarchical clustering method to identify the most frequent gesture pattern without any prior knowledge of the data. Also, the visual exploration of gesture features enabled comparison of the various aspects of gestures, and supported identification of representative gesture features. A case study on motion tracking data obtained from elicitation studies is conducted to demonstrate the utility of GestureAnalyzer. In our future work, we plan to further investigate the usability of the system via expert reviews, and compare it with traditional analysis methods. We will also expand the analytics capability to other motion data types such as finer finger motions or sensor-based motion tracking data. The knowledge discovered from the motion tracking data can be directly used in training gesture classifiers. Integrating gesture classification into GestureAnalyzer will provide a way to understand the analysis results and use it toward interaction design.

**ACKNOWLEDGMENTS**

This work was partially supported by the NSF Award No. 1235232 from CMMI and 1329979 from CPS, as well as the Donald W. Feddersen Chaired Professorship from Purdue School of Mechanical Engineering. Any opinions, findings, and conclusions or recommendations expressed in this material are those of the authors and do not necessarily reflect the views of the sponsors.

**REFERENCES**

1. Ankerst, M., Breunig, M. M., Kriegel, H.-P., and Sander, J. Optics: ordering points to identify the clustering structure. *ACM SIGMOD Record 28*, 2 (1999), 49–60.

2. Ashbrook, D., and Starner, T. MAGIC: a motion gesture design tool. In *Proceedings of the ACM Conference on Human Factors in Computing Systems* (2010), 2159–2168.

3. Bernard, J., Wilhelm, N., Kruger, B., May, T., Schreck, T., and Kohlhammer, J. MotionExplorer: Exploratory search in human motion capture data based on hierarchical aggregation. *IEEE Transactions on Visualization and Computer Graphics 19*, 12 (2013), 2257–2266.

4. Buchmann, V., Violich, S., Billinghurst, M., and Cockburn, A. FingARtips: gesture based direct manipulation in augmented reality. In *Proceedings of the ACM Conference on Computer Graphics and Interactive Techniques in Australasia and South East Asia* (2004), 212–221.

5. Chen, C., Zhuang, Y., Nie, F., Yang, Y., Wu, F., and Xiao, J. Learning a 3D human pose distance metric from geometric pose descriptor. *IEEE Transactions on Visualization and Computer Graphics 17*, 11 (2011), 1676–1689.

6. Dahlbäck, N., Jönsson, A., and Ahrenberg, L. Wizard of Oz studies—why and how. *Knowledge-Based Systems 6*, 4 (1993), 258–266.

7. Gerling, K., Livingston, I., Nacke, L., and Mandryk, R. Full-body motion-based game interaction for older adults. In *Proceedings of the ACM Conference on Human Factors in Computing Systems* (2012), 1873–1882.

8. Guo, D., Peuquet, D., and Gahegan, M. Opening the black box: interactive hierarchical clustering for multivariate spatial patterns. In *Proceedings of the ACM Symposium on Advances in Geographic Information Systems* (2002), 131–136.

9. Hansen, L. A. Full-body movement as material for interaction design. *Digital Creativity 22*, 4 (2011), 247–262.

10. Hartmann, B., Abdulla, L., Mittal, M., and Klemmer, S. R. Authoring sensor-based interactions by demonstration with direct manipulation and pattern recognition. In *Proceedings of the ACM Conference on Human Factors in Computing Systems* (2007), 145–154.

11. Heinrich, J., Vehlow, C., Battke, F., Jäger, G., Weiskopf, D., and Nieselt, K. iHAT: interactive hierarchical aggregation table for genetic association data. *BMC Bioinformatics 13*, Suppl 8 (2012), S2.

12. Hinckley, K., Ramos, G., Guimbretiere, F., Baudisch, P., and Smith, M. Stitching: pen gestures that span multiple displays. In *Proceedings of the ACM Conference on Advanced Visual Interfaces* (2004), 23–31.

13. Höysniemi, J., Hämäläinen, P., and Turkki, L. Wizard of Oz prototyping of computer vision based action games for children. In *Proceedings of the ACM Conference on Interaction Design and Children* (2004), 27–34.

14. Keim, D., Andrienko, G., Fekete, J.-D., Görg, C., Kohlhammer, J., and Melançon, G. Visual analytics: Definition, process, and challenges. In *Information Visualization*, A. Kerren, J. Stasko, J.-D. Fekete, and C. North, Eds., vol. 4950 of *Lecture Notes in Computer Science*. Springer Berlin Heidelberg, 2008, 154–175.

15. Khoshelham, K., and Elberink, S. O. Accuracy and resolution of kinect depth data for indoor mapping applications. *Sensors 12*, 2 (2012), 1437–1454.

16. Kim, J.-W., and Nam, T.-J. EventHurdle: supporting designers' exploratory interaction prototyping with gesture-based sensors. In *Proceedings of the ACM Conference on Human Factors in Computing Systems* (2013), 267–276.

17. Kin, K., Hartmann, B., DeRose, T., and Agrawala, M. Proton++: a customizable declarative multitouch framework. In *Proceedings of the ACM Symposium on User Interface Software and Technology* (2012), 477–486.

18. Konrad, T., Demirdjian, D., and Darrell, T. Gesture+ play: full-body interaction for virtual environments. In *Extended Abstracts of the ACM Conference on Human Factors in Computing Systems* (2003), 620–621.

19. Kovar, L., Gleicher, M., and Pighin, F. Motion graphs. *ACM Transactions on Graphics 21*, 3 (2002), 473–482.

20. Lü, H., and Li, Y. Gesture coder: a tool for programming multi-touch gestures by demonstration. In *Proceedings of the ACM Conference on Human Factors in Computing Systems* (2012), 2875–2884.

21. McArdle, G., Tahir, A., and Bertolotto, M. Spatio-temporal clustering of movement data: An application to trajectories generated by human-computer interaction. *ISPRS Annals of Photogrammetry, Remote Sensing and Spatial Information Sciences I-2* (2012), 147–152.

22. Mitra, S., and Acharya, T. Gesture recognition: A survey. *IEEE Transactions on Systems, Man, and Cybernetics 37*, 3 (2007), 311–324.

23. Morris, M. R., Danielescu, A., Drucker, S., Fisher, D., Lee, B., Wobbrock, J. O., et al. Reducing legacy bias in gesture elicitation studies. *Interactions 21*, 3 (2014), 40–45.

24. Needleman, S. B., and Wunsch, C. D. A general method applicable to the search for similarities in the amino acid sequence of two proteins. *Journal of Molecular Biology 48*, 3 (1970), 443–453.

25. Ofli, F., Chaudhry, R., Kurillo, G., Vidal, R., and Bajcsy, R. Sequence of the most informative joints (SMIJ): A new representation for human skeletal action recognition. *Journal of Visual Communication and Image Representation 25*, 1 (2014), 24–38.

26. Ooms, K., Andrienko, G., Andrienko, N., De Maeyer, P., and Fack, V. Analysing the spatial dimension of eye movement data using a visual analytic approach. *Expert Systems with Applications 39*, 1 (2012), 1324–1332.

27. Piumsomboon, T., Clark, A., Billinghurst, M., and Cockburn, A. User-defined gestures for augmented reality. In *Human-Computer Interaction–INTERACT*. Springer, 2013, 282–299.

28. Rinzivillo, S., Pedreschi, D., Nanni, M., Giannotti, F., Andrienko, N., and Andrienko, G. Visually driven analysis of movement data by progressive clustering. *Information Visualization 7*, 3-4 (2008), 225–239.

29. Robertson, G., Fernandez, R., Fisher, D., Lee, B., and Stasko, J. Effectiveness of animation in trend visualization. *IEEE Transactions on Visualization and Computer Graphics 14*, 6 (2008), 1325–1332.

30. Ruiz, J., Li, Y., and Lank, E. User-defined motion gestures for mobile interaction. In *Proceedings of the ACM Conference on Human Factors in Computing Systems* (2011), 197–206.

31. Savitzky, A., and Golay, M. J. Smoothing and differentiation of data by simplified least squares procedures. *Analytical chemistry 36*, 8 (1964), 1627–1639.

32. Schrammel, J., Paletta, L., and Tscheligi, M. Exploring the possibilities of body motion data for human computer interaction research. In *HCI in Work and Learning, Life and Leisure*. Springer, 2010, 305–317.

33. Schreck, T., Tekušová, T., Kohlhammer, J., and Fellner, D. Trajectory-based visual analysis of large financial time series data. *ACM SIGKDD Explorations Newsletter 9*, 2 (2007), 30–37.

34. Seo, J., and Shneiderman, B. Interactively exploring hierarchical clustering results [gene identification]. *IEEE Computer 35*, 7 (2002), 80–86.

35. Takeoka, Y., Miyaki, T., and Rekimoto, J. Z-touch: an infrastructure for 3D gesture interaction in the proximity of tabletop surfaces. In *Proceedings of the ACM Conference on Interactive Tabletops and Surfaces* (2010), 91–94.

36. Vatavu, R.-D. User-defined gestures for free-hand TV control. In *Proceedings of the European Conference on Interactive TV and Video* (2012), 45–48.

37. Wang, H.-C., and Lai, C.-T. Kinect-taped communication: using motion sensing to study gesture use and similarity in face-to-face and computer-mediated brainstorming. In *Proceedings of the ACM Conference on Human Factors in Computing Systems* (2014), 3205–3214.

38. Warren Liao, T. Clustering of time series data—a survey. *Pattern Recognition 38*, 11 (2005), 1857–1874.

39. Wobbrock, J. O., Aung, H. H., Rothrock, B., and Myers, B. A. Maximizing the guessability of symbolic input. In *Extended Abstracts of the ACM Conference on Human Factors in Computing Systems* (2005), 1869–1872.

40. Wobbrock, J. O., Morris, M. R., and Wilson, A. D. User-defined gestures for surface computing. In *Proceedings of the ACM Conference on Human Factors in Computing Systems* (2009), 1083–1092.

41. Worsley, M., and Blikstein, P. Towards the development of multimodal action based assessment. In *Proceedings of the ACM Conference on Learning Analytics and Knowledge* (2013), 94–101.

42. Wu, W., Yu, C., Doan, A., and Meng, W. An interactive clustering-based approach to integrating source query interfaces on the deep web. In *Proceedings of the ACM SIGMOD Conference on Management of Data* (2004), 95–106.

# Exploring Gestural Interaction in Smart Spaces using Head Mounted Devices with Ego-Centric Sensing

**Barry Kollee**
University of Amsterdam
Faculty of Science
Amsterdam, Netherlands
barrykollee@gmail.com

**Sven Kratz**
FX Palo Alto Laboratory
3174, Porter Drive
Palo Alto, USA
kratz@fxpal.com

**Tony Dunnigan**
FX Palo Alto Laboratory
3174, Porter Drive
Palo Alto, USA
tonyd@fxpal.com

## ABSTRACT

It is now possible to develop head-mounted devices (HMDs) that allow for ego-centric sensing of mid-air gestural input. Therefore, we explore the use of HMD-based gestural input techniques in smart space environments. We developed a usage scenario to evaluate HMD-based gestural interactions and conducted a user study to elicit qualitative feedback on several HMD-based gestural input techniques. Our results show that for the proposed scenario, mid-air hand gestures are preferred to head gestures for input and rated more favorably compared to non-gestural input techniques available on existing HMDs. Informed by these study results, we developed a prototype HMD system that supports gestural interactions as proposed in our scenario. We conducted a second user study to quantitatively evaluate our prototype comparing several gestural and non-gestural input techniques. The results of this study show no clear advantage or disadvantage of gestural inputs vs. non-gestural input techniques on HMDs. We did find that voice control as (sole) input modality performed worst compared to the other input techniques we evaluated. Lastly, we present two further applications implemented with our system, demonstrating 3D scene viewing and ambient light control. We conclude by briefly discussing the implications of ego-centric vs. exo-centric tracking for interaction in smart spaces.

## ACM Classification Keywords

H.5.2 User Interfaces: Input devices and strategies

## Author Keywords

head-mounted device (HMD);smart spaces;interaction techniques;modalities;ego-centric;hand gestures

Figure 1. An experimental setup of a "smart" office environment. Users, such as the person on the right (1) can use their HMD to interact with the displays (2, 3).

## INTRODUCTION

Wearable devices are currently increasing in popularity. An indication of this the increase of the number of head-mounted devices (HMD) and other wearables such as smart watches that are becoming available commercially. At the same time, many spaces within office buildings are becoming "smart", i.e., spaces such as meeting rooms are being equipped with a proliferation of devices, such as displays, wireless speakerphones and remotely-controlled lighting, that can be interconnected via network over wireless or wired connections.

In this paper, we explore the use of wearable devices, specifically HMDs, for interaction in such *smart spaces*. Most currently available commercial HMDs, such as Google Glass, have a relatively limited array of input options. The Google Glass devices, for instance, rely mainly on voice commands and a rim-mounted touch pad, although there is also support for head-tilt gestures using third party libraries[1]. In the context of smart space interaction this poses usability problems, as, for instance, it can be difficult to select external devices in the environment. Previous works have already tried to address this problem [6], although the interactions presented there still seem cumbersome as they still rely on the limited existing input mechanisms provided by the HMD they used. A further issue which we touch tangentially is the question whether smart spaces should be instrumented to (externally) track users, or if the users

---

[1]E.g., "Head Gesture Detector",
https://github.com/thorikawa/glass-head-gesture-detector

themselves should be instrumented for input tracking in an ego-centric manner, which is possible using HMDs with embedded sensors, e.g., depth cameras, that are able to track gestural input. Although, in this paper, we do not make a direct comparison between ego-centric and external (i.e., exo-centric) tracking, we do highlight some of the interaction possibilities for ego-centrically tracked users working in smart spaces.

We propose the use of in-air hand gestures to increase the input possibilities for HMDs. We believe that hand gestures have the potential to make interaction easier not only with the HMD itself, but also with external devices and displays in a smart space scenario. However, since there are several modalities besides gestures available to user interface designers of HMDs or other types of wearables, e.g., touch pad, voice commands, head gestures and hand gestures, we are also interested in evaluating the usability of these different modalities for input tasks on HMDs with a focus on interaction in smart spaces.

Specifically, we contribute an interaction scenario that we use as a test bed for gestural interactions with external displays, using an HMD that allows ego-centric sensing of gestural input by the user. To realize this scenario, we contribute a prototype HMD system that uses ego-centric tracking to enable in-air hand gestures as input, in addition to the other modalities mentioned previously. Furthermore, we present the results of two user studies centered around a smart-space interaction scenario. In the studies, we examine the usability of a range of input techniques available through our prototype for smart space interaction.

In the first study, we gather qualitative feedback through an elicitation study on the usability of several gestural input techniques for an interaction scenario involving and HMD and a smart space. Based on the insights gained in the first study, we conducted a second user study using the prototype HMD system we developed. In this study, we intended to find out if the results of the elicitation study are reflected in an user evaluation of an actually running software and hardware prototype.

Lastly, we describe two further applications of our prototype application: a 3D scene viewer on a large display, and abient light control.

## RELATED WORK
In the following, we provide an overview of related work, with a focus on the interaction techniques we study in this paper.

## Head Orientation
Chen et al. [6] showed ways how physical home appliances could be controlled by using head orientation as input for their prototype. They compared head orientation selection versus the device's touchpad (i.e. list-view selection) to control these home appliances. They found that if more than 6 home appliances are selectable, head

orientation input outperformed the list view of the device's touchpad. Meaning that home appliances could be selected and controlled faster with head orientation input than with touchpad input. We thus incorporated head orientation as a candidate technique for our prestudy.

## Hand Tracking and Gestures on Wearable Devices
Hand tracking is not yet implemented in mainstream HMDs (such as Google Glass) and is still an ongoing field of research as seen, e.g., in the MIME prototype by Colaco et al. [7]. In contrast to MIME, the sensing setup used by our system allows dual-handed applications as we can track both the user's hands. In contrast to the present paper, MIME does not address how external devices could be controlled using in-air gestures through HMD-based tracking.

Bailly et al.'s ShoeSense [2] is a shoe-mounted wearable system that explored gestural interactions in the space in front of the user. While ShoeSense did solve many problems associated with minimum range limitations of the depth sensors at that time, we believe that a head-mounted sensor might be more practical and, in certain situations, more socially acceptable. One reason for this is that shoe-mounted cameras can be perceived as obtrusive, due to their "upskirt" orientation.

Mistry et al. presented a chest-worn projector/camera system that could track the user's hand gestures [14]. However, this system required colored markers on the user's fingers for tracking, which in many cases cumbersome and should be avoided, according to the design considerations proposed by Colaco et al. [7].

A further, highly related work was carried out by Piumsomboon et al. They conducted an elicitation study for hand gestures in AR [15]. In exploring HMD-based gestures in smart spaces, the current work address a somewhat different domain, nevertheless many of the gestures elicited the authors could be incorporated into our system.

## Touch Control
The most common form of input on current mobile devices of the phone or tablet class is touch input. Multitouch allows users to interact using multiple fingers and enables relatively complex gestures to be entered and also provides the opportunity to provide physical analogies (i.e., *Reality-Based Interfaces* [11]) in the interfaces to improve the usability. Thus, it is not surprising that current HMDs have moved towards using touch as the main input modality, seen, e.g., in the rim-mounted touchpad of the Google Glass device [10]. We argue, however, that touch might not be the best way of interacting, as, for example, the size of the touchpad on head-worn devices such as Glass is limited by the form factor of the device, and can only support relatively coarse input. Lastly, Malik et al. studied multi-touch input for control of distant displays [13].

## Interaction with External Devices

HMDs can communicate with external devices via a wired or wireless connections. Examples of such devices could be small embedded wireless devices, e.g., Chen et al. [6] or and smartphones [10].

A large body of work has been completed on the topic of interaction across multiple devices. In this paper, we present a prototype that uses interactions similar to Rekimoto's "Pick and Drop" [16]. This allows the user, through a selection and a deselection technique, to "pick" a digital item on one device or display, and "drop" it on another device or display.

## Multi-Display Environments and Smart Spaces

A large body of related work has discussed interaction in multi-display environments. For instance *PointRight* [12] discusses the implementation of input redirection such environments. We believe that many issues in input direction could be solved by using direct manipulation via gestures, as suggested in this paper. With the *LightSpace* project, Wilson et al. [19] realized the direct manipulation concept in a highly instrumented space. Our current research works in the direction of realizing such interactions through ego-centric tracking.

## PROTOTYPE ENVIRONMENT AND SCENARIO

Modern work environments contain spaces such as conference rooms that are equipped with a large amount of technology, such as displays, projectors, audio and telecommunication systems, climate control and lighting systems. However, the interface to this technology is often cumbersome and heterogeneous. Thus, we believe that new and improved ways of interacting with infrastructure that is present in such *smart* spaces need to be found. Therefore, we devised a scenario that allows us to prototype and evaluate HMD-based gestural interactions in smart work spaces.

Specifically, our scenario describes a brainstorming session in a modern architect's office. The architects are trying to decide what type of stone pattern they want to use in an interior design project. Our proposed smart office space allows the architects to organize and compare the types of stone patterns by means of placing images of the patterns next to each other on multiple displays in a "smart" conference room. Instead of a normal desktop-based interface, they make use of an HMD that can track mid-air hand gestures and also control the displays in the conference room (Figure 1). Our implementation of this scenario consists of a conference room with multiple displays that allow interaction using a HMD (as in Figure 1).

Boring et al. [3] previously showed how visual content could be selected, controlled and transferred from one screen to another by using a smartphone and the embedded camera from the device. Our prototype environment replicates this setup in some aspects. However, we have replaced the mobile device by an HMD, and input on the phone's touch screen with in-air gesture input. In

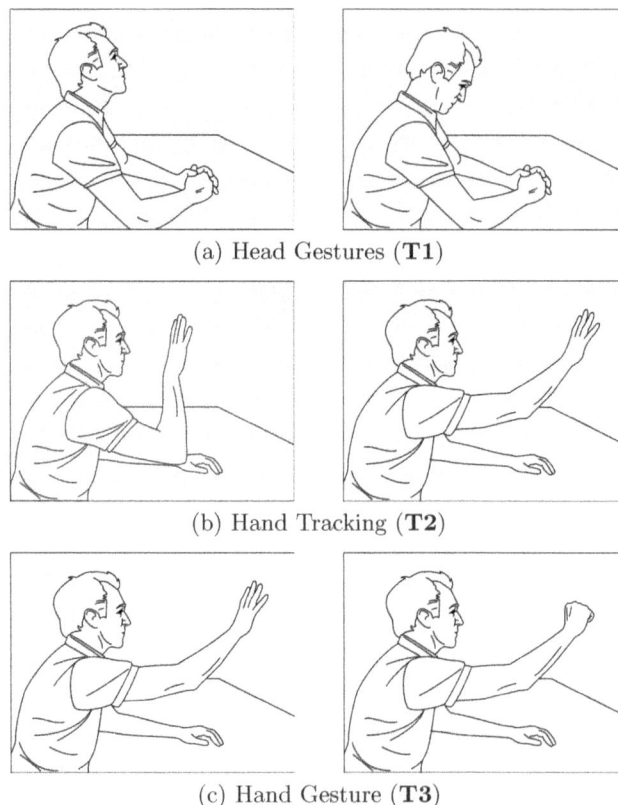

(a) Head Gestures (**T1**)

(b) Hand Tracking (**T2**)

(c) Hand Gesture (**T3**)

**Figure 2. Proposed gestural techniques for gestural interaction with external devices using an HMD with ego-centric tracking.**

this paper, we investigate whether a set of input tasks as required by our scenario can be accomplished by a HMD using two types of hand gestures as well as voice and HMD-based GUI input.

## Interaction Techniques and Tasks

In our scenario, the task (i.e. moving an image thumbnail from one screen to another) that needs to be performed by the user consists of three input steps: (1) Select the display, which holds the image thumbnail that needs to be transferred, (2) select the desired image thumbnail on the selected display and (3) select the display to which the image thumbnail needs to be transferred to.

To accomplish these tasks, we propose two mid-air gestural input techniques, *hand gestures* and *hand tracking* as well as *head gestures*, *voice commands* and the use of the rim-mounted *touchpad* on a Google Glass device. In the following, we will will explain the proposed interaction techniques in more detail:

### Head Gestures

When using head gestures in our scenario, the user gazes towards the display or image thumbnail that needs to be selected (Figure 2(a)). Selection takes place by means of a "nod" gesture (i.e., moving the head up and down).

*Hand Tracking*

This interaction technique consists of the tracking of the hand's position with respect to the HMD (Figure 2(b)). By means of a push movement in space (i.e., a rapid shift in z-axis position) a selection takes place.

*Hand Gestures*

By hand gestures we refer to detecting certain poses of the hand. Colaco et al., proposed detecting hand gestures for interaction [7]. For our tasks, we chose to use a grasp gesture (opening and closing the hand) to select items on the displays or the displays themselves (Figure 2(c)). We believe that grasp gestures are appropriate for content manipulation on an external display as this follows the Natural User Interface (NUI) paradigm [18]. A typical interaction using hand gestures would work as follows:

1. The user selects the display by looking at the display and grasping it in space

2. The user opens up his hand and hovers over the thumbnails. When the desired image thumbnail is in the view of the user, the user grasps the thumbnail by holding his or her hand as a fist.

3. The user looks towards the display where the image thumbnail needs to be transferred to and opens his or her hand again.

*Voice Commands*

We assume that many future HMDs will incorporate voice command functionality. Thus, we decided to allow voice commands in our scenario. Because we cannot predict the ability of future devices to recognize complex grammatical constructs, e.g., "Select item 3 on display 1 and transfer it to display 2", we chose very simple commands that follow a verb and noun structure, e.g., "Select display 1". Furthermore, the choice of voice commands allows the user to replicate the same (atomic) interaction steps as in the other modalities we propose, thus making a comparison easier.

*Touchpad*

As a baseline technique, we use the existing touchpad input capabilities of Google Glass. The touchpad is used to interact with a selection list that contains all the selectable screens and display items. The list is displayed in the Glass device's display. The selectable displays are displayed (in numerical order) at the beginning of the list, and the selectable items are displayed (in numerical order) in the remainder of the list.

## ELICITATION STUDY

Before implementing the previously discussed scenario as a software prototype, we conducted a prestudy to elicit qualitative user feedback on the gestural input techniques we discussed in the previous section, i.e., head gestures (**T1**), hand tracking (**T2**) and hand gestures (**T3**). The reason we wanted qualitative feedback was to gain an insight into which gestural input technique might be acceptable to users for the proposed scenario.

## Methodology

To elicit qualitative feedback from test subjects, we explained the scenario to them and then, using a within-subjects design, showed each test subject three videos[2] demonstrating the use of **T1**–**T3**, respectively.

After viewing the video for each technique, participants were asked to fill out a questionnaire. The questionnaire consisted of three parts. In the first part, participants were asked to fill in five Likert-Scale questions with respect to *Effectiveness*, *Learnability*, *Practicality*, *Intuitiveness* and *Comfort*.

In the second part of the questionnaire, we elicited emotional reponses to the interaction examples shown using a custom variant of the *EmoCard* approach [1]. In this method, we allowed the test subjects to distribute up to three "points" to any emotion on the EmoCard scale. We believe that this approach allows users to either express a wider range of emotions or strongly express single emotions while rating a technique.

Finally, we asked users, after viewing the demonstration video and filling out the questionnaires described previously, to provide three preference rankings of the current gestural technique vs. baseline[3] commands, which were *Voice Command* (**B1**) and *Touchpad* (**B2**), for the following tasks: "Select a display", "Select a visual item on the display" and "Transfer the visual item to another display".

In total, 16 participants from an industrial research lab participated in the study. The age range was 22–55 years, 4 participants were female.

## Hypotheses

Prior to our study, we assumed that the techniques using in-air hand gestures would be superior to head gestures, and that hand gestures would possibly be rated superior to voice commands or using the HMD's touchpad. Thus, we formulated the following hypotheses:

- **H1:** the input techniques using in-air hand gestures (**T2** and **T3**) are rated more favorably in the Likert Scale questions as well as receive more positive EmoCard emotion ratings than head gestures **T1**.

- **H2:** gestural input techniques are ranked first more often than the baseline techniques **B1** and **B2**.

## Findings

The results of the Likert-scale questionnaires indicate that head gestures were rated less favorably than hand gestures in terms of *intuitiveness*, *comfort* and *effectiveness* (Figure 4). A nonparametric Friedman test on the rating data shows a significant difference within these measures with $p = 0.001$ for *intuitiveness* and $p < 0.001$ for *comfort*, $p = 0.001$ for *effectiveness* and $p < 0.001$ for

---

[2] The videos shown to the test subjects can be viewed online at https://vimeo.com/102943456.

[3] We derived the baseline techniques from the set of input capabilities currently available in Google Glass HMDs.

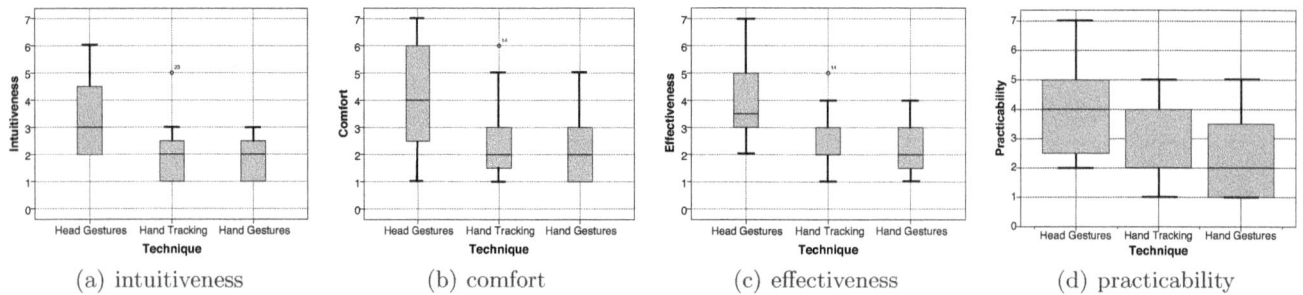

(a) intuitiveness    (b) comfort    (c) effectiveness    (d) practicability

Figure 4. Box plots of the results of the prestudy Likert scale questionnaires rating the *intuitiveness*, *comfort*, *effectiveness* and *practicability* of the interaction techniques. A *lower* rating is better.

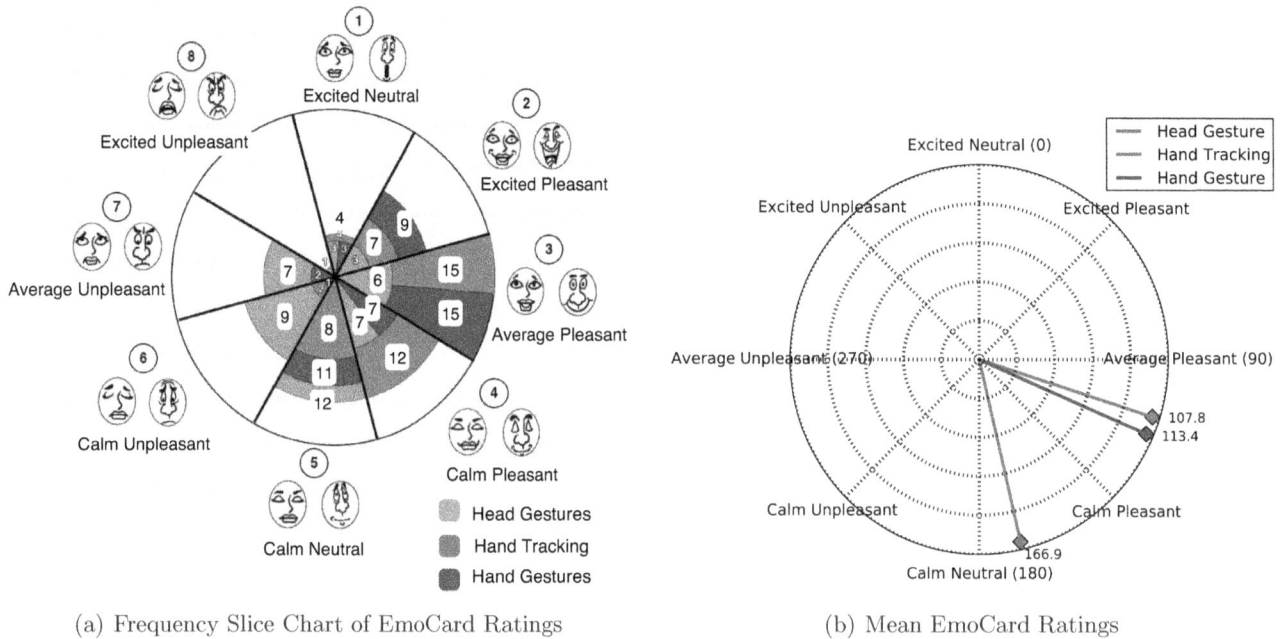

(a) Frequency Slice Chart of EmoCard Ratings    (b) Mean EmoCard Ratings

Figure 5. (a) Frequency slice chart of ratings on EmoCard sectors. (b) Mean EmoCard Ratings plotted as angles on the EmoCard scale.

*practicability*. We did not obtain significant results for *learnability*.

We received a total of 48 emotion ratings for head gestures using the custom method we described previously (i.e., 16 participants×3 distributed emotions for head gestures). 28 ratings (58%) were given in the "Average Unpleasant" to "Calm Neutral" sectors (Figure 5(a)). The EmoCard results (Figure 5) are consistent with the results for intuitiveness, comfort and effectiveness of the Likert scale questionnaires. Figure 5(a) shows a frequency slice chart that presents a histogram of the test subjects' ratings plotted on the EmoCard sectors. We can see that head gestures (green color) were rated more towards the neutral/unpleasant side of the EmoCard scale.

In an alternative analysis, we assigned an angle value to each EmoCard emotion (e.g., "Excited Neutral" = 0, "Calm Neutral" = 180, etc.) and calculated the average angle. Figure 5(b) shows the average Emo-

Card angles plotted on polar coordinates. It is clear that head gestures (green) are centered mostly around the "Calm Neutral" sector and the hand gesture techniques are on average in the sector between "Calm Pleasant" and "Average Pleasant". An ANOVA on the converted EmoCard ratings shows a significant difference ($f_{1,44} = 4.666$, $p = 0.036$). A Bonferroni post-hoc comparison shows a significant difference between Head Gestures (**T1**) and **T2** ($p = 0.030$) as well as a marginally significant difference between (**T1**) and **T3** ($p = 0.056$).

In summary, the elicitation study indicates that input via head gestures (**T1**) was rated less favorably by the test subjects in terms of *intuitiveness*, *comfort* and *effectiveness* as well as EmoCard-based emotional response than hand tracking (**T2**) or hand gestures (**T3**). Furthermore, gestural techniques (**T1**–**T3**) were ranked first more often than the baseline techniques **B1** and **B2**. We can thus confirm our hypotheses **H1** and **H2**.

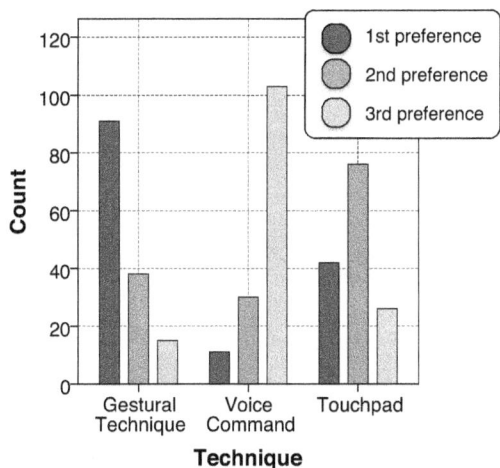

Figure 3.　Ranking frequency of gestural techniques vs. basline techniques.

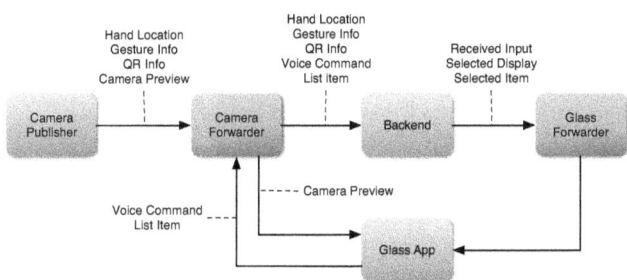

Figure 6. This system diagram shows the direction and type of messages that are sent between the three software components that comprise the prototype.

## PROTOTYPE

We developed a software and hardware prototype to implement the scenario and interaction techniques proposed earlier. Because head gestures (**T1**) were rated unfavorably in the elicitation study, we decided not to implement them in our prototype and also not to study head gestures as an input technique in the subsequent evaluation. The prototype software consists of three intercommunicating applications: a C++ application that publishes depth sensor tracking data, a Java backend application for state management and graphical output on large displays and an Android application running on a Google Glass device. Figure 6 provides an overview of how the system components communicate with each other. In the following, we describe each component and associated hardware of the prototype in more detail:

### Gestural Input using Head-Mounted Depth Camera

Currently available HMDs, such as Google Glass, do not have the capability to capture depth information or provide spatial hand tracking information. Therefore, we used a Creative SENZ3D short-range depth camera[4] to fetch the spatial position (i.e., real-world $x$, $y$

[4]The maximum IR depth resolution of this sensor is 320x240 and its diagonal field of view is 73°. The sensor captures depth and RGB images at a rate of 30 Hz.

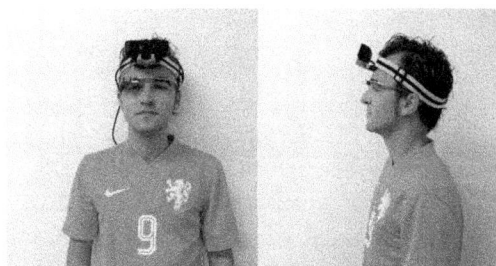

Figure 7. Depth camera head strap as a substitution for embedded hand tracking in the HMD.

and $z$ coordinates) of the user's hands. We developed a C++ application using the Intel Perceptual Computing SDK[5] (PCSDK), OpenCV[6] and ZBar[7] libraries to publish hand tracking information, a low-resolution camera preview image stream and QR Code information for use by the backend application.

The PCSDK is used to fetch finger tracking information from the depth sensor and to provide simple gesture recognition capabilities, e.g., "hand close", "hand open" or "thumbs up" gestures. OpenCV is used to generate a low-resolution preview of a $256 \times 256$ camera center region shown in the Glass Device's display (shown in Figure 8), which is intended to ease targeting of QR Codes for display or item selection, as the camera view can be slightly misaligned with respect to the user's gaze direction. ZBar is used to detect QR codes based on the depth sensor's RGB image stream.

We engineered a customized strap that enables the user to head-mount the depth sensor in order for hand tracking and gesture recognition to function (Figure 7). This is intended to be a substitute for future HMD hardware with built-in sensing capabilities for user hand tracking. Users are able to wear the head strap at the same time as a Google Glass device, which completes the hardware of our prototype.

### Backend Application

The backend application is implemented in Java. It makes use of the Processing Library[8] for graphical output and manages the interaction state. The backend application receives hand tracking and gesture events from the camera publisher module, voice command and selection events from the HMD.

In addition to processing user input events, the backend produces the graphical output shown on the displays of the smart office environment. On these displays the backend displays visual identifiers (QR Codes) that can be observed by the depth sensor. This is used as a simple way of determining the item the user wants to select on the display. As previously mentioned, as a targeting

[5]https://software.intel.com/en-us/vcsource/tools/ perceptual-computing-sdk/home
[6]http://opencv.org/
[7]http://zbar.sourceforge.net/
[8]http://www.processing.org/

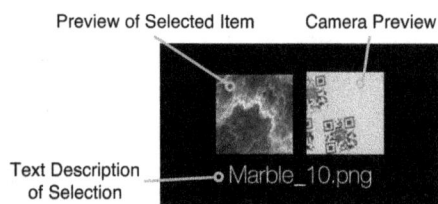

**Figure 8. Screenshot of the HMD application.**

aid for the user, a $256 \times 256$ pixel image of the center region of the RGB image captured by the depth sensor is shown in the HMDs display (Figure 8).[9]

### HMD Application

To realize the HMD portion of our proposed scenario, we implemented an Android-based HMD application for Google Glass that provides visual feedback to the user while interacting in the smart office. In addition to a visual and textual description of the currently selected item, the HMD application shows a camera live view to aid target selection using hand gestures.

The HMD application also allows the user to use voice commands or a list-based selection mechanism that uses Glass' rim-mounted touchpad. Voice commands use Google's voice recognition service, which samples user audio, sends it to a cloud service and returns the recognized voice input as a string. To improve the detection accuracy for our voice command set, we use a *Hamming Distance* measure to enable somewhat more relaxed string matching for detected voice commands. We defined a Hamming Distance of 2 to still be acceptable for matching voice commands. The list-based selection mechanism presents the user with a vertical list that contains all known displays and selection items. The user can swipe through this list and on each tap event a message is forwarded to the Backend application containing the unique identifier of the selected item.

### Messaging

Since the three software components of our prototype are required to communicate with each other, we use ZeroMQ[10] (ZMQ) to implement messaging via sockets. We designed the messaging architecture in our prototype using publish/ subscribe semantics. The blue boxes in Figure 6 represent ZMQ "forwarder devices" that implement the messaging semantics. Our system uses a local WiFi hotspot to transmit messages.

### USER STUDY

We conducted a second user study to obtain quantitative usability information on an actual prototype that implements the scenario outlined in Section . Specifically, we

wanted to find out if there was a difference between the two proposed gestural techniques **T2** (Hand Tracking) and **T3** (hand gestures) and the baseline techniques **B1** (voice command) and **B2** (list view), and generally, if the gestural techniques would be feasible alternatives to **B1** and **B2**. We decided against comparing our proposed gestural techniques with a more traditional baseline technique, such as mouse input. Mouse input on large and distant displays has been extensively studied in the literature. Robertson et al. illuminate a number of user experience issues of mouse input on large displays in [17]. As an alternative, Forlines et al. as well as Malik et al. argue for using touch input when interacting with tabletop-size or distant displays in situations where more than one user is using the displays [9, 13]. Lastly, we are specifically interested in comparing input techniques that are supported by current or potential future HMDs, so studying mouse our touch pad input would not gain us further insight into interaction tasks with HMDs.

### Participants and Apparatus

We recruited a total of 12 participants (2 female) from an industrial research lab. Their age range was 23-44 years old.

The study was set up using the prototype described in the previous section. The backend application was used to visualize the application output on two external 60 inch HD displays, placed in a modern conference room environment. In keeping with the "architect" scenario, the study application allowed participants to move visual items (i.e., pictures of different stone patterns) between the two displays. The list view for **B2** was set up to maximize its effectiveness: we listed the two displays as the first two items on the list and the selectable items following those. Thus, the list had only a single selection level, and the number of items (12 stone patterns and two displays) was low enough such that the users could scroll the list effectively.

### Procedure and Design

To simulate a typical interaction sequence of our scenario, participants were asked to perform two tasks using each interaction technique, thus following a within-subjects design. The two tasks were (1) move a visual item from display 1 to display 2, and (2) to move a visual item from display 1 to display 2 and then back to display 1. The reason for only asking for one task repetition was that the two task were set up in such a way such that each interaction technique was repeated several times per task (e.g., repeated selection of visual items during a task). This way, the users performed the same action per interaction technique multiple times.

We measured (total) task completion time and error count (i.e., the number of missed selections) per task as performance measured and also asked participants to answer a System Usability Scale (SUS) [4] questionnaire for each input technique.

---

[9]We note here that with complete camera-hand-display calibration, which might be a complex task to achieve, a direct item selection based solely on pointing towards an item would be possible. We believe, however, that the setup we use in this paper is sufficient for the goals of our user study.

[10]http://zeromq.org

(a) Total Time Task (1)

(b) Total Time Task (2)

(c) Errors Task (1)

(d) Errors Task (2)

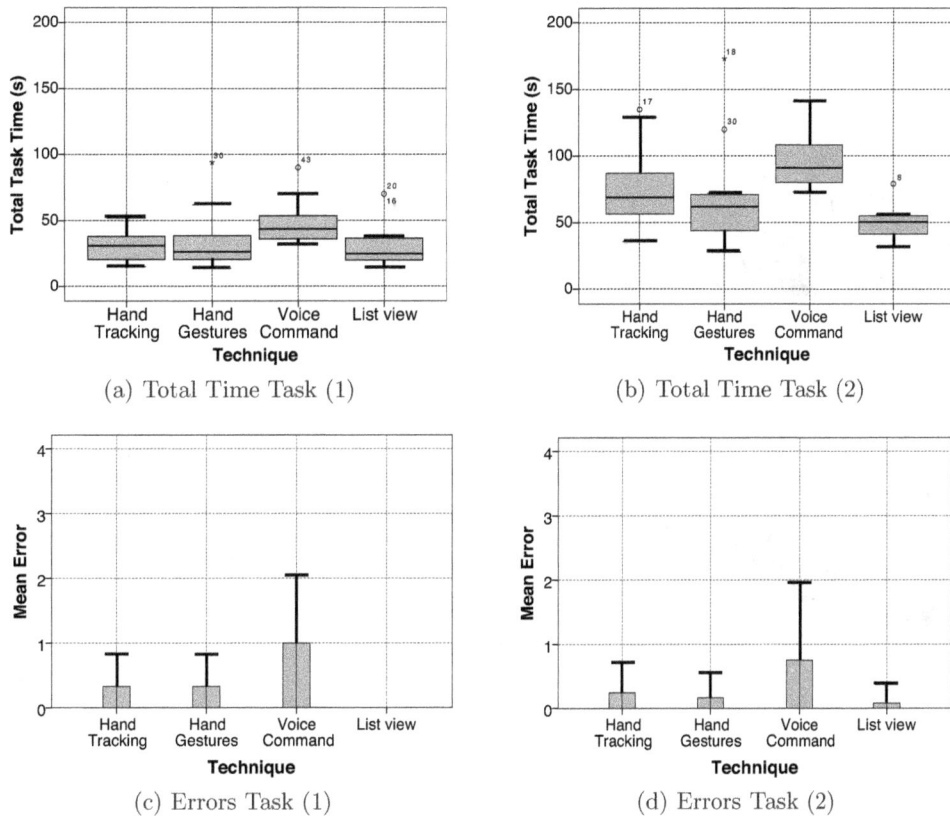

**Figure 9. Quantitative results of our main user study. Note: the error bars on boxplots (a) and (b) show the 95 % confidence interval, whereas the bars on plots (c) and (d) show one standard deviation from the mean.**

Before starting the main tasks, each participant was instructed to practice with the system for about 15 minutes until he or she became familiar with all the proposed input techniques.

**Hypothesis**

Our initial hypothesis (**H3**) was that **T2** and **T3** would have shorter task execution times and lower error counts than the baseline techniques **B1** and **B2**.

**Findings and Discussion**

Figures 9(a) and 9(b) show the total task time for tasks (1) and (2). An ANOVA shows that there was a significant difference in the task completion times for task (2) ($F_{3,44} = 5.516$, $p = 0.003$). For task (2), list view (**B2**) was the technique with the lowest (average) total execution time of 49.92 s, followed by hand gestures (**T3**) at 69.33 s and hand tracking (**T2**) at 75.92 s. Voice commands (**B1**) had the highest total execution time at 95.92 s. However, a Bonferroni pairwise comparison showed only a significant difference between techniques **B2** and **B1**.

We conducted an ANOVA on the error count measure. The only observable statistically significant difference ($F_{3,44} = 5.359$, $p = 0.003$) was for task (1), where **B1** and **B2** differed significantly according to a Bonferroni post-hoc test (p = 0.002).

We obtained an average SUS score of 51 for **B1**, **B2** and **T3** as well as 49 for **T2**. Not surprisingly, an ANOVA showed that there was no statistical significant difference for the SUS score. We should note, however that the score for all techniques was rather low on the SUS scale (which ranges from 0 to 100). The somewhat diffuse SUS results suggest that this questionnaire might not be entirely suitable to evaluate the usability of the post-desktop interactions we discuss in this paper.

Our results do not validate our initial hypothesis **H3**. Although **T2** and **T3** did show a lower average execution time for tasks (1) and (2) than **B1**, **B2** had the lowest average task execution time. We should note, however, that there was no significant difference to **B2**. Although not provable with our statistical analysis, we can hypothesize that **T2** and **T3** performed more or less on par with **B2**. This is also reflected by the significantly higher error rate observed for **B1** (see Figures 9(c) and 9(d)). Although we chose a very simple vocabulary and syntax for the speech-based interface, and allowed for recognition errors in the speech commands, there were still a lot of errors stemming from misrecognized voice commands. Nevertheless, voice recognition on current devices like Google Glass is not instantaneous, as voice recognition is performed in the cloud, which causes a delay that may have contributed to the somewhat longer average task execution times, an effect which we have

(a) Interaction with 3D content on large display.

(b) Ambient light control through in-air gestures.

**Figure 10. Two demonstration applications we implemented using our prototype.**

considered to be an intrinsic property of voice-based interfaces for the purposes of this study.

We should also note that, as mentioned previously, the list view of **B2** was set up in a very effective way. We believe however, that the list view interface will not scale effectively if the number of selectable targets grows. Scrolling actions will get proportionally longer. Furthermore, the time to choose an appropriate item (i.e., a list item that corresponds to a desired selection item in the environment) in the list view will increase as the number of selectable items increases (Hick's Law [5]). Here, we believe that a gestural approach would be the most effective as users can directly select items they see rather than searching for a correspondence between the desired item on an external screen and an item on their HMD's display. Future work will need to asses under which conditions selection via hand gestures will become more effective than the current list view interface.

## FURTHER SPATIAL INTERACTION APPLICATIONS
Apart from the application and scenario we have already discussed in this paper, there are numerous possibilities of leveraging the spacial input properties afforded by our prototype. With ego-centric tracking, users can perform spatial interactions with any type of connected device (i.e., reachable via TCP/IP or other communication channel) in the environment, without requiring further instrumentation of the device to track user inputs. In the following, we describe two demonstration applications we have developed based on our prototype.

As our prototype allows full 3D capture of the user's hand, we can, for example, implement user interfaces for 3D scene viewing on ubiquitous displays very easily (see the demo application in Figure 10(a)). A further advantage for ego-centric tracking here is that, e.g., for very large displays (e.g., in public spaces) supporting interaction by larger numbers of users there is no sensor scalability or coverage problem as each user is equipped with a personal sensing device.

Another application example for our prototype is controlling smart room appliances such as ambient lighting (see Figure 10(b)). In contrast to previous work in this domain [6], we believe that interacting directly through gestures can be more effective than using GUI-based controls on the HMD. Gestures, for example, allow more possibilities to fine tune certain parameters that are of interest when controlling ambient lighting, for instance, fine-tuning the lights' brightness and hue settings. Also, targeting the ambient devices can be accomplished by visual selection, i.e., turning the head towards the device, or direct pointing via a gesture.

## CONCLUSION AND FUTURE WORK
In this work we presented a prototype scenario for HMD-based gestural interactions in a smart office environment. We described our implementation of a prototype system for use in this environment. The development of the prototype was informed by a preliminary study that elicited user emotions towards several proposed gestural input techniques and also provided user preference ranking feedback of HMD gestural input techniques vs. a set of baseline techniques. In a second study implementing the proposed scenario we quantitatively evaluated the usability our prototype.

The results of our first study indicate that gesture-based interaction techniques were accepted by the user both in preference, as shown by the ranking and Likert-scale results, and emotional feedback, where the input techniques using in-air hand gestures elicited a positive emotional response.

The results of our second study, however, are more difficult to interpret due to the unclear statistical results. However, the statistically significant results for audio do indicate that this modality (used by itself) is at a disadvantage vs. gestural input and the baseline GUI "list view" technique, both in terms of execution speed and error count. The comparison between gestures and the baseline technique does not show a clear winner. Nevertheless, we believe that the list view may at a certain point (e.g., at a certain level of available targets, or for more complex nested selection tasks) show disadvantages vs. gestural input. A reason for this is that using gestures, users potentially have a larger space to perform inputs, and furthermore, when not using a HMD that covers the user's entire field of view, using gestures in conjunction with the external display provides a much larger space for displaying information, which might also speed up selection tasks.

A future study that varies the number of targets on the display and that also implements nested selection tasks will be needed to answer detailed questions comparing the list view to gestural interactions. However, the knowledge gained in this study may be limited, as the insights would be applicable mostly to HMDs with limited display areas, such as the Google Glass device we used in this work. It is likely that the view area of future devices will be larger, and thus allow the implementation of more effective menu structures, such as dropdown menus or pie menus. Therefore, it would arguably be more interesting to conduct a future study with a slightly more capable HMD, such as the Epson Moverio Series of devices [8], which, in contrast to Google Glass, have a significantly wider viewing angle and a handheld large touch pad for interaction.

Lastly, we presented two demonstrator application that make use of our ego-centric tracking technique for HMDs. We believe that ego-centric tracking has advantages over exo-centric tracking as spaces do not need to be specially instrumented with sensors. Furthermore, the input capabilities of a space can scale with the number of users when using ego-centric tracking. However, one issue to address is how to detect and interface with external interactive devices in a seamless way. In this paper, we used visual codes as a helper to address devices and content. Using natural image features, BLE beacon technology, ultrasound, IR or visual light signaling, etc., could be used to address this problem in more elegant ways.

In the future, we are interested in more directly studying the difference between exo- and ego-centric tracking in terms of tracking performance, e.g., making a comparison of our prototype vs. a standard depth sensor such as the Kinect. We also wish to explore further applications for controlling ambient devices, and, correspondingly, investigate what further gestures may be useful given those applications.

## REFERENCES

1. Agarwal, A., and Meyer, A. Beyond usability: evaluating emotional response as an integral part of the user experience. In *CHI 2009 Extended Abstracts*, ACM (2009), 2919–2930.

2. Bailly, G., Müller, J., Rohs, M., Wigdor, D., and Kratz, S. Shoesense: a new perspective on gestural interaction and wearable applications. In *Proc. CHI 2012*, ACM (2012), 1239–1248.

3. Boring, S., Baur, D., Butz, A., Gustafson, S., and Baudisch, P. Touch projector: mobile interaction through video. In *Proc. CHI 2010*, ACM (2010), 2287–2296.

4. Brooke, J. Sus-a quick and dirty usability scale. *Usability evaluation in industry 189* (1996), 194.

5. Card, S. K., Newell, A., and Moran, T. P. The psychology of human-computer interaction.

6. Chen, Y.-H., Zhang, B., Tuna, C., Li, Y., Lee, E. A., and Hartmann, B. A context menu for the real world: Controlling physical appliances through head-worn infrared targeting. Tech. rep., DTIC Document, 2013.

7. Colaço, A., Kirmani, A., Yang, H. S., Gong, N.-W., Schmandt, C., and Goyal, V. K. Mime: compact, low power 3d gesture sensing for interaction with head mounted displays. In *Proc. UIST 2013*, ACM (2013), 227–236.

8. Epson. Epson Moverio BT-200. http://ow.ly/Ag2Y4, Aug. 2014.

9. Forlines, C., Wigdor, D., Shen, C., and Balakrishnan, R. Direct-touch vs. mouse input for tabletop displays. In *Proc. CHI 2007*, ACM (2007), 647–656.

10. Google. Google glass. http://www.google.com/glass/start/, July 2014.

11. Jacob, R. J., Girouard, A., Hirshfield, L. M., Horn, M. S., Shaer, O., Solovey, E. T., and Zigelbaum, J. Reality-based interaction: a framework for post-wimp interfaces. In *Proc. CHI 2008*, ACM (2008), 201–210.

12. Johanson, B., Hutchins, G., Winograd, T., and Stone, M. Pointright: experience with flexible input redirection in interactive workspaces. In *Proc. UIST 2002*, ACM (2002), 227–234.

13. Malik, S., Ranjan, A., and Balakrishnan, R. Interacting with large displays from a distance with vision-tracked multi-finger gestural input. In *Proc. UIST 2005*, ACM (2005), 43–52.

14. Mistry, P., Maes, P., and Chang, L. WUW-wear Ur world: a wearable gestural interface. In *CHI Extended Abstracts 2009*, ACM (2009), 4111–4116.

15. Piumsomboon, T., Clark, A., Billinghurst, M., and Cockburn, A. User-defined gestures for augmented reality. In *Human-Computer Interaction–INTERACT 2013*. Springer, 2013, 282–299.

16. Rekimoto, J. Pick-and-drop: a direct manipulation technique for multiple computer environments. In *Proc. UIST 1997*, ACM (1997), 31–39.

17. Robertson, G., Czerwinski, M., Baudisch, P., Meyers, B., Robbins, D., Smith, G., and Tan, D. The large-display user experience. *Computer Graphics and Applications, IEEE 25*, 4 (2005), 44–51.

18. Wigdor, D., and Wixon, D. *Brave NUI world: designing natural user interfaces for touch and gesture*. Morgan Kaufmann, 2011.

19. Wilson, A. D., and Benko, H. Combining multiple depth cameras and projectors for interactions on, above and between surfaces. In *Proceedings of the 23nd annual ACM symposium on User interface software and technology*, ACM (2010), 273–282.

# *VideoHandles*: Replicating Gestures to Search through Action-Camera Video

**Jarrod Knibbe, Sue Ann Seah, Mike Fraser**

Department of Computer Science, University of Bristol, UK

{Jarrod.Knibbe, s.a.seah, Mike.Fraser}@bristol.ac.uk

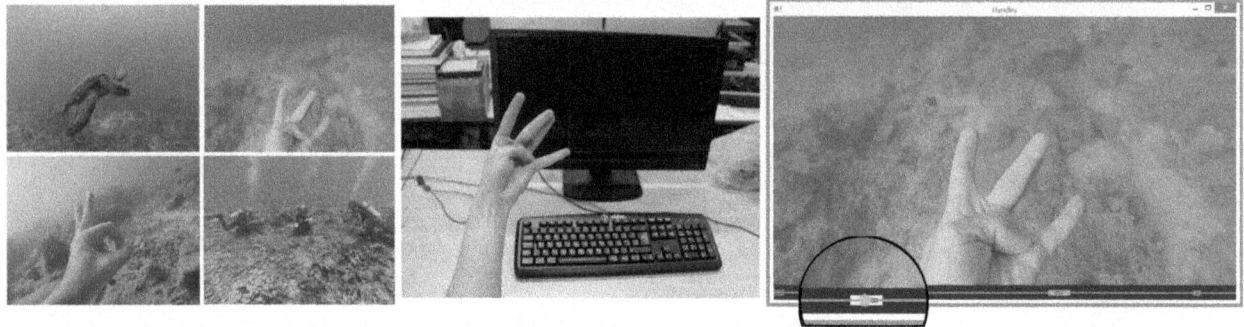

**Figure 1. VideoHandles interaction technique: a) Max records his diving activities, b) upon returning home, he repeats a gesture he remembers performing as a search query and c) the system compares the query with the original footage, returning a range of possible results (shown by highlighted yellow spans in the time bar).**

## ABSTRACT

We present *VideoHandles*, a novel interaction technique to support rapid review of wearable video camera data by re-performing gestures as a search query. The availability of wearable video capture devices has led to a significant increase in activity logging across a range of domains. However, searching through and reviewing footage for data curation can be a laborious and painstaking process. In this paper we showcase the use of gestures as search queries to support review and navigation of video data. By exploring example self-captured footage across a range of activities, we propose two video data navigation styles using gestures: *prospective gesture tagging* and *retrospective gesture searching*. We describe *VideoHandles'* interaction design, motivation and results of a pilot study.

## INTRODUCTION

*Max, a marine zoologist, is performing a scuba dive to record some underwater footage using an action camera. During the dive Max performs various hand gestures for his buddy, indicating aquatic life of interest. On one occasion, he sees a trigger fish and performs a fish swimming gesture followed by a trigger mime. On another occasion, he sees a*

*puffer fish and performs the gesture (fish swimming gesture followed by a two-handed mimicked inflation) to his dive buddy so that she can identify it too. Upon returning home, Max uploads the footage to his computer in order to analyse some of the key moments. He performs a puffer fish gesture as a search query and VideoHandles produces the puffer fish footage as a top ranking result among other results that include the fish swimming gesture. In the results, Max notices the trigger fish and decides to review that footage as well.*

A wide variety of users, from amateurs to professionals, have adopted action cameras across a diverse range of activities, from mountain biking and scuba diving through to professional fieldwork. These cameras, such as the GoPro [6], are frequently mounted on head-gear or fixed to the chest and record throughout an activity, often for $1 - 2$ hours, with little or no additional interaction. From these positions, and given a wide field of view (circa 170 degrees), the cameras are able to catch the majority of the wearer's view including any interactions or gestures they may be performing with their hands.

Where professionals may capture footage in order to maintain a clear record of their actions, others (e.g. sports enthusiasts) are more likely capture footage for key exciting moments. Although these are different motivations, all scenarios necessitate review in order to locate desired moments. Current approaches for video review are limited, with the widely adopted traditional method of video scrubbing (i.e. clicking through a timeline) being an inefficient process. As lifelogging becomes more pervasive, this process is clearly not scalable.

In this paper we present *VideoHandles*, a novel video search technique to expedite the review of specific moments in wearable video camera data. By exploiting the camera's view of the wearer's interactions and gestures, our system allows users to query their footage by repeating interactions and gestures performed during capture. The user re-attaches the action camera to the original position, and re-performs their target gesture. These reproduced gestures are matched to instances in the original footage.

From observing footage across a range of activities, we propose two video data navigation styles using gestures: *prospective gesture tagging*, where gestures are specifically performed to 'tag' moments in the footage, and *retrospective gesture searching*, where gestures are simply a part of the activity, recalled through muscle memory. We describe *VideoHandles'* interaction design, motivation and results of a pilot study.

## RELATED WORK

The most widely adopted method for video data navigation and review is video scrubbing. As a technique, it has been shown to be very fast in low latency systems where the video output updates perfectly in time with a moved slider [11]. Further, user knowledge of the footage (temporal, contextual and spatial) helps to increase the speed of navigation [11]. However, scrubbing has its limitations and these become increasingly apparent as video duration increases. As one example, the mapping between the scrubbing slider and the corresponding video timeline is rarely one-to-one [9]. The slider is limited in size by the window width, itself defined by the video's resolution. As the video length increases, each pixel of slider movement corresponds to a longer time step within the video. For example, given a 2.5 hour 1080p recording, each pixel of slider movement corresponds to 4.69 seconds. Assuming the video is viewed at full resolution on a 24-inch 1080p monitor, a pixel measures 0.28 mm. Moving 1 cm along the slider thus represents a time step of 2 minutes 47 seconds. These time steps make it easy to miss interesting moments of footage even with small slider movements.

*VideoHandles* aims to assist video navigation by providing location markers in a video based on user's input gesture. In this way, *VideoHandles* not only provides navigation cues, but also functions as a video search interface.

Traditionally, in an attempt to align with other online search forms, video search has been based on a query-by-text approach [13]. This technique requires pre-defined textual annotations that necessitate unacceptable initial time expenditure [12]. Furthermore, the annotations encode user perception, making their sharing difficult between multiple users difficult [7]. Recently, video search has moved to focus on a combination of different approaches, such as visual and audio cues [15], concept search [17], and image search [5]. While video search results are improving, the best results are often achieved using a combination of image processing and human interaction [7].

As gestural interfaces have grown in popularity, so too has research on image processing, specifically gesture segmentation and matching. The approaches typically vary based on camera type [1, 8] or key algorithmic features [e.g. 4, 10]. As yet there is no one-size-fits all solution and the design decisions of any proposed algorithm need to be closely tied to that of the setting.

## AN EXPLORATION OF ACTION CAM FOOTAGE

In order to motivate the design of our technique and to identify different styles of candidate gestures, we observed more than 50 hours of footage captured from a range of activities, including snowboarding, cycling, scuba diving and archaeological excavation. The footage was collated from 5 existing users of this type of camera.

*Observation 1: Activity-based Gestures*

Our first observation is that the style of gestures naturally performed varies significantly across usage scenarios. For example at one end of the spectrum, scuba diving includes frequent sign-language gestures, where meaning is directly encoded in the hand-shape and motion. In the middle of the spectrum are activities such as archaeological excavation, tennis and windsurfing. Whilst these activities do not have a clear gestural vocabulary (like scuba diving), the majority of the skill is performed manually (i.e. embodied action performed specifically with the hands). For example, this could be careful trowel movements in archaeology, the various shots in tennis (forehand vs. backhand) or the different hand-holds for mast and boom positioning in windsurfing. As the motion of the hands plays a key role in these activities, these gestures are also good candidates for *VideoHandles*.

*Observation 2: Non-activity-based Gestures*

At the other end of the spectrum, where manual variation is limited, are activities such as mountain biking and running. In these activities, the primary execution of the skill is non-hand based and thus the participant's hands perform a limited variety of movements. For this reason, the 'normal' opportunities for gesture or action repetition are more limited without the performance of additional deliberate gestures for use as prospective gesture tags for later searching.

Even during those activities whose skill is less manually-performed, one key similarity observed between all the activities is the frequent and continued use of social or 'pantomime' gestures. These settings showcase frequent language-like gestures, such as congratulatory 'high-fives' or 'fist-bumps.' These same activities also utilized language-tied and deictic gestures, such as *"that time you went left and I went the other way."* Gestures of this kind also provide good candidates for our technique.

### *VIDEO HANDLES*

The *VideoHandles* video search technique enables users to remember, or specifically plan, gestures produced during recording and to reproduce these gestures as search criteria to relocate specific moments in footage. Our technique reduces the requirement for human time and effort in reviewing vast reams of video data.

Users can search their footage by repeating any hand-actions / gestures from a similar viewpoint to which they were originally captured. By not making any assumptions about the style of gestures performed or their meaning, our technique can support a wide variety of gestures, including sign-language like scuba-diving gestures and manual skill based actions, such as trowelling in archaeology.

Based on our observations in the previous section, we propose two video data navigation styles using gestures: *prospective gesture tagging* and *retrospective gesture searching*.

### Prospective Gesture Tagging

As users become accustomed to *VideoHandles*, gaining an understanding of the gestures that are matched most successfully by the system, we foresee increased performance of gestures during recording specifically designed for later retrieval. We term these gestures *prospective tagging*. For example, if a moment of immediate interest occurs during mountain biking, the rider could pre-emptively perform a gesture to 'tag' the moment and increase the accuracy of later retrieval (e.g. a gesture that would not normally occur during the activity). Gesturing has been shown to assist our ability to remember [3], and thus prospective tagging of this kind further aids users' memory of the gesture for search, ensuring more accurate search results.

### Retrospective Gesture Searching

*VideoHandles* is also able to support occasions where gestures are simply a part of the activity. In some instances, prospective marking will not be possible, perhaps because the event only acquires importance and meaning for the user in retrospect rather than at the time, or because the user is not interested only in a single event, but wishes to review and compare all examples of a particular activity (such as trowelling in archaeology). In these cases, the user can use VideoHandles to perform a *retrospective search*. One of the benefits of this mode of searching is that the user may be able to rely on visual and muscle memory to perform the query. If the search is for one or more instances of a well-rehearsed manual skill, then the previous practice will also enhance the consistency of the search query.

### Multiple Results

Just as a web search provides multiple results, *VideoHandles* does not intend to provide only 'exact' matches; rather it supports reflection and comparison between hits by returning a ranked range of results. In this way, *VideoHandles* also serves to better support 'chance finds' when clicking through footage and specifically supports 'middle-spectrum' activity-based gestures.

### PROTOTYPE SYSTEM

We developed a prototype system to explore the feasibility of our concept and its value from an HCI perspective. We used a combination of existing computer vision algorithms to track, segment, and shape- and motion-match gestures in different videos. The technical approach we adopt is just one of many possible approaches and any appropriate computer vision algorithm could be used.

We segment gestural information from the scene based on motion (using Farneback optical flow [5]) and color (a combination of RGB and HSV skin color detection). Identified skin regions are tracked over a series of frames (typically 10 frames or 0.33 seconds) and subsequently saved as a 'gesture chunk.' When gesture chunks have been located in both the raw and query footage, these chunks are compared (in both shape and motion) to determine suitable matches.

The shape match is calculated using Fourier Descriptors of the contours [16] and chamfer matching [2]. Both of our matching techniques are rotation and scale invariant and by varying the examined 'gesture chunk' window size our techniques are also time invariant. Motion matching is conducted using the $ gesture recognizer [14]. Similarly to our shape matching, this is invariant to time, scale and location. Combined scores (from both shape and motion matching) below a given threshold are considered a match.

Once the footage has been processed, temporally and spatially co-located matched chunks are grouped together and time-period scores are returned based on frequency of matches.

### PILOT STUDY OF *VIDEOHANDLES* IN THE WILD

To further explore our interaction technique and to begin to evaluate our prototype, we conducted an initial study of *VideoHandles* in realistic use. A participant wore a GoPro action camera on a chest mount whilst cycling, recording 42 minutes of footage. The participant was asked to perform a gesture of their choosing, indicating: every time they saw a red car, when they were feeling energetic and when they felt tired. After the activity was completed, the participant reviewed their footage using video scrubbing, recording the time and meaning of every gesture they saw. While not all gestures were revisited, a subset were noted to provide correspondences for our *VideoHandles* software. In total, 28 gestures were identified. After review, an example of each type of gesture was recorded as a search query for our system.

*Results*

Our participant indicated 28 'two-finger gun' style gestures corresponding to red cars. Our prototype algorithm returned 89% of these gestures and 1 false-positive gesture. Our participant performed 3 'OK' gestures and our prototype algorithm returned 2 correct matches and 16 false-positive gestures, including both car gestures and 'tired' gestures.

### DISCUSSION

Our exploration and evaluation has highlighted a number of interesting features for further consideration in the design of our approach.

Firstly, our study highlighted the importance of shot framing and camera mounting. Even with the camera's wide field of view, our study participant (an inexperienced action camera user) repeatedly performed their 'tagging' gestures at the very top of the frame, resulting in part of the shape detail being lost and making any matching difficult. Given increasing use of these cameras and our technique, we foresee users becoming more accustomed to the camera's field of view, thus purposefully positioning their gestures more accurately.

Secondly, our study highlighted differences between human and computer interpretation of gestures. For example, where humans understand a clear distinction between 'thumbs up' and 'thumbs down' gestures, these are interpreted the same in our system (due to rotation invariance). The same is true for gestures of similar outer shape, such as 'thumbs up' and 'OK.' While improvements could be made in our prototype, users would benefit from selecting gestures that are shape and rotation unique, rather than human meaning unique.

Thirdly, our sample footage and pilot study demonstrated the variations in lighting and color palette of captured videos. Our technique could be extended such that users could specify a target 'search' color in an example frame. By selecting an example frame from the raw footage, the user could specify their own skin color (thus increasing accuracy given the lighting and color conditions). Further, non-skin color sections could be selected for tracking and comparison, extending our approach to be applicable to gloves or specific equipment details. As an example, an archaeologist could choose whether to search for trowelling by providing a 'troweling-like' action or by selecting the handle color of the trowel as a search criteria.

Due to the continuous capture style of these cameras and the often repetitive nature of the activities recorded, our users benefit from a system supporting both searching and filtering. Our system was not intended to only return correct matches (searching), rather to also highlight similar moments (filtering), thus supporting wider exploration of the footage. This further supports our archaeologist, above, allowing them to not only locate exact gestures but also segment all moments of trowelling.

Finally, our sample footage highlighted the frequently social nature of the activities recorded. There is an opportunity for our work to be extended to support the repetition of any captured gesture, not only that of the wearer. In turn, this would allow for a more complex range of queries from a wider audience and thus support wider results and reflection.

## CONCLUSION

*VideoHandles* is a novel search interaction technique for action camera footage which allows users to search through footage by repeating actions performed during the original recording. *VideoHandles* allows real-time tagging and categorizing of data, thus reducing time spent on post-processing, whilst facilitating wider exploration of recorded footage by supporting comparison between search matches. Our technique also supports a range of usage methods, allowing for both retrospective searching through memory of actions or prospective marking of footage with specific gestures during the initial capture.

We have highlighted and explored the style of footage captured by the action-camera community, described the implementation of our prototype system and explored the feasibility of its use in one study in the wild where our prototype has demonstrated promising initial results.

## REFERENCES

1. Baran, J., Gauch, J., Motion Tracking in Video Sequences Using Watershed Regions and SURF Features, in *Proc. Of SE*, 2012.
2. Barrow, HG., et al, Parametric correspondence and chamfer matching: Two new techniques for image matching, in *Proc. 5th Int. Joint Conf. AI*, 1977.
3. Cook, SW, Yip, TK, Goldin-Meadow, S., Gesturing Makes Memories that Last, *Journal of Memory and Language*, 1996.
4. Endres, D., et al., Emulating human observers with Bayesian binning: Segmentation of Action Streams, in *Trans. A.P.*, 2011.
5. Flickner, M. et al, Query by Image and Video Content: the QBIC System, *Computer 28.9*, 1995.
6. GoPro Action Cameras , http://gopro.com/
7. Halvey, M., Joemon, MJ., The role of expertise in aiding video search, in *Proc. CIVR*, 2009.
8. Hanlu, L., et al, Contour Cue Based Particle Filter for Monocular Human Motion Tracking, in *VRCAI*, 2010.
9. Hürst, W., Interactive Audio-Visual Video Browsing, in *Proc. Of MM*, 2006.
10. Li, C., Kitani, K., Pixel-level Hand Detection in Ego-Centric Videos, in *Proc. Of CVPR*, 2013.
11. Matejka, J., Grossman, T., Fitzmaurice, G., Swift: Reducing the Effects of Latency in Online Video Scrubbing, in *CHI*, 2012.
12. Shim, JC., Dorai, C., Bolle, R. Automatic Text Extraction from Video for Content-based Annotation and Retrieval, in *PR*, 1998.
13. Tian, X. et al, Bayesian Video Search Reranking, in *MM*, 2008
14. Wobbrock, JO., Wilson, AD., Li, Y., Gestures without Libraries, Toolkits or Training: a $1 Recognizer for User Interface Prototypes, *Proc. UIST*, 2007.
15. Yuan, J., Tian, Q., Ranganath, S., Fast and Robust Search Methods for Short Video Clips from Large Video Collection, in *Proc. Of PR*, 2004.
16. Zhang, D., Lu, G., A comparative study on shape retrieval using Fourier descriptors with different shape signatures, in *Proc. Of ICIMADE*, 2001.
17. Zhong, D, Chang, SF., Spatio-temporal Video Search Using the Object Based Video Representation, in *Proc of IP*, 1997.

# Fisheye Vision: Peripheral Spatial Compression for Improved Field of View in Head Mounted Displays

**Jason Orlosky, Qifan Wu, Kiyoshi Kiyokawa,**
**Haruo Takemura**
Osaka University, Japan
{orlosky@lab., wu@lab., kiyo@, takemura@}
ime.cmc.osaka-u.ac.jp

**Christian Nitschke**
Kyoto University, Japan
christian.nitschke@
i.kyoto-u.ac.jp

## ABSTRACT

A current problem with many video see-through displays is the lack of a wide field of view, which can make them dangerous to use in real world augmented reality applications since peripheral vision is severely limited. Existing wide field of view displays are often bulky, lack stereoscopy, or require complex setups.

To solve this problem, we introduce a prototype that utilizes fisheye lenses to expand a user's peripheral vision inside a video see-through head mounted display. Our system provides an undistorted central field of view, so that natural stereoscopy and depth judgment can occur. The peripheral areas of the display show content through the curvature of each of two fisheye lenses using a modified compression algorithm so that objects outside of the inherent viewing angle of the display become visible. We first test an initial prototype with 180° field of view lenses, and then build an improved version with 238° lenses. We also describe solutions to several problems associated with aligning undistorted binocular vision and the compressed periphery, and finally compare our prototype to natural human vision in a series of visual acuity experiments. Results show that users can effectively see objects up to 180°, and that overall detection rate is 62.2% for the display versus 89.7% for the naked eye.

### Author Keywords

Wide field of view; fisheye lens; spatial compression; augmented reality; safety; head mounted display.

### ACM Classification Keywords

H.5.2 [User Interfaces]: Prototyping

## INTRODUCTION

In recent years, head mounted displays (HMDs) have finally achieved a form factor that can be worn comfortably

for long periods of time. Products like Google's Glass, Epson's Moverio, Vizux's Wrap, and Oculus's Rift are becoming commercially available, and increasingly commonplace. However, a number of problems with these devices remain. In the case of video see-through displays, problems like limited resolution, pixel persistence, narrow field of view (FOV), and delay can make devices unsafe to use for everyday augmented reality (AR) applications. In particular, the narrow FOV of most see-through displays poses a problem to user safety when conducting simple tasks like walking, navigating, or checking for oncoming traffic. Current solutions to this problem include prototypes designed to provide a wide FOV, but are often bulky or do not provide good binocular vision [1, 5, 9, 13].

In this paper, we propose the use of fisheye lenses to expand a user's peripheral field of view for both general and outdoor augmented reality (AR) applications. We use a setup that somewhat resembles other stereo AR displays such as those by Kiyokawa et. al and Fan et. al [7, 9]. However, our prototypes include several major differences, including the use of ultra wide angle fisheye lenses and modified undistortion algorithms for images in the peripheral region of the display. The prototypes, which are modified versions of the Oculus Rift, are shown in A and B of Figure 1. In our design, binocular vision is achieved by undistorting the pixels in the central field of view, as in other models. The big difference is that images presented in the peripheral view are shown to the user as if viewed through a fisheye lens, as can be seen through the left eye camera in D of Figure 2, but with several modifications.

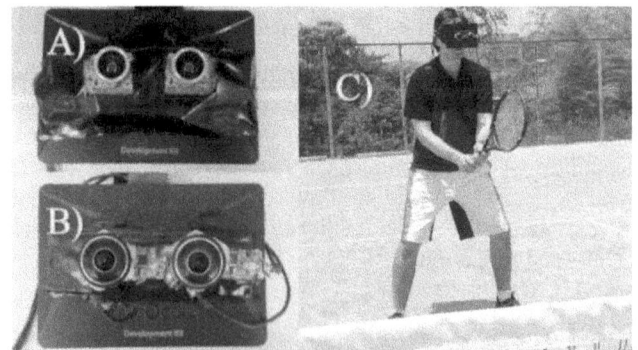

**Figure 1. Our A) first and B) second prototypes of the Fisheye Vision display with 180° and 238° FOV lenses, and C) testing of the 238° prototype in a tennis rally.**

Wide angle lens distortion would introduce a number of problems such as reduced depth perception and skewed direction estimation if it were in the binocular field [4, 10, 21]. However, acuity in human peripheral vision is already low and does not have a binocular component, so a fisheye view of the periphery can escape many of these problems. The great benefit of this expanded view is that objects such as cars and pedestrians that are beyond the HMD screen's angular viewing plane become visible to the user. This means that peripheral objects of interest come into view more quickly, and in most cases are noticed at angles similar to those of normal human vision.

Additionally, our prototype is lighter than most helmet-based and catadioptric systems, is inexpensive to construct, and can be used for outdoor AR for extended periods of time. In the following sections, we describe the detailed setup of an initial prototype using 180° FOV lenses and an improved design using 238° FOV lenses. We then present the results of a series of experiments testing a user's ability to notice peripheral objects of different sizes and at different angles in the redesigned display. Users conduct the same tasks with both the display and naked eye to provide an objective comparison to natural human vision.

## RELATED WORK
Related research primarily falls into two categories. These include 1) expanding a user's virtual FOV through hardware or software and 2) studying displayed objects and perception in expanded or modified peripheral views.

### Field of View Expansion
One of many attempts at expanding a user's FOV in a head mounted display was in 1999 by Yamazaki et. al. They prototyped a prism based display that offered a 51° wide FOV [24]. Subsequently, a number of other design guidelines and display prototypes were created that used mirror and lens systems to expand the physical FOV to the periphery [5, 17]. In 2006, Nagahara et al. developed a display that converts the image from a 360° catadioptric camera system into two stereoscopically aligned images [13]. These images, which compensate for distortion, are subsequently projected onto two hemispherical lenses, and provide a near 180° field of view. Another recent attempt to accomplish a wide FOV using projective displays was carried out by Kiyokawa et al. This display was developed using hyperbolic half-silvered mirrors in combination with a retro-reflective screen, which gives users optical see-through capability [9]. Both designs by Nagahara et al. and Kiyokawa et al. are relatively bulky, and require separate projectors and mirrors for each eye.

A similar display proposed by Ardouin et al. in 2012 also uses a catadioptric camera to compress 360° of viewing field into a 45° FOV display [1]. Unfortunately, this introduces significant distortion into the user's binocular vision, and only a short quantitative experiment was carried out. To our knowledge, the most recent attempt at providing an expanded field of vision is that of Fan et al. in

2014 [7]. They present a single 100° wide field of view camera image to both eyes (biocular view). Instead of a user being able to view his or her peripheral environment, a number of different indicators are blended into the displayed image to indicate objects of interest. In contrast, our prototype provides binocular stereoscopy and a simultaneous compressed view of the peripheral, allowing users to constantly view objects up to 180°. Furthermore, we conduct a number of studies on perception and visual acuity of compressed objects displayed in the periphery, such as the effect of lens compression on reaction time.

### Studies on Modified Peripheral Views
Most past studies on virtual peripheral vision in wearable displays have been limited due to physical restrictions of display technology. However, a number of studies are available that examine various projected objects or modified physical peripheral views in non-virtual environments. Human peripheral vision has been very widely studied, with one of the first relevant studies from Brandt et al., who showed that rotations of the periphery result in a perceived self-rotation [4]. This type of perceptual study has been extended into the virtual domain, such as the work by Draper et al., which showed that changes in scale can lead to simulation sickness in virtual displays [6]. Based on the results of these studies, we sought to avoid major rotations or changes in scale when designing our compression methodology.

More recently, researchers have begun to consider virtual displays for the modification of the periphery. For example, Vargas-martin et. al, used an HMD to add peripheral information to the central field of view to help patients with severe tunnel vision [19]. A more recent study by Loomis et. al in 2008 studied perceptions of gaze in human peripheral vision. It was discovered that, to some degree, humans can determine the gaze direction of an onlooker despite the fact that the onlooker's face is in the periphery [12]. Even more recently, the predator-prey vision metaphor has been proposed as a method for modifying the periphery by varying the camera angle to simultaneously increase the peripheral FOV while decreasing the binocular FOV [16]. Our model tries to avoid this modification of camera angle to ensure the user has a more natural and consistent binocular view, but can still reap the benefits of an expanded periphery. Annotation discovery rate has also been studied in wide FOV optical see-through displays by Kishishita et. al [8]. This provides further evidence that effective use of both binocular and peripheral view spaces is essential when users need to notice objects beyond the binocular field of vision.

### Further Motivation
Up to now, a number of catadioptric and view modification systems have been proposed to expand a user's field of view, but these attempts do not always provide good binocular stereoscopy, which is desired for correct projection and augmentation in real-world AR [2].

Other existing studies have yet to compare the apparent benefits of these prototypes to human vision [1, 13, 20]. In comparison to catadioptric displays, our design has a smaller form factor and requires less hardware. Additionally, problems associated with binocular display techniques have been well studied, but only recently have portable wide FOV displays become commercially available. This allows us to conduct improved studies of the virtual peripheral field, and take advantage of the pixels in the display that are in the periphery.

## SYSTEM DESIGN

To build a usable prototype, we sought a lightweight, portable display that had at least an 80° horizontal field of view. Secondly, stereo cameras had to have an appropriate frame rate and wide enough field of view to match the opening of the fisheye lenses. To provide a decent initial FOV, we selected the Oculus Rift, primarily for its 90° horizontal viewing angle. This allows us to utilize 60° of binocular vision, and the remaining 30° of peripheral vision for each eye. It is in these remaining 30° sections that we compress approximately 60° of peripheral vision per eye. Depending on the user's exact range of binocular vision, different angular ratios can be used.

### Prototype with 180° Lenses

Our first prototype, shown in A of Figure 1, was designed with two 180° FOV wide angle lenses, and was intended to expand a user's vision to 180°, though we later learned that wider angle lenses are necessary. These lenses and web cameras can be purchased for under $50 each. As already mentioned, our setup is similar to some other emerging AR stereo rigs in the sense that we provide binocular vision.

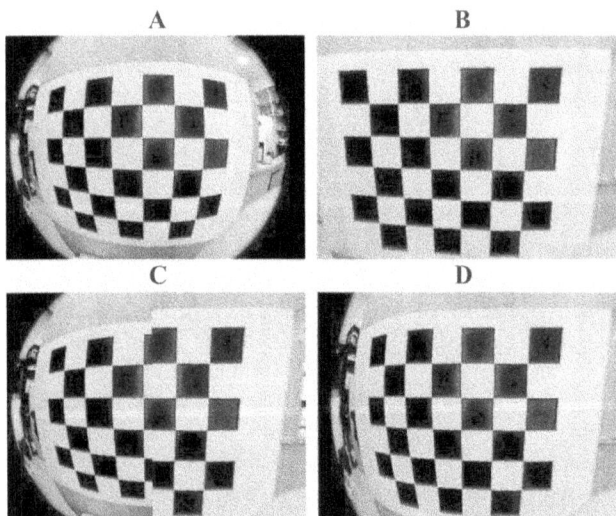

**Figure 2. Screenshots from the left-eye camera showing the A) view through the fisheye lens, B) completely undistorted image, C) image using peripheral compression, but with misalignment due to variation in compression and undistortion functions (center line), and D) corrected image with modified horizontal peripheral compression.**

However, where most other setups seek to achieve a perfect one-to-one mapping between the environment and each pixel viewed by the user [11, 18], we provide this exclusively for a user's binocular vision. Regarding peripheral vision, our prototype varies greatly from other setups. Rather than providing a standard one-to-one mapping, we modify the pixels in a user's peripheral vision to look as they are to some extent viewed through the fisheye lens. This presents a number of benefits, such as the ability to notice objects past the inherent FOV of the display. It also raises a number of interesting questions, such as: To what extent will users notice peripheral objects and how does this compare with the naked eye? Will this affect the time it takes to notice an object? Can users complete everyday tasks with relative ease with this modified view?

### Peripheral Spatial Compression

Since our display design is atypical for see-through displays, a number of problems arose when trying to correctly display the camera images, including several that are not solvable with normal use of existing computer vision functions such as the stereoalign or undistort functions provided by OpenCV [3].

Some setups call for vertical alignment of cameras since they align with the Oculus Rift's pixel distribution for binocular vision. This presents a major problem for our design since we are trying to achieve a higher horizontal FOV, and since some parts of the fisheye lens are not visible when aligned with many standard web cameras, as can be seen at the top and bottom of A in Figure 2. Therefore, we opted for horizontal alignment of the cameras, which allows us to neatly fit a majority of the fisheye lens's horizontal FOV into the camera's input. Vertical FOV is slightly cut off due to the fact that the fisheye lens does not fit perfectly, but this is not a problem since we are primarily concerned with horizontal FOV. Though this orientation results in a minor decrease in resolution due to the mapping between camera and display, we gain control of a much wider horizontal viewing angle.

### Undistortion Algorithms

The initial methods we used for undistortion and compression can be summarized in four distinct steps, including binocular undistortion, peripheral partial compression, misalignment correction, and peripheral linear compression, the latter of which is described along with the second prototype.

*Binocular*

The binocular view of 60° is corrected using standard OpenCV functionality [3]. A camera image through the fisheye lens is first faced toward a checkerboard to obtain camera parameters, as shown in A of Figure 2. After obtaining radial and tangential distortion coefficients for each lens, the imageundistort function is then applied in real time to both video streams for all pixels located within the binocular FOV.

Although the standard undistort function worked well for the 180° FOV lenses, getting accurate parameters for the 238° lens system was more difficult. OpenCV's standard functionality actually cannot handle a FOV of over 180°, so if a perfect undistortion of all peripheral pixels is required, a different undistortion algorithm would be necessary. Luckily, a majority of the binocular view presented to the user is viewed through the fisheye lens center, where the distortion is less pronounced.

*Peripheral*

The more complex part of our design lies in the manipulation of the peripheral FOV. Here, we must effectively compress over 60° of environmental FOV into 30° or less of virtual FOV. First, we left a portion of the virtual image untouched, as if viewed through the fisheye lens. Unfortunately, this results in a very obvious line where the compressed and non-compressed images meet, which is visible in C of Figure 2. So, we were left with an interesting problem: How can we present a compressed image in the periphery and smoothly connect it to the undistorted binocular image?

After considering a number of image-stitching and mosaic algorithms to merge the misaligned portion, we found a much more efficient solution, which also provides a more natural view for the user. Instead of running a time consuming alignment algorithm, we run the undistortion using only the *y* values of the coordinate map. This results in both a relatively clean alignment and a less distorted perspective in the vertical domain, as shown in D of Figure 2. In order to accomplish this, we modify the input map to OpenCV's undistort function as follows [3]. First, we start with the standard formula used to undistort an image, where $(x_p, y_p)$ represent undistorted points, and $(x_d, y_d)$ are the points viewed by the camera through the fisheye lens. Here, $k_1$, $k_2$, and $k_3$ are the radial and $p_1$ and $p_2$ are the tangential distortion coefficients obtained from the checkerboard calibration. The result of $y_p$ is obtained by compensating for radial and tangential distortion using the standard remap function, as in the following

$$[y_p] = (1 + k_1 r^2 + k_2 r^4 + k_3 r^6)[y_d] + [p_1(r^2 + 2y_d^2) + 2p_2 x_d y_d].$$

The result of $x_p$ is obtained by only compensating for tangential distortion, leaving *x* values in their compressed state, with

$$[x_p] = [x_d] + [2p_1 x_d y_d + p_2(r^2 + 2x_d^2)].$$

In code, this undistortion is normally carried out by the *Remap* function,

*Remap(dst, image, mapx_mod, mapy, CV_INTER_LINEAR | CV_WARP_FILL_OUTLIERS, cvScalarAll(0));,*

where *dst* is the destination image, *image* is the original image, *mapx* is the map containing new undistorted point locations in the *x* domain, and *mapy* is the matrix containing new undistorted points in the *y* domain.

Our modification is accomplished by substituting the default *mapx* parameter with *mapx_mod*, which contains new distortion values. This *mapx_mod* matrix is produced using the undistort function with the radial distortion coefficients set to zero.

As a result, the virtual peripheral view still compresses objects horizontally, the vertical ratio of environmental objects to virtual objects becomes closer to one, and the peripheral and binocular images align, as shown in D of Figure 2. Additionally, the complete virtual image more accurately represents the limits of the human field of view, which are more rectangular than circular as can be seen in the differences between the left hand borders of C and D. Note that the border is still somewhat rounded, due to the fact that the *mapy* values are reassigned based on the modified *mapx_mod*. This actually works in our favor, since more vertical content becomes visible towards the edge of the virtual FOV. At this point, we had come up with an effective method for displaying objects outside the native FOV of the display.

However, upon testing the display outside and with a number of different users, we quickly learned that 180° (advertised) lenses do not always provide a true 180° field of view, partially because the web camera FOV does not perfectly fit the fisheye lens inlets. Additionally, objects towards the outer edge of the fisheye lens appeared extraordinarily small and were barely visible. We then ordered a pair of 238° super-wide angle fisheye lenses, which provided a good solution to this problem, and resulted in an improved second prototype, as shown in B of Figure 1.

**Improved 238° Lens Design**

In comparison with our first design, we made three primary modifications to both hardware and software in the second prototype. The first main difference is the use of 238° instead of 180° FOV lenses. This was a good choice since objects placed around 180° no longer appeared infinitesimally small, and were relatively noticeable on the raw camera image. The second change was with the cameras themselves, which were originally Logitech C500s, chosen since to fit the inlets of the 180° FOV lenses. These were upgraded to Logitech C310s, which are more suited to the 238° FOV lenses, and provide easier manipulation of exposure and brightness via software. The last change was to the algorithm managing peripheral compression. Because of the differences between users' interpupillary distances and spacing between the Oculus lenses and the eyes, some people could not see the entire peripheral camera image during informal testing.

*Linear Compression Compensation*

To compensate for this deficit and in order to conduct more consistent experiments, we applied a small linear compression (equivalent to a perspective change) in addition to radial compression to ensure that data would fill the virtual FOV for all participants.

We first compute a perspective matrix $M$ using getPerspectiveTransform [3], which solves for $M$ in

$$\begin{bmatrix} t_i x_i' \\ t_i y_i' \\ t_i \end{bmatrix} = M \cdot \begin{bmatrix} x_i \\ y_i \\ 1 \end{bmatrix},$$

where $x_1$ and $x_2$ are the $x$ coordinates representing the vertical division between peripheral and binocular in the display $x_0$ and $x_3$ represent the outermost pixel showing content through the display lens. The last computation is done using the previously described $(x_p, y_p)$ as parameters in OpenCV's warpPerspective function, as in

$$(x_f, y_f) =$$

$$\left( \frac{M_{11}x_p + M_{12}y_p + M_{13}}{M_{31}x_p + M_{32}y_p + M_{33}}, \frac{M_{21}x_p + M_{22}y_p + M_{23}}{M_{31}x_p + M_{32}y_p + M_{33}} \right)$$

where pixels in the final image are represented by $(x_f, y_f)$. All of this processing occurs in about 11ms on a laptop with a Core-i7 3520m processor running at 2.9 gigahertz, allowing for display at over 30 frames per second (fps). Although current smartphones may not be able to run the undistortion algorithms at over 30 fps, small form factor laptops or tablets likely have enough power to run Fisheye Vision for mobile AR applications.

## EXPERIMENTS

In our experiments, we sought to evaluate the ability of users to notice objects in the improved prototype and compare this with human vision in terms of both acuity and reaction time. To test this, we displayed a number of icons of different sizes and at different angles in each participant's periphery, and recorded whether or not they were noticed, as well as the time it took to notice them. The results of this experiment have important implications for safety, since someone using an AR application outdoors that fails to notice an oncoming vehicle may be severely injured or killed.

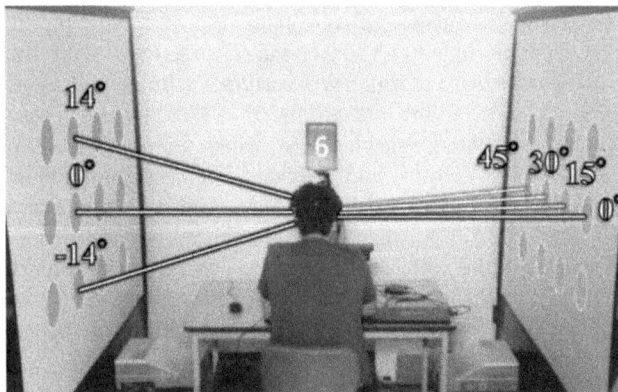

**Figure 3. Experiment setup showing projector screens, numbers displayed on the tablet for the concentration task, and a participant. A simulated view of display angles and large icons at every position is overlaid for reference.**

## Setup

We tested a total of 10 individuals, 3 female, 7 male, all of who willingly volunteered. The experiment task was to press a button when an icon came into view, and we recorded detection rate and reaction time for correctly detected icons for both the 238° fisheye display (referred to as "display" condition) and the naked eye (referred to as the "eye" condition). The setup is shown in Figure 3, with a simulated view of all large icons and angles overlaid at the same time for reference. The two projector screens were stationed at 105 centimeters (cm) to the left and right of the user and a 70cm high table was centered between the two projector screens. A headrest was fitted and centered on top of the table so that participants' heads would remain at 104cm above the floor.

Directly in front of the participant at a distance of 140 cm was a tablet PC, which displayed random numbers between 0 and 9 every three seconds. Participants read these numbers aloud to ensure that they were concentrating on their central field of view. A single semi-ambient light was positioned behind the user, and luminance was set to approximately 50 lumens (lx) for a blank projector screen, and 55 lx for the wall where the tablet was located, as measured from the headrest. This luminance was selected through informal testing to ensure that a number of icons would likely be missed for both eye and display, allowing us to effectively observe differences in error between conditions. Icons were solid red circles, and were displayed at 0°, 15°, 30°, and 45° in the horizontal, and at -14°, 0°, and 14° in the vertical, for a total of 12 different positions on each side of the periphery, as designated by the lines and angles overlaid onto Figure 3. Three different circle diameters, 3.5 cm, 7.0 cm, and 10.5 cm were presented, which represent an approximate cone of 1.9°, 3.9°, and 5.8° of FOV respectively, though perspective was slightly shifted for icons over 0°. For reference, a 1.5 meter wide vehicle at 10 meters away can fit in approximately 8° of FOV, and at 50 meters away, 1.7° of FOV. With these conditions, we cover a large range of object sizes and peripheral locations.

Each individual icon was displayed at a random interval between 3 and 8 seconds, and remained on the screen for one second. Conditions were randomized to prevent any ordering effects. The same projector models and settings were used to show images on both screens, and icon positions were calibrated individually to ensure left and right angles were consistent. Each participant completed all tasks in less than one hour.

## Results

From the experiments, we were able to evaluate the display in terms of both visual acuity and reaction time in comparison with the naked eye. This let us evaluate how the spatial compression would affect users in an environment that requires peripheral attention.

*Visual Acuity*

To clearly show significant tendencies regarding acuity, we first plot detection rate of the display versus eye according to icon size and display angle, as shown in Figures 4 and 5. A two way analysis of variance (ANOVA) showed a main effect of device ($F_{(1,9)}$=204.4, P<.01), and a slight interaction of size and angle conditions ($F_{(9,180)}$=2.28, P<.02). Although there is a relatively large difference between eye and display for small icons, the difference decreases as object size increases. For objects over 5.8° of FOV, the difference was only 15.8%. This means that pedestrians would likely notice a peripheral car or bicycle at 10 meters away, but would be less likely to notice objects as distance increases. As shown in Figure 5, there is a relatively consistent difference in error rate for all angles, suggesting that the compression of objects into peripheral space works for objects at any angle, potentially over 180°.

*Delay*

It should first be noted that because of camera throughput, processing, and display rendering, there is an inherent delay of approximately 150-180 ms between the time an object appears on the projector and the time it was rendered on the display screen. As such, in Figure 6 we show average reaction times for the eye, display, and display minus the inherent delay to provide a more objective comparison. A two way ANOVA on delay times also revealed both a main effect of device ($F_{(1,9)}$=216.33, P<.01) and slight interaction of size and angle conditions ($F_{(9,180)}$=2.26, P<.01).

Unlike acuity, a very interesting trend occurred with respect to angle and delay. In contrast to the consistent difference in error rates shown in Figure 5, the differences in reaction times between display and eye at 0° and 45° were significantly lower. It is very likely that because different regions of peripheral vision have different sensitivities, delay was higher for the eye at 0° and 45°. This means that placing virtual objects at more central peripheral angles can improve reaction times, which is an important finding for the field of view management. Though other minor tendencies for accuracy were observed, the results discussed above will likely have the biggest impact on future iterations of spatial compression displays. Unexpectedly, no learning effects or improvements in reaction time or detection rate were found for display or eye over time.

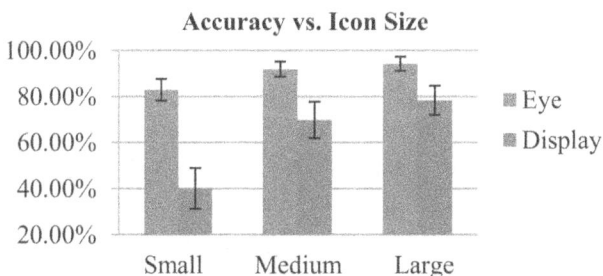

**Figure 4. Graph showing accuracy (correctly detected icons) according to icon size and standard deviation.**

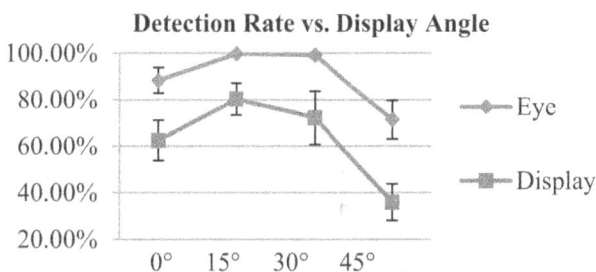

**Figure 5. Graph showing averages for correctly detected icons according to horizontal display angle for all icon sizes, with standard deviation.**

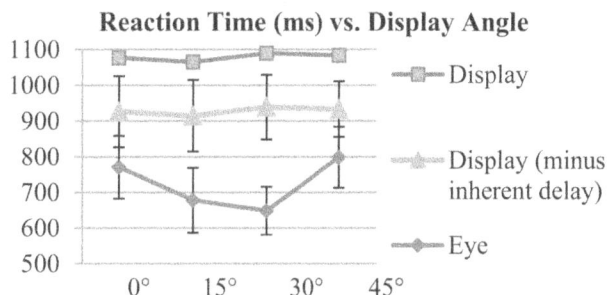

**Figure 6. Graph showing average reaction times for all icon sizes for the display (red), for the display minus the inherent delay (green), and for the eye (blue), and standard deviation, with respect to horizontal angle.**

**DISCUSSION**

Through this experiment, we were able to show that Fisheye Vision enables users to see objects at 180°. With further camera and parameter optimization, this can potentially be expanded past the human visual field. However, based on our results, a number of objects, particularly small objects, will not be noticed with this kind of compression. Part of this difference is probably due to the resolution limitations of the display and camera, so improvements in display technology will likely reduce the disparity between head mounted displays utilizing this method and the human eye. We look forward to testing how close we can come to human vision as technology improves.

In many respects, our method functions like parabolic mirrors on street corners or the curved mirrors attached to many side mirrors on cars nowadays. Although these spatial compression methods provide a better view of the environment, warnings such as "objects are closer than they appear" are often necessary. A similar notice may be beneficial for Fisheye Vision. Also, when testing the 238° fisheye lenses, we made an interesting discovery. If both lenses (not virtual, just the lenses) are placed and aligned directly in front of a user's eyes, the brain can still easily maintain stereoscopy. This means that the brain can stitch together two radially distorted images, which is very interesting physiologically, especially considering the mechanisms behind binocular summation are not yet fully understood [14, 22].

Lastly, studies show that variations in linear scale can cause simulation sickness [6], however the same is not necessarily true for non-linear distortion, such as that of a fisheye lens. This may be even less so when distorted information is only displayed in the periphery. We also conducted several informal tests with the display such as shopping at a convenience store and playing tennis, as shown in C of Figure 1. Initial results indicate that simulation sickness is not a problem, but eye fatigue occurs with prolonged use. As future work, we plan to test fatigue, naturalness, and required mental workload of linear versus radial distortion in a number of concentration intensive outdoor tasks.

## CONCLUSION

In this paper, we introduce Fisheye Vision, a method for expanding a user's effective field of view in see-through displays using fisheye lenses. We take advantage of the compressed nature of the lens, but only in the periphery, allowing users a wider field of view without sacrificing binocular vision. Experiments show that users can effectively see up to 180°, and that the larger the object, the smaller the difference between the display and the naked eye in terms of visual acuity. This method can not only be used to expand a user's virtual field of view, but can serve as a cornerstone for the development and study of new peripheral spatial compression functions and applications.

## ACKNOWLEDGMENTS

This research was funded in part by Grant-in-Aid for Scientific Research (B), #24300048 from the Japan society for the Promotion of Science (JSPS), Japan.

## REFERENCES

1. Ardouin, J., Lécuyer, A., Marchal, M., Riant, C., & Marchand, E. (2012, December). FlyVIZ: a novel display device to provide humans with 360° vision by coupling catadioptric camera with hmd. In Proceedings of the 18th ACM symposium on virtual reality software and technology (pp. 41-44). ACM.

2. Bimber, O., Wetzstein, G., Emmerling, A., & Nitschke, C. (2005, October). Enabling view-dependent stereoscopic projection in real environments. In Proceedings of the 4th IEEE/ACM International Symposium on Mixed and Augmented Reality (pp. 14-23). IEEE Computer Society.

3. Bradski, G., & Kaehler, A. (2008). Learning OpenCV: Computer vision with the OpenCV library. O'Reilly Media, Inc.

4. Brandt, T., Dichgans, J., & Koenig, E. (1973). Differential effects of central versus peripheral vision on egocentric and exocentric motion perception. Experimental Brain Research, 16(5), (pp. 476-491).

5. Chen, C. B. (2002, December). Wide field of view, wide spectral band off-axis helmet-mounted display optical design. In International Optical Design Conference 2002 (pp. 61-66). International Society for Optics and Photonics.

6. Draper, M. H., Viirre, E. S., Furness, T. A., & Gawron, V. J. (2001). Effects of image scale and system time delay on simulator sickness within head-coupled virtual environments. Human Factors: The Journal of the Human Factors and Ergonomics Society, 43(1), (pp. 129-146).

7. Fan, K., Huber, J., Nanayakkara, S., & Inami, M. (2014, March). SpiderVision: extending the human field of view for augmented awareness. In Proceedings of the 5th Augmented Human International Conference (p. 49). ACM.

8. Kishishita, N., Orlosky, J., Mashita, T., Kiyokawa, K., & Takemura, H. (2013, March). Investigation on the peripheral visual field for information display with real and virtual wide field-of-view see-through HMDs. In 3D User Interfaces (3DUI), 2013 IEEE Symposium on (pp. 143-144). IEEE.

9. Kiyokawa, K. (2007, November). A wide field-of-view head mounted projective display using hyperbolic half-silvered mirrors. In Proceedings of the 2007 6th IEEE and ACM International Symposium on Mixed and Augmented Reality (pp. 1-4). IEEE Computer Society.

10. Kruijff, E., Swan II, J. E., & Feiner, S. (2010, October). Perceptual issues in augmented reality revisited. In Proceedings of the 2007 6th IEEE and ACM International Symposium on Mixed and Augmented Reality (pp. 3-12).

11. Li, S. (2008). Binocular spherical stereo. Intelligent Transportation Systems, IEEE Transactions on, 9(4), (pp. 589-600).

12. Loomis, J. M., Kelly, J. W., Pusch, M., Bailenson, J. N., & Beall, A. C. (2008). Psychophysics of perceiving eye-gaze and head direction with peripheral vision: Implications for the dynamics of eye-gaze behavior. Perception, 37(9), (pp. 1443-1457).

13. Nagahara, H., Yagi, Y., & Yachida, M. (2006). A wide-field-of-view catadioptrical head-mounted display. Electronics and Communications in Japan (Part II: Electronics), 89(9), (pp 33-43).

14. Pardhan, S., & Whitaker, A. (2000). Binocular summation in the fovea and peripheral field of anisometropic amblyopes. Current eye research, 20(1), (pp. 35-44).

15. Prothero, J. D., & Hoffman, H. G. (1995). Widening the field-of-view increases the sense of presence in immersive virtual environments. Human Interface Technology Laboratory Technical Report TR-95, 2.

16. Sherstyuk, A., Treskunov, A., & Gavrilova, M. (2012, March). Predator-prey vision metaphor for multi-tasking virtual environments. In 3D User Interfaces (3DUI), 2012 IEEE Symposium on (pp. 81-84). IEEE.

17. Shum, H. Y., Kang, S. B., & Chan, S. C. (2003). Survey of image-based representations and compression

techniques. Circuits and Systems for Video Technology, IEEE Transactions on, 13(11), (pp. 1020-1037).

18. Takagi, A., Yamazaki, S., Saito, Y., & Taniguchi, N. (2000). Development of a stereo video see-through HMD for AR systems. In Augmented Reality, 2000.(ISAR 2000). Proceedings. IEEE and ACM International Symposium on (pp. 68-77). IEEE.

19. Vargas-Martin, F., & Peli, E. (2002). Augmented-view for restricted visual field: multiple device implementations. Optometry & Vision Science, 79(11), (pp. 715-723).

20. Veas, E., Grasset, R., Kruijff, E., & Schmalstieg, D. (2012). Extended overview techniques for outdoor augmented reality. Visualization and Computer Graphics, IEEE Transactions on, 18(4), (pp. 565-572).

21. Watson, B. A., Walker, N., & Hodges, L. F. (1995). A user study evaluating level of detail degradation in the periphery of head-mounted displays. In Proceedings of Framework for Interactive Virtual Environments (FIVE) Conference.

22. Wood, J. M., Collins, M. J., & Carkeet, A. (1992). Regional variations in binocular summation across the visual field. Ophthalmic and Physiological Optics, 12(1), 46-51.

23. Xiong, Y., & Turkowski, K. (1997, June). Creating image-based VR using a self-calibrating fisheye lens. In Computer Vision and Pattern Recognition, 1997. (pp. 237-243). IEEE.

24. Yamazaki, S., Inoguchi, K., Saito, Y., Morishima, H., & Taniguchi, N. (1999, May). Thin wide-field-of-view HMD with free-form-surface prism and applications. In Electronic Imaging'99 (pp. 453-462). International Society for Optics and Photonics.

# Human Sensitivity to Dynamic Translational Gains in Head-Mounted Displays

**Ruimin Zhang**
Michigan Technological
University
ruiminz@mtu.edu

**Bochao Li**
Michigan Technological
University
bochaol@mtu.edu

**Scott A. Kuhl**
Michigan Technological
University
kuhl@mtu.edu

## ABSTRACT

Translational gains in head-mounted display (HMD) systems allow a user to walk at one rate in the real world while seeing themselves move at a faster or slower rate. Although several studies have measured how large gains must be for people to recognize them, little is known about how quickly the gains can be changed without people noticing. We conducted an experiment where participants were asked to walk on a straight path while wearing an HMD while we dynamically increased or decreased their virtual world translation speed. Participants indicated if their speed increased or decreased during their walk. In general, we found that the starting gain affected the detection and that, in most cases, there was little difference between gradual and instantaneous gain changes. The results of this work can help inform redirected walking implementations and other HMD applications where translational gains are not constant.

## ACM Classification Keywords

I.3.3 Computer Graphics: Three-Dimensional Graphics and RealismVirtual Reality

## Author Keywords

Virtual reality, translation, redirected walking, perceptual threshold, gain, head-mounted display

## INTRODUCTION AND BACKGROUND

Head-mounted displays (HMDs) are portable display devices that are useful for many virtual reality applications including virtual prototyping, training, education and gaming. While wearing a typical HMD, a user is able to see a virtual environment without seeing the real world. When the HMD's position is tracked, a user can walk and navigate through the virtual space. Typically, one centimeter of real world movement results in the same amount of virtual world movement. Redirected walking [2, 3, 5, 6, 7, 10, 11] breaks this direct mapping to allow a user to safely navigate virtual spaces that are

larger than real spaces and frequently use translational gain manipulations. For example, a fixed translation gain (i.e., the virtual world speed divided by real world speed) of two can support a user who wants to explore a virtual space that is four times larger than the real space. Translational gain values that are less than one can also be useful in some situations. If a user is walking toward a virtual wall that is four meters away and the edge of the tracking system is six meters away, dampening the user's virtual movement can improve the alignment between the wall and boundary and thus increase the amount of tracked space behind the user so that there is more navigable space when they turn around.

When gains are introduced the visual information presented to the HMD user conflicts with vestibular and proprioceptive cues. As a result, people might notice the gain, find it distracting, or feel simulator sickness during navigation. A couple of studies attempt to investigate users' sensitivity thresholds for gain manipulations [8, 9] and provide guidelines for how small gains must be to prevent people from reliably detecting them. These existing guidelines, however, provide little information about how rapidly gains can be changed without people noticing. For example, a fixed translation gain of 0.8 or 1.3 may go unnoticed, but it is unknown if instantly changing from a gain of 0.8 to 1.3 would go unnoticed. A recent study [12] asked users to detect rotation gain changes which were applied to the virtual world either gradually or instantaneously during their rotation in the real world. Their results indicate that users do not reliably detect the gain changes regardless of the conditions that gain changes occur gradually or instantaneously. Users were more likely to view a stable virtual world to be changing when using dynamic rotation gains. This result agrees with previous studies [1, 4] in which users were asked to adjust scene motion until the scenes appeared to be the most stable when they walk or turn.

In this study, we investigate users' sensitivity to four types of dynamic translation gains. Participants walk on a straight path and report if they notice the virtual world has been slowed down or sped up. Similar to the previous work [12] on rotational gains, the gain changes are applied either gradually or instantaneously and we either increase or decrease them. The goal of this experiment is to provide a basic guideline for dynamically changing translational gains without HMD user's detecting the change.

## EXPERIMENT

**Hardware setup:** Many aspects of this experiment were similar to that of a previous study which examined dynamic rotation gains [12]. All experiments were performed in a lab-

Figure 1. A screen shot of the virtual world. Furniture was placed along the white walk path in the virtual world.

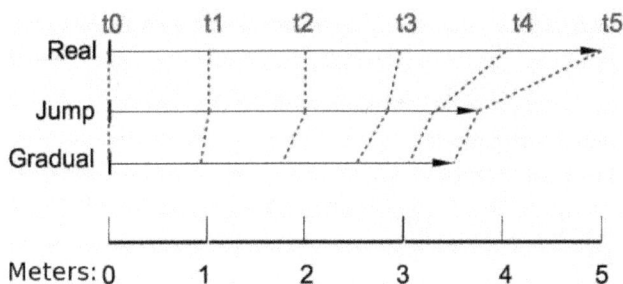

Figure 2. Participants' walk paths in the virtual world when gains were applied from 1.0 to 0.5 gradually (labeled as gradual) or instantaneously (labeled as jump) compared to their walk path in the real world (labeled as real). $t_0$ to $t_5$ are six observation times.

oratory with a 5 × 6 meter tracked space. The virtual world was a high fidelity virtual classroom, 30m × 35m large (see Figure 1). The virtual world was displayed through an NVIS nVisor ST HMD that was set up in a non-see-through configuration and tracked by the WorldViz PPT-H tracking system and an InterSense InertialCube2. The field of view of the HMD was measured to be 47.40 × 39.85 degrees in the horizontal and vertical directions respectively. The HMD was surrounded with fabric and the laboratory was darkened to prevent participants from seeing the real world. Participants wore noise-canceling headphones which played white noise to cover any ambient noise in the lab. They could also hear the experimenter's voice through the headphones.

**Participants:** A total of twenty-four participants between the ages of 18 and 35 participated in this experiment and were recruited from our university's psychology participant pool. After participants provided informed consent, they were screened to ensure that they had normal vision or corrected-to-normal vision. The participants read written instructions and listened to verbal instructions from the experimenter. All of these interactions with the participant occurred in a lobby area outside the laboratory. After the instructions were complete, the experimenter instructed the participant to walk into the lab blindfolded so they could not see the lab prior to the experiment. Each experiment took approximately one hour to complete. Each participant was assigned to ei-

ther the Gradual-Gain condition or the Gain-Jump condition. Twelve participants successfully completed the Gain-Jump condition and ten completed the Gradual-Gain condition (two participants were not included in our analysis because they did not walk straight and they had to be stopped by the experimenter to avoid collisions).

**Methods:** Participants walked on a straight 5 meter path through the middle of the laboratory. A line was drawn in the virtual world (see Figure 1) which aligned with the real world path. Participants were instructed to walk at a constant speed and at a normal walking speed while they were traversing the path. In each trial, participants were given a few seconds to look around the virtual world, orally indicated when they were ready to walk, and then began walking. Our software automatically displayed "stop" on the HMD screen once they had walked five meters in the real world. Then participants stopped walking and orally indicated if the virtual world "sped up" or "slowed down". Next, participants closed their eyes, the HMD screen was blanked, and the experimenter led them back to the starting position in the real world. Participants completed three practice trials before we collected data. The trials demonstrated an extreme gain increase, an extreme gain decrease, and then a practice trial where the participant made a judgment on their own (without feedback). We conducted a brief pilot study to help select which gain changes we should study. We wanted to include gain changes that were very noticeable and changes that were very subtle. To limit the number of trials, we decided to fix the starting gain to 0.7, 1.0 and 2.0 and then select a set of ending gains for each starting gain. To make it easier to compare the results from the different starting gains, the same ratio of gain changes were used (i.e., each starting gain had a trial where the ending gain was half the starting gain). We initially tried using a starting gain of 0.5 instead of 0.7, but found that people had difficulty determining if they moved at all when the starting gain was 0.5 and the ending gain was even smaller (for example, an ending gain of 0.25). The participants performed 33 official trials in random order for this experiment. Among these trials, eleven had gains that began at 0.7 and ended at gains 0.35, 0.42, 0.49, ..., 1.05. Eleven trials start with a gain of 1 and ended with gains 0.5, 0.6, 0.7, ..., 1.5. Finally, eleven trials started with a gain of 2 and ended with gains of 1, 1.2, 1.4, ..., 3. Each starting gain included a trail where there was no gain change (i.e., start at a gain of 2 and end at a gain of 2). Participants started at the same positions in the real world and the virtual world. However, they could not simply rely on their ending places in the virtual world to determine if the gain increased or decreased. For example, a participant would walk approximately the same distance when the gain starts at 1 and ends at 0.7 as they would when the gain starts at 0.7 and ends at 0.98 or 1.05.

In the Gain-Jump condition, the ending gain was applied instantaneously when the user had walked 2.5 meters in the real world. In the Gradual-Gain condition, the gain was gradually changed until they had walked five meters in the real world. Figure 2 illustrates the difference between Gradual-Gain and Gain-Jump with a starting gain of 1.0 and an ending gain of 0.5. The Gradual-Gain was implemented with the equation:

$$\text{Gain} = \text{EndGain} \times (\text{Dist}/5.0) + (1 - \text{Dist}/5.0) \times \text{StartGain}$$
where 'Gain' is the gain that we would like to apply for each point in time while the participant is walking, 'Dist' is the distance (in meters) that a participant has walked in the real world. Gains were applied only to forward and backward translation. If we applied gains to all directions of motion, movements of the head on the frontal plane would be amplified. As a result, head bobbing motions would be amplified or dampened in a way that might provide additional information about the gain changes were measuring and could potentially lead to unnecessary imbalance and simulator sickness.

**Results and Discussion**
Figure 3 shows the results on the Gain-Jump condition with a starting gain of 0.7, 1.0 and 2.0 respectively. The $x$-axis is calculated as $(\text{EndGain} - \text{StartGain})/\text{StartGain}$, so positive numbers indicate an increasing gain and negative numbers indicate a decreasing gain. The $y$-axis shows the percentage of responses which indicated that the virtual translation sped up as participants completed the walk-path in the real world. This figure shows participants' biased judgments with different starting gains. The DTL and DTH represent the 25% and 75% detection thresholds respectively. The value that marked by a "*" denotes results which fall outside of the gain changes that we tested. The difference between DTL and DTH provides an indication of the range of gain changes which might not be reliably detected by participants. The PSE (Point of Subjective Equality) indicates the gain change where participants have a 50-50 chance of indicating that the gain increased or decreased. For example, a PSE value of zero indicates participants accurately detected the gain changes on average and a value less than zero indicates that participants detected no gain changes when the gains were actually decreasing. The PSE values are -0.24, 0.29 and 0.45 when participants walked from the gain of 2.0, 1.0 and 0.7. Or stated differently, for trials where the gain started at 2.0, people tended to indicate that the gains were constant when they were actually decreasing. When the gain started at 0.7, participants indicated that the gains were constant when they were actually increasing. This demonstrates a trend that participants' judgments on the translation changes in speed were biased to the opposite direction as the starting gains increase. Figure 4 shows a similar trend when participants performed the trials on Gradual-Gain condition. The psychometric curves of the starting gain of 1 (or 2) on Gain-Jump and Gradual-Gain conditions presented similar shape and PSE values. This result suggests that participants are not more sensitive to gradual gain changes than instantaneous changes although gradual gain changes are much more subtle than instantaneous changes. One noticeable difference between the Gradual-Gain and Gain-Jump results is that when the starting gain was 0.7, participants were very likely to indicate that the virtual world was slowing down regardless of the amount of dynamic gain change—suggesting that it might be possible to gradually increase gains by a large amount without the user recognizing it if the starting gain is small.

Our results are similar to a similar study investigating dynamic rotational gains [12]. While rotation and translation are different types of motion, participants in both studies showed a similar degree of sensitivity to gradual and instantaneous changes to the rotations or translations when the virtual world was applied with a starting gain of one or two. In addition, participants in both studies displayed a trend to accept an acceleration of rotations or translations when the starting gain is one and a deceleration when the starting gain is two. Taken together, the results of these two dynamic gain studies complement existing work on fixed gain thresholds [8] and by providing insights into how dynamic gain changes might effectively be used in applications such as redirected walking.

Participants were instructed to walk at a consistent speed in the experiments. We wanted to know if their virtual world velocity impacted their real world walking speed. For example, did large gains cause people to walk slower? To answer these questions, we recorded the walking speed of the participants (excluding the first meter and last meter of walking to reduce the impact of acceleration and deceleration). On average, participants walked 1.08 meters per second. To analyze the velocity data, we averaged the StartGain and EndGain for each trial to get an average gain for the trial and compared that with the participants' walking speed. Our analysis found that individual participants react to the gains differently. Some participants walked slower when the gains increased while others walked faster. We found no direct connection between walking speed and gains.

**CONCLUSIONS**
This study investigated participants' sensitivity to dynamically changing translational gains while participants were walking on a straight path. Our results show that participants do not reliably detect translational gain changes in a large range and that a stable virtual world can be judged to be changing. This result is consistent to previous studies [1, 4, 12]. The magnitude of the gain at the start of the participants' walk also had a significant impact on how participants detected the gain changes. Our study, together with the previous studies [5, 12], might indicate an opportunity to exploit the dynamically changed gains of translation, rotation and curvature in order to allow a user to naturally navigate a larger virtual world space than using the fixed gains.

**REFERENCES**
1. D. Engel, C. Curio, L. Tcheang, B. Mohler, and H. H. Bülthoff. A psychophysically calibrated controller for navigating through large environments in a limited free-walking space. In *Proceedings of the 2008 ACM symposium on Virtual reality software and technology*, VRST '08, pages 157–164, New York, NY, USA, 2008. ACM.

2. E. Hodgson, E. Bachmann, and D. Waller. Redirected walking to explore virtual environments: assessing the potential for spatial interference. In *ACM Transactions on Applied Perception (TAP)*, volume 8(4), pages 22:1–11, Nov. 2011.

3. V. Interrante, B. Ries, and L. Anderson. Seven league boots: A new metaphor for augmented locomotion through large scale immersive virtual environment. In

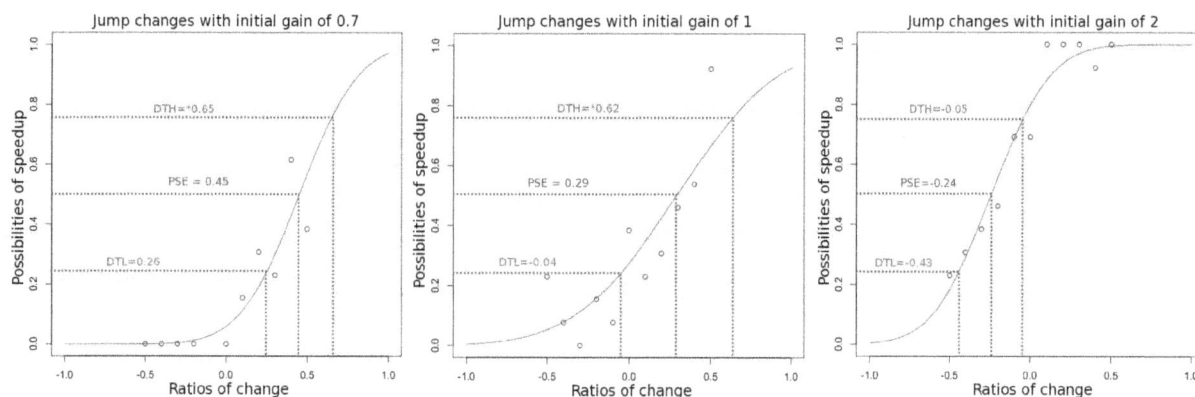

**Figure 3. Psychometric curves of three initial gains on jump conditions. Initial gain of 0.7 on jump condition (left), initial gain of 1.0 on jump condition (middle), initial gain of 2.0 on jump condition (right).**

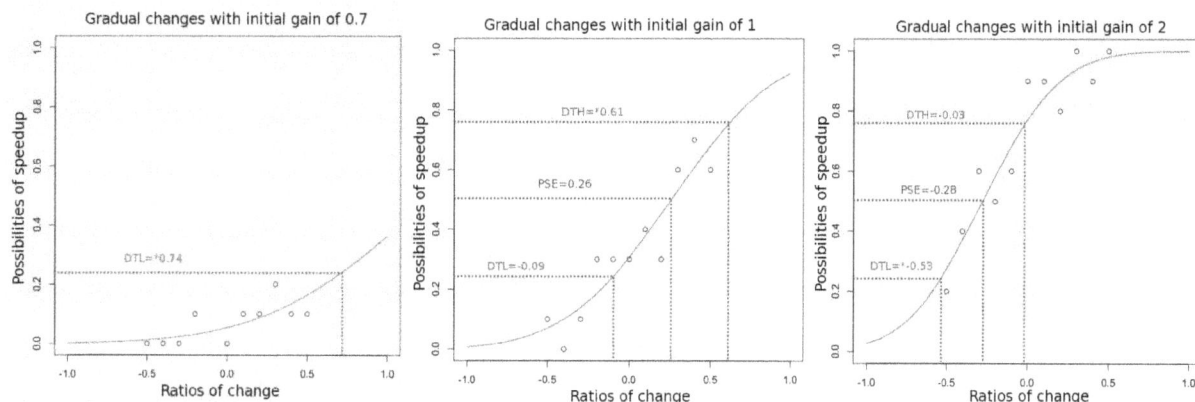

**Figure 4. Psychometric curves of three initial gains on gradual conditions. Initial gain of 0.7 on gradual condition (left), initial gain of 1.0 on gradual condition (middle), initial gain of 2.0 on gradual condition (right).**

*Proc. IEEE Symposium on 3D User Interfaces*, pages 169–172, 2007.

4. P. M. Jaekl, M. R. Jenkin, and L. R. Harris. Perceiving a stable world during active rotational and translational head movements. *Experimental Brain Research*, 163:388–399, 2005.

5. C. Neth, J. Souman, D. Engel, U. Kloos, H. Bulthoff, and B. Mohler. Velocity-dependent dynamic curvature gain for redirected walking. In *IEEE Virtual Reality (VR)*, pages 1–8, 2011.

6. T. C. Peck, H. Fuchs, and M. C. Whitton. Improved redirection with distractors: A large-scale-real-walking locomotion interface and its effect on navigation in virtual environments. In *Proc. IEEE Virtual Reality*, pages 35–38, Mar. 2010.

7. S. Razzaque, Z. Kohn, and M. C. Whitton. Redirected walking. In *Proc. Eurographics 2001*, pages 289–294, 2001.

8. F. Steinicke, G. Bruder, J. Jerald, H. Frenz, and M. Lappe. Analyses of human sensitivity to redirected walking. In *Proceedings of the 2008 ACM symposium on Virtual Reality Software and Technology*, VRST '08, pages 149–156, New York, NY, USA, 2008. ACM.

9. F. Steinicke, G. Bruder, T. Ropiński, and K. Hinrichs. Moving towards generally applicable redirected walking. In *Proc. Virtual Reality International Conference (VRIC)*, pages 15–24. IEEE Press, 2008.

10. E. A. Suma, G. Bruder, F. Steinicke, D. M. Krum, and M. Bolas. A taxonomy for deploying redirection techniques in immersive virtual environments. In *IEEE Virtual Reality*, pages 43–46, 2012.

11. B. Williams, G. Narasimaham, B. Rump, T. P. McNamara, T. H. Carr, J. Rieser, and B. Bodenheimer. Exploring large virtual environments with an HMD on foot. In *Proc. Fourth Symposium on Applied Perception in Graphics and Visualization*, pages 41–48, 2007.

12. R. Zhang and S. A. Kuhl. Human sensitivity to dynamic rotation gains in head-mounted displays. In *Proc. Proceedings of the ACM Symposium on Applied Perception (SAP)*, pages 71–74, 2013.

# A Self-Experimentation Report about Long-Term Use of Fully-Immersive Technology

**Frank Steinicke**
Human-Computer Interaction
Department of Informatics
University of Hamburg, Germany
frank.steinicke@uni-hamburg.de

**Gerd Bruder**
Human-Computer Interaction
Department of Informatics
University of Hamburg, Germany
gerd.bruder@uni-hamburg.de

## ABSTRACT

Virtual and digital worlds have become an essential part of our daily life, and many activities that we used to perform in the real world such as communication, e-commerce, or games, have been transferred to the virtual world nowadays. This transition has been addressed many times by science fiction literature and cinematographic works, which often show dystopic visions in which humans live their lives in a virtual reality (VR)-based setup, while they are immersed into a virtual or remote location by means of avatars or surrogates.

In order to gain a better understanding of how living in such a virtual environment (VE) would impact human beings, we conducted a self-experiment in which we exposed a single participant in an immersive VR setup for 24 hours (divided into repeated sessions of two hours VR exposure followed by ten minutes breaks), which is to our knowledge the longest documented use of an immersive VEs so far. We measured different metrics to analyze how human perception, behavior, cognition, and motor system change over time in a fully isolated virtual world.

## Author Keywords

Self-experiment; immersive user interfaces; virtual reality; head-mounted display; presence; simulator sickness

## ACM Classification Keywords

H.5.m. Information Interfaces and Presentation (e.g. HCI): Miscellaneous

## INTRODUCTION

While computer games provide the means to immerse someone into an interactive computer-generated space, virtual reality (VR) pushes this idea to the next level [4]. For instance, with immersive head-mounted displays (HMD) and tracking systems combined with computer graphics environments it becomes possible to fully immerse a user into a spatial VE and decouple the user's perception from the real world (see Figure 1). The user only perceives the visual scene displayed

on the HMD (see Figure 1(left and bottom right inset)), while all movements of the user in the real world such as walking or head movements are transferred to corresponding motions of the virtual camera providing an updated virtual view [2]. Such applications seek to invoke a *place illusion*, i. e., having the sensation of being in a real place, as well as *plausibility illusion*, i. e., having the sensation that the scenario being depicted is actually occurring [4]. These illusions occur despite the fact that the user is aware that the environment is a simulation [4].

So far, immersive VEs are usually only used by experts in very specific application domains such as training or simulation, or by subjects during experiments [2]. Furthermore, these systems are mostly used for a very limited amount of time, typically ranging from 30 minutes to a maximum of approximately four hours, for instance to investigate the effects of collaboration for an extended period of time [5]. With current technology trends such as the Oculus Rift HMD or the Microsoft Kinect tracking device, it becomes obvious that soon more and more people will spend significant amount of their time particularly for communication or entertainment in such immersive systems.

However, to our knowledge, nobody has spent more than three to four hours with a donned HMD in an immersive VR system as described above. Hence, it is an open question how long a human can use immersive technology and remain isolated in a fully-immersive system. Furthermore, the question arises, what happens to the human perception, behavior, cognition, and motor system during and after using such user interfaces (UIs) for a longer period of time.

In order to get a notion how such scenarios would impact human beings, we conducted a self-experiment in which we exposed a single participant in an immersive VE in eleven two-hour blocks for an entire day. The UI consisted of an optically tracked Oculus Rift HMD for displaying a computer-generated virtual living space as well as virtual island. Inside the tracked lab space we arranged physical objects, such as a chair, bed, table and couch, which provide passive haptic feedback for their registered virtual objects [6]. While the participant stayed in the VE, we measured different metrics to analyze the impact of long-term use of a fully-immersive VE. The results provide implications for current and future immersive VEs, software, and technology.

# EXPERIMENT

Due to the enormous effort to immerse and supervise someone for a long time in a continuously running fully-immersive VR setup, we decided to conduct a case study as a self-experiment in which a single participant was exposed to the immersive VE. We choose this special case of a single-subject scientific experimentation as it is used extensively in the experimental analysis of behavior and applied behavior analysis with both human and non-human participants [1]. We chose the AB design as principal method, which is a two phase design composed of a baseline phase (in our case: no VR exposure) with no changes, and a treatment or intervention phase (in our case: VR exposure).

## Participant

One of the authors of this paper volunteered as the participant. The male participant (age: 37, height: 1.86m, weight: 89kg, body mass index: 25.7, right-handed) of our experiment is a professional in computer science with more than a decade of experience in HCI, VR, 3D and spatial user interfaces, which allows a professional valuation of certain effects, which might occur. According to a health check, the participant was healthy prior to the experiment without known disorders or physical challenges. Before the experiment, the participant signed an informed consent form and he was allowed to abort the experiment at any time. We measured his interpupillary distance (IPD) of the participant, which revealed an IPD of 6.4cm. We used this IPD for the generation of correct head-coupled perspectives in the stereoscopically displayed VE. The participant was not involved in the design of the VE, but was briefly introduced to the VE and the features one day before the experiment.

## Materials

As depicted in Figure 1 (top middle and top right inset) the experiment was conducted with the participant wearing an Oculus Rift DK1 HMD with an attached active infrared (IR) target. The target was tracked by an optical WorldViz Precision Position Tracking (PPT X4) system with sub-millimeter precision for position and orientation data in an 8m×8m laboratory room. We fused the PPT's optical heading with the inertial orientation of the Oculus Rift in order to provide robust head tracking without drifts. The Oculus Rift offers a horizontal FOV of approximately 90° and a vertical FOV of 110° at a resolution of $1280 \times 800$ pixels ($640 \times 800$ for each eye). This setup supports wireless video transmission at high interactive frame rates. We used an Asus WAVI wireless transmitter box to transmit the rendered images at 60Hz from the graphics card of a rendering computer via the HDMI protocol to the HMD. A Wii remote controller was available to the participant, which could be used to control different settings in the VE (in particular, turn on/off lights, radio or movies, change volume etc.). Additionally, we used the same wireless transmitter to transfer the real-time data from the head orientation sensor in the Oculus Rift HMD back to the rendering computer. The HMD and wireless transmitter box were powered by an Anker Astro Pro2 20,000mAh long-life portable battery. The boxes were carried in a small belt bag during the experiment. We used a 5.1 surround sound setup

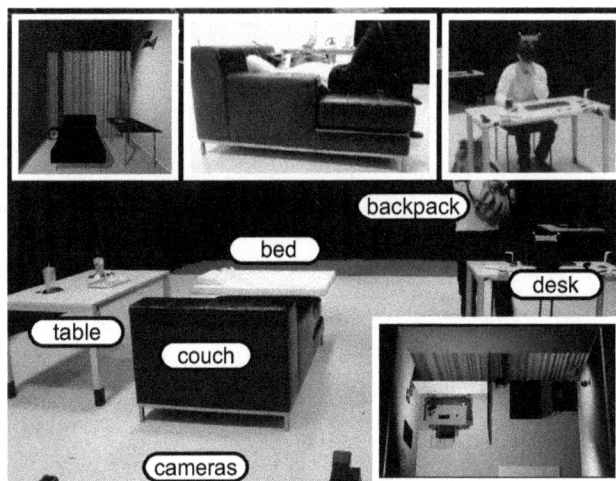

Figure 1. Pictures of the experiment with real and virtual tables, chair, couch, and bed. The insets show (top left) the participant's virtual view, (top middle) the participant during the experiment while laying on the couch, (top right) sitting at the desk as captured by the cameras, and (bottom right) a top view of the entire virtual living space.

for auditive feedback. The computers and experimental observers were spatially separated from the participant in an adjacent room with a large window screen to eliminate acoustic interferences from outside the virtual world.

The virtual stimulus (see Figure 1) in the experiment consisted of a 3D scene, which was rendered with Unity3D Pro[1] and our own software on an Intel computer with a Core i7 3.8GHz CPU, 8GB of main memory and Nvidia GeForce GTX580 graphics card. As illustrated in Figure 1 the basis of the VE was a virtual room furnished with a bed, chair and tables, which were registered with corresponding real-world objects allowing the participant to sit or to rest on them in the virtual and real world respectively. We implemented a virtual computer (with registered physical mouse and keyboard), which was connected to a real computer using a virtual network computing simulation. The virtual room itself provided a means for tele-transportation to another virtual location, which we modeled as a virtual island. Hence, the participant could transport himself between both VEs, and walk around, work at the desk or enjoy the beach.

## Methods

The participant spent a timespan of 24 hours in the immersive system. We split the time in the immersive VE setup in two types of blocks: (1) VR block and (2) break block. The VR blocks lasted for two hours in which the participant had to wear the tracked HMD on which the VE was continuously displayed. During the entire time (except for the breaks), the participant needed to stay within the range of the optical tracking system wearing the HMD on his head, so that constant virtual feedback was provided; even during sleeping the HMD had to be worn. No communication with persons in the real world was allowed except for an abort code. Each VR block was followed by a 10 minutes break block (without HMD), which allowed for bathroom usage. During

[1]see **http://unity3d.com**

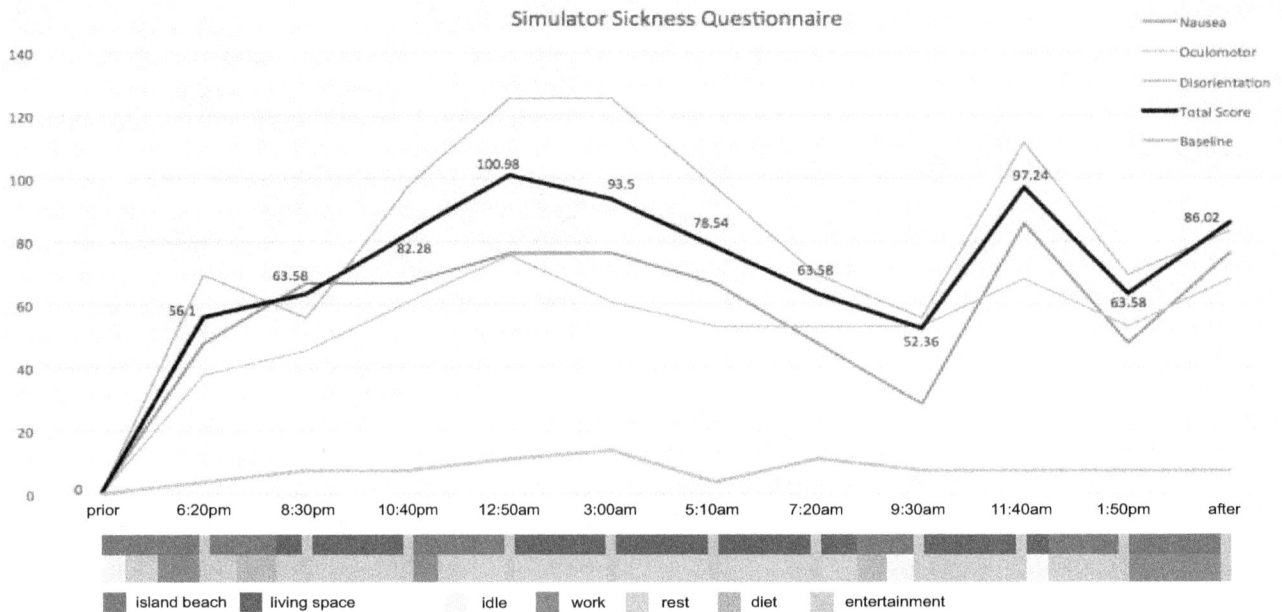

Figure 2. Results of SSQ questionnaires during the self-experimentation. The combined total score for the situation with immersive technology is shown as black line, whereas the baseline (without usage of immersive technology) is shown by the gray line. The bottom rows show the participant's dominant activities during the time span.

these short breaks, the participant answered questionnaires and informal questions, and we took photos of the participant. Hence, the breaks were mandatory for the participant even during sleeping periods, and (if required) the participant was woken. The experiment started on March 22, 2014 at 4:20pm.

Since nobody ever spent such a long time period in a fully immersive system, for safety concerns at least two experimental observers monitored the participant and the setup from an adjacent room all the time. The participant was provided with food and beverages with an amount of ca. 1.969 kcal according to his metabolic rate at rest.

### Data Gathering
We measured qualitative and quantitive data. At least two experimental observers watched the hard- and software setup as well as a camera feed during the entire experiment. The participant was allowed to continually speak aloud his thoughts whenever desired. We also used retrospective probing, in which the experimental observers asked questions during the breaks and after completion of the experiment. We asked the participant to complete subjective questionnaires at the beginning, during each break block and after the experiment. The participant had to complete Kennedy-Lane Simulator Sickness Questionnaires (SSQ) [3] and Slater-Usoh-Steed (SUS) presence questionnaires [7]. Finally, the participant had to judge his subjective level of comfort on a five point Likert-scale ranging from very discomfortable to very comfortable.

### RESULTS
Since only a single subject participated in the experiment, we visually analyzed the data to consider level, trend and variability of activities, simulator sickness and sense of presence.

### Activities
Figure 2 (bottom rows) illustrates the participant's activities during the experiment. We categorized these activities into predominant activities over the corresponding time frames based on the recorded videos as well as notes and observations made by the experimental observers. The participants switched between virtual living space and a virtual island several times, but preferred the virtual living room about 60% of the time. In about 35% of the overall VR exposure time the participant used the various entertainment options such as watching movies, listing to radio stations or audio books. Dinner and breakfast required about 7% percent of the VR exposure time. At the beginning and at the end, the participant was working at the virtual desk, in particular reading and writing emails. Finally, about 37% of the VR exposure time, the participant was laying in bed and rested or slept. Overall, the participant spent only about 5% in an idle mode, for instance walking around, exploring the different spaces.

### Simulator Sickness
Figure 2 shows the results for nausea, oculomotor, disorientation and total score when the participant was equipped with the immersive technology and the total score for the baseline phase without immersive equipment, which was performed two weeks after the experiment. In this baseline phase, we exposed the participant with a congeneric setup (including similar activities and timings as in the VR blocks), but without any immersive equipment that the participant had to wear. The baseline phase in which the participant was not exposed to any immersive technology shows a flat slope. Linear regression revealed a slight increase of simulator sickness during the baseline phase ($y = 0.37 \cdot x + 4.97$). In contrast, simulator sickness shows a trend to increase when the partici-

pant was exposed to the immersive system. Linear regression of the total SSQ score revealed a significant increase of simulator sickness ($y = 3.4 \cdot x + 47.71$), i.e., 10 times higher.

Visual analyses of the graph shows a cyclical behavior, i.e., alternate periods of increase and decrease, which approximately corresponds to sleeping and resting phases during the experiment. Simulator sickness decreased in particular during the periods in which the participant was resting and/or sleeping in more or less stable horizontal poses.

### Sense of Presence
The average score of the SUS presence questionnaires during the experiment was 5.59, which underlines that the participant had a high sense of presence during the entire experiment. A linear regression reveals almost a flat slope ($y = 0.09 \cdot x + 5.08$), which underlines that the sense of presence was rarely affected over time. According to the subjective comments, no significant breaks in presence occurred during the experiment, which is also supported by the results from the questionnaires.

### DISCUSSION
According to the participant's comments and responses, we identified the following main observation:

- *Simulator sickness*: The participant reported serious, but not harmful simulator sickness symptoms, in particular after periods of moving around extensively in the VE. In contrast, simulator sickness symptoms were soon decreased when the participant rested on the bed or on the couch.

- *Perceived accommodation*: After about four hours in the VE, the participant started to report that the accommodation distance seemed to vary from the fix accommodation distance (160cm) of the HMD. In particular, the participant reported the illusion of staying in a virtual sphere with a radius of 5 meters on which the virtual scene is projected.

- *Ergonomics of HMD*: The only concern of the participant about the HMD was the latency causing simulator sickness during exhaustive movements and the limited resolution during working at the desk. During the first and second VR block, the participant perceived a dry eye syndrome on both eyes, which may result from decreased tear production due to the sealed HMD setup.

- *Place and Plausibility illusion*: Several times during the experiment the participant was confused about being in the VE or in the real world, and mixed certain artifacts and events between both worlds.

The self-experiment revealed some first insights into how "living" in a virtual world with immersive technology would impact human beings. We were surprised that the participant did not suffer more from simulator sickness. An interesting finding is that according to the participant's feedback a comfortable and stable pose has the potential to enormously reduce simulator sickness. This may be due to the fact that in these poses the body senses (vestibular and kinesthetic feedback) inform the user that he is not moving. The participant's comments about the ergonomics of the HMD revealed that latency is by far the most important aspect, which must be improved for long-term use. In most situations, higher resolution appears to be more important than a larger field of view for long-term use. The limited resolution was clearly a problem when working at the virtual desk. For other activities such as watching a movie or walking around, the resolution was sufficient to provide compelling place and plausibility illusions.

### CONCLUSION AND FUTURE WORK
To our knowledge, for the first time we document a self-experiment in which a participant has spent such a long duration in an immersive system. The results of this explorative self-experiment give interesting insights into the design of immersive VEs. First, one needs to analyze the several effects reported by the participant and found in the results. In particular, we would like to investigate the potential of reduced simulator sickness due to the horizontal and/or stable body poses during an immersive exposure. For further future work, it might be interesting to repeat the experiment with different participants for longer periods such as several days, and more triangulation of data (heart rate, skin conductance etc.). With the raise of new immersive technology, more and more people will use these systems for longer periods of time. Our findings have shown some shortcomings and open challenges, which need to be addressed before these systems can be used or even recommended for long-term usage.

### REFERENCES
1. Altman, L. *Who Goes First? The Story of Self-Experimentation in Medicine*. No. ISBN 0-520-21281-9. University of California Press, (1998).

2. Bowman, D., Kruijff, E., LaViola, Jr., J., and Poupyrev, I. *3D User Interfaces: Theory and Practice*. Addison-Wesley Professional, 2004.

3. Kennedy, R., Lane, N., Berbaum, K., and Lilienthal, M. Simulator Sickness Questionnaire: An Enhanced Method for Quantifying Simulator Sickness. *The International Journal of Aviation Psychology 3*, 3 (1993), 203–220.

4. Slater, M. Place illusion and plausibility can lead to realistic behaviour in immersive virtual environments. *Philosophical Transactions of the Royal Society Biological Science 364*, 1535 (2009), 3549–3557.

5. Steed, A., Spante, M., Heldal, I., Axelsson, A.-S., and Schroeder, R. Strangers and friends in CAVEs: an exploratory study of collaboration in networked IPT systems for extended periods of time. In *Proceedings of the Symposium on Interactive 3D Graphics (I3D)* (2003), 51–54.

6. Steinicke, F., Bruder, G., Hinrichs, K., Jerald, J., Frenz, H., and Lappe, M. Real walking through virtual environments by redirection techniques. *Journal of Virtual Reality and Broadcasting 6*, 2 (2009).

7. Usoh, M., Catena, E., Arman, S., and Slater, M. Using Presence Questionaires in Reality. *Presence: Teleoperators & Virtual Environments 9*, 5 (1999), 497–503.

# Coordinated 3D Interaction in Tablet- and HMD-Based Hybrid Virtual Environments

**Jia Wang**
HIVE Lab
Worcester Polytechnic Institute
wangjia@wpi.edu

**Robert Lindeman**
HIVE Lab
Worcester Polytechnic Institute
gogo@wpi.edu

## ABSTRACT

Traditional 3D User Interfaces (3DUI) in immersive virtual reality can be inefficient in tasks that involve diversities in scale, perspective, reference frame, and dimension. This paper proposes a solution to this problem using a coordinated, tablet- and HMD-based, hybrid virtual environment system. Wearing a non-occlusive HMD, the user is able to view and interact with a tablet mounted on the non-dominant forearm, which provides a multi-touch interaction surface, as well as an exocentric God view of the virtual world. To reduce transition gaps across 3D interaction tasks and interfaces, four coordination mechanisms are proposed, two of which were implemented, and one was evaluated in a user study featuring complex level-editing tasks. Based on subjective ratings, task performance, interview feedback, and video analysis, we found that having multiple Interaction Contexts (ICs) with complementary benefits can lead to good performance and user experience, despite the complexity of learning and using the hybrid system. The results also suggest keeping 3DUI tasks synchronized across the ICs, as this can help users understand their relationships, smoothen within- and between-task IC transitions, and inspire more creative use of different interfaces.

## Author Keywords

Hybrid virtual environments; 3D user interface; Tablet interface; Transitional continuity; Virtual reality

## ACM Classification Keywords

H.5.1 [**Information Interfaces and Presentation**]: Multimedia Information Systems – *artificial, augmented, and virtual realities*; H.5.2 [**Information Interfaces and Presentation**]: User Interfaces – *evaluation/methodology, input devices and strategies, interaction styles, user-centered design*.

## INTRODUCTION

Immersive virtual reality (VR) technology has been gaining great popularity recently thanks to a new generation of low-cost Head-Mounted Displays (HMD). Besides the high fidelity of the displays, the performance and usability of 3D User Interfaces (3DUIs) also play a critical role in the overall immersive experience delivered to the end user. Through decades of research, various input devices and interaction techniques have been proposed and evaluated for the basic 3DUI tasks of navigation, selection, manipulation, system control, and symbolic input [5]. But despite the realistic experience of grabbing and manipulating a virtual object using your hand [23], or real walking in a Virtual Environment (VE) [34], researchers also realize that interaction in VR can be just as confusing, limiting, and ambiguous as in the real world, when it comes to tasks with diverse requirements [28]. For example, it is difficult to select and manipulate objects of different sizes, from multiple angles, and at different distances, without spending significant time and effort on navigation.

One way to overcome such limitations is to develop Hybrid Virtual Environment (HVE) systems, which incorporate multiple and complementary virtual and/or physical interface elements appropriate for a set of tasks. For example, the World-In-Miniature (WIM) interaction technique renders an interactive miniature world in the left hand of the user to complement the immersive context with quick teleportation, range-less object selection, and large scale object translation [28]. HVE systems with different physical interfaces are inspired by Hybrid User Interface (HUI) systems [13]. A common example is the pen-and-tablet interface which uses a tracked surface to complement the spatial pen input for 2D tasks such as system control, symbolic input, and map-based way-finding [6].

The rapid progress of mobile technology has inspired a recent research trend of offloading 3DUI tasks to mobile phone and tablet devices, to take advantage of their growing computing power, high resolution, multi-touch touch screens, and various built-in motion sensors [4, 26, 33]. However, most of these techniques have been focused on very simple scenarios, where only one or two UI functions are assigned to the tablet to aid the primary spatial interface used in the immersive environment. Few studies have been conducted to investigate the overhead involved in transitioning between the multiple interface elements [14].

In this paper, we propose a novel HVE system that aims to join the strengths of a tablet device and an HMD-and-wand-based immersive setup. Instead of a supplementary tool, the tablet is designed and implemented as a complete Interaction Context (IC), formally defined later, which renders the entire virtual world on its own, and supports all 3DUI tasks through multi-touch gestures and 2D GUI elements. To reduce the perceptual, cognitive, and functional overhead [12] caused by complex 3DUI transitions across multiple ICs, a *coordination mechanism* featuring 3DUI task synchronization is proposed. Lastly, the results of a user study are presented, which suggest that task synchronization can lead to smoother transitions across ICs, and that user performance can be increased by using multiple complementary ICs in an HVE system.

## RELATED WORK

### Tablet-Based 3D Interfaces

Interactive tablets have been demonstrated as powerful tools for interaction in VR. By displaying an interactive 2D map on a tracked touchpad, early pen-and-tablet prototypes made way-finding and travel efficient in cluttered indoor spaces [1], as well as in large-scale outdoor scenes [6]. The Personal-Interaction-Panel (PIP) proposed concepts of a hybrid approach for object selection and manipulation, system control, and interaction with volumetric data [29]. The main idea was to augment virtual objects with 3D widgets and 2D GUI elements on the tablet, both of which could be interacted with using a stylus. Transparent pen and pad props have also been developed to enable Through-The-Lens (TTL) interaction with virtual content displayed on a tabletop [24]. From a usability point of view, an empirical study of a UI manipulation task has shown that bimanual interaction and passive haptic feedback offered by a physical surface held in the non-dominant hand can significantly increase precision and efficiency, as well as reduce fatigue [16]. Based on these advantages, the design guideline of *dimensional congruence* was proposed, which advocates matching the dimensionality of the 3DUI tasks to that of the input devices [11].

With no tethers attached, mobile phone and tablet devices can provide more flexibility than traditional pen-and-tablet interfaces. The use of mobile devices in VR has grown with the advancement of mobile technologies. Early work of Watsen *et al.* demonstrated a handheld computer used as an interaction device, which only contained simple 2D GUI widgets to aid system control tasks in the VE [32]. As the computing power increased, researchers started to experiment with rendering interactive virtual objects on the screen of mobile devices, based on PIP [4] or TTL [17] metaphors. Recently, many mobile devices contain high-performance, multi-touch touchscreens. To take advantage of this, various 3D interfaces have been proposed that combine multi-touch gestures with spatial tracking of mobile phones or tablets for object manipulation [33],

volume data annotation, and textual data visualization [26]. Furthering this trend, a different design perspective is taken in this paper, which treats the mobile device not as a supplementary tool, but a complete interaction system, with computing power, display technology, and interaction richness comparable to that of an HMD-based, immersive VR system. This new approach is also expected to inspire new design possibilities of HVE systems for handling complex and highly diverse interaction tasks more effectively in 3D spaces.

### Hybrid Virtual Environments

The early seminal work of Feiner & Shamash defined the term HUI as interface systems that combine heterogeneous display and interaction devices in a complementary way to compensate for the limitations of the individual devices [13]. Like HUI, HVE systems also strive to seamlessly integrate multiple representations of the same VE, in order to facilitate 3D interactions from different angles, scales, distances, reference frames, and dimensions. The multiple VE representations in HVE systems are often related based on some natural metaphor. For example, the WIM technique combines an egocentric and an exocentric view of the virtual world through a "handheld miniature world" metaphor [28]. The Voodoo Dolls technique creates a second instance of a remote object in the local space following a well-known fictional metaphor [20]. The SEAMs technique defines a portal which can be traveled through, or reached in to, to translate objects across two distinct spaces [25]. The Magic Lenses adopts an x-ray see-through metaphor to offer different visualizations of the same virtual content side by side [30].

HVE systems can also incorporate different physical interface components alongside the VE representations. The HVE system presented in this paper coordinates two VE representations contained in two ICs: a tablet device with multi-touch input and a 2D GUI, and an HMD-based VR system with wand input. Two closely related works are the HybridDesk, which surrounds a traditional desktop computer with a desktop CAVE display [9], and SCAPE, which puts a see-through workbench display in the center of a room with projection walls [7]. However, the former limited its ICs to exclusive 3DUI tasks, forcing the user to make unnecessary switches, and the latter mainly focused on view management, instead of rich 3D interactions.

Much research work in transitional user interfaces and Collaborative Virtual Environments (CVE) is closely related to HVEs. Transitional user interface systems present multiple representations of the virtual world in a linear, time-multiplexed way [14]. The MagicBook is a classic demonstration of a transitional experience between an exocentric view of the VE in Augmented Reality (AR) to an egocentric view represented in immersive VR [3]. Many CVEs can be considered as HVEs with their multiple VEs assigned to different users. A well-known metaphor is the combination of a God-user and a Hero-user, who possess complementary views and reference frames in the shared VE to aid each other towards a common goal [15]. The unique challenge of designing CVE systems is to ensure the collaborators are well aware of each other's viewpoints and interaction intentions as tasks are carried out, and avatars and artificial cues have been found effective [10]. Finally, it is also possible to merge hybrid, transitional, and collaborative virtual environments together into a hybrid collaborative system, such as the VITA system [2].

## Cross-Context Transitions

Compared to traditional VR, one main challenge for HVE systems is the perceptual, cognitive, and functional overhead induced by transitions across multiple virtual and physical components [12]. The challenge is also present in coordinated multiple view (CMV) systems, where multiple views of the same dataset are generated and displayed to help the data analyst discover unforeseen patterns. The key to reduce the transition gap in CMV systems is to coordinate the visualizations of, and the interactions with, the multiple views [31]. For example, multiple views can be "snapped together" to better reveal their relationships and ease the gap between transitions [19]. Multiple views of 3D data can also be linked [22], or integrated through frame-of-reference interaction [21]. Guidelines for view management have been provided to minimize the cognitive overhead of context switching [31]. Applications and study results have demonstrated improvements in user performance when coordination mechanisms are implemented [27]. These findings inspired us to design and develop coordination mechanisms that can keep the complex 3D interaction transitions simple and smooth in the proposed HVE system.

## METHODOLOGY

### HVE Level Editor

Level editing was selected as the test bed to drive the design and study of our HVE system. It was selected for several reasons. First, level editing plays a key role in many real world applications, such as video game design, animation production, and urban planning. Second, many level-editing tasks feature diverse and complementary requirements, which makes them good candidates to adopt HVE approaches [6, 27]. Third, unlike the simple and monotonous tasks most VR studies have been designed for (e.g., travel from A to B [34]), level editing actually involves all 3DUI tasks (i.e., navigation, selection, manipulation, system control, and symbolic input) and combines them in various ways. This grants us an opportunity to study complex *3D interaction transitions across multiple ICs, and the overhead involved in the process.* The specific level-editing tasks supported in the proposed HVE system include editing of terrain (height and texture), foliage (grass and trees), objects, time-of-day, and spotlights.

## Interaction Context

We introduce the concept of an Interaction Context (IC) here to represent *a conceptual integration of input and output devices, techniques, and parameters, which offers one representation of the VE and a set of interaction rules.* HVE systems are formed by relating multiple ICs under a unified metaphor. The metaphor defines the conceptual relationship between the ICs, making it more likely for the user to consider the overall HVE system as an integrated whole. Common HVE metaphors include WIM [28], portal [25], Voodoo Doll [20], see-through [30], and information surround [13]. For our HVE level editor, we selected WIM as the metaphor to combine the exocentric God view with the egocentric first person Hero view. An IC can be formed by specifying the following components:

- **Medium:** The type of medium adopted by the IC on the reality-virtuality continuum [18], such as VR, AR, or mixed reality.

- **Display device:** The multi-sensorial devices used to display the virtual world to the user's sensory organs, such as HMD, CAVE, headphones, haptic stylus, etc.

- **Rendering technique:** The technique used to represent the virtual content (e.g., shaders for visual display).

- **Input device:** The device used to express commands, such as a data glove or a multi-touch touch pad.

- **Interaction technique:** The software that maps the input data to control parameters in the virtual world. For example, wand input devices usually uses ray-casting based interaction techniques [23].

- **Perspective:** The position, orientation, and other parameters of a virtual camera that determines the IC's view of the virtual world. Immersive VR systems usually offer an in-the-world, first person perspective.

- **Reference frame:** The coordinate system that determines the perception of the virtual world and the effect of interaction. Egocentric (body-centered) and exocentric (object-centered) are two reference frames commonly discussed in VR [21].

This list of components defines a taxonomy that can be used to categorize HVE systems. For example, the original WIM interaction technique includes two ICs [28]. Both ICs use VR as the medium, and render their views of the VE in the same HMD, using a photorealistic shader. In addition, a buttonball prop is used in both ICs to interact with virtual objects, using a collision-based pick-and-drop technique. However, the two ICs are different in their perspectives and reference frames. The immersive IC has an in-the-world, first person view where all interactions are based on the user's egocentric body, while the miniature IC adopts an above-the-world, God view with object-centered exocentric reference frame. The HVE level editor presented in this paper incorporates an immersive IC and a tablet IC, whose components are specified in Table 1.

| Components | Immersive IC | Tablet IC |
|---|---|---|
| **Medium** | Virtual reality | Virtual reality |
| **Display device** | HMD, fans | Tablet screen |
| **Rendering technique** | Photorealistic | Photorealistic |
| **Input device** | 6-DOF wand | Touch screen |
| **Interaction technique** | Ray-casting & button based | 2D GUI and multi-touch gestures |
| **Perspective** | In the world | Above the world |
| **Reference frame** | Egocentric (body-centered) | Exocentric (object-centered) |

Table 1. The IC components of the HVE level editor

### Immersive IC

As shown in Figure 1, an eMagin Z800 HMD is used to display a first-person, in-the-world view of a photorealistic VE, with a 60-degree horizontal field-of-view (FOV). The HMD utilizes two 800x600 OLED screens to render monoscopic images to both eyes with a 40-degree diagonal FOV. It is tracked in six degrees of freedom (DOF) using the PhaseSpace motion capture system. A constellation of four active LED markers is attached to the top of the HMD and tracked by sixteen cameras surrounding an octagon-shaped cage space, with the user seated in a swivel chair in the center. Since the HMD is non-occlusive, the user is able to see the display in the center of his/her field of view, as well as look at the screen of the tablet by gazing down.

A wand interface is provided to the dominant hand of the user to enable 3D interaction in the immersive VE. The wand is made by attaching a 6-DOF tracking constellation to a Wii Remote controller. 3DUI tasks are performed by pointing the wand and pressing buttons to issue commands. To navigate within the VE, the user can point the wand in different directions, and press down the D-pad buttons to travel in that direction at a constant speed. To reserve the realistic feeling, virtual locomotion is always constrained to the ground, but the swivel chair gives extra flexibility to point the wand easily at all directions. While the user is traveling, a group of fans corresponding to the direction of the locomotion are turned on, and blow wind at a constant speed to enhance the sense of motion in the virtual world.

To select an editing mode, the user can call out a floating menu as shown in Figure 1b, by holding down the "home" button on the Wii Remote controller. The tile pointed to by the wand is highlighted, and the corresponding editing mode is selected upon release of the "home" button. In the modes of terrain shape, texture, grass, or tree editing, a ray is cast from the tip of the wand to the intersection on the terrain surface, and a terrain brush is visualized to indicate the effective range. The size of the terrain brush can be changed

using the "+" and "-" buttons on the wand controller. The "A" and "B" buttons have opposite effects. The former is used to raise, align, and plant trees and grass, while the latter is used to lower, sample, and remove trees and grass. In object editing mode, the objects in the VE, such as houses, can be selected by ray-casting and pressing the "A" button, or deselected by pressing the "B" button. Objects are highlighted in light blue when being pointed at, and in bright blue when actually selected. Once selected, the user can drag the object on the terrain surface by holding the "A" button, rotate it around the up-axis by pressing the left and right buttons on the D-pad, or scale it by pressing the "+" and "-" buttons. Lastly, the user can paint subparts of the virtual objects with different textures, as well as changing the scale of each texture.

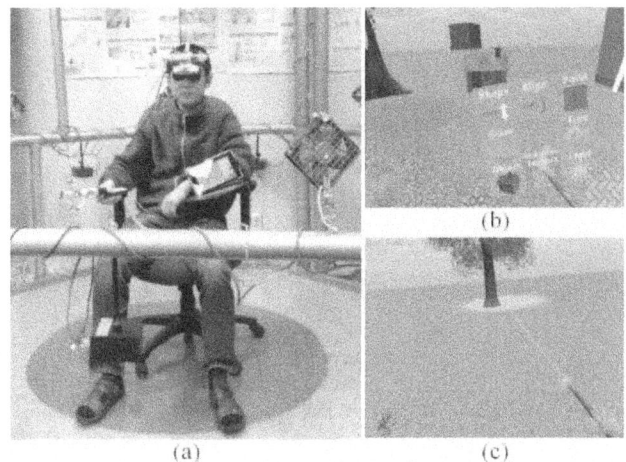

Figure 1. The hardware setup (a), the floating menu (b) and terrain brush (c) of the HVE level editor.

### Tablet IC

Figure 1a shows a user wearing a Google Nexus-7 tablet on his left forearm, and resting it on an arm pad to reduce fatigue. To leverage bimanual interaction [16], the user is asked to hold the wand interface temporarily in the left hand, or place it between the legs, and use the right hand to apply multi-touch gestures to the touch screen.

The interface on the tablet is illustrated in Figure 2. It consists of a three-tier GUI menu, a WIM view of the VE, and a shortcut bar. The top tier (1) is a tool bar for switching between the general editing modes. The tool bar at the second tier (2) displays further sub-modes, such as height, texture, grass, and trees for terrain editing. Based on the selection in the first two tiers, the third tier (3) shows specific GUI elements that can be used to perform the current task, such as a slider to resize the terrain brush, a selection grid to choose a type of grass to plant, and a broom button to clean grass from the terrain. Note that the immersive IC and the tablet IC each have their own terrain brush, so that terrain editing can be performed at different scales. To the right of the third-tier panel, an above-the-world, photorealistic, third person view of the VE is presented (4), whose camera has a 60-degree horizontal FOV in the VE, and can be manipulated using multi-touch gestures. These include a pinch gesture for zoom, a rotate gesture for orbit, a two-finger all-direction swipe gesture for pan, and a three-finger up-and-down swipe gesture for pitch. The one finger tap and swipe gestures are reserved for level editing, such as painting the terrain, or dragging an object on the terrain surface. The functionality of the shortcut buttons (5) will be discussed later.

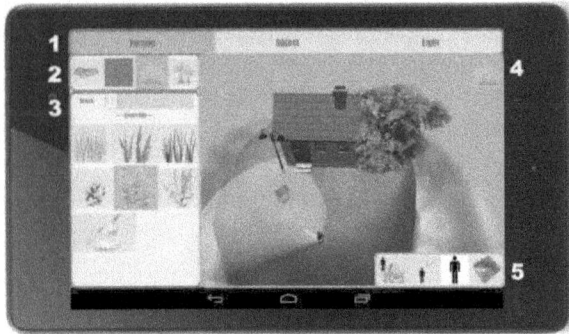

**Figure 2. The tablet IC used to edit the VE from the God view**

Regarding the software implementation, the HVE system was developed using the Unity game engine as a multi-player game running separately on the desktop and the tablet platforms. The hardware devices of the immersive IC are connected to the desktop computer through USB and Bluetooth connections. The input data from the PhaseSpace motion capture system and the Wii Remote controller are collected and streamed to the game process through VRPN and the Unity Indie VRPN Adapter (UIVA). Both the desktop and the tablet simulate the VE locally, and keep each other synchronized by sending UDP data streams and RPC calls over a local WiFi network. This way, both ICs can run the game at a steady 30 frames per second, and editing performed in one IC can be propagated to the other IC in real time, giving the user a convincing experience that they are viewing and interacting with the same virtual world, only from two different perspectives.

**Coordination Mechanisms**

The advantages of the two ICs can complement each other to support diverse tasks efficiently. For example, a fast way of moving a small object across a long distance in the VE is to select the object in the local space using the wand, and drag it to the destination using the tablet. However, such process involves frequent switches between the ICs, and the mental overhead of adapting to different IC components cannot be overlooked. The challenges to create smooth transition experiences in the HVE level editor are further illustrated in Figure 3, in which each level-editing task is decomposed into a set of basic 3DUI tasks. The user's workflow may start with any task in one IC and end with another task in a different IC. During transitions, the user needs to understand the relationship between the two VE representations, and adapt to distinctly different display

devices, input devices, interaction techniques, reference frames, and perspectives. To reduce this transition gap, we propose the following four coordination mechanisms.

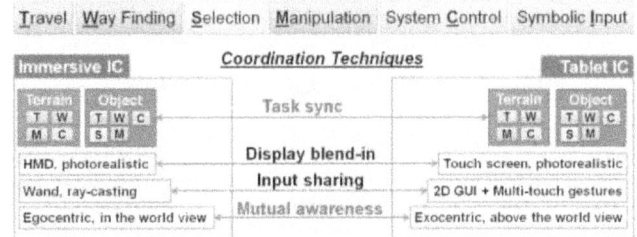

**Figure 3. The coordination mechanism to smooth the complex cross-task, cross-IC transitions in the HVE level editor**

- **Task synchronization:** The multiple data views in CMV systems are often coordinated to be consistent during user interaction [19, 22, 31]. Similarly, the effect of 3D interaction in one IC should also be propagated to all other ICs, to keep the workflow continuous during transitions. For example, when a user changes to object editing mode and selects an object using the wand, the tablet should also update to the same mode and select the same object, so that the user can directly continue to manipulate this object after changing the IC. Without task synchronization, the user's work would be interrupted, forcing her to repeat actions already made in the other IC.

- **Display blend-in:** The change of display device can cause perceptual gaps between ICs due to differences in screen size, resolution, brightness, and other parameters. Using mixed reality technology [8], the image of one IC's display device can be embedded into another IC's view to reduce this discrepancy. For example, compared to viewing the tablet screen from the peripheral vision, a better experience may be promised by tracking and rendering a virtual tablet in the HMD view, in place of the physical tablet itself.

- **Input sharing:** Some generic input devices, such as the mouse and keyboard, can be optimal to use in multiple ICs [2]. For example, a similar HVE system can be formed using a desktop computer and a tablet. In this situation, the mouse and keyboard could be efficient tools for controlling both the first-person view on the monitor and the God view on the tablet. Sharing input among ICs may not only reduce the mental overhead of transitions between interfaces, but also the physical effort of switching between devices.

- **Mutual awareness:** Research in CVE systems has stressed mutual awareness as the key to efficient human collaborations in VR [10, 15]. This rule can also be applied to HVE systems where different views are assigned to the same user. By knowing the whereabouts of the other view and the status of its interfaces, the user can better determine when to make the IC transition, and be more prepared to adapt to the new IC once the transition is made. Examples of effective mutual awareness cues include avatars, viewing frusta, pointing rays, and editing brushes (see Figure 4).

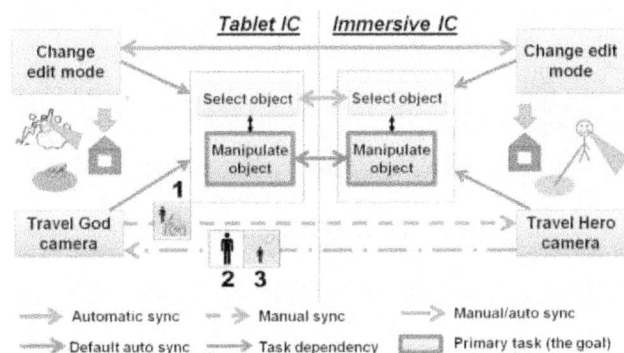

**Figure 4. An example of task synchronization and mutual awareness cues implemented in the HVE level editor**

Of the four coordination mechanisms, task synchronization and mutual awareness cues have been implemented in the current version of the HVE level editor. Figure 4 shows an example of the implementation in object-editing mode. The ultimate goal of this mode is to properly arrange virtual objects in the scene, through manipulation of the objects' positions, orientations, and scales. Manipulation is preceded by enabling object-editing mode (system control), moving to an appropriate spot (travel), and selecting the objet (selection). By default, the effect of object manipulation is synchronized between the two ICs, as the VE needs to look the same on both displays. However, synchronization of the preceding steps is optional, and very much dependent on the level of multi-tasking a hybrid system aims to support. We hypothesize that by synchronizing the effects of all 3DUI basic tasks, the working-memory demands required to keep track of the status of 3D interactions across ICs can be effectively reduced, leading to better task performance and user experience. Thus, task synchronization was implemented, with the goal of minimizing the interaction gap between the ICs. As illustrated in Figure 4, changing the editing mode or selecting a virtual object in one IC is always automatically synchronized to the other IC. Teleporting the user's Hero avatar to the field of the God view is done manually with the tap of a shortcut button (1) on the tablet, because previous research has indicated that constantly changing an immersive view can cause disorientation and even motion sickness symptoms [28]. To synchronize the God view with the space surrounding the Hero avatar, the user can either tap a button (2) for one-time teleporting, or switch a toggle (3) to enable/disable camera following.

## EVALUATION

### Hypotheses

The HVE system aims to combine the strengths of an immersive VR setup and a multi-touch tablet device. Being inside the virtual world, the user can better understand the space, judge scales of objects, and do manipulation of finer details [15]. Meanwhile, from the God view, the user can better navigate the VE, investigate the overall layout, and perform large-scale manipulations [28]. The two ICs are unified under the WIM metaphor, and coordinated through mutual awareness cues and task synchronization. Based on these analyses, we made the following hypotheses. *H2* and *H3* are trying to capture higher-level processes, such as user behavior, as opposed to low-level, performance-based claims as in *H1*.

*H1*: Having the effects of basic 3DUI tasks synchronized between the ICs can make the transitions more continuous, and lead to better task performance and user experience.

*H2*: The users are able to learn the HVE system, and use both ICs to handle tasks with diverse requirements.

*H3*: The users are able to decompose a complex, high-level task into a series of basic 3DUI tasks, and find step-by-step strategies to efficiently use both ICs.

**Figure 5. The task is to fix design flaws in an unfinished VE.**

### User Study

Instead of building a virtual world from scratch, the study presented the subjects an unfinished virtual world (see Figure 5), and asked them to find and fix five different types of design flaws in the VE as quickly and precisely as possible. This task approach was chosen for several reasons. First of all, based on natural metaphors, the design flaws were clear to identify, and the goals easy to understand and remember. Secondly, compared to building a VE from scratch, fixing existing design flaws takes less time to complete, making the threats such as user fatigue and motion sickness much more manageable. Finally, to complete the tasks efficiently, the subject needed to take different angles, interact at different scales and reference frames, and use different interfaces. This encouraged the subjects to learn both ICs, and explore different ways to use their complementary advantages.

With approval from the institutional review board (IRB), 24 university students were recruited with no remuneration. The study employed a within-subjects approach to compare the HVE level editor with and without task synchronization (indicated by green lines in Figure 4). The study began with the subject reading and signing the consent form, followed by a demographic questionnaire that asked about gender, age, and handedness, as well as experiences with immersive VR, multi-touch devices, multi-screen devices (e.g. the Nintendo WiiU), and first-person world building games (e.g., Minecraft). The subject was then introduced to the hardware used in the study, including the HMD, the wand, the tablet, and the fans. While having the freedom to swivel the chair, the subject was asked to stay in the center of the cage, to keep the best tracking quality of the motion capture cameras. The experimenter also explained the five world-fixing tasks as illustrated in Figure 6. The subject then put on the equipment, and learned the interfaces and the tasks in a 20-minute training session. To guide the subjects effectively, the VE in the training session had the five types of design flaws and the goals shown side by side as in Figure 6, where the experimenter explained different ways of solving each task, using either the wand or the tablet.

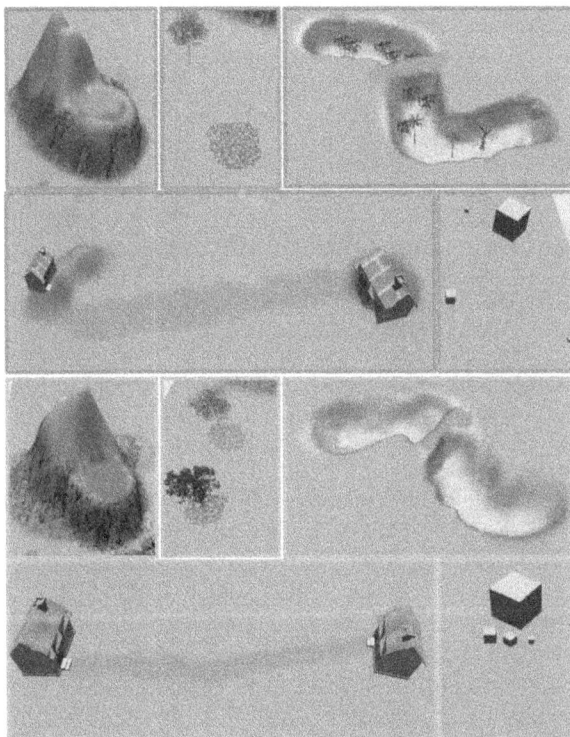

Figure 6. The five types of design flaws to fix in the study.

After the training session, the subject took a five-minute break, and then continued through two experimental conditions, each of which had one trial of world editing tasks. The conditions were presented to the subject in counterbalanced order, and only one of them had task synchronization enabled. To get used to the HVE system with different configurations, the subject spent eight minutes in a practice scene prior to each trial. In each trial, the subject had up to 15 minutes to fix the virtual world, and could end the trial early when they felt all design flaws had been addressed. After completing both conditions, the subject was asked to fill in a questionnaire to compare the

HVE level editor with and without task synchronizations enabled, and to rate them on a one to six scale regarding eight different questions (see Figure 8). In the end, the subject was interviewed to give comments about the benefits and drawbacks of having multiple ICs, and the effectiveness of task synchronization.

## Results

### Task Performance
At the end of each trial, the system recorded the total time spent, and saved the edited VE into a data file. All VE data files were then reloaded and rated by two graders, who followed the same rubric to compare the completed VEs with the goals. The inter-rater reliability was evaluated using Pearson's correlation analysis and the result showed high agreement (R=0.92). As indicators of task performance, the task time, task score, and score-per-minute of the two conditions were compared using two-sided, paired t-test, with a threshold of 0.05 for significance. Score-per-minute was calculated by dividing score by time, and used as a measure of user efficiency. As indicated in Figure 7, subjects spent less time, and achieved higher task completeness, with task synchronization. The results are statistically significant for score-per-minute (p=0.02), and showed trends for task time (p=0.08) and score (p=0.07).

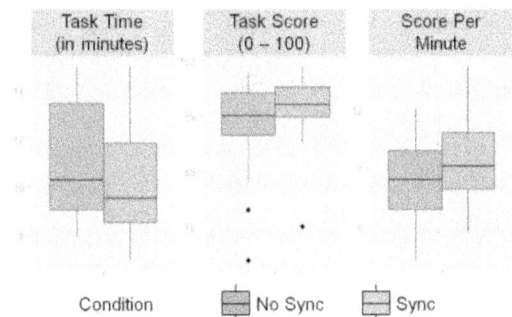

Figure 7. The analysis results of task performance indicators

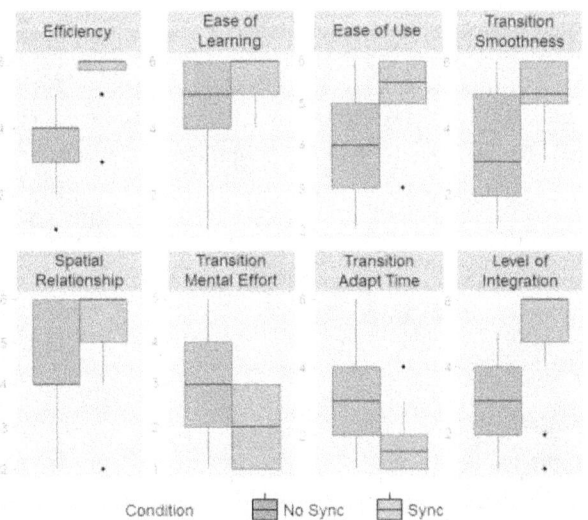

Figure 8. The analysis results of subjective rating scores

*Post Questionnaire*

The six-point rating scores of the two conditions were analyzed using two-sided Wilcoxon signed-rank tests with a threshold of 0.05 for significance on all questions. As indicated in Figure 8, the HVE system with task synchronization was considered to be more efficient, easier to learn, and easier to use, and the transitions between ICs smoother, and less time and mental effort demanding. In addition, the subjects felt the task synchronization mechanisms made it easier to understand the spatial relationship between the two VE representations, and the ICs were better integrated in the HVE system. All results were strongly statistically significant ($p < 0.01$).

*Interview Feedback*

In the interview, subjects were asked about whether they felt perceptual, cognitive, or functional disconnections between the ICs when transitions were made. The summary of their answers indicated better transitional continuity when task synchronization was enabled. The number of subjects who reported disconnected experiences, comparing "Sync" with "No-Sync", were 6 and 11 for perceptual disconnection, 1 and 7 for cognitive disconnection, and 2 and 16 for functional disconnection. For the "Sync" condition, eight subjects complimented the synchronization of the editing mode, for emphasizing strong connection between the ICs, and making sure the non-active IC always kept up with the user's workflow in the active IC. The travel synchronization buttons on the tablet (teleport, focus, and follow) also had significant contributions to the smooth transition experiences, according to eight subjects who claimed that "the two views were spatially connected with these buttons" and that "the appropriate camera view was always available at hand when I tapped these buttons". Synchronization of selected objects was also liked by four subjects, as it enabled effortless within-task transitions, such as picking up a small cube using the wand and dragging it across the virtual world on the tablet screen. For the "No-Sync" condition, seven subjects felt the ICs were disconnected, and the overall HVE system was confusing and awkward to learn and use. Because the editing mode and the selected object did not get updated in both ICs, the subjects had to keep track of their individual status, and repeat actions they already took before the transitions. Four subjects even gave up using both ICs, and stayed with one interface throughout the trial. However, four subjects did point out one advantage of working in the "No-Sync" mode, which is the ability to simultaneously work on two different tasks and/or in two different spaces. When asked about preference of ICs in "Sync" mode, 22 subjects preferred to use both ICs, two subjects preferred tablet only, and no subject selected VR only. Different answers were given in the "No-Sync" mode, with nine for both ICs, four for tablet only, and 11 for VR only. In other words, subjects preferred using both ICs with task synchronization, but staying with one IC without it.

The subjects were also asked to give general comments about the HVE level editor. Eleven subjects appreciated the complementary benefits offered by the heterogeneous views and interfaces. They suggested 2D tasks (e.g., painting and menu control), long distance navigation, and large scale manipulation to be performed on the tablet, and 3D tasks (e.g., object selection and scaling), local space locomotion, and small scale adjustment to be performed using immersive VR. Having redundant functionality on both ICs was acknowledged by two subjects, for it granted them freedom to perform the tasks differently in different situations. Lastly, suggestions to improve the HVE level editor were given in the interviews, such as undo and redo (three subjects), ambient sound and sound effects (two subjects), teleport in VR (three subjects), flying in VR (two subjects), showing a virtual tablet in the HMD (one subject), and combining the wand and tablet into a single interface like the Nintendo WiiU controller (one subject).

*Video Analysis*

To understand how the subjects used the two ICs, we captured videos of the experiment trials from three sources. A web camera was mounted on the ceiling to capture the subject from the top, and screen capture software was installed on the desktop computer and the tablet to capture from both screens. The three streams of video footage for each trial were then merged, timeline-synchronized, and analyzed by the authors. The videos showed that subjects were able to connect the two views in the shared 3D space, and take advantage of both ICs for different tasks. For example, after painting the mountain with the wand, many subjects immediately switched to the tablet, located the river near the mountain, and continued to clean the foliage in it. With task synchronization, the subjects did not need much time to plan such sequences of transitional actions, and were able to execute smoothly. On the other hand, although all subjects eventually adapted to the absence of task synchronization, many of them expressed confusion and awkwardness to repeat actions that had already been done, and some even made a few mistakes when they lost track of the ICs' individual statuses. The videos also showed that subjects made fewer transitions without task synchronization. They grouped all appropriate tasks for one IC, and completed them before changing to the other IC.

There was also no within-task transition for the cube collecting task in "No Sync" mode. Many subjects chose to stay at the wand, and traveled long distances to carry the cubes to their destinations. This is probably because they had to reselect the same cube on the tablet, which is just why the wand was used in the first place. In contrast, several subjects were able to discover some efficient strategies to leverage both ICs with task synchronization enabled. For example, three subjects completed the cube collecting task quickly by using the tablet to teleport the Hero avatar near a small cube, selecting it with the wand, teleporting with the tablet again near the destination, and dropping the cube. Another interesting approach was taken by two subjects, who positioned the Hero avatar near the destination, and used the wand to drop cubes that have been selected using the tablet from a zoomed-in view.

The "teleport" and "focus" buttons were used a lot in the experiment. Using these two buttons, a subject demonstrated an interesting strategy to speed up multi-scale navigation on the tablet. Instead of panning and zooming in the God camera, the subject teleported his Hero avatar, and tapped the focused button. This allowed him to instantly navigate to an area of interest. However, the "follow" toggle was not used as much, probably because our test bed did not include any "focus + context" task.

Lastly, the video analysis gave us insight about how the interfaces were used for the five test bed tasks. In general, the tablet was mainly used for 2D tasks that needed to be done from different angles, and at large scales, such as painting textures on the terrain, clearing foliage in the rivers, and moving cubes across the VE. In contrast, the wand and HMD were used to edit details of objects in 3D spaces, such as selecting cubes, smoothing terrain surfaces, scaling houses, and planting flowers under trees. These interaction patterns agreed with the subjects' comments in the interview, and clearly indicated the complementary benefits of the two ICs for 3D interaction tasks with diverse requirements.

*Discussion*

All three hypotheses were confirmed by the user study results. Similar interaction patterns were discovered in the interview feedback and the video analysis, proving that the subjects were able to connect the Hero and God views in the shared virtual space, and learn and use both ICs effectively to perform tasks with diverse and complementary requirements (*H2*). However, the transitions between ICs were much more continuous with task synchronization enabled, as suggested by comparative ratings, user comments in the interview, and video analysis of the experiment trials (*H1*). In comparison, the HVE system without task synchronization was perceived to be confusing, awkward, and inefficient to learn and use in a hybrid way. In essence, the absence of task synchronization broke the hybrid system into two separate tools. Although it was still beneficial to use both ICs for complementary task requirements, subjects tended to avoid transitions as much as possible. The video analysis showed them doing so by dividing the tasks into two groups, and finishing all tasks in one IC before transitioning to a different one. And when some subjects attempted to add more transitional interactions to their workflows, mistakes were made, because they forgot to constantly invest more working memory to keep track of the status of both systems. The synchronization of travel and object selection also enabled and inspired various within-task transition strategies to perform the cube-collecting task efficiently (*H3*). In comparison, these strategies were abandoned when task

synchronizations were absent, because subjects had to reselect the cubes in the second IC, which was the reason why it was not used in the first place.

## CONCLUSION

To conclude, this paper proposed a novel HVE system to overcome the limitations of traditional immersive VR systems, in task scenarios that involved diverse scales, angles, perspectives, reference frames, or dimensions. The system leveraged the power and rich interactivity of a tablet device to complement the natural yet limiting 3D interfaces in a traditional HMD and wand-based immersive VR setup. The definition of interaction context (IC) was given, and a taxonomy of IC components was presented. Based on research findings in related fields, four coordination mechanisms were proposed to increase the transition continuity between the ICs. And two of them, namely, mutual awareness and task synchronization, were implemented in the current version of the HVE system. Lastly, a user study was conducted based on five level-editing tasks, to validate the benefits of multiple ICs, and compare the transition experience with and without task synchronization enabled. The study results confirmed that complex HVE systems can be learnt and used to perform diverse 3D tasks efficiently, and suggested that task synchronization is necessary to keep continuous and effortless transitions across ICs.

Regarding future work, we are looking to further optimize the transition experience between the ICs through input sharing, and display blend-in techniques, and evaluate the effectiveness of these coordination mechanisms through similar user studies. In addition, we are also interested in applying the same methodology to non-occlusive HMD devices or CAVE based VR systems, as well as experimenting with HVE systems with more than two ICs.

## REFERENCES

1.  Angus, I. G., and Sowizral H. A. Embedding the 2D interaction metaphor in a real 3D virtual environment. *Proc. IS&T/SPIE's Symposium on Electronic Imaging: Science & Tech. '95.* 282-293.

2.  Benko, H., Ishak, E. W., and Feiner, S. Collaborative mixed reality visualization of an archaeological excavation. *Proc. IEEE ISMAR'04*, 132-140.

3.  Billinghurst, M., Kato, H., and Poupyrev, I. The MagicBook: a transitional AR interface. *Computers & Graphics, 25*, 5 (2001), 745-753.

4.  Bornik, A., Beichel, R., Kruijff, E., Reitinger, B., and Schmalstieg, D. A hybrid user interface for manipulation of volumetric medical data. *Proc. IEEE 3DUI'06*, 29-36.

5.  Bowman, D. A., Kruijff, E., LaViola, J. J., and Poupyrev, I. *3D User Interfaces: Theory and Practice.* Addison-Wesley Professional, 2004.

6.  Bowman, D. A., Wineman, J., Hodges, L. F., and Allison, D. Designing animal habitats within an immersive VE. *IEEE Computer Graphics and Applications, 18*, 5 (1998), 9-13.

7.  Brown, L. and Hua, H. Magic lenses for augmented virtual environments. *IEEE Computer Graphics and Applications, 26*, 4 (2006), 64-73.

8.  Bruder, G., Steinicke, F., Valkov, D., and Hinrichs, K. Augmented virtual studio for architectural exploration. *Proc. VRIC'10*, 43-50.

9.  Carvalho, F. G., Trevisan, D. G., and Raposo, A. Toward the design of transitional interfaces: an exploratory study on a semi-immersive hybrid user interface. *Virtual Reality, 16*, 4 (2012), 271-288.

10. Churchill, E. F., and Snowdon D. Collaborative virtual environments: an introductory review of issues and systems. *Virtual Reality, 3*, 1 (1998), 3-15.

11. Darken, R. and Durost, R. Mixed-dimension interaction in virtual environments. *Proc. ACM VRST'05*, 38-45.

12. Dubois, E., Nigay, L., and Troccaz, J. Assessing continuity and compatibility in augmented reality systems. *Universal Access in the Information Society, 1*, 4 (2002), 263-273.

13. Feiner, S. and Shamash, A. Hybrid user interfaces: breeding virtually bigger interfaces for physically smaller computers. *Proc. ACM UIST'91*, 9-17.

14. Grasset, R., Dunster, A., and Billinghurst, M. Moving between contexts - a user evaluation of a transitional interface. *Proc. IEEE Artificial Reality and Telexistence'08*, 137-143.

15. Holm, R., Stauder, E., Wagner, R., Priglinger, M., and Volkert, J. A combined immersive and desktop authoring tool for virtual environments. *Proc. IEEE VR'02*, 93-100.

16. Lindeman, R., Sibert, J., and Hahn, J. Towards usable VR: an empirical study of user interfaces for immersive virtual environments. *Proc. ACM CHI'99*, 64-71.

17. Miguel, M. M., Ogawa, T., Kiyokawa, K., and Takemura, H. A PDA-based see-through interface within an immersive environment. *Proc. IEEE Artificial Reality and Telexistence'07*, 113-118.

18. Milgram, P., Takemura, H., Utsumi, A., and Kishino, F. Augmented reality: a class of displays on the reality-virtuality continuum. *Proc. Photonics for Industrial Applications'95*, 282-292.

19. North, C. and Shneiderman, B. Snap-together visualization: a user interface for coordinating visualizations via relational schemata. *Proc. ACM AVI'00*, 128-135.

20. Pierce, J. S., Steams, B. C., and Pausch, R. Voodoo dolls: seamless interaction at multiple scales in virtual environments. *Proc. ACM i3D'99*, 141–145.

21. Plumlee, M. and Ware, C. Integrating multiple 3D views through frame-of-reference interaction. *Proc. IEEE CMV'03*, 34-43.

22. Plumlee, M. and Ware, C. An evaluation of methods for linking 3D views. *Proc. ACM i3D'03*, 193-201.

23. Poupyrev, I., Ichikawa, T., Weghorst, S., and Billinghurst, M. Egocentric object manipulation in virtual environments: empirical evaluation of interaction techniques. *Computer Graphics Forum, 17*, 3 (1998), 41-52.

24. Schmalstieg, D., Encarnacao, M., and Szalavari, Z. Using transparent props for interaction with the virtual table. *Proc. ACM i3D'99*, 147-154.

25. Schmalstieg, D. and Schaufler, G. Sewing worlds together with SEAMS: a mechanism to construct complex virtual environments. *Presence: Teleoperators and Virtual Environments, 8*, 4 (1999), 449-461.

26. Song, P., Goh, W., and Fu, C. WYSIWYF: exploring and annotating volume data with a tangible handheld device. *Proc. ACM CHI'11*, 1333-1342.

27. Steinicke, F., Ropinski, T., Hinrichs, K., and Bruder, G. A multiple view system for modeling building entities. *Proc. IEEE CMV'06*, 69-78.

28. Stoakley, R., Conway, M., and Pausch, R. Virtual reality on a WIM: interactive worlds in miniature. *Proc. ACM CHI'95*, 265-272.

29. Szalavári, Z. and Gervautz, M. The personal interaction panel - a two-handed interface for augmented reality. *Computer Graphics Forum, 16*, 3 (1997), C335-C346.

30. Viega, J., Conway, M. J., Williams, G., and Pausch, R. 3D magic lenses. *Proc. ACM UIST'96*, 51-58.

31. Wang Baldonado, M. Q., Woodruff, A., and Kuchinsky, A. Guidelines for using multiple views in information visualization. *Proc. ACM AVI'00*, 110-119.

32. Watsen, K., Darken, R., and Capps, M. A handheld computer as an interaction device to a virtual environment. *International Immersive Projection Technology Workshop*, 1999.

33. Wilkes, C.B., Tilden, D., and Bowman, D. A. 3D user interfaces using tracked multi-touch mobile devices. *Proc. JVRC of ICAT-EGVE-EuroVR'12*, 65-72.

34. Zanbaka, C. A., Lok, B. C., Babu, S. V., Ulinski, A. C., and Hodges, L. F. Comparison of path visualizations and cognitive measures relative to travel technique in a virtual environment. *IEEE Transactions on Visualization and Computer Graphics, 11*, 6 (2005), 694-705.

# Making VR Work: Building a Real-World Immersive Modeling Application in the Virtual World

**Mark Mine**
Walt Disney Imagineering
1401 Flower Street
Glendale, CA 91201
mark.mine@disney.com

**Arun Yoganandan**
Walt Disney Imagineering
1401 Flower Street
Glendale, CA 91201
ayogan2@gmail.com

**Dane Coffey**
Walt Disney Imagineering
1401 Flower Street
Glendale, CA 91201
dcoffey86@gmail.com

## ABSTRACT

Building a real-world immersive 3D modeling application is hard. In spite of the many supposed advantages of working in the virtual world, users quickly tire of waving their arms about and the resulting models remain simplistic at best. The dream of creation at the speed of thought has largely remained unfulfilled due to numerous factors such as the lack of suitable menu and system controls, inability to perform precise manipulations, lack of numeric input, challenges with ergonomics, and difficulties with maintaining user focus and preserving immersion. The focus of our research is on the building of virtual world applications that can go beyond the demo and can be used to do real-world work. The goal is to develop interaction techniques that support the richness and complexity required to build complex 3D models, yet minimize expenditure of user energy and maximize user comfort. We present an approach that combines the natural and intuitive power of VR interaction, the precision and control of 2D touch surfaces, and the richness of a commercial modeling package. We also discuss the benefits of collocating 2D touch with 3D bimanual spatial input, the challenges in designing a custom controller targeted at achieving the same, and the new avenues that this collocation creates.

## Author Keywords

Virtual Reality; 3D user interaction; Selection; Graphical User Interfaces; Controller design; Immersive 3D modeling.

## ACM Classification Keywords

H.5.1 [Information Interfaces and Presentation]: Multimedia Information Systems – Artificial, augmented and virtual realities.

## INTRODUCTION

From making cars to designing theme park rides, pre-visualization and virtual prototyping have become an integral part of the design process. Commercial-off-the-shelf (COTS) desktop modeling tools like Maya and SketchUp are extensively used in such processes to design and develop 3D assets. Unfortunately, when using these tools, a wealth of spatial information is unavailable to the designer since they are constrained to viewing and interacting through a 2D window. Conversely, there is compelling evidence that tracked 3D interaction offers a much more intuitive and quicker way to work in 3D [18], but unfortunately most immersive modeling applications are built from scratch and do not provide the wealth of tools and plugins that COTS applications provide. In this paper, we share our experiences trying to bring those two worlds together by converting the COTS application SketchUp into a virtual reality application: VR SketchUp. Beyond that, we

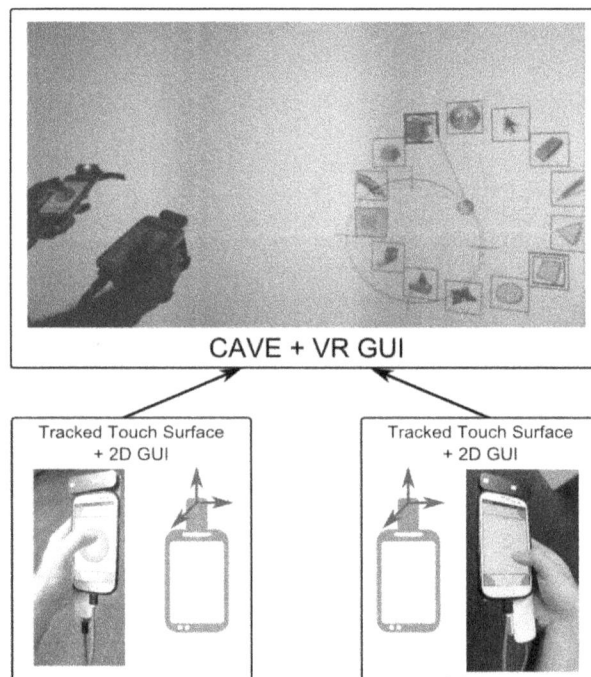

**Figure 1. SketchUp VR Interface**
**Top: Floating VR GUI**
**Lower left: Non-dominant Hand Controller (ND-HC),**
**Lower right: Dominant Hand Controller (D-HC)**

endeavor to develop interaction techniques that can run across a spectrum of displays, ranging from the desktop, to head-mounted displays to large CAVE environments, while responsively adapting to the unique input mechanisms and interaction styles afforded by each. That way, designers can switch between these displays based on their current stage in the process such as design, review, showcase etc., but still retain the same familiar tools and capabilities across them. We use synchronous and asynchronous bimanual input for view, object and menu manipulation.

We also share lessons learned from our efforts to build expressive, easy to use, and ergonomic input devices. Immersive modeling tools from the past have mostly relied on tracked wands and game controllers with only physical inputs such as buttons, triggers and joystick. This can both limit the expressiveness of user interaction due to the simplistic nature of these types of inputs while simultaneously complicating the interface due to the large number of inputs and the need for the user to remember complex functional mappings. We detail here our approach in building a hybrid controller that collocates a touch display, a casing with physical buttons, and 6 degrees of freedom (DoF) tracking to enable a dynamic and rich medium of interaction. The presence of two touch screens and floating virtual menus (Fig 1) provide a great avenue to perform much of the system control and menu navigation without dividing attention between the displays, and we share our design practices for the same. Furthermore, we have found that collocating spatial tracking and touch on two hands enables opportunities for novel tools and new forms of interaction. We describe several new widgets for object manipulation that were developed from this opportunity.

## RELATED WORK

Immersive 3D modeling has been of interest for almost two decades now. Butterworth et al. [1] developed a 3D modeling system for head-mounted displays, with a 6-DoF 2-button mouse. Mine [11] explored scene composition within Virtual Environments (VE) with ISAAC. Hughes et al. [6] developed CaveCAD, an application to build architectural models with 3D interaction inside a CAVE environment. Ponto et al. [14] developed a system for freeform virtual sculpting of organic shapes with 3D interaction.

Multigen [15] pioneered the SmartScene modeling system that enabled fully immersive modeling using two tracked hands. Jerald et al. [7] also demonstrated a two-handed 3D modeling system with magnetically tracked controllers. There has been evidence of interest in using commercial-off-the-shelf applications within VEs. Takala et al. [22] adapted Blender, an open-source desktop modeling application by incorporating 3D interactions into it with the PlayStation Move controllers. The immersive desktop holographic system - ZSpace [24] has enabled support for Maya.

Menu selection and navigation are important components of an immersive modeling tool to facilitate quick and efficient workflows. Ni et al. [13] developed the rapMenu system that used tracked pinch gloves to interact with hierarchical pie menus. Menu selection with 6-DoF magnetically tracked controllers was examined by [16] with the rAirFlow menus. Many researchers have investigated the use of touch screens for menuing within VEs in the past. Medeiros et al. [10] explored using a tracked tablet for view manipulation, object selection and manipulation and for symbolic input in a virtual engineering environment. The application required having the tablet lifted up to perform object manipulation. Wang et al. [23] used a tablet strapped to the arm for menu and attribute selection. A 3D tracked controller on the other hand controlled navigation. Gebhardt et al. [5] studied the usage of smartphones for system control within VE. Their menus were represented only on the smartphone and not within the VE.

Researchers both within and outside of Virtual Reality have investigated combining spatial tracking and touch. Marquardt et al. [9] defined the continuous interaction space between 2D touch surfaces and the 3D tracked spaces above them. De Araujo et al. [4] expanded on [9] to create an intuitive bimanual application that combined on and above surface interactions along with gaze and posture to facilitate creation of 3D models. Additionally, they also segregated interactions between hands, with system control and menu selection performed on the non-dominant (ND) hand and sketching or spatial modeling gestures on the dominant (D) hand. Coffey et al. [3] examined the use of multi-touch surfaces as an input device for manipulating view and widgets in a VE on a distant display. Controlling virtual widgets with a tracked, unseen touch screen was explored by Steed et al. [21]. Seifert et al. [19] extensively investigated using smartphones as pointers to large displays. Song et al. [20] defined the concept of a handle bar metaphor to manipulate virtual objects at a distance. Rashid et al. [17] studied the effectiveness of mobile devices for proximal and distal selection tasks on a remote large display. They found touch interactions on mobile devices to be easier when many widgets needed to be modified, but introduced the issue of attention switching between the phone and the large display. In this paper, we expand on research reported in our previous work [12].

## SYSTEM

### Hardware

Our system has been developed and used in 3 environments:

- The DISH - a 360° CAVE environment with 5 stereo projected surfaces – 4 walls and a floor.
- The Wall – A stereo rear-projected curved display wall.
- A regular desktop without stereo rendering

Phasespace Inc's optical and sensor fusion tracking systems were used for 6-DoF head and hand tracking within the large environments. A Polhemus Fastrak magnetic system was used on the desktop version. Hybrid input devices known as Hand Controllers (HC) were designed and developed in-house. They each consist of a Samsung Galaxy S3 smartphone, an Arduino Nano microcontroller, and 3 physical buttons, all connected with each other and housed in a custom casing that was 3D printed. The physical buttons are reserved for fundamental actions or events that remain consistent throughout the application such as object manipulation, view manipulation and menu reset. The controller design was iterated for ergonomic comfort and for prolonged usage.

## Software

TechViz, an openGL intercept application and cluster renderer like [2] was used to adapt SketchUp for VR displays. SketchUp runs a custom plugin that manages the tracking information, communicates with the TechViz API to update graphical transformations, emulates the mouse and keyboard inputs, provides 3D representations of hands, generates floating menu interfaces, and manages the state of the system. A modified version of Mape's Two Handed Interface (THI) [8] was implemented to achieve bimanual view manipulation. The HCs run custom Android applications that manage touch and button presses. Thus SketchUp and HCs communicate with each other over Wi-Fi to update the state of the system and adapt dynamically.

## VR SKETCHUP

There are several benefits that can be achieved from adapting SketchUp into VEs. Head tracking provides a quick and natural way of making minor viewpoint changes to look around a model to study and absorb it, resulting in a better understanding of the 3D space. With the combination of head and hand tracking, users can manipulate both the object and the viewpoint at the same time. Direct 6-DoF interactions enable intuitive 3D manipulation of objects in the scene, and a bimanual system allows the user to take great advantage of proprioception for the interactions.

These benefits, however, come at a cost. There are several challenges associated with immersive 3D modeling specifically, and all immersive applications in general, the primary of which is system control. The lack of the familiar WIMP interface within VR environments makes it difficult to navigate about menus and tool options. Additionally, the absence of the familiar mouse and keyboard only serves to deepen this issue. As a result, even operations that do not require 3D interaction such as precise numeric input, textural input and symbolic input are often achieved with complicated 3D widgets, resulting in a cumbersome and unintuitive user experience. Finally, even though spatial interaction offers an intuitive mechanism for design, their control is still restricted to coarse interactions. Thus precise alignment and positioning in a VE still remain as a largely unsolved problem.

In addition to the above, one of the main challenges in adapting COTS applications to VEs arises from the fact that

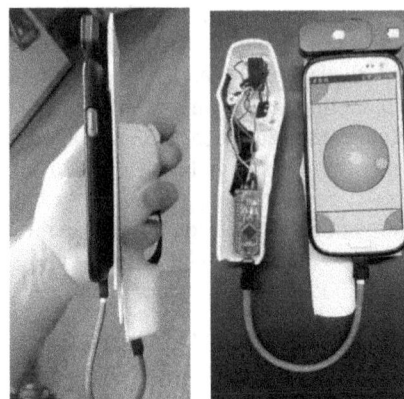

**Figure 2. Hand Controller**

these applications are not designed or meant to be used in VEs. Very quickly, VR developers start to face limitations with respect to rendering, interactions and the software architecture. For example, SketchUp does not have a way to classify 3D objects as either scene objects or 3D GUI elements. As a result, simple operations such as picking and ray collisions end up acting on these GUI elements unintentionally. Also, native tools for such applications are usually closed source and are not available for the developer to extend or customize for VR. As a result, mouse emulation is resorted to in native tools, where spatial interaction could have very well made a big difference.

## Hand Controllers

As mentioned in the Introduction, the challenges associated with using traditional game controllers such as the Nintendo Wii and the Razor Hydra as input devices for immersive modeling applications motivated us to develop custom hand-held controllers that combine a smartphone, full 6-DoF tracking and a casing with physical buttons (Fig 2).

We incorporated touch screens because they provide a rich dynamic interface that allows for higher bandwidth of input and output. In addition, they support both unseen touch interactions and the more traditional visual widgets for 1D and 2D interaction, informational readouts, numeric input etc. They allow for dynamic affordances, enabling a wide option of widget choices that can be more or less complicated depending on the task at hand. The touch screens also provide tangible steadying surfaces for fine manipulation, which is often an issue in pure spatial interaction.

The smartphone form factor was chosen because users could easily hold one in each hand (allowing for bi-manual interaction) and carry them wherever they went. In the early stages of our project, we experimented with a larger touch tablet for this purpose, but the size of the device and the necessity to hold it with one hand for interacting with the other proved to be limiting. Similarly, we considered a larger pen-based input device mounted on a wheeled platform. This would enable rich forms of interaction, but we found that the device was never where one wanted it to be when physically moving around in the VE.

We also tested skipping the physical buttons and just relying on the soft buttons for all of our interactions, but the loss of tactile feedback in addition to the attention required to visually locate buttons resulted in reduced focus and immersion. The physical buttons provide consistent access to system features that are tool agnostic and are constantly accessed throughout the application such as view and object manipulation, system control, and modifiers. By tools, we refer to the different class of actions within SketchUp such as the rectangle tool, circle tool etc. The number of buttons was deliberately kept low to minimize user confusion.

On extended use, ergonomics and shape of the device have proven to be critically important. The controllers were designed to be lightweight and to fit comfortably within a single hand. Additionally, since touch interactions have to happen with the thumb of the same hand that holds the HC, design changes were made to ensure that the thumb could reach as much of the touch screen as possible without much strain. Factors such as wrap around radius, angle of the physical button surface, angle at which the HC is being held at neutral position, size and resistance of the button, number of fingers dedicated for physical gripping, distribution of work load between fingers operating on physical buttons were all iterated upon through multiple revisions to arrive at a design that satisfies our needs. The HC still has issues related to unintentional touch screen presses when pushing physical buttons that we are continuing to work on. Other modalities that are available from a smartphone such as voice and gestural input were investigated and found to be more suitable for one-off operations; for more frequently used interactions, they were found to be either ambiguous or to slow down the interactions.

## Interaction Design Philosophy

Considering that our system is made up of multiple input and output mechanisms with varying levels of controls, we found it important to build the user experience based on certain design guidelines.

### Minimize energy

3D modeling by its nature calls for extended hours of design, iteration and modification. Therefore, conserving energy is important. Even though the user's head and hands are tracked, it is in our interest to design for minimum locomotion and physical exertion. Animated hand gestures could be used for virtual menu selection, but they will soon tire the user out. We restrict such frequent actions to the touch screen, where only small movements of the thumb are used to perform the same selection. Similarly, much of the user's energy is going to be spent in navigating from place to place if a system is designed such that objects can only be manipulated when within arm's reach. Therefore, we lean heavily towards action at a distance and image plane interaction techniques. Additionally, we provide quick access to most frequently used system controls and tools in order to reduce time spent in menu navigation.

We designed our system to be used in a comfortable seating posture in all display environments. The THI allows users to grab and pull the world towards them, essentially moving their viewpoint forward. The same action when performed alternately with two hands results in a movement that is akin to walking with two hands within the virtual world. That combined with THI's ability to rotate, scale and translate about the user helps reduce the need for physical locomotion. Also, wherever possible 2D touch alternatives are provided for spatial interactions.

### Maximize comfort

Issues of ergonomics and comfort play an important role in the success of any immersive modeling system. Due to the inherent limitations of the movement style and reach available for the thumb, the touch interfaces were correspondingly designed to work within these limitations. For example, widgets are typically placed within the area of the touch screen that is comfortably swept by the thumb; placements in regions that require extensive reach are avoided as much as possible. It was also observed that a simultaneous physical button press and touch screen interaction on the same hand resulted in some physical strain; as such these were avoided or used in a limited fashion. Instead, interaction patterns that required simultaneous use of physical and soft buttons were distributed across the hands such that one hand engages the physical button and the other engages the soft buttons.

### 3D spatial interaction for coarse input

3D spatial interactions are inherently intuitive for 3D tasks. Users do not need to have a mental map that translates 2D interactions to 3D in an awkward manner. On the contrary, spatial interactions are not a good fit for precision operations due to the lack of tangible support surfaces and the existence of superfluous degrees of freedom. We use 3D spatial input to achieve a coarse but intuitive starting step.

### 2D touch for precision input

2D touch interactions are very well suited for controls such as precision numeric input, textural input etc. We adapt the methodology of performing spatial work to achieve coarse results and then tweaking them with precise interactions on touch surfaces.

### Combine modalities and use what works

Every modality has its strengths and weaknesses. Our system is designed to combine multiple modalities in a manner that each modality is only utilized for controls for which they are naturally suited. For example, touch screens are great for selecting colors and textures but are not independently suited for view manipulation due to the differences in the number of degrees of freedom. Overall, depending on the task at hand, it is important to eliminate and avoid superfluous DoFs to achieve consistent mapping between user's interactions and output.

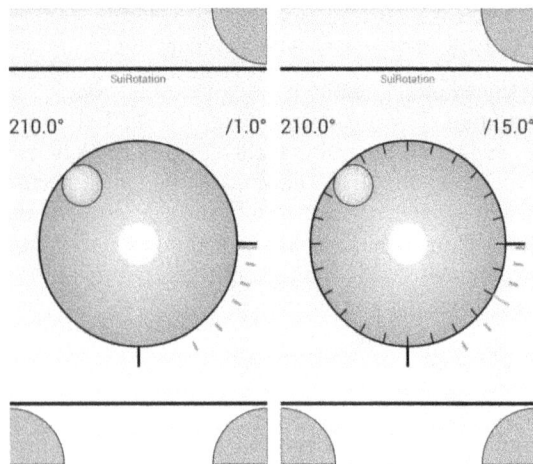

**Figure 3. Left: radial widget for setting the angle, Right: Precision modifier set to 15° interval between increments**

*Constrain yourself*

Great control comes with good constraints. The rotary dial in Fig 3 for example has additional controls around the outer edge of the dial that can be used to set the angle of increment and hence the precision of the operation. On the move tool interface (Fig 4), users can depress the record button to record the current vector between the two hands and use either that vector or the closest primary world axis as a constraint along which the object should move. Alternatively, they can use the constraint hot spot (see below) to constrain movement along the X, Y or Z axis.

*Preserve immersion (as much as you can)*

Preserving immersion and retaining focus and context on the current task at hand is crucial for immersive modeling. Therefore, it is important that the system's interactions divert the attention of the user away from the VE as little as possible. This being one of our top requirements, our system is designed such that menu navigation is represented by floating GUIs in the VE that are invoked by interactions on the touch surface that do not require the user to have to look down at them. Users only need to look at the touch screen for tool specific context menus.

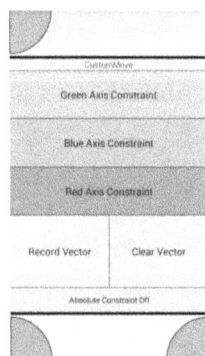

**Figure 4. Constraint options menu for the move tool**

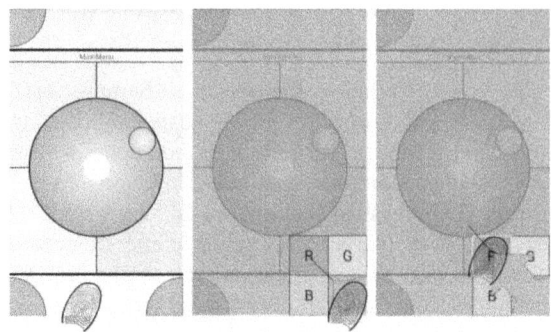

**Figure 5. Region surrounding menu dial broken into zones for quick access to certain menu levels. Corners of screens contain hot spots from where hot keys are evoked as marking menus**

*Capitalize on proprioception*

Human beings are very good at sensing the position of their body and remembering body relative information; we have tried to take advantage of this factor in our application design. For example, the area around the system control dial menu is divided into four hot zones that can be used to invoke frequently used menus (Fig 5). The user's sense of his or her hand position is usually all the user needs to select any one of these hot zones without looking at the touch screens.

*Use haptic feedback*

Within moments of holding the hand controller, the tactile feedback associated with the sides and the corners help one to uniquely identify and access them without the need for visual cues. To make use of this, our touch surfaces are divided into static and dynamic regions. The static regions lie at the corners of the screen (Fig 5) and remain in place throughout the application. They house hot spots, which when touched invoke marking menus with hot keys and system controls, such that one can access them without having to look down at the touch surface. For example in Fig 5, the user reaches to the right-bottom corner of the touch screen to touch a hot spot and slides across to activate a modifier via the marking menu. The farthest corners are usually not quickly reachable by the thumb and hence hot spots are avoided there. Hot spots provide a clean and intuitive way to add up to 3 modifiers or hot keys per corner without crowding the interface, yet taking full advantage of proprioception and haptic feedback. Similarly, using large touch buttons as modifiers (Fig 4) provides the advantage that once the user learns how to use them they are easy to remember spatially and can often be used without having to look down at the screens.

**System Control**

As shown in Fig 1, the system can be broken down to a head-tracked VR Display, and two touch-screen-enabled Hand Controllers. The GUI floating in the VE is controlled by touch interactions performed on the Hand Controllers. System interactions can be divided into 2 categories:

*Menu Navigation*

An important part of any application is the ability to navigate menus and select appropriate tools. In place of the traditional WIMP interface, system menus in VR SketchUp are represented as pie menus floating in the VE.

Users can invoke the menu navigation radial dial (Fig 5) by touching a dedicated hot spot on the top left corner of the touch screen that remains there all through the application. Instead of one tap for invoking the menu navigation page and another to start interaction with the dial, the interactions are programmed such that the user can start the touch on the hot spot and drag their thumb to the center of the screen. By the time their thumb reaches the center, the widgets would have changed to that of menu navigation dial, allowing a tap-drag-circle style interaction.

For menu navigation, touch screens are used as primarily unseen touch surfaces and users can fully rely on the visual feedback from the GUI floating in the VE for selection. The system displays a dial at the center of the non-dominant Hand Controller (ND-HC) touch screen that invokes the pie menu when touched and a large button on the dominant Hand Controller (D-HC) that can be used to either navigate

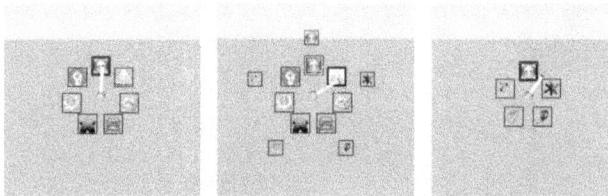

**Figure 6. Multi-level pie menu navigation; scroll to sub-menu option, preview menu level, and tap to enter**

to a different level in the menu hierarchy or to confirm tool selection (Fig 6). We find this to be a fast way to navigate, preview and select hierarchical menus while still preserving immersion. Furthermore, the region immediately surrounding the dial is broken down into quick access zones (Fig 5) that have specific menu levels assigned to them previously. When a user starts touch on one of these zones and slides into the dial, they are immediately taken to the assigned menu irrespective of their current state.

While the DISH with its 360° view facilitated placement of visual menu elements in almost any view direction, this was not the case with the more limited displays such as the Wall and the desktop monitor. Therefore, placement of floating GUI was constrained and configured differently based on the display in use.

*Context Menus*

Upon selecting a particular tool, the touch screens update to display the corresponding context menus that are used to specify and control parameters particular to the active tool. The dynamic nature of touch devices makes it possible to use a wide variety of 2D widgets to perform many different

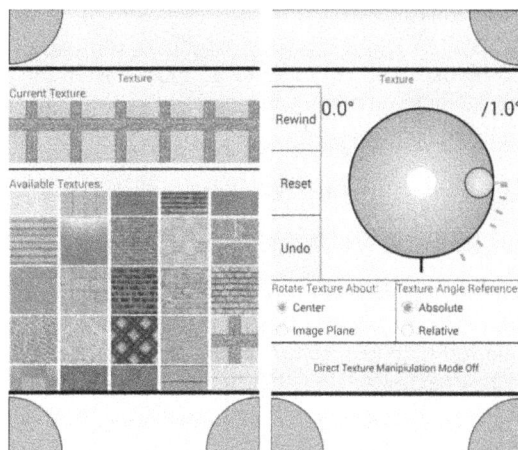

**Figure 7. ND and D screens for texture tool context menus.**

tasks such as: texture selection, numeric input, and color selection to name a few (Fig 7).

When a large number of 2D widgets are required to control a particular tool it becomes hard to fit them all in a single touch screen. In this case, the widgets are distributed across the touch screens on the two Hand Controllers. 2D widgets that require involved interaction are as much as possible retained on the D-HC, while the widgets that require coarse selection such as large modifier buttons are assigned to the ND-HC. The context menu for the texture tool (Fig 7) is a good example where the widgets can neatly be split across the screens, with the ND-HC focusing on texture selection and application, while the D-HC focuses on texture manipulation. The split across two screens also enables the simultaneous two-handed control of multiple parameters; the color selection context menu for example, has a hue widget on the ND-HC and a saturation and value widget on the D-HC. All three parameters can be adjusted at once.

In the case of complicated menus such as numerical input, splitting a tool's widgets across multiple screens would result in the user having to constantly shift their attention back and forth between the two Hand Controllers. In these situations, we split a tool's widgets across multiple layers on the D-HC instead (Fig 8). A modifying tap button on the ND-HC is used to switch between the two layers. Given

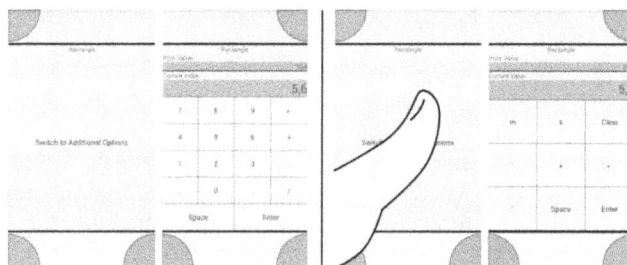

**Figure 8. ND and D screens for multi-layer context menus.**
**Left: Input layer before pressing modifier button.**
**Right: Popup layer after pressing modifier button.**

that the interactions with the touch screens are limited to the thumb, we find using these tap modifiers on the alternate hand to invoke a popup layer to be much faster and more convenient than swiping the screen with the thumb to go from one page to the other.

## Object Manipulation

There are three important ways in which objects can be manipulated within VR SketchUp:

- *Direct 6-DoF Manipulation* Where the user grabs objects within arm's reach and positions and rotates them in a manner similar to the real world. Scaling of the object can be achieved using bi-manual interaction. DoF constraints, rotational axes, and special behavior such as position-only manipulation are specified using the touch-screen interface.

- *Image Plane Interaction* Where movement of the user's hand within their field of view is mapped to screen space interactions. Note that the screen space is defined to be a rectangular region perpendicular to the user's current gaze direction. It roughly corresponds to the SketchUp active modeling window.

- *Track Pad Interaction* Where the user manipulates objects via a touchpad widget on the touch screen to emulate mouse interactions within the user's screen space.

VR SketchUp and the HC are in constant communication with each other, synchronizing information such as hand collision with virtual objects, screen space picking information and touch activity on the track pad. Using these, the application can identify which object manipulation mode the user is interested in working in and transition to it automatically.

In large virtual worlds, scene objects are often dispersed at various distances and directions. Physically or virtually moving to within arm's reach of an object every time one needs to interact with it is a tiring experience and often not practical for extended hours of interaction. Also, it is sometimes important to tweak an object's position and orientation while still needing to have the rest of the scene or other objects in context, making physical or virtual proximity to the object not an option. Therefore, image plane and other action-at-a-distance interaction techniques are essential for effective object manipulation. It is to be noted that our system leverages the benefits of mouse style input with image plane interactions but adds spatial input on top of that for additional expressiveness and control. World In Miniature style input was considered and experimented with, but proved to be less elegant to implement due to SketchUp's architectural limitations.

## SUI Tools

We developed several action-at-a-distance tools for the translation, rotation, and spatial arrangement of objects within the VE that take advantage of the colocation of 2D touch with 3D spatial user interaction (SUI) afforded by the application. We categorize them as SUI tools and we detail them here.

### Action Plane Widget

All of our SUI tools depend on a custom 3D widget called the Action Plane Widget (APW). The APW widget allows users to define the coordinate space in which the selected object is to be translated and/or rotated. Visually, the APW (Fig 9) consists of a 2D plane represented by a grid and a normal to the plane. The Center of Action (CoA) of the APW is defined to be the root of the plane's normal vector. The CoA as its name suggests, is the point about which all transformations are intended to happen. The user interacts with the APW using a combination of 6-DoF and image plane interactions with touch as a modifier.

To position the CoA the user pushes a dedicated physical button on the ND-HC and then uses 6-DoF or image plane interaction techniques to specify the exact location of the CoA within the scene. SketchUp's picking and inference mechanisms make it easy for users to snap the CoA to features of interest in the scene.

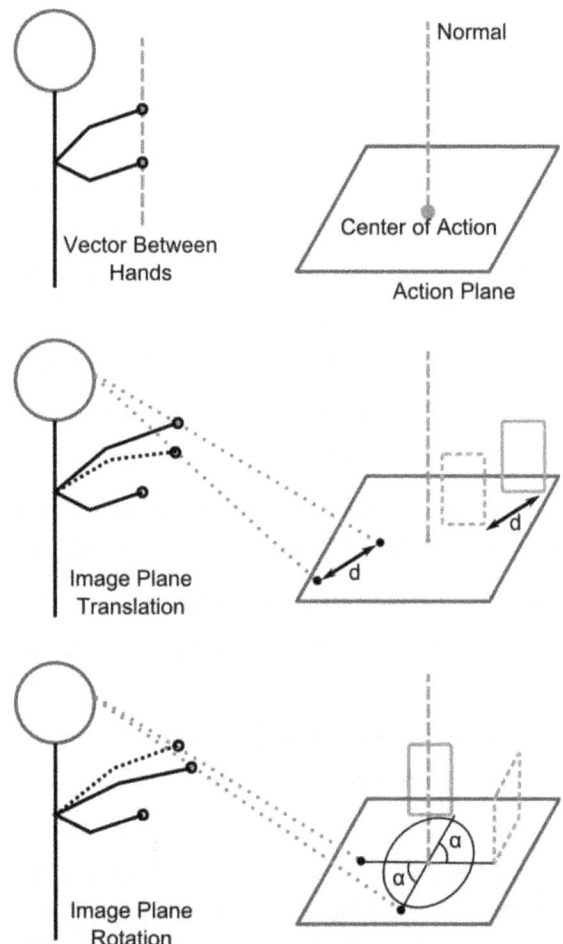

**Figure 9. Top: APW normal definition via bimanual spatial input, Middle: SUI translation, Bottom: SUI Rotation**

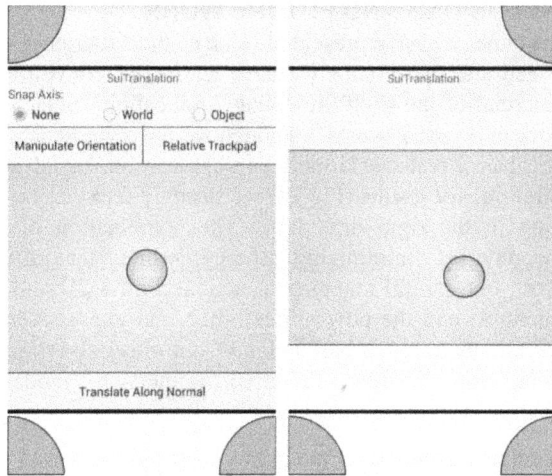

Figure 10. ND and D screens for SUI Translation tool

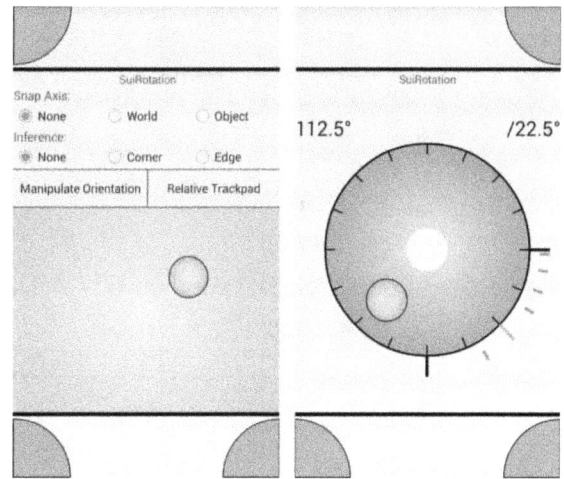

Figure 11. ND and D screens for SUI Rotation tool

The orientation of the APW is set when the user presses the "Manipulate Orientation" button on the ND-HC touch screen (Fig 10, 11 Left) and is defined by the vector between the user's two hands. (Fig 9 Top) The APW's orientation can be set freely or can be aligned relative to scene features such as a primary world axis, a primary object axis or any other feature in the scene. Radio buttons on the touch interface (Fig 11 Left) are used to control which types of inferences are currently active.

Using these techniques, one can define the APW transformation space in a very detailed manner, for example: CoA at the corner of one object in the scene, normal aligned to the edge of a different object; alternately, CoA at the corner of one object, normal aligned to a primary world axis and so on.

The CoA can also be manipulated using track pad interaction on the ND-HC (Fig 10, 11 Left). Interaction on the track pad moves the CoA correspondingly in the user's screen space. While using the track pad to place CoA within the user's screen space, the jitter from head tracking can significantly reduce the effectiveness of placement. We deal with this problem by temporarily suspending the update of screen space pose the moment the user touches the track pad. Note that this only suspends update of the screen-space interaction plane pose but does not suspend normal head tracking. If the user does not significantly stray from the pose of the head at the start of interaction this doesn't cause any problems. The tracking picks up again when the user's finger releases from the track pad's surface or when the user strays beyond a threshold.

### SUI Manipulation general strategy

To use the SUI tools one must first indicate the object to be manipulated using image plane interaction and select it using the physical action button on the D-HC.

Then, if necessary, the pose of the APW can be modified using the techniques described above, or the user can continue with the APW in its existing pose.

Once the pose of the APW is satisfactory, the user can employ either image plane interactions or the touch screen widgets (described below) to perform the desired manipulation. Typically, users begin with image plane interaction for coarse manipulation until the object is almost at the desired transformation and then switch to touch interaction to perform fine grain manipulations and adjustments until the precise effect is achieved

To ensure a consistent experience using the SUI tools we adopted the following strategy:

- Manipulation of the APW is performed by interactions initiated on the ND-HC

- Real object manipulation is performed by interaction initiated on the D-HC

### SUI Translation tool

Translation of the object happens either on the APW's plane or in another plane parallel to it. Translation can also happen along the normal to the APW plane. Image plane interaction for translation is relative as well, the distance between the start and end points of the image plane intersection point on the APW grid determines the distance by which the selected object is moved (Fig 9 Middle). The "Translate Along Normal" modifier (Fig 10 Left) can be depressed to make the object move along the normal direction to the APW plane. Projection of the vector from the user's head to his or her dominant hand onto the APW's normal defines the amount of vertical traversal of the object. Users can switch back and forth between translation along the plane and traversal in the direction of the normal seamlessly by simply depressing and releasing the Translate Along Normal modifier without breaking their interaction.

Additionally, users can also use the large 2D (Fig 10 Right) track pad widget on the D-HC to translate the object along the plane with respect to the user's screen space. We have found that differences in head orientation and the orientation with which users hold the touch screen can

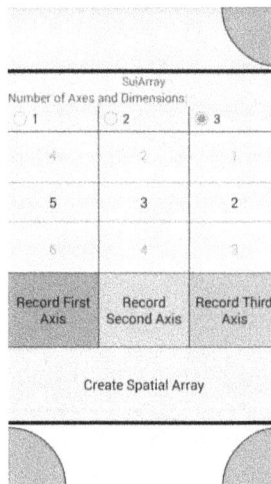

**Figure 12. D screen for SUI spatial array tool**

affect their perception of what is up-down-left-right and will on occasion provide less than satisfactory results.

*SUI Rotation tool*

Rotation of the object is relative to the APW normal. Vectors from the start and end points of the image plane intersection point on the APW grid with respect to the CoA define the angle of rotation (Fig 9 Bottom). The selected object is correspondingly rotated by the same amount with respect to the CoA. Similarly the radial menu on the D-HC touch screen (Fig 11 Right) can also be used to perform the same action.

*SUI Spatial Array tool*

Copying objects to form a 1D, 2D or a 3D array is a task that benefits greatly from a hybrid touch-SUI interface. As with the above tools, the user can first pose the APW about the point of interest. Then he or she can use the widgets on screen (Fig 12) to define the number of axes the array will have and the divisions on each of those axes. The user can then press the soft button that corresponds to the axis of interest and move his or her hand in space to redefine the direction of the axis while simultaneously pre-visualizing the arrangement of the copies (Fig 13). Once satisfied with the layout, pressing the confirm button actually creates the array.

**CONCLUSIONS AND FUTURE WORK**

In this paper we have presented some of the experiences we have had and the lessons we have learned in converting a commercial-of-the-shelf modeling application, SketchUp, to work in a virtual world. Though we have yet to achieve our goal of a real-world modeling application, based upon our preliminary results (Fig 14) we strongly feel that we are moving in the right direction. The combination of our philosophy of minimizing energy while maximizing comfort; our careful mapping of actions across 2D and 3D interactions; and the power, flexibility, and expressiveness of our bimanual touch-based Hand Controllers shows great promise for creating effective immersive modeling environments in the future.

Depending on the size of the user's hands, we observed that reaching the opposite corners of the touch screens proved difficult at times. We hope to alleviate this issue by using smaller smartphones. We also suffer from noticeable latency in button presses, since the communication is happening across Wi-Fi. We would like to experiment with other low latency wireless communication methods to resolve this issue.

We feel that we have just begun to explore the potential of the collocation of 2D touch with 3D spatial input. We continue to explore potential tools and interaction techniques that exploit their coexistence to the fullest. We continue to refine the design of our Hand Controllers, working to minimize user strain and maximize long-term use. We would like to further explore using tactile cues on the screen surface such as dots or thin transparent frames that can further our spatial understanding of our touch screens and help with unseen touch interactions.

**REFERENCES**

1. Butterworth, J., Davidson, A., Hench, S., & Olano, M. T. (1992, June). 3DM: A three dimensional modeler using a head-mounted display. In *Proceedings of the 1992 Symposium on Interactive 3D graphics* (pp. 135-138). ACM.

2. http://chromium.sourceforge.net/

3. Coffey, D., Malbraaten, N., Le, T. B., Borazjani, I.,

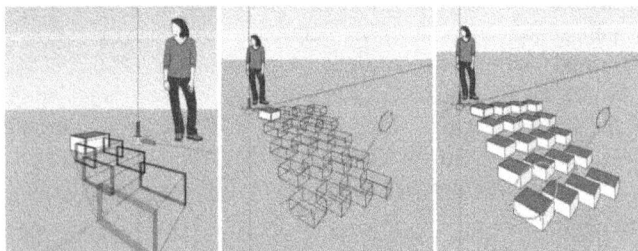

**Figure 13. SUI Spatial Array tool. Left: Set first axis and divisions. Middle: Set second axis and division. Right: Resulting array**

**Figure 14. Models created with VR SketchUp**

Sotiropoulos, F., Erdman, A. G., & Keefe, D. F. (2012). Interactive slice wim: Navigating and interrogating volume data sets using a multisurface, multitouch VR interface. *Visualization and Computer Graphics, IEEE Transactions on, 18*(10), 1614-1626.

4.  De Araùjo, B. R., Casiez, G., & Jorge, J. A. (2012, May). Mockup builder: direct 3D modeling on and above the surface in a continuous interaction space. In *Proceedings of Graphics Interface 2012* (pp. 173-180). Canadian Information Processing Society.

5.  Gebhardt, S., Pick, S., Oster, T., Hentschel, B., & Kuhlen, T. (2014, March). An evaluation of a smart-phone-based menu system for immersive virtual environments. In *3D User Interfaces (3DUI), 2014 IEEE Symposium on* (pp. 31-34). IEEE.

6.  Hughes, C. E., Zhang, L., Schulze, J. P., Edelstein, E., & Macagno CAVE. In *3D User Interfaces (3DUI), 2013 IEEE Symposium on* (pp. 193-194). IEEE. (2013, March). CaveCAD: Architectural design in the

7.  Jerald, J., Mlyniec, P., Yoganandan, A., Rubin, A., Paullus, D., Solotko, S., MakeVR: A 3D World-Building Interface. 3DUI 2013

8.  Mapes, D. P., & Moshell, J. M. (1995). A two-handed interface for object manipulation in virtual environments. *Presence: Teleoperators and Virtual Environments, 4*(4), 403-416.

9.  Marquardt, N., Jota, R., Greenberg, S., & Jorge, J. A. (2011). The continuous interaction space: interaction techniques unifying touch and gesture on and above a digital surface. In *Human-Computer Interaction–INTERACT 2011* (pp. 461-476). Springer Berlin Heidelberg.

10. Medeiros, D., Teixeira, L., Carvalho, F., Santos, I., and Raposo, A. 2013. A tablet-based 3D interaction tool for virtual engineering environments. In *Proceedings of the 12th ACM SIGGRAPH International Conference on Virtual-Reality Continuum and Its Applications in Industry* (VRCAI '13). ACM, New York, NY, USA, 211-218

11. Mine, M., "ISAAC: a meta-CAD system for virtual environments." *Computer-Aided Design* 29.8 (1997): 547-553.

12. Mine, M., and Yoganandan, A., "Building (Disney) Castles in the Air", Proceedings of Interactive Surfaces for Interaction with Stereoscopic 3D (ISIS3D), 2013.

13. Ni, T., McMahan, R. P., & Bowman, D. A. (2008). Tech-note: rapMenu: Remote menu selection using freehand gestural input. In *3D User Interfaces, 2008. 3DUI 2008. IEEE Symposium on* (pp. 55-58). IEEE.

14. Ponto, K., Tredinnick, R., Bartholomew, A., Roy, C., Szafir, D., Greenheck, D., & Kohlmann, J. (2013, March). SculptUp: A rapid, immersive 3D modeling environment. In *3D User Interfaces (3DUI), 2013 IEEE Symposium on* (pp. 199-200). IEEE.

15. http://www.presagis.com/

16. Rado, D., & Keefe, D. F. (2009, August). rAir flow menus: toward reliable 3D gestural input for radial marking menus. In *SIGGRAPH'09: Posters* (p. 26). ACM

17. Rashid, U., Kauko, J., Häkkilä, J., & Quigley, A. (2011, August). Proximal and distal selection of widgets: designing distributed UI for mobile interaction with large display. In *Proceedings of the 13th International Conference on Human Computer Interaction with Mobile Devices and Services* (pp. 495-498). ACM.

18. Schultheis, U., Jerald, J., Toledo, F., Yoganandan, A., & Mlyniec, P. (2012, March). Comparison of a two-handed interface to a wand interface and a mouse interface for fundamental 3D tasks. In *3D User Interfaces (3DUI), 2012 IEEE Symposium on* (pp. 117-124). IEEE.

19. Seifert, J., Bayer, A., & Rukzio, E. (2013). PointerPhone: Using Mobile Phones for Direct Pointing Interactions with Remote Displays. In *Human-Computer Interaction–INTERACT 2013* (pp. 18-35). Springer Berlin Heidelberg.

20. Song, P., Goh, W. B., Hutama, W., Fu, C. W., & Liu, X. (2012, May). A handle bar metaphor for virtual object manipulation with mid-air interaction. In *Proceedings of the 2012 ACM annual conference on Human Factors in Computing Systems* (pp. 1297-1306). ACM.

21. Steed, A., & Julier, S. (2013, March). Design and implementation of an immersive virtual reality system based on a smartphone platform. In *3D User Interfaces (3DUI), 2013 IEEE Symposium on* (pp. 43-46). IEEE.

22. Takala, T. M., Makarainen, M., & Hamalainen, P. (2013, March). Immersive 3D modeling with Blender and off-the-shelf hardware. In *3D User Interfaces (3DUI), 2013 IEEE Symposium on* (pp. 191-192). IEEE.

23. Wang, J., Leach, O., & Lindeman, R. W. (2013, March). DIY World Builder: An immersive level-editing system. In *3D User Interfaces (3DUI), 2013 IEEE Symposium on* (pp. 195-196). IEEE.

24. http://zspace.com

# T(ether): Spatially-Aware Handhelds, Gestures and Proprioception for Multi-User 3D Modeling and Animation

**Dávid Lakatos[1], Matthew Blackshaw[1], Alex Olwal[1,3,4], Zachary Barryte[1], Ken Perlin[2], Hiroshi Ishii[1]**

[1] Tangible Media Group, MIT Media Lab
Cambridge, MA, USA
{dlakatos, mab, olwal, zbarryte, ishii}@media.mit.edu

[2] Media Research Lab, NYU
New York, NY, USA
perlin@mrl.nyu.edu

a) Collaborative 3D manipulation and animation in the physical space.    b) Gesture space    c) VR viewport and pinch mapping

Figure. 1: a) T(ether) is a system for spatially-aware handhelds that emphasizes multi-user collaboration, e.g., when animating a shared 3D scene. b) Gestural interaction *above*, on the *surface*, and *behind* the handheld leverages proprioception and a body-centric frame of reference. (c) The UI provides a perspective-correct VR view of the tracked hands and 3D objects through the head-tracked viewport, with direct control through the spatial 3D UI.

## ABSTRACT

T(ether) is a spatially-aware display system for multi-user, collaborative manipulation and animation of virtual 3D objects. The handheld display acts as a window into virtual reality, providing users with a perspective view of 3D data. T(ether) tracks users' heads, hands, fingers and pinching, in addition to a handheld touch screen, to enable rich interaction with the virtual scene.

We introduce gestural interaction techniques that exploit proprioception to adapt the UI based on the hand's position *above*, *behind* or on the *surface* of the display. These spatial interactions use a tangible frame of reference to help users manipulate and animate the model in addition to controlling environment properties. We report on initial user observations from an experiment for 3D modeling, which indicate T(ether)'s potential for embodied viewport control and 3D modeling interactions.

## Author Keywords

3D user interfaces, Spatially-aware displays, Gestural interaction, Multi-user, Collaborative, 3D modeling, VR.

[3] KTH, Royal Institute of Technology, Stockholm, Sweden
[4] Google [x], Mountain View, CA, USA

## ACM Classification Keywords

H.5.2 User Interfaces: Interaction styles; I.3.6 [Methodology and Techniques]: Interaction techniques.

## INTRODUCTION

We are seeing an increasing amount of devices that have the capability for advanced context and spatial awareness thanks to advances in embedded sensors and available infrastructure. Recent advances have made many relevant technologies available in a portable and mobile context, including magnetometers, accelerometers, gyroscopes, GPS, proximity sensing, depth-sensing cameras, and numerous other approaches for tracking and interaction. Previous work has extensively explored the use of spatially aware displays, but primarily focuses on single-user scenarios and how the display's tracked position in the 3D space can be used to interact with virtual contents.

In this paper, we introduce T(ether), a prototype system that specifically focuses on novel interaction techniques for spatially aware handhelds. It leverages proprioception to exploit body-centric awareness, and it is specifically designed to support concurrent and co-located multi-user interaction with virtual 3D contents in the physical space, while maintaining natural communication and eye contact.

We report on initial user observations from our 3D modeling applications that explores viewport control and object manipulation.

## RELATED WORK

The concepts of using tracked displays as viewports into Virtual Reality (VR), as introduced by McKenna [8] and Fitzmaurice [4], has inspired numerous related projects.

### Spatially-Aware Displays

The Personal Interaction Panel [15] is a tracked handheld surface that enables a portable stereoscopic 3D workbench for immersive VR. Boom Chameleon's [16] mechanically tracked VR viewport on a counter-balanced boom frees the user from holding the device, but limits motion with mechanical constraints. Yee [17] investigates spatial interaction with a tracked device and stylus. Collaborative AR has been explored with head-mounted displays (HMDs) [14] and on mobile phones [6]. Yokokohji et al. [18] add haptic feedback to the virtual environment observed through a spatial display. Spindler et al. [13] combine a large tabletop with projected perspective-correct viewports. The authors present several interesting concepts but also describe interaction issues with their implemented passive handheld displays due to lack of tactile feedback, constrained tracking and projection volume, and limited image quality. T(ether) focuses specifically on supporting rich interaction, high-quality graphics and tactile feedback. We therefore extend the stylus, touch and buttons used in the above-mentioned projects, with proprioceptive interaction techniques on and around active displays that form a tangible frame of reference in 3D space.

### Gestural Interaction and Proprioception

Early research in immersive VR demonstrated powerful interactions that exploited 3D widgets, remote pointing and body-centric proprioception [3, 9, 11]. Advancements in tracking and display has allowed the use of more complex gestural input for wall-sized user interfaces (UIs), shape displays [8], augmented reality [10], and volumetric displays [5]. T(ether) emphasizes proprioceptive cues for multi-user interactions with unhindered, natural communication and eye contact.

### Multi-user Interaction

Related work on multi-user 3D UIs with support for face-to-face interaction [1, 5] focuses on workspaces with support for a small number of users, while T(ether) emphasizes a technical infrastructure to support large groups of users for room-scale interaction with full body movement for navigation.

### INTERACTION TECHIQUES

T(ether) extends previous work through an exploration of gestures that exploit proprioception to advance the interaction with spatially aware displays. By tracking the user's head, hands, fingers and their pinching, in addition to a handheld touch screen, we enable multiple possibilities for interaction with virtual contents. Head tracking relative to the display further enhances realism in lieu of stereoscopy by enabling perspective-correct rendering [8].

For body-centric, proprioceptive interaction, we use the tablet to separate the interaction into three spaces:

- *Behind.* Direct manipulation of objects in 3D.
- *Above.* Spatial control of global parameters (e.g., time).
- *Surface.* GUI elements, properties and tactile feedback.

The available functions in each of these spaces are mutually exclusive by design, and the switch between them is implicit. The view of the interactive virtual 3D environment is shown on the display when the user's hand is behind the tablet, while the GUI appears when the hand is moved above or in front of it.

We use a 6DOF-tracked glove with pinch-detection for 3D control and actuation in the spirit of previous work [10]. Our initial user observations indicate that pinch works well also in our system. Pinching an object maps to different functions based on whether the thumb pinches the index (select), middle (create) or ring (delete) finger (Figure 1c).

### Behind: Direct manipulation of virtual 3D shapes

*Create.* Pinching the middle finger to the thumb adds a new shape primitive. The shape is created at the point of the pinch, while the orientation defaults to align with the X-Y plane of the virtual world. The distance between the start and release of the pinch determines object size. When the user begins creating a shape, other entities in the scene (objects, hand representations and other users' positions) become transparent to decrease visual load and for an unhindered view of the current operation. T(ether) currently supports lines, spheres, cubes and tri-meshes.

*Select.* As the user moves their hand "behind" the screen, the "cursor" (a wire-frame box) indicates the closest entity, and allows selection of objects, or vertices of a mesh.

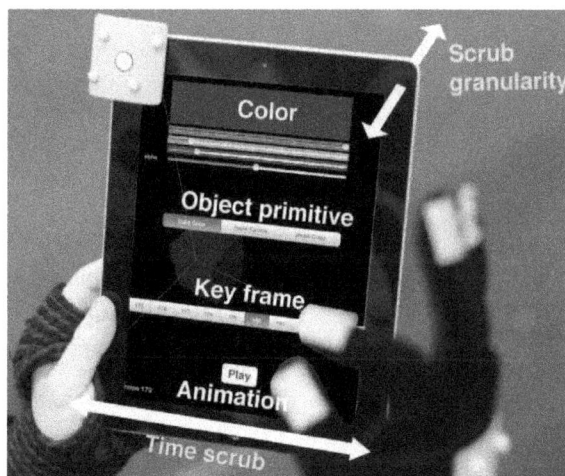

**Figure 2: T(ether) adapts the spatial UI for the most relevant interactions based on the location of the user's hand. In our 3D modeling and animation application, gestures for navigating time are available *above* (yellow) the display, while settings and GUI controls are available on its *surface* (white).**

*Manipulate.* After selection, the user can pinch the index finger to the thumb for 1:1 manipulation. Objects are translated and rotated by hand movement while pinched. Transformations are relative to the starting pinch pose. Users can select and manipulate vertices to deform meshes.

*Delete.* Pinching of ring finger and thumb deletes entities.

**Above: Spatial 3D parameter control**

A key-frame based animation layer built into our system allows users to animate virtual objects. Key frames are recorded automatically when a user modifies the scene. The user can animate an object by recording its position in one key frame, transforming it and moving the current key frame to match the desired duration of the animation. The user has access to the key frame engine through the pinch gesture above the screen, as shown in Figure 2.

The user can scrub through key frames by pinching the index finger and moving it left (rewind) or right (fast forward) relative to the tablet. The user can adjust the granularity of scrubbing by moving the pinched hand away from the tablet. By anchoring hand motions relative to the tablet, the tablet becomes a tangible frame of reference. Similarly to how the ubiquitous "pinch to zoom" touch gesture couples translation and zooming, we couple the time scrubbing and its granularity in order to allow users to rapidly and precisely control key frames.

**Surface: GUI and Tactile Surface for 2D Interaction**

*Object properties.* A UI fades in when the hand moves from *behind* to *above* the screen. Here, users configure settings for new objects, such as primitive type (cube, sphere or mesh cube) and color.

*Animation.* The 2D GUI also provides control over the animation engine and related temporal information, such as indication of the current key frame and scrubbing granularity. Users manipulate animation playback through different controls, such as the on-screen Play/Stop button.

*Annotation.* Freehand content can be draw on the tablet's plane and will be mapped to the virtual environment based on the tablet's pose [11]. The user can annotate the scene and create spatial drawings by simultaneously moving the tablet in space while touching the surface.

**IMPLEMENTATION**

Our handheld display software is implemented using C++ and the Cinder low-level OpenGL-wrapper with our custom Objective-C scene graph, to allow native Cocoa UI elements on Apple iPad 2 (600 g). We obtain the position and orientation of tablets, users' heads and hands through attached retro-reflective tags that are tracked with 19 cameras in a G-speak motion capture system (http://www.oblong.com/), covering a space of 14×12×9 ft. Our gloves use one tag for each finger and one for the palm. We enable capacitive pinch-sensing with a woven conductive thread through each fingertip.

Our server software is implemented in Node.js (http://nodejs.org/) and handles tag location broadcasts and synchronization of device activity (sketching, model manipulation, etc.) and wirelessly transmits this data to the tablets (802.11n). System performance is related to scene complexity, but in our experiences with user testing and hundreds of objects and multiple collaborators, frame rates have been consistently above 30 Hz.

**INITIAL USER OBSERVATIONS**

To assess the potential of T(ether), we conducted an experiment to explore its 3D modeling capabilities.

**3D Modeling**

*Participants.* We recruited 12 participants, 19–40 years old (3 females), from our institution that were compensated with a $50 gift card. All were familiar with tablets, 8 had used traditional CAD software, and none had experience with T(ether). Session lasted approximately 40-90 min.

*Procedure.* In a brief introduction (10–15 min), we demonstrated T(ether)'s gestural modeling capabilities. Once participants got familiar with the gestural interaction, we introduced them to the on-surface GUI for modifying object properties. Participants received training (15–30 min) in the Rhinoceros (Rhino3D) desktop 3D CAD software (http://www.rhino3d.com/), unless they were experts in it.

*Conditions.* Participants performed three tasks, first with T(ether) and then in Rhino3D. In the sorting task, participants sorted a random mix of 10 cubes and 10 spheres into two groups. In the stacking task, participants were instructed to create two cubes of similar size and stack and align them on top of each other. Then they repeated this task for 10 cubes. In the third task, participants recreated a random 3D arrangement of 6 cubes and 3 spheres with some of the objects stacked.

*Observations.* Participants were able to perform all functions in both interfaces. Using the body for "walking through data" was "a very appealing" approach to viewport manipulation and was considered easier than in traditional CAD. Some participants especially appreciated that they "regained peripheral awareness", since the "body is the tool" for viewport control. Shape creation and manipulation was generally "easy" and "straight-forward". They enjoyed the "unprecedented" freedom of the system, although some of them commented that the alignment relative to other objects was "tricky" and suggested inclusion of common features from traditional CAD, such as grids, snapping and guided alignment operations.

**Discussion**

Our experiment confirmed that with little training, participants could indeed perform basic 3D modeling tasks in our spatial UI. The observations especially highlight how participants appreciate the embodied interface and viewport control for navigating the 3D scene in the physical space.

While more complex 3D modeling would benefit from widgets, constraints and interaction techniques found in traditional CAD, we believe that the experiment illustrates the potential of spatially aware handhelds, as discussed in previous work [8, 4, 16], while leveraging modern, high-resolution widely available multi-touch displays, and a massively scalable infrastructure.

# LIMITATIONS AND FUTURE WORK

Our system is currently using an untethered tablet to support multi-user interaction and mobility. Similarly to previous work [8, 4, 15, 11, 17] and handheld mobile augmented reality systems, there is, however, a risk for fatigue when using a handheld device as a viewport and interaction surface. This could be of particular importance for 3D modeling scenarios, where participants may be expected to interact for extended time. We believe that these issues will be partially addressed through advances in hardware with increasingly lighter handhelds or by using projection surfaces [13]. Mid-air interaction can, however, also affect precision and the quality of interaction, issues that require additional investigation to assess their impact on our scenarios. THRED [12] indicates that carefully designed bi-manual mid-air interaction does not necessarily need to result in more pain or fatigue than a mouse-based interface. If mobility is not required, then counterbalanced mechanical arms could also be introduced [16].

In future work we would like to extend collaborative spatial modeling by integrating advanced functionality from Open Source tools like Blender (http://www.blender.org/) and Verse (http://www.quelsolaar.com/verse/). State-of-the-art software and hardware for location and mapping, e.g., Project Tango (https://www.google.com/atap/projecttango), are natural next steps to implement our techniques without infrastructure. Similarly, mobile depth cameras and eye tracking would enable improved perspective tracking and detailed shape capture of hand geometry. This could, e.g., enable more freeform clay-like deformation of virtual contents. Gaze tracking could also improve multi-user scenarios by rendering collaborators' field-of-view and attention. For improved feedback from virtual content, we believe that the passive feedback from the physical tablet surface could be complemented with techniques like TeslaTouch [2], instrumented gloves, and passive or actuated tangible objects in the environment. In fact, some of our study participants already used physical objects in the space for reference when placing and retrieving virtual content. Physical objects not only have the benefit of tactile feedback, but also improve legibility for collaborators with or without a personal T(ether) display.

We believe that much potential lies in further exploring massive collaborative scenarios with a large number of participants and complex scenes. Our network-distributed architecture would also make it straightforward to explore our techniques for remote collaboration scenarios, with distributed teams for various types of applications, such as architectural visualizations, augmented reality and virtual cameras for movie production.

# CONCLUSIONS

Today's interfaces for interacting with 3D data are typically designed for stationary displays that limit movements and interaction to a single co-located user. T(ether) builds on previous research for spatially aware handheld displays, but with an emphasis on gestural interaction and proprioception in its use of the display as a tangible frame of reference. T(ether) was also designed for multi-user, collaborative, concurrent and co-located spatial interaction with 3D data and focuses on technology that minimizes interference with human-human interaction.

# ACKNOWNALEDGMENTS

We thank the members of the Tangible Media group and the MIT Media Lab. Alex Olwal was supported by the Swedish Research Council.

# REFERENCES

1. Agrawala, M., Beers, A., McDowall, I., Fröhlich, B., Bolas, M., and Hanrahan, P. The two-user Responsive Workbench: support for collaboration through individual views of a shared space. Proc. SIGGRAPH '97, 327-332.

2. Bau, O., Poupyrev, I., Israr, A., and Harrison, C. TeslaTouch: electrovibration for touch surfaces. Proc. UIST '10. 283-292.

3. Bowman, D., and Hodges, L., F. An evaluation of techniques for grabbing and manipulating remote objects in immersive virtual environments. Proc. I3D '97, 35-39.

4. Fitzmaurice, G.W. Situated Information Spaces and Spatially Aware Palmtop Computers. Com. ACM (1993), 36(7), 38-49.

5. Grossman, T. and Balakrishnan, R.. Collaborative interaction with volumetric displays. Proc. CHI '08, 383-392.

6. Henrysson, A., Billinghurst, M., and Ollila, M. Virtual object manipulation using a mobile phone. Proc. ICAT '05, 164-171.

7. Leithinger, D., Lakatos, D., DeVincenzi, A., Blackshaw, M., and Ishii, H. Direct and gestural interaction with relief: a 2.5D shape display. Proc. UIST '11, 541-548.

8. McKenna, M. Interactive viewpoint control and three-dimensional operations. Proc. I3D '92, 53-56.

9. Mine, M. R. 1996. Working in a Virtual World: Interaction Techniques Used in the Chapel Hill Immersive Modeling Program. Technical Report.

10. Piekarski, W., Thomas, B. H. Through-Walls Collaboration. IEEE Pervasive Computing 8(3), 42-49.

11. Poupyrev, I., Tomokazu, N., Weghorst, S., Virtual Notepad: handwriting in immersive VR. Proc. VR '98. 126-132.

12. Shaw, C. Pain and Fatigue in Desktop VR. Proc. GI '98. 185-192.

13. Spindler, M., Büschel, W., and Dachselt, R. Use Your Head: Tangible Windows for 3D Information Spaces in a Tabletop environment. Proc. ITS '12, 245-254.

14. Szalavári, Z., Schmalstieg, D., Fuhrmann, A. and Gervautz, M. Studierstube: An environment for collaboration in augmented reality. Virtual Reality (1998), 3:37-48.

15. Szalavári, Zs,, Gervautz, M. The Personal Interaction Panel – a Two-Handed Interface for Augmented Reality. Computer Graphics Forum (1997), 16(3).

16. Tsang, M., Fitzmaurice, G, Kurtenbach, G., Khan A., and Buxton, B. Boom chameleon: simultaneous capture of 3D viewpoint, voice and gesture annotations on a spatially-aware display. Proc. UIST '02, 111-120.

17. Yee, K-P. Peephole displays: pen interaction on spatially aware handheld computers. Proc. CHI '03, 1-8.

18. Yokokohji, Y., Hollis, R. L., and Kanade, T. What you can see is what you can feel - Development of a visual/haptic interface to virtual environment. Proc. VRAIS '96, 46-53.

# RUIS – A Toolkit for Developing Virtual Reality Applications with Spatial Interaction

**Tuukka M. Takala**

Department of Media Technology, Aalto University

Otaniementie 17, 02150 Espoo, Finland

tuukka.takala@aalto.fi

## ABSTRACT

We introduce Reality-based User Interface System (RUIS), a virtual reality (VR) toolkit aimed for students and hobbyists, which we have used in an annually organized VR course for the past four years. RUIS toolkit provides 3D user interface building blocks for creating immersive VR applications with spatial interaction and stereo 3D graphics, while supporting affordable VR peripherals like Kinect, PlayStation Move, Razer Hydra, and Oculus Rift. We describe a novel spatial interaction scheme that combines freeform, full-body interaction with traditional video game locomotion, which can be easily implemented with RUIS. We also discuss the specific challenges associated with developing VR applications, and how they relate to the design principles behind RUIS. Finally, we validate our toolkit by comparing development difficulties experienced by users of different software toolkits, and by presenting several VR applications created with RUIS, demonstrating a variety of spatial user interfaces that it can produce.

## Author Keywords

3D user interface; software toolkit; Unity.

## ACM Classification Keywords

H.5.2 **[Information Interfaces and Presentation]**: User Interfaces – *Interaction styles (e.g., commands, menus, forms, direct manipulation)*; I.3.7 **[Computer Graphics]**: Three-Dimensional Graphics and Realism – *Virtual reality*.

## INTRODUCTION

In the past virtual reality (VR) applications were developed mostly by researchers and industry professionals, because the required hardware was expensive. This has changed with the advent of affordable display technology and inexpensive interaction devices, such as Kinect and Leap Motion, which have become available to consumers. The release of Oculus Rift head-mounted display (HMD) in

2013 attracted considerable public attention; over 50,000 units of the $300 developer kit have been sold [15]. The accomplishments of Oculus Rift has inspired other companies to bring forth VR peripheral devices like Virtuix Omni treadmill and Sixense STEM controller that were both successfully funded through Kickstarter crowdfunding campaigns. While it is too early to say how much traction these peripherals will gather, it is clear that this revolution in consumer VR is increasing interest towards spatial user interfaces.

Despite the advances in affordable hardware, the number of hobbyists developing VR and 3D user interface (3DUI) applications is still restricted by the difficulty of using unnecessarily complex software toolkits that have not been designed for the development of spatial user interfaces. Furthermore, the design and implementation of VR applications is ridden with unsolved issues [31], even with decades of virtual environment research behind us. With these issues in mind we have created Reality-based User Interface System (RUIS), a toolkit for developing VR applications with spatial user interfaces. Our main aspiration has been to make it easier for students and hobbyists to implement VR applications.

## BACKGROUND

For the past four years RUIS has been used in a VR course that we have been organizing annually in Aalto University. First we briefly describe our course, and then we list the challenges that affect VR application development.

### Virtual Reality Course

The students of our course focus on learning VR concepts and application development by building working VR applications in cross-disciplinary student groups, where the students can have varied backgrounds. The VR course is designed around a capstone project where each student group develops an interactive VR application with a 3DUI in 11 weeks of time. The group sizes have ranged from two to five students, who had the freedom to plan and implement any VR application of their choosing.

Our purpose has been to offer a holistic course that covers the whole VR application creation process from planning to implementation. We want students to experience different facets of VR application development, putting emphasis on those areas that are unique to VR applications – mainly immersion, virtual worlds, and 3DUIs. To facilitate this, we have provided our students with an access to immersive technologies: so far the VR applications have been intended to work in Aalto University's virtual environment, which has two stereo-walls. This environment has also been equipped with inexpensive 6-degrees-of-freedom (6DOF) controllers through all four years, a Kinect sensor in the last three years, and an Oculus Rift HMD in 2014.

Near the end of each course we have organized a public demonstration event where the student groups presented their VR applications and willing members of the audience could use them. In this paper we present some of the best student-created VR applications and their spatial user interfaces.

### Challenges in VR Development
Despite decades of research and advances in software engineering, VR application development remains difficult, as acknowledged by researchers: several papers extensively highlight the challenges in VR application development [23, 28, 31].

Firstly, development of a VR application involves many tasks and skills that are common with computer game development: building and testing a user interface through an iterative process, programming the application itself, using computer graphics knowledge and 3D mathematics such as 3D rotations (rotation matrices, quaternions), and finding or creating 3D models and other content to be included into the application. Each of these tasks contains challenges of their own. Secondly, there are also VR specific development challenges, such as taking advantage of novel display devices (e.g. stereo 3D projection walls) and employing novel input devices (e.g. motion tracked controllers),

Thirdly, VR applications commonly embody a 3DUI, where the user operates in a spatial 3D context [3]; this often involves tracking the 3D position and orientation of user's hands and head. This implies that, in contrast to developing 2D WIMP-interfaces (windows, icons, menus, pointer), 3DUI developers are missing high-level "building blocks" and established interaction metaphors [31]. This is especially unfortunate for novice 3DUI developers, who are forced into a low-level trial and error development process. Fifthly, novice developers usually have very limited experience of using 3DUIs, meaning that they struggle to imagine how a good 3DUI should function. In figurative terms we liken a novice developer's task of designing and implementing a 3DUI to that of using sheet metal to build an automobile without a blueprint or experience in driving.

Finally, testing of VR applications also has its issues: proper 3DUI testing is not automatable [31] and can only be conducted with the intended, full hardware setup. Often a developer team has access to only one such setup that contains the required VR peripherals. In these cases developers are limited to conduct user interface tests one at a time, and only at the location of the hardware setup. This

is a huge contrast to traditional user interface development, where practically any computer with a keyboard and a mouse can be used for testing the interface.

The above mentioned challenges strongly characterize VR application development. Students and hobbyists who develop VR applications face these challenges head-on and are commonly on their own when it comes to finding solutions. For some this is a daunting task. It is then up to the teacher to educate students about the intricacies of VR development, and help them navigate through the challenges.

### RUIS - VR SOFTWARE TOOLKIT
RUIS is a VR toolkit developed by us in Aalto University. This toolkit has been constantly developed during the four years that we have organized our VR course.

The name of RUIS and the philosophy behind it is inspired by a paper from Jacob et al. [9], who introduced "Reality-Based Interaction" (RBI), which is a conceptual framework for non-traditional interfaces involving the following themes: naïve physics, body awareness, environment awareness, and social awareness. The RBI themes influenced us to strive for a VR toolkit that enables developers to utilize a physics engine and full-body tracking in their VR applications.

RUIS grew out of our own frustrations with difficulties in VR development. Before its conception we had been developing VR applications for three successive years and witnessed several technical hurdles: interfacing with exotic VR devices and their equally exotic drivers, having to rely on low-level input data, issues with compiling software and linking programming libraries, idiosyncrasies of C++ programming language, etc. Senior staff members in our faculty had complaints about VR Juggler [2], a toolkit that had been used for several years in previous research. These experiences left us wanting for a VR toolkit with a *low barrier of entry*, which could be adopted with very little effort. This led us to create a list of requirements for such a toolkit:

R1. Developing applications is possible without any knowledge about compilers or linkers

R2. Development is possible with a normal PC or laptop

R3. Motion trackers can be simulated with a mouse and a keyboard

R4. Input devices are abstracted and high-level data is provided

R5. 3D selection and manipulation utilities are provided

R6. The toolkit is free

R7. Applications can be tested without a slow build process

R8. Applications can be easily exported to a different computer

We created RUIS toolkit to meet these requirements, with the purpose of simplifying VR application development. Our idea is to enable hobbyist developers to implement their VR concepts in a way where minimum effort is spent on coping with technical challenges related to hardware or development tools. Since most hobbyists and our VR laboratory have budgetary constraints, we had to build RUIS to support affordable, off-the-shelf hardware from the start.

The presence of requirements R1 – R6 makes it easier to get started with VR development. Requirement R7 ensures that a tight iterative development process is possible, and R8 eases the application testing and deployment. Getting started with VR development is very straightforward in the current version of RUIS: the application developer only needs to install Unity 3D game development software suite from an automatic installer, unpack RUIS package, and open one of our examples in the RUIS subfolders. The examples and any of their derivatives can be run simply by clicking a play button.

Not surprisingly, the above requirements are valuable in a toolkit also when teaching VR application development. Since our students had varied backgrounds, it was preferable to have a low barrier of entry into the domain of VR development; this applies for requirements regarding students' computer hardware (R2-R3) and technical knowledge about software compilation (R1) or 3D mathematics (R4-R5). Our requirement of being able to develop VR applications without any knowledge about compilers or linkers (R1) is quite strict, and as such this cannot be required from all VR toolkits. We agree with Burdea [4] that it is not practical for universities to pay for VR toolkit licenses (nor for hobbyists), and hence the requirement R6.

Portability (R8) helps the students to move the working copy of their project between their home computers and the ones in teaching laboratory, which in turn facilitates teamwork. In an ideal case it would be enough just to copy the latest working version from internet or a USB-stick, which could be run with a click of a button.

Some of our requirements tackle the VR application development challenges mentioned in the previous section. The 3D selection and manipulation utilities (R5) act as building blocks for a 3DUI, and motion tracker simulation (R3) enables rudimentary application testing even without the intended VR peripherals.

In 2010 when we started developing RUIS there were no VR toolkits that we were aware of, which would have had all of our desirable requirements R1-R8. According to our current review, there are four such VR toolkits besides RUIS: Bespoke 3DUI Framework [29] could have been of use in our 2011 VR course, but its development was discontinued in 2010 and it does not support hand-held 6DOF controllers or more recent input devices like Kinect or PlayStation (PS) Move. Studierstube [19] toolkit also satisfies our requirements R1-R8, but its developement was stopped in 2008. More recently we have become aware of two VR toolkits that are still being updated and fill all of our toolkit requirements: Instantreality framework [7] relies

on an extended version of the X3D markup language and enables VR application development with a text editor. OpenSpace3D[1] on the other hand provides a graphical editor interface, which is very similar to Unity 3D development environment in its appearance, and offers many equivalent features (e.g. physics engine, asset importing, and scripting). OpenSpace3D and the underlying Ogre3D game engine are open source, which has its benefits when compared to Unity and other proprietary platforms. Conversely, Ogre3D has a smaller online community than Unity, and in our subjective view OpenSpace3D is less powerful for application development.

There are multiple low-level toolkits like CalVR [20], VRPN [27], and FreeVR [22] that lack many of our requirements (R1, R5, R7, and R8). There are also a number of VR toolkits with high-level features (e.g. AVANGO [12], DIVERSE [10], and VR Juggler [2]), which involve a bothersome code compilation process (often with a multitude of library dependencies) either in the toolkit installation or application development phase, violating requirements R1 and R8. Then there are VR toolkits created by researchers, which are not available online, either because they have been abandoned or they have not been released publicly. Some such examples include ARTiFICe [14], DIVE [5], MR Toolkit [21], and VARU Framework [8]. Alice [16] was a VR toolkit that over the years has morphed into a 3D teaching tool for programming education, shedding support for spatial input devices or immersive displays in the process.

We know of several VR toolkits that require a license and are not freely available to our students: COVISE [17], CAVELib, EON Studio, getReal3D, TechViz, and WorldViz Vizard[2]. MiddleVR[3] is a promising commercial toolkit that has a free version, but developers are restricted to maximum of one stereo camera viewport and two VRPN trackers, which we found to be too limiting for our purposes. There is also H3D[4] toolkit, which is open source and focuses on haptic devices, but can act as a full-fledged VR toolkit when extended with its VR modules.

Vrui toolkit [11] supports many state-of-the-art VR peripherals and offers a high-level of abstraction, but application development with Vrui is confined to C++. As such it violates our requirements R1, R7, and R8. Table 1 presents a summary of how our VR toolkit requirements relate to the investigated toolkits that are available online and do not need a license.

---

[1] OpenSpace3D, http://www.openspace3d.com/

[2] CAVELib, http://www.mechdyne.com/cavelib.aspx
   Eon Studio, http://www.eonreality.com/eon-studio
   getReal3D, http://www.mechdyne.com/getreal3d.aspx
   TechViz, http://www.techviz.net
   WorldViz Vizard, http://www.worldviz.com

[3] MiddleVR, http://www.imin-vr.com/middlevr/

[4] H3D, http://www.h3dapi.org/

| VR Toolkit | R1 | R2 | R3 | R4 | R5 | R6 | R7 | R8 |
|---|---|---|---|---|---|---|---|---|
| AVANGO | | x | x | x | x | x | x | |
| Bespoke 3DUI Framework | x | x | x | x | x | x | x | x |
| CalVR | | x | x | x | | x | | |
| DIVERSE | | x | x | x | x | x | | |
| FreeVR | | x | x | x | | x | | |
| H3D | x | x | x | x | | x | x | x |
| Instantreality | x | x | x | x | | x | x | x |
| OpenSpace3D | x | x | x | x | | x | x | x |
| RUIS | x | x | x | x | | x | x | x |
| Studierstube | x | x | x | x | | x | x | x |
| VR Juggler | | x | x | x | x | x | x | |
| VRPN | | x | x | x | | x | | |
| Vrui | | x | x | x | x | x | | |

**Table 1. Freely available VR toolkits and how they match our toolkit requirements R1-R8.**

## RUIS for Processing

RUIS toolkit evolved from a collection of code that we were using when developing simple VR applications for our university's virtual environment. At the time we used Processing, which is a free, easy-to-use computer graphics development environment for designers and artists [18]. Processing offers a simple integrated coding environment for creating applications that can be run just by pressing a play button in the editor. According to Zagal and Sharp's 2011 survey, 8.3% of game development capstone courses used Processing as one of the toolkits [32].

In 2011 the students of our VR course used an early version of RUIS for Processing that relied on a custom, camera-based motion tracker that followed the position of the user's head and two hand-held Nintendo Wiimotes with LEDs attached to them [25]. Essentially these modified Wiimotes acted as 6DOF controllers. In the 2012 course we launched a new version of RUIS for Processing, where the Wiimotes were replaced with PS Move controllers and our custom motion tracker was substituted with a PS Eye camera.

## RUIS for Unity

Unity 3D is a widely used game development software suite behind popular games such as Bad Piggies, Kerbal Space Program, and Temple Run. It has also gained traction among VR researchers [1, 30]. In the survey conducted by Zagal and Sharp, 55.6% of game development capstone course instructors reported that Unity 3D was used as one of the toolkits [32].

After the 2012 course we realized that Processing is not an ideal platform for developing VR applications: it was very slow at rendering real-time 3D graphics, and it did not have a scenegraph, an integrated physics engine, an ingrained audio engine, a thorough 3D programming library, or a built-in 3D model importer. This forced students to work at a very low level when it came to 3D content, which took time and effort at the expense of building more immersive interfaces and virtual worlds. We got past these problems

by porting RUIS to Unity 3D, which is very fast at rendering graphics, offers the above-mentioned features that are missing from Processing, and contains a powerful development environment that is easy to use. Content, scripts, and game objects can be created, modified, and duplicated within Unity Editor's drag and drop interface. And just like in Processing, applications can be run by clicking a play button.

Unity 3D is available as a Pro version that costs $1500 (more affordable academic licenses also exist) and as a Free version that lacks the more advanced features like shadows. It is not necessarily imperative for students or hobbyists to purchase the commercial Unity Pro version, because the Free version can be used indefinitely and it is enough for many VR and game development purposes. In 2013 and 2014 students of our course used RUIS for Unity, which at the time supported Kinect and PS Move controllers, as well as different stereo 3D displays. Oculus Rift support was added for the 2014 course.

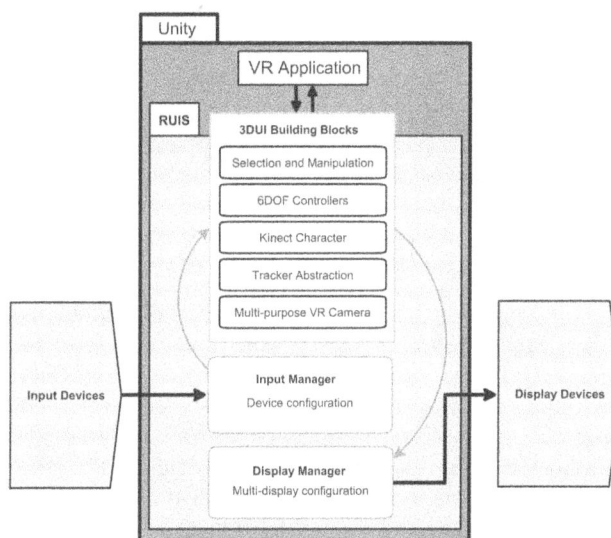

**Figure 1. Outline of RUIS for Unity toolkit architecture, where arrows depict data flow.**

A general outline of RUIS for Unity is illustrated in Figure 1, which shows the coupling of RUIS' internal components, and how RUIS relates to input and display devices. From a software architecture point of view, RUIS is implemented on top of Unity software. For developers RUIS is just like any Unity add-on, and developing a VR application is no different from developing a normal Unity application. Using components of RUIS, the VR developer assigns 3D displays and VR input devices that the application relies on, and creates a 3DUI with Unity's graphical editor interface. RUIS for Unity provides the developer with specialized editors for input and display management, as well as scripts and *prefabs* that act as 3DUI building blocks. In Unity's vocabulary prefabs are prefabricated templates of objects that can contain any number of custom components, and which can be easily included to scenes or instantiated in real-time.

Unity applications, and therefore RUIS applications, run in a single thread where function invocation order is deterministic and can be easily changed. Generally speaking, every Unity application has a main loop that updates all scene objects and runs one update-iteration of developer's scripts before rendering a new frame of graphics. At each main loop iteration, before executing other scripts, RUIS fetches the most recent input device states and stores them into corresponding RUIS' input abstractions that can be read at any time by custom scripts. A RUIS developer would need to get involved with event-handling only if they modify RUIS' selection and manipulation scripts, where different behavior can be invoked depending on the input device state. However, in many cases it is sufficient to use Unity's graphical editor interface to add RUIS prefabs and adjust their settings, when implementing typical VR application functionality.

*3D User Interface Building Blocks*
Our interest lies in such spatial user interfaces, where full-body tracking is combined with hand-held 6DOF motion controllers. In order to facilitate the development of such hybrid interfaces, RUIS supports the use of Kinect and PS Move together in the same coordinate system regardless of the sensor locations, as long as their tracking volumes intersect. This is achieved via a simple calibration procedure, where a PS Move controller is moved in front of Kinect and PS Eye sensors. The calibration needs to be performed only once as its results are saved in an XML-file.

In our experience PS Move controllers complement Kinect's motion capture perfectly: they are very precise and responsive in conveying 6DOF input data, whereas Kinect tracking suffers from high latency, inaccuracy, and noticeable spatial jitter. Tracking of the user's body can be utilized for controlling an avatar in a virtual world, which increases the awareness of body and environment, two of the themes emphasized in the RBI framework by Jacob et al. [9]. The motion data from Kinect – even with its shortcomings – is well-suited for establishing coarse-grained spatial relations in actions such as pointing, gesturing shape, or performing other continuous gestures.

Hand-held controllers are appealing, because most humans are naturally accustomed to using hand tools. They also provide greater tracking accuracy with less latency than inexpensive full-body tracking devices such as Kinect. Additionally, hand-held controllers are equipped with buttons that offer multiple benefits when compared to issuing commands via gesture recognition: buttons allow instantaneous and error-free signaling with haptic feedback.

We have implemented several 3DUI building blocks into RUIS in order to ease the creation of spatial interfaces that simultaneously employ full-body tracking and hand-held motion controllers. These building blocks are presented in the subsequent sections.

*Wand Controllers*
At the moment RUIS for Unity supports the following hand-held controllers: 2D mouse, PS Move, and Razer Hydra. These devices are abstracted as 6DOF wand controllers that can be accessed via scripts or prefab objects. The two-axis input of a 2D mouse can be augmented with simulated input to cover for the missing four degrees of freedom if necessary. Individual body parts tracked with Kinect can also be chosen to represent 6DOF wand controllers, in which case a holding gesture can be used to signify controller button signals. RUIS converts the location and rotation input data of the supported devices, so that their units of measure and axis directions are congruent with each other.

The wand controllers in RUIS come equipped with basic components for developers to create their own 3DUIs. The most important component is a ray-based selection algorithm, which detects when a ray cast from a wand controller intersects with the nearest 3D item that is defined as selectable. Developers can define any number of selectable item archetypes with RUIS, and program them with custom behaviors that are invoked in any of the five stages of item selection:

S1.　Selectable item is unselected

S2.　Selecting wand is pointing at unselected item

S3.　Selection button is pressed down and item becomes selected

S4.　Selection button is being held down and item is selected

S5.　Selection button is released and item becomes unselected

The default selectable item behavior in RUIS is for the item to follow the location and rotation of the wand that selects it during selection stage S4. Several predefined 3D item manipulation schemes can be chosen by the developer from the graphical menus of RUIS for Unity, from affecting absolute or relative pose of the item, to attaching the item to the selection ray, like a marshmallow is attached to the end of a stick.

*Kinect Controlled Avatar*
RUIS for Unity contains a versatile Kinect character prefab that we have designed specifically for avatar control. We have named the prefab as *MecanimBlendedCharacter*, because it embodies an interface for developers to control how a humanoid avatar is animated by blending Kinect's real-time motion tracking data with predefined skeletal animation clips using Unity's Mecanim animation system. Developers are free to substitute RUIS' default 3D model and its animations with any humanoid 3D model and skeletal animation clips of their choosing. Real-time Kinect measurements are used to pose and scale the 3D model's body parts in order to match them with the dimensions of the user's body. Avatars implemented with MecanimBlendedCharacter can be included in Unity's physics simulation, and hence the avatar can step down or drop from high places, push or kick objects, and even climb on objects.

All major limbs of the avatar have motion source blending weights that can be controlled via scripts. This makes it possible, for example, for the avatar to be fully Kinect controlled until a hand-held controller button is pressed to move it forward, animating only the legs with a walking animation clip, while keeping rest of the body under Kinect control. In fact, this is how the default MecanimBlendedCharacter of RUIS behaves when a user is tracked with Kinect while controlling the avatar's locomotion via a keyboard, a gamepad, a Razer Hydra, or a PS Navigation controller.

The locomotion controls also allow strafing, turning, sprinting, and jumping. The RUIS' avatar locomotion controls are identical to that of modern video games, as far as MecanimBlendedCharacter's hand-held controller scheme is concerned.

As a whole, our avatar prefab allows hybrid locomotion: if the application user moves within Kinect's tracking range, the virtual avatar moves accordingly. Thus, users can walk, turn, sidestep, crouch, jump, peak around a corner, interact with virtual objects, and perform any human motions, as long as they stay in the view of Kinect, and their avatars will faithfully follow suite. If the user needs to walk further than the range of Kinect allows, then a hand-held controller can be used to make the avatar run, walk, or perform other actions. We hypothesize that many players will prefer this locomotion scheme over omnidirectional treadmills in those full-body action games where traveling distances are several kilometers, simply because walking such lengths is physically exhaustive and quickly becomes tedious.

Multiple MecanimBlendedCharacter prefabs can be used simultaneously, both for first- and third-person view schemes. Positional tracking for Oculus Rift is supported in RUIS by Kinect's skeletal tracking, or by attaching a Razer Hydra or PS Move controller to the HMD. Alternatively, any device that can supply positional tracking data to Unity can also be utilized. The MecanimBlendedCharacter prefab's scripts automatically choose the best positional tracking device after running the application, based on which devices are enabled in RUIS. Since Oculus Rift and Razer Hydra are not wireless, they need to be equipped with extension cords when used in conjunction with Kinect.

*Multiscreen Stereo 3D Rendering*
In RUIS it is simple to configure a heterogeneous collection of display devices consisting of mono and stereo projectors, LCDs, and HMDs in any spatial configuration, whether they are part of a professional cave automatic virtual environment (CAVE) system [6] or a home VR setup. The only limitation is rendering speed; distributed rendering is not currently supported. For stereo 3D displays, side-by-side and top-and-bottom modes are incorporated. Oculus Rift HMD is also supported in RUIS for Unity, and can be used as an additional "screen" along other displays.

In order to correct projectors' keystone effect, RUIS supports keystone calibration, where the developer drags each rendered viewport corner to the corresponding physical corner of the projector's silver screen. The correction is achieved through calculating a modification for each corrected view's projection matrix, as described by Lancelle et al. [13]. Keystone correction calibration data is saved to a separate XML-file for each viewport, and the calibration needs to be performed only once. An example of a 4-wall CAVE's rendered frame with keystone correction is presented in Figure 2.

**Figure 2. A panoramic view from a RUIS application with projector keystone corrections for a 4-display CAVE setup**.

*Head-tracked Off-axis Perspective Projection*
Displays in RUIS can be designated as CAVE-displays, where information about each display's spatial location and the user's tracked head pose is utilized to calculate off-axis perspective projection for all the viewports. DisplayManager of RUIS performs this calculation in a similar fashion to what Cruz-Neira et al. did with their CAVE [6], but a more complex procedure is required due to the arbitrary display configurations and simultaneously applied keystone correction.

Figure 2 illustrates how the off-axis perspective projection behaves when the application user's tracked head gets close to display walls: The two views in the middle have a pronounced projective distortion, and the rendered virtual world proportions remain correct in the eyes of the user as he approaches the corner between the walls.

**RESULTS**

**Comparison of Toolkit Difficulties**
In order to compare RUIS for Processing and RUIS for Unity to other VR toolkits, we utilized data from a 3DUI questionnaire that we have used in the past for surveying 3DUI applications [26]. For this paper's toolkit comparison, we chose three subsets of participants from a total of 140 people who had answered the survey between 2011 and 2014: 26 were our students who had used RUIS for Processing, 45 were our students who had used RUIS for Unity, and 17 participants had independently found the questionnaire and reported using other high-level software toolkits. In the latter subset four participants had used Vizard, three Studierstube, three VR Juggler, and seven participants were sole users of Bespoke 3DUI Framework,

CAVElib, DIVERSE, EON SDK, MiddleVR, OpenSpace3D, and Virtools.

Answering the 3DUI questionnaire was mandatory for the students of our VR course. After deciding course grades, we emailed the students a link to the questionnaire, explaining that the grades had been decided and that they would not be revealed until everyone had answered the questionnaire. The purpose of this was to try to get as objective answers as possible from the students, by letting them know that their answers could not affect their grade, and by preventing each student's knowledge about their grade to affect their answers.

The 3DUI questionnaire participants rated a number of statements regarding 3DUI application development difficulties on a seven point Likert scale (where 1 indicated strong disagreement and 7 indicated strong agreement), basing their ratings on the experience of developing a 3DUI application. Each statement was constructed in a way where a higher rating signifies that more difficulty was experienced. The following 10 statements of our 3DUI questionnaire were used to compare the toolkits:

D1. Getting input device drivers to work was difficult

D2. There were too many steps required between connecting the input device for the first time and successfully streaming data from the device into my application

D3. Device input data was too low-level for quickly getting started with my 3DUI application

D4. Lack of documentation or tutorials about the 3DUI toolkit made the development difficult

D5. The 3DUI toolkit had a steep learning curve

D6. The development was difficult because the 3DUI toolkit had a bad programming interface

D7. There were bugs in the 3DUI toolkit that I used for developing my 3DUI application, making the development difficult

D8. Lack of proper 3DUI building blocks made it difficult to develop my 3DUI application

D9. Each added 3D interaction feature increased application complexity, making the development difficult

D10. Testing of the application's 3DUI could not be carried out properly with just mouse and keyboard, making the development difficult

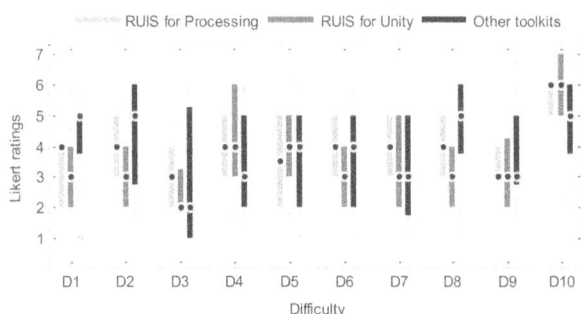

Figure 3. Severity of development difficulties in VR application development (boxplot of Likert ratings).

Figure 3 presents the above statements' Likert ratings from questionnaire participants who used different toolkits. Statistically significant differences were found with a Kruskall-Wallis test in ratings of statements D6 ($\chi^2(2)$ = 10.2, p = 0.006) and D8 ($\chi^2(2)$ = 8.3, p = 0.016). Post-tests with Tukey-Kramer correction revealed that statement D6 was rated significantly less severe by RUIS for Unity developers than RUIS for Processing developers, and statement D8 was rated significantly less severe by RUIS for Unity developers than by the 17 developers who had used other high-level toolkits.

### TurboTuscany

We created TurboTuscany [24] VR game with RUIS for Unity, to demonstrate our spatial user interface ideas in action; the game contains both the Kinect controlled full-body avatar with hand-held 6DOF controllers and our hybrid locomotion scheme, where the avatar can be moved by walking within Kinect's tracking range or by directional buttons of the hand-held controllers. The demo has a first-person perspective and it is meant to be viewed with Oculus Rift. Because of the full-body Kinect tracking, the user can look down in the virtual world and see his virtual body match the pose of his real body, as illustrated in Figure 4.

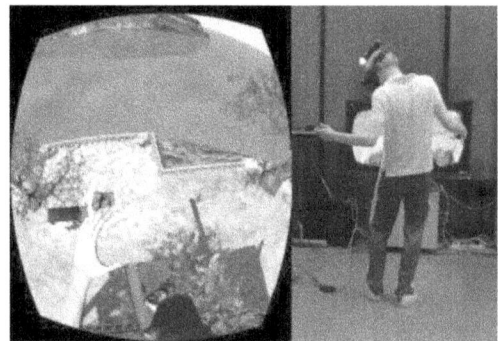

Figure 4. TurboTuscany demo from the user's point of view (left) and behind the user (right).

At the core TurboTuscany is a sandbox demo for experiencing a virtual avatar's interactions in a virtual world. The Kinect tracked avatar reflects the user's actions, who can play with soccer balls, hit a punching bag, manipulate and stack objects, climb a ladder, swing at balls with a baseball bat, and walk on top of a giant circus ball. PS Move and Razer Hydra controllers can be used for grabbing and manipulating objects with precision. All the aforementioned actions utilize Unity's physics engine. A video[1] of TurboTuscany, as well as the demo[2] itself, are available online.

### Student-created VR Applications

In the four years that we have been organizing our VR course, 71 students have taken part in the creation of 22 VR applications. Next we describe our personal top six of those applications, highlighting their differences both in terms of

---

[1] http://youtu.be/wMEaJWsowfQ

[2] http://blog.ruisystem.net/download/

using immersive technologies, as well as their qualitative nature. Table 2 summarizes the six applications, listing their course year, name, features, and the included spatial interaction. Each listed feature and form of spatial interaction was implemented using RUIS.

| Year | Application | Features | Spatial interaction |
|------|-------------|----------|---------------------|
| 2011 | Room Planner | • stereo 3D<br>• 1st-person view<br>• head-tracking | • two-handed 3DUI<br>• 6DOF object manipulation |
| 2012 | Air Supremacy | • stereo 3D<br>• 3rd-person view<br>• multiuser application | • two-handed 3DUI<br>• 3DOF shooting |
| 2013 | Cutout Duel | • stereo 3D<br>• 3rd-person view<br>• multiuser application | • full-body interaction<br>• "laser cutting" |
| 2014 | Wheelchair Champion | • stereo 3D<br>• 1st-person view<br>• head-tracking | • two-handed, tangible 3DUI<br>• upper-body interaction |

Table 2. Summary of the selected VR applications created by students with RUIS.

The six applications' success was reflected in the audience participation and interest during the courses' public demonstration events where they were presented. Names of the VR applications have been changed to provide better anonymity for our students. We encourage our readers to see a compilation video[1] of our students' VR applications from 2013, for acquiring a more complete understanding of the spatial interfaces incorporated in the applications.

Figure 5. Room Planner, 2011.

*Room Planner*
Room Planner application created in the 2011 VR course (Figure 5) provided a two-handed interface with a head-tracked stereo 3D view, where the user could choose pieces of furniture from a drop-down 3D menu and place them into a 3D scene. The student group behind the application created a powerful 3DUI where one Wiimote was used to control the viewpoint while the other was used to manipulate the furniture. Nearly all of the buttons on the two Wiimotes were mapped to different commands in the application interface. The application used audio very scarcely, but it utilized several 3D models of furniture that

the two-person group had acquired from internet. We felt that Room Planner worked very well, and that with relatively little extra work the students could have expanded it into a research project or a prototype for an interior design company.

Figure 6. Air Supremacy, 2012.

*Air Supremacy*
In 2012 VR course a group of students created a game called Air Supremacy (Figure 6 ), where one student used two PS Move controllers to fly a warplane through an obstacle course of hoops, while another student acted as a gunner who shot down enemy planes with a third controller attached to a rifle peripheral. The warplane was maneuvered by altering the pitch angle of the two PS Move controllers and by changing their positions. Throttle of the warplane could be adjusted via two buttons. The gunner could feel the kick of the rifle through the controller's rumble motor that was activated upon shooting. Both the terrain 3D model and the obstacle course path were randomly generated on each run of the game. The intuitive flight controls of the warplane did have some bugs, but overall Air Supremacy was fun to play and pleasant to look at. The game employed 3D models and textures acquired from internet, and it was the best looking application from all the applications created with RUIS for Processing in 2011 and 2012.

Figure 7. Cutout Duel, 2013.

*Cutout Duel*
The Cutout Duel game from 2013 (Figure 7) was a competitive third-person action game for two, where the

---

[1] http://youtu.be/Ptq9F1nnUaI

players used PS Move controllers to draw a hole for each other on an opposing wall. The wall would then start moving towards the players, who had to pass through the holes without their Kinect-controlled avatars touching the wall. Winner of each round was the player who passed through the hole that their adversary had drawn, as well as the hole of their own creation. While the Cutout Duel had simple gameplay mechanics, it was fun to play and gathered the most volunteer players from the audience in the 2013 VR course's live demonstration event.

Figure 8. Wheelchair Champion, 2014.

*Wheelchair Champion*
In Wheelchair Champion game of 2014 (Figure 8) the player sat down on a real, manual wheelchair that was lifted from the ground, and wore a position tracked Oculus Rift HMD with a PS Move attached to it. The player assumed the first-person view of a Kinect-controlled avatar bound to a virtual wheelchair, which was maneuvered by physically rotating the real wheelchair's wheels that each had a PS Move controller bound to them. The object of the game was to roam around a virtual town, collecting treasures while fending of enemies with a baseball bat, which was represented by another PS Move controller that was tracked in 6DOF. Since Wheelchair Champion was a single player HMD game, we used the stereo 3D walls only for displaying the game to the audience in the VR course's live demonstration event. There were no buttons to be pressed in the user interface: the physical wheelchair acted as a tangible interface to the virtual wheelchair, which was programmed to be more agile and faster than a real wheelchair ever could. The idea was to empower the player who could cruise at high speeds around the town, rooftops of buildings, and the surrounding nature.

**CONCLUSIONS**
In this paper we have discussed the range of challenges that are specific to developing VR applications with spatial interaction. We introduced RUIS toolkit, which we have created to address those challenges and to simplify VR application development for students and hobbyist developers. We described the principles behind RUIS, its 3DUI building blocks, and presented example VR applications that have been created with it, demonstrating the toolkit's capabilities for developing spatial interfaces.

We statistically analyzed development difficulty statement ratings from 88 3DUI application developers, finding evidence to our subjective assessment that porting RUIS from Processing to Unity has improved the VR application development experience for our students. Furthermore, RUIS did not fare any worse when compared to a group of other high-level VR toolkits; in fact RUIS for Unity was rated as significantly better when it came to difficulties caused by lack of 3DUI building blocks.

Our hybrid locomotion scheme that is implemented in RUIS allows 3DUIs where traditional, effortless video game locomotion is combined with unrestricted human motion within the range of a full-body tracker such as Kinect. This offers an alternative to omnidirectional treadmills where the user is restricted by safety harnesses, and also for desktop VR where the user is sitting down.

According to our preliminary tests with a Kinect 2 sensor's hand tracking, hand-held controllers like PS Move and Razer Hydra are still more responsive, accurate, and better suited for precision tasks than purely non-invasive motion trackers. We believe that the combination of full-body motion trackers and hand-held 6DOF controllers have their place in spatial interfaces, as long as haptic feedback cannot be induced remotely with sufficient plausibility. In the future we plan to provide developers with more responsive and accurate full-body tracking by implementing Kinect 2 support for RUIS.

**REFERENCES**
1. Bednarz, T.P., Caris, C. and Dranga, O. 2009. Human-computer interaction experiments in an immersive virtual reality environment for e-learning applications. *20th Annual Conference for the Australasian Association for Engineering Education, 6-9 December 2009: Engineering the Curriculum* (2009), 834.
2. Bierbaum, A., Just, C., Hartling, P., Meinert, K., Baker, A. and Cruz-Neira, C. 2001. VR Juggler: A virtual platform for virtual reality application development. *Virtual Reality, 2001. Proceedings. IEEE* (2001), 89–96.
3. Bowman, D.A., Kruijff, E., LaViola Jr, J.J. and Poupyrev, I. 2004. *3D user interfaces: theory and practice*. Addison-Wesley.
4. Burdea, G.C. 2004. Teaching Virtual Reality: Why and How? *Presence: Teleoperators and Virtual Environments*. 13, 4 (Aug. 2004), 463–483.
5. Carlsson, C. and Hagsand, O. 1993. DIVE A multi-user virtual reality system. *Virtual Reality Annual International Symposium, 1993., 1993 IEEE* (1993), 394–400.
6. Cruz-Neira, C., Sandin, D.J. and DeFanti, T.A. 1993. Surround-screen projection-based virtual reality: the design and implementation of the CAVE. *Proc. conference on Computer graphics and interactive techniques* (1993), 135–142.

7. Fellner, D.W., Behr, J. and Bockholt, U. 2009. Instantreality - A Framework for Industrial Augmented and Virtual Reality Applications. *Proceedings of the 2nd Sino-German Workshop on Virtual Reality & Augmented Reality in Industry* (2009), 78–83.

8. Irawati, S., Ahn, S., Kim, J. and Ko, H. 2008. Varu framework: Enabling rapid prototyping of VR, AR and ubiquitous applications. *Virtual Reality Conference, 2008. VR'08. IEEE* (2008), 201–208.

9. Jacob, R.J., Girouard, A., Hirshfield, L.M., Horn, M.S., Shaer, O., Solovey, E.T. and Zigelbaum, J. 2008. Reality-based interaction: a framework for post-WIMP interfaces. *Proceedings of the SIGCHI conference on Human factors in computing systems* (2008), 201–210.

10. Kelso, J., Arsenault, L.E., Satterfield, S.G. and Kriz, R.D. 2002. Diverse: A framework for building extensible and reconfigurable device independent virtual environments. *Virtual Reality, 2002. Proceedings. IEEE* (2002), 183–190.

11. Kreylos, O. 2008. Environment-independent VR development. *Advances in Visual Computing*. Springer. 901–912.

12. Kuck, R., Wind, J., Riege, K., Bogen, M. and Birlinghoven, S. 2008. Improving the avango vr/ar framework: Lessons learned. *5th Workshop of the GI-VR/AR Group* (2008), 209–220.

13. Lancelle, M., Offen, L., Ullrich, T., Techmann, T. and Fellner, D.W. 2006. *Minimally Invasive Projector Calibration for 3D Applications*.

14. Mossel, A., Schönauer, C., Gerstweiler, G. and Kaufmann, H. 2013. Artifice-augmented reality framework for distributed collaboration. *International Journal of Virtual Reality*. (2013).

15. Palmer Luckey interview: The new Oculus Rift prototype and the future of VR: 2014. *http://www.pcgamer.com/2014/01/15/interview-oculus-rift-founder-palmer-lucky/*. Accessed: 2014-02-17.

16. Pausch, R., Burnette, T., Capeheart, A., Conway, M., Cosgrove, D., DeLine, R., Durbin, J., Gossweiler, R., Koga, S. and White, J. 1995. Alice: Rapid prototyping system for virtual reality. *IEEE Computer Graphics and Applications*. 15, 3 (1995), 8–11.

17. Rantzau, D., Lang, U., Lang, R., Nebel, H., Wierse, A. and Ruehle, R. 1996. Collaborative and interactive visualization in a distributed high performance software environment. *High Performance Computing for Computer Graphics and Visualisation*. Springer. 207–216.

18. Reas, C. and Fry, B. 2007. *Processing: a programming handbook for visual designers and artists*. Mit Press.

19. Schmalstieg, D., Fuhrmann, A., Hesina, G., Szalavári, Z., Encarnaçao, L.M., Gervautz, M. and Purgathofer, W. 2002. The studierstube augmented reality project. *Presence: Teleoperators and Virtual Environments*. 11, 1 (2002), 33–54.

20. Schulze, J.P., Prudhomme, A., Weber, P. and DeFanti, T.A. 2013. CalVR: an advanced open source virtual reality software framework. *IS&T/SPIE Electronic Imaging* (2013), 864902–864902.

21. Shaw, C., Green, M., Liang, J. and Sun, Y. 1993. Decoupled Simulation in Virtual Reality with The MR Toolkit. *ACM TRANSACTIONS ON INFORMATION SYSTEMS*. 11, 3 (1993), 287–317.

22. Sherman, W.R., Coming, D. and Su, S. 2013. FreeVR: honoring the past, looking to the future. *IS&T/SPIE Electronic Imaging* (2013), 864906–864906.

23. Steed, A. 2008. Some useful abstractions for re-usable virtual environment platforms. *Software Engineering and Architectures for Realtime Interactive Systems-SEARIS*. (2008).

24. Takala, T.M. and Matveinen, M. 2014. Full body interaction in virtual reality with affordable hardware. *Virtual Reality (VR), 2014 iEEE* (2014), 157–157.

25. Takala, T.M., Pugliese, R., Rauhamaa, P. and Takala, T. 2011. Reality-based User Interface System (RUIS). *Proceedings of the IEEE Symposium on 3D User Interfaces 2011* (Mar. 2011), 141–142.

26. Takala, T.M., Rauhamaa, P. and Takala, T. 2012. Survey of 3DUI applications and development challenges. *Proceedings of the IEEE Symposium on 3D User Interfaces 2012* (Mar. 2012), 89–96.

27. Taylor II, R.M., Hudson, T.C., Seeger, A., Weber, H., Juliano, J. and Helser, A.T. 2001. VRPN: a device-independent, network-transparent VR peripheral system. *Proceedings of the ACM symposium on Virtual reality software and technology* (2001), 55–61.

28. Taylor, R.M., Jerald, J., VanderKnyff, C., Wendt, J., Borland, D., Marshburn, D., Sherman, W.R. and Whitton, M.C. 2010. Lessons about virtual environment software systems from 20 years of ve building. *Presence: Teleoperators and Virtual Environments*. 19, 2 (2010), 162–178.

29. Varcholik, P.D., LaViola Jr, J.J. and Hughes, C. 2009. The Bespoke 3DUI XNA Framework: a low-cost platform for prototyping 3D spatial interfaces in video games. *Proceedings of the 2009 ACM SIGGRAPH Symposium on Video Games* (2009), 55–61.

30. Williamson, B.M., Wingrave, C., LaViola, J.J., Roberts, T. and Garrity, P. 2011. Natural full body interaction for navigation in dismounted soldier training. *The Interservice/Industry Training, Simulation & Education Conference (I/ITSEC)* (2011).

31. Wingrave, C.A. and LaViola Jr, J.J. 2010. Reflecting on the design and implementation issues of virtual environments. *Presence: Teleoperators and Virtual Environments*. 19, 2 (2010), 179–195.

32. Zagal, J.P. and Sharp, J. 2011. A Survey of Final Project Courses in Game Programs: Considerations for Teaching Capstone. *Digital Games Research Association Conference* (2011).

# Void Shadows: Multi-Touch Interaction with Stereoscopic Objects on the Tabletop

## Alexander Giesler, Dimitar Valkov and Klaus Hinrichs

Visualization and Computer Graphics (VisCG) Research Group
University of Münster, Germany
[alexander.giesler, dimitar.valkov, khh]@uni-muenster.de

## ABSTRACT

In this paper we present the *Void Shadows* interaction – a novel stereoscopic 3D interaction paradigm in which each virtual object casts a shadow on a touch-enabled display surface. The user can conveniently interact with such a shadow, and her actions are transferred to the associated object. Since all interactive tasks are carried out on the zero-parallax plane, there are no accommodation-convergence or related 2D/3D interaction problems, while the user is still able to "directly" manipulate objects at different 3D positions, without first having to position a cursor and to select an object.

In an initial user study we have proved the applicability of the metaphor for some common tasks, and we have found that compared to in-air 3D interaction techniques the users performed up to 28% more precisely using about the same amount of time.

## Author Keywords

3D Interaction; Multi-Touch Interaction; Selection Technique; Stereoscopic Displays; Tabletop Displays.

## ACM Classification Keywords

H.5.2 Information Interfaces and Presentation: User Interfaces – Input Devices and Strategies, Interaction Styles.

## General Terms

Design; Human Factors

## INTRODUCTION

Multi-touch enabled tabletop surfaces have shown significant potential for exploring complex content in an easy and natural manner, supporting expressive interaction without any instrumentation. In particular, the inherent tactile feedback and the ability to directly touch virtual objects increase the acceptance of such techniques and usually allow novices to attain more advanced skill levels swiftly [4].

Although multi-touch surfaces could exhibit limitations in the context of stereoscopically rendered projections because the

Figure 1. Illustration of the *Void Shadows* technique in action. Objects cast virtual shadows on the (in 3D invisible) touch sensitive display surface, i. e., they cast shadows in the void. These *void shadows* are then used to manipulate the objects.

input is inherently constrained to the 2D surface, the benefits of the combination of these two technologies have recently been emphasized in many publications [6, 11, 27, 28], and even first commercial products are already available [1]. Furthermore, interdisciplinary research projects have addressed the question of touch interaction with stereoscopic content on a two-dimensional surface [2, 3]. Stereoscopy is of particular interest in many application domains, since stereoscopically rendered content provides the user with additional depth cues, which usually decrease the overall cognitive load for understanding complex scenes [18]. Recent studies have also motivated that stereoscopy may increase the perceived image quality and supports the separation of the content from the background [21, 25]. Nevertheless, multi-touch based interaction with stereoscopic visualization is inherently difficult, since the displayed objects are floating freely in the vicinity in front of or behind the display surface, while touch is only available upon direct contact with the display. While one could simply use a 3D tracking technique to capture the user's finger motions in front of the display surface, it has been shown that the passive haptic feedback provided by touching the display surface has the potential to considerably enhance the user's experience and her overall performance [4, 26].

In this paper we present the *Void Shadows* interaction (cf. Figure 1), a novel interaction paradigm primarily aimed to enable object selection and manipulation for stereoscopic interactive tabletops. The basic idea behind the *Void Shadows* is that each interactive object casts a shadow onto the zero parallax plane, which is aligned with the touch enabled display surface, but is usually invisible in stereoscopic environments. The user can interact conveniently with such a shadow, and her actions are transferred to the associated object. Since all interactive tasks are carried out on the zero-parallax plane, there are no accommodation-convergence problems or perceived displacements of the touch point, as described for instance by Möller et al. [22]. Furthermore, using shadows as interactive representation has many advantages over other types of proxies or widgets [14]. For instance, the form of the shadow helps the user to identify which object is represented, and its size is closely related to the object's depth, which allows to directly interact with objects at different 3D positions, without first having to position a cursor and select an object.

We have proved the applicability of the metaphor for some common tasks in an initial usability study, and we have measured its quantitative performance against the Hand-Shadow technique proposed by Hilliges et al. [15] in a formal experiment. Our results have confirmed our initial expectations. Users considered the metaphor to be intuitive and adequate for the tested tasks, and they have performed the tasks up to 28% more precisely using about the same amount of time.

## RELATED WORK

An extensive review of the existing work on interactive tabletops has been presented by Grossman and Wigdor [10] who also developed a taxonomy for classification of this research. This framework takes into account the perceived and the actual display space, the input space and the physical properties of an interactive surface. While initially mainly considered in a 2D context (e.g., [5]), multiple touch and multi-touch interfaces have been developed for interaction with 3D scenes [12, 13, 19] and recently with stereoscopically rendered 3D content [11, 24, 27]. For instance, Schöning et al. [24] have investigated stereo visualization on a multi-touch enabled wall and discussed approaches based on mobile devices for addressing the formulated parallax problems. Furthermore, Valkov et al. [27, 28] and Bruder et al. [6] investigated humans' sensibility to stereoscopic depth in touch environments, and how the parallax changes the touch behavior and precision.

Extension of the interaction space beyond the touch surface has been addressed mainly by two different approaches: free-hand interaction above the surface [15, 20], or indirect interaction with the object, possibly using physical props [17] or widgets [4, 7, 8]. Following the first approach, Wilson and Benko [29] have proposed to use multiple cameras and projectors to enable interaction on, above and between multiple surfaces. Indirect interaction with the shadows of stereoscopically rendered objects on a multi-touch tabletop setup has been addressed by Coffey and Keefe [7]. They have combined a monoscopic tabletop projection with a large scale horizontal stereo display to explore complex medical data sets

with an extended world-in-miniature metaphor. The *Balloon Selection* metaphor, which has been proposed by Benko et al. [4] for augmented reality setups and which was extended by Daiber et al. [9] for stereoscopic data on tabletops supports precise object selection and manipulation. The metaphor imitates a small helium balloon, which the user is holding on a string above the surface. By pulling the string with a second finger, the height of the balloon is controlled. Although such indirect techniques usually provide better precision and lower levels of fatigue compared to free-hand interaction [16], they could suffer from occlusion artifacts and fat finger problems. These problems might be solved by using an adjustable cursor offset, as in the Triangle Cursor proposed by Strothoff et. al [26]. The orthogonal approach – to use the hand shadow as a distant "cursor" instead of the object shadow as a proxy – was investigated by Hilliges et al. [15], who have tested two depth sensing techniques to enrich the multi-touch interaction on a tabletop setup with monoscopic projection.

In this paper we propose a shadow interaction technique which was initially inspired by the Balloon Selection and the Triangle Cursor, but which is designed to support more direct object interaction without initial cursor positioning and selection phase. Although *Void Shadows* uses a similar approach for object manipulation as existing direct [12, 13] or indirect [4, 26] techniques, we expect that the underlying mental model of interacting with objects' shadows might be more beneficial in the context of 3D stereoscopic multi-touch applications.

## VOID SHADOWS

In the *Void Shadows* interaction, each interactive object casts a shadow on the touch-enabled display. An object's geometry, orientation and spatial location in the scene controls its shadow's shape and size and helps the user to identify which object is represented. In order to interact with an object, the user manipulates the associated shadow. Therefore, *Void Shadows* uses the objects' fake shadows as mental model, similar to the shadow metaphor of Herndon et al. [14]. Furthermore, the display surface is typically invisible in 3D stereo applications. However, *Void Shadows* visualizes the interactive shadows on the zero parallax plane, which is aligned to the display surface. Thus, the metaphor implicitly associates some semantical meaning with the interactive surface and facilitates planing and execution of the touch gesture [27].

With this technique touch and multi-touch gestures performed on a virtual shadow are transferred to the object casting this shadow. For instance, if the user moves a void shadow on the surface with one finger, the object will be translated in the X/Y-plane, while the shadow always remains under the user's finger. If she scales the shadow up or down with two fingers by a stretch or pinch gesture, the associated object will be lifted or lowered, respectively, in the Z-coordinate. Furthermore, rotating the shadow on the display surface with two fingers will rotate the object around the Z-axis. Thus, the technique separates the degrees-of-freedom between different modes in order to reduce unwanted operations [19, 23]. Obviously, users can move both fingers simultaneously, com-

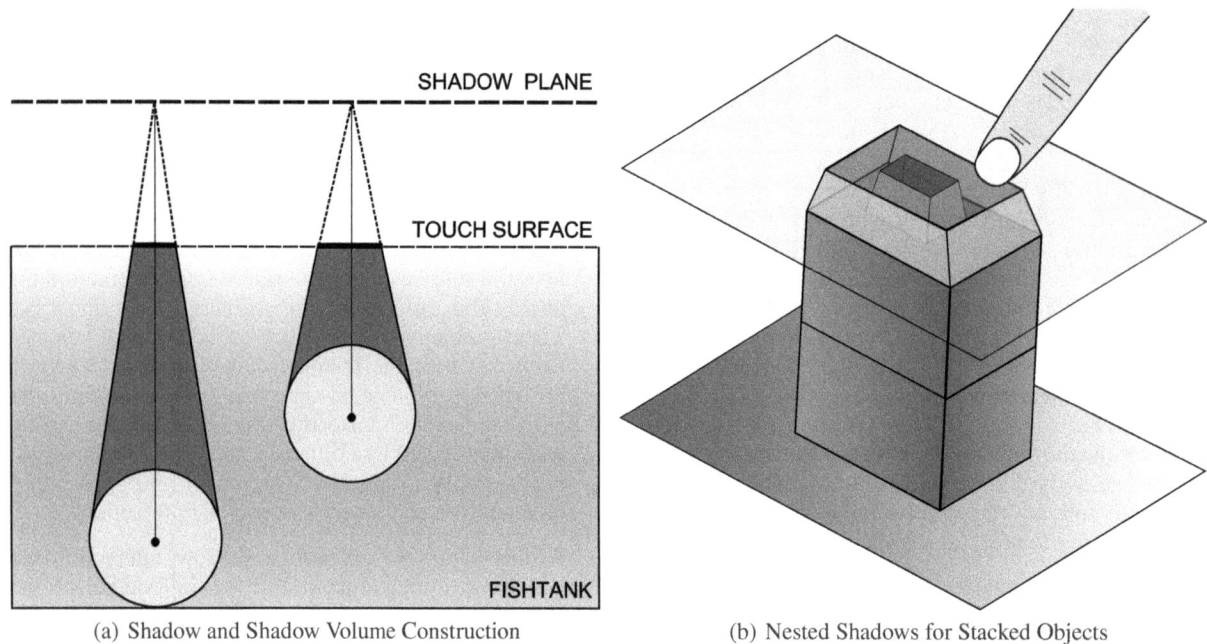

(a) Shadow and Shadow Volume Construction  (b) Nested Shadows for Stacked Objects

**Figure 2. Illustration of the *Void Shadows* concept. Each interactive object casts a shadow onto the touch sensitive display surface. *(a)* From a projection of the object's center onto an imaginary shadow plane the void shadows are cast onto the interactive surface; the shadow volume under the surface is rendered to highlight the link between the object and its shadow. *(b)* Stacked objects have different shadows, which may be manipulated independently.**

bining position, rotation and height manipulation at the same time.

The *Void Shadows* metaphor uses a non-realistic shadow rendering technique, i.e., the shadows are always projected orthogonally onto the touch surface. As Figure 2(a) shows, this projection is controlled by an imaginary plane above the touch surface, called the *shadow plane*, in which each object is represented by a single point. By construction, the shadow volume is generated by this point and the object's silhouette. The void shadow is then the intersection of this shadow volume and the zero parallax plane on the touch surface. To simplify the understanding of the shadow-object link even further, the part of the shadow volume lying below the display surface is rendered with a semi-transparent light gray color. With decreasing distance to the display surface, objects generate a more obtuse angled shadow volume, which results in a larger shadow. In contrast, objects that are more distant from the surface will generate a more acute angled volume and therefore a smaller shadow (cf. Figure 2(a)).

Furthermore, if objects are stacked on top of each other, the resulting void shadows will be nested (cf. Figure 2(b)). Nevertheless, it is still possible to select and manipulate individual objects by touching the associated shadow. For instance, touching the innermost shadow will select the bottommost object, while touching the outermost shadow will select the topmost object. Of course, since the shadows are by their nature 2D projections of 3D geometry, there will always be constellations of objects where the shadows are not clearly separable, e.g., stacked objects having different size or geometry. Nevertheless, in many real world applications such object arrangements are rather rare. Furthermore, the technique may be extended to compensate for this, e.g., by allowing to modify the height of the shadow plane.

*Void Shadows* is primarily designed for objects at positive parallax, i.e., below the screen surface, but may also work for objects at negative parallax, i.e., above the surface. In this case, the shadow plane is conceptually below the display surface (at the same distance), and the shadow volume is rendered above the surface. However, a stretch gesture on shadows for objects above the display will decrease their size. Furthermore, objects that are located above the display may occlude the interactive shadow. To address this, objects above the display are rendered semi-transparently. Thus, the void shadows appear "inside the objects" (but are still correctly ordered due to the stereoscopic cues) and are still accessible in full size for interaction.

Since fingers might occlude an object rendered with negative parallax, which may disturb stereoscopic perception [27], we have decided to extend the gesture set to support an offset technique. This can be activated by first using two fingers (e.g., for height adjustment) and then releasing the first finger from the shadow. In this case, the formerly second finger that remains on the surface can be used to manipulate the object's position, and a further finger touching the surface can be used to adjust the height and orientation. Since the fingers can be placed anywhere on the surface, the object can be manipulated without stereoscopic perception issues that arise by occlusion of the finger.

Furthermore, the offset feature can be very useful for moving objects over larger distances by consecutively repeating this procedure, e.g., on large tabletops where some parts of the display surface might be unreachable otherwise.

However, since each object casts a shadow onto the display surface, the metaphor might involve a limitation on the number of objects in the scene, i.e., the shadows may block the user's view of the objects. As an extension it might be possible to track the user's hands in order to detect a non-interactive user state or to hide shadows of unselected objects during interaction.

## USER STUDY

The *Void Shadows* technique uses the objects' shadows as metaphor for interaction and allows users to directly select an object by touching its associated shadow. Although the technique uses a similar approach for object manipulation as existing 3D multi-touch techniques (e.g., [4, 26]), the underlying shadow metaphor distinguishes *Void Shadows* from existing multi-touch metaphors. Therefore, we were particularly interested in the comparison of *Void Shadows* to a shadow based in-air interaction technique [15] that uses an orthogonal approach as shadow interaction metaphor.

We performed a formal user study consisting of two experiments to quantitatively evaluate the performance of *Void Shadows* (VOID) and to compare it with a shadow based in-air interaction technique (HAND) that uses the hand's shadow and a grasp gesture to interact with objects. Both techniques have been designed primarily to target objects below the tabletop surface, and they are based on interaction with shadows, i.e, *Void Shadows* uses an object's shadow as proxy for interaction on the display surface, and the in-air interaction technique casts a shadow from the user's hand into the scene that acts as a distant cursor for interaction. We divided the user study into two experiments, testing both techniques in a synthetic docking task and in a more real-world-like assembly and object dropping task. Since our HAND implementation does not support precise object rotation, we deactivated the rotation gesture in VOID for better comparability and only tested performance for 3D translation tasks.

## Participants

14 participants (13 male, 1 female), ages 21–59 (M = 29.4, SD = 9.0), sizes 169cm–188cm (M = 177.7cm, SD = 6.7) participated in the study and were the same in both experiments. All participants were undergraduate, graduate or PhD students or professionals in computer science. All participants were frequent computer users, and all reported to have experience with stereoscopic projections and multi-touch devices, and most participants reported to have experience with in-air interaction, e.g., from earlier experiments. All participants had normal or corrected to normal vision, none reported amblyopia or another stereopsis disruption. Six participants wore glasses or contact lenses and were instructed to also wear glasses during the experiment under the 3D glasses. Completing the experiments, including training, instructions, questionnaire and debriefing took about 45-60 minutes per participant. The participants were allowed to take breaks at any time.

## Experimental Setup

The experiments were performed using our prototype stereoscopic multi-touch tabletop setup. A PC running Windows 7 with an NVIDIA Quadro FX 4800 graphics card was used for the experiments. For visualization we used a 46" Toshiba LED 3D TV mounted on a table at the height of 100cm. The 3D TV had a resolution of 1920 × 1080 with frame-sequential stereoscopic visualization at 120 Hz with Toshiba active 3D glasses. The physical dimensions of the touch surface were 102 cm × 57.5 cm, resulting in a pixel size of approximately 0.5 mm. To enable touch detection on our table setup we used a PQ Labs G4 Basic multi-touch bezel, which was mounted above the 3D TV display, providing touch detection with a sampling rate of up to 200 fps and an accuracy of 2.7 mm. We tracked a subject's head with the WorldViz PPT-X8 optical tracker, which provides millimeter precision and sub-millimeter accuracy, and adjusted the position of the virtual cameras for the left and for the right eye relative to the position of one tracked marker. We mounted a mouse at a convenient position for the dominant hand of the user, and in each experiment participants had to start the next trial by a mouse click. For the in-air technique a participant's hand was tracked with our in-house tracker implementation based on the Kinect depth camera.

The rendered virtual fish tank was 102 cm × 57.5 cm × 31 cm. We utilized a physics engine, which we could activate or deactivate for the experiments. The rear wall of the virtual fish tank was tilted in order to push objects that are too far away for reaching closer to the user by utilizing gravity of the physics engine. In the tasks where the physics engine was enabled, selecting an object automatically paused the global physics simulation, which allowed the user to move the object freely in the scene. In contrast, releasing the object reactivated the physics simulation again. Furthermore, objects that were moved outside of the fish tank were automatically pushed back into the scene. We displayed a transparent and nearly invisible noisy texture on the screen surface for the *Void Shadows* technique in order to create a reference of the touch surface in the virtual scene.

## In-Air Technique

The in-air interaction technique (HAND), which was used in the experiments, is based on the work of Hilliges et al. [15] and was extended for use with our stereoscopic fish tank VR setup. In the HAND technique a user's hand casts a virtual shadow into the scene and activates an invisible distant cursor with an offset below the tabletop surface, which can be positioned in the vicinity of an object for selection. Furthermore, the technique was extended with the grasp gesture proposed by [15] for object selection. The grasp gesture couples the distant cursor to the object and allows to move the object freely in the scene by mapping the hand movements to equivalent object translations, after which the object can be released by opening the hand. Furthermore, we added visual feedback for selectable objects in the vicinity of the distant cursor such that users can adjust their hand position in order to select the intended object. We did not project the cast hand shadow on objects above the distant cursor to improve the sensing of the current position.

Our implementation of the HAND technique is based on the Kinect sensor, which was mounted above the tabletop dis-

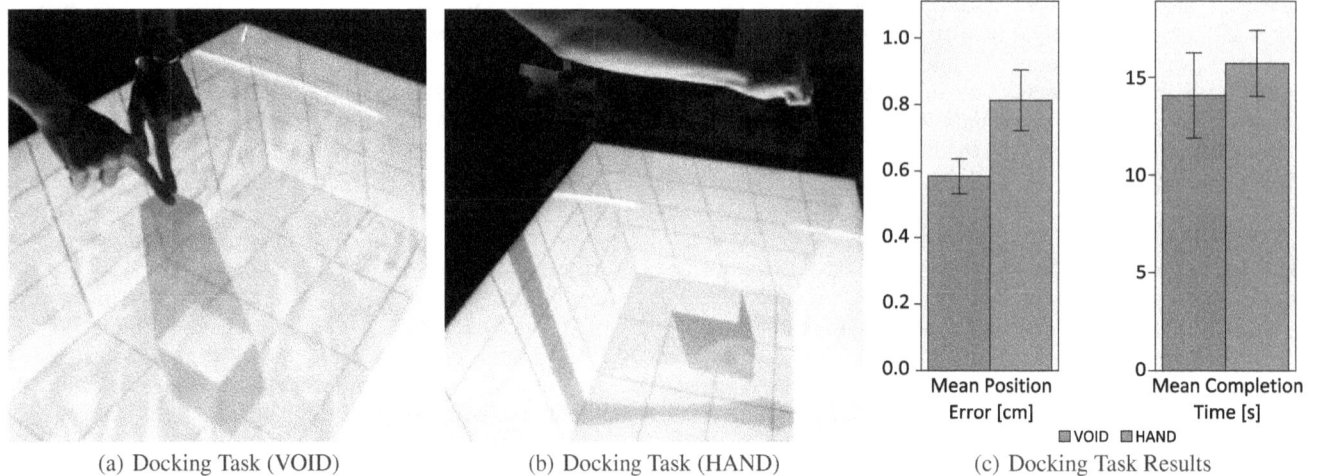

(a) Docking Task (VOID)          (b) Docking Task (HAND)          (c) Docking Task Results

**Figure 3. Illustration of participant performing the docking task with VOID *(a)* and HAND *(b)* technique (a monoscopic projection was used while these images were captured). *(c)* Mean position error and mean task completion time for both techniques in the docking task. (Error bars = ± SE)**

play. We tracked the user's hand and projected the masked depth image as texture from the sensor position into the scene to simulate the shadow. After detection of the user's hand in the depth image, the implementation analyzes the convex hull and convexity defects to classify a hand as opened or closed. Furthermore, we used the detected hand center as distant cursor position. Since the depth image is affected by noise, we used a dynamic filter as jitter compensation for precise positioning tasks and fast object movement, i.e., we applied a stronger filter during slow hand motions against jitter and a weaker filter during quick hand motions. However, as the user's hand alters its shape during the transition from a closed to an opened state, the hand's center and therefore the distant cursor are suddenly moved, which results in a displaced object upon releasing. In order to compensate for this issue, we take the most recent value in the history of positions before the hand changes its state, which results in surprisingly correct object placement and grabbing. Users who have tested the technique described this as magical snapping effect and they had the feeling that the in-air technique automatically snaps the object into the target position.

### Experiment 1: Docking

Participants were asked to use both interaction techniques to move a green colored box displayed under the table and drag it to a target position, which is indicated by a red colored semi-transparent box of the same size (cf. Figure 3(a) and 3(b)). We deactivated the physics engine during this task to test target positions with different heights.

A within-subjects, repeated measures design was used consisting of 2 techniques and 9 positions in 3 different depths, resulting in a total of 27 target positions. All trials were repeated twice. The target positions were aligned on a 3 × 3 grid near the center of the fish tank floor and could be easily reached by all participants for both techniques. The start position of the green colored box was the same for all trials and was located near the center of the fish tank floor, but different from any positions in the grid. When the participants were

satisfied with the alignment of the box at the target they had to complete the trial by pressing with their dominant hand the left button of a mouse located next to the tabletop setup. Furthermore, the participants were instructed to try to maintain the same speed-precision ratio during all trials. The use of the mouse button ensured the same starting position of the user's dominant hand in all trials. The order in which the techniques were tested was counterbalanced to avoid ordering effects. To eliminate the effects of switching interaction techniques the first three trials were marked as training and were discarded from the results for each trial set, resulting in a total number of 108 trials per subject. The completion time for each trial, i. e, the time between the button presses at the beginning and the end, was recorded. Additionally, the distance of the box to the target position was recorded.

### Results

The mean completion time and position error were calculated for each subject and are shown in Figure 3(c). We encountered 10 trials in the results which showed either a high position error (7 trials with error $\geq 20cm$) or an unrealistic short task completion time (3 trials with time $\leq 0.5s$). Debriefing with the participants revealed that these trials (with short completion time) were skipped accidentally by a click on the mouse button before task completion, therefore we excluded these trials from evaluation. The position errors were all related to the HAND technique and were more than 3 SDs larger than the mean for this technique. We excluded these trials from evaluation to not unfairly decrease precision of the HAND technique.

With a two sided t-test over subject means we found that VOID performed better in terms of position error ($T_{26} = -2.17$, $p = 0.039 < 0.05$). The mean position error was approximately 2.3mm smaller with VOID ($M = 0.58cm$, $SD = 0.19$) than with HAND ($M = 0.81cm$, $SD = 0.34$). We have not found a significant difference for task completion time ($T_{26} = -0.6$, $p = 0.55$) between VOID ($M = 14.06s$, $SD = 8.16$) and HAND ($M = 15.71s$, $SD = 6.27$).

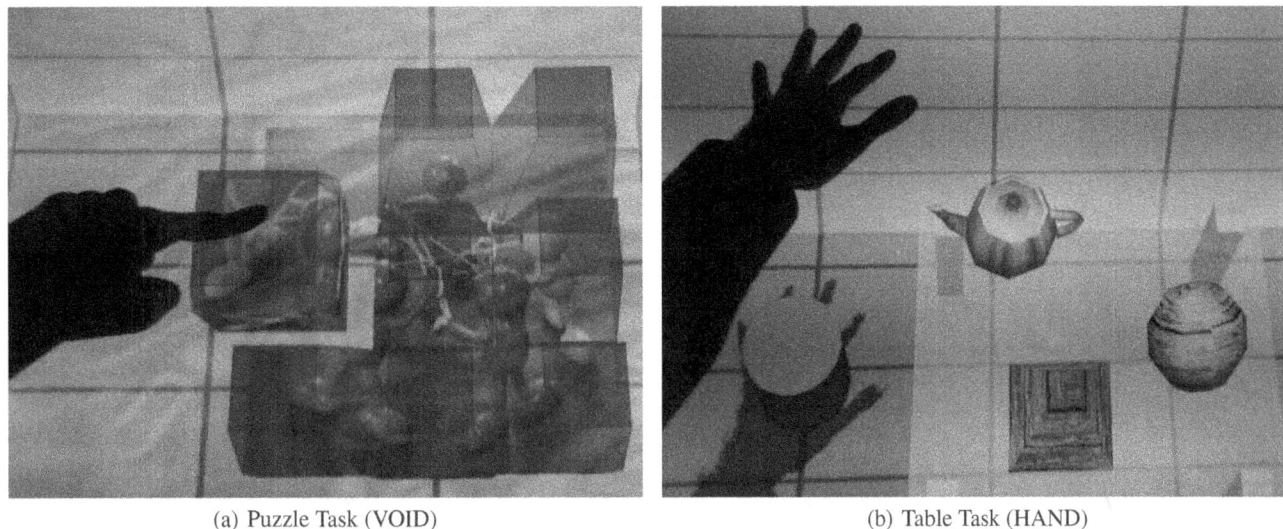

(a) Puzzle Task (VOID)                                    (b) Table Task (HAND)

**Figure 4. In the puzzle task, participants had to assemble 8 boxes into a puzzle around a stationary reference puzzle piece. The illustration *(a)* shows the VOID technique in action during this task. In the table task *(b)*, illustrated with the HAND technique, participants had to drop four objects on the table (a monoscopic projection was used while these images were captured).**

## Experiment 2: Assembly And Dropping

In this experiment, we tested both techniques in more real-world-like scenarios. In order to test both techniques for construction and assembly scenarios, participants had to complete a puzzle in the first block. In order to test the techniques for imprecise tasks such as sorting and arrangement, participants had to move objects into a target region in the second block.

In the first block (PUZZLE), nine boxes were displayed. Each box contained on all its faces the same part of an image. The participants were asked to assemble the complete image by aligning the boxes (cf. Figure 4(a)) on the floor. Furthermore, the top-left part of the puzzle was placed into the scene as reference point, which could not be selected or moved by the participants. The other eight boxes dropped randomly into the scene with random orientation and activated physics, i. e, the boxes fell into the scene and collided with other objects or the floor after releasing. However, when a participant selected one object, its orientation was reset to the orientation of the reference object, such that no rotation was required to complete the task. The participants had to click on the left mouse button to start a trial, and once they were satisfied with the arrangement of the boxes, the trial was ended by pressing the button again. There was no predefined order in which the boxes had to be moved, and the users could align the boxes freely.

We used a within-subjects, repeated measures design. The participants were asked to perform 2 trials with each technique, resulting in a total of 4 trials per user. To eliminate the effects of switching techniques a practice trial was added for each technique that was excluded from the evaluation. The order in which the techniques were tested was randomized to avoid providing a bias for one technique. The task completion time and the box positions were recorded.

In the second experiment block (TABLE), four different objects were placed at four fixed positions on the left and right side of a semi-transparent table, which was placed as stationary object into the scene. Participants were asked to place the objects onto the table surface (cf. Figure 4(b)), while the physics engine was activated. The objects were distributed randomly among the four positions. The participants had to click on the left mouse button to start a trial, and once they were satisfied with the arrangement of the objects the trial was ended by pressing the button again. Each object had to be selected and moved onto the table surface. Since physics was activated during this experiment block, we encouraged participants to utilize simulated gravity and to release the objects somewhere above the table surface for faster task completion, since objects will automatically drop onto the table's surface. There was no predefined order in which the objects had to be moved, and the users could align the objects freely in random order.

Again, we used a within-subjects, repeated measures design. The participants were asked to perform 5 trials with each technique, resulting in a total of 10 trials per subject. To eliminate the effects of switching techniques a practice trial was added for each technique that was excluded from the results. Again, the order in which the techniques were tested was randomized to avoid providing a bias for one technique. The task completion time and the success of placing individual objects correctly on the table was recorded.

## Results

For PUZZLE the mean completion time and accumulated position error were calculated for each subject and interaction technique and are shown in Figure 5(a). The accumulated error was calculated by summarizing the error distances of adjacent boxes, i. e, two adjacent boxes will result in zero error for perfect alignment, in order to reduce error propagation in the assembled puzzle. We observed one trial that showed an

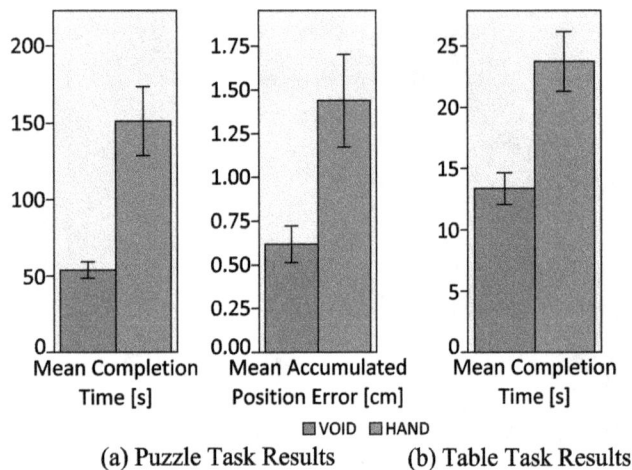

(a) Puzzle Task Results    (b) Table Task Results

**Figure 5.** *(a)* **Mean accumulated position error and mean task completion time for both techniques in the puzzle assembly task.** *(b)* **Mean task completion time for both techniques in the table task. Success rate for the table task was 100% for both techniques. (Error bars = ± SE)**

outlier in the position of two puzzle pieces. However, reconstruction of this trial showed that the participant exchanged two puzzle pieces accidentally, therefore we exchanged these two positions with each other in the results and recalculated the position error.

With a two sided t-test over subject means we found that VOID ($M = 53.57s, SD = 19.69$) was significantly faster ($T_{14.43} = -4.20, p < 0.01$) compared to HAND ($M = 150.25s, SD = 83.81$). VOID also performed better in terms of accumulated position error ($T_{26} = -2.89, p < 0.01$). The mean accumulated position error for the whole puzzle was approximately 0.81cm smaller with VOID ($M = 0.62cm, SD = 0.39$) than with HAND ($M = 1.43cm, SD = 0.98$).

For TABLE the mean completion time and success for placing objects were calculated for each subject and interaction technique for all movable objects and are shown in Figure 5(b). We excluded one trial from evaluation, which showed an unrealistic short trial completion time ($t < 0.2s$) where a misclick ended the trial before task completion. All participants placed the objects correctly on the table in all trials for both techniques (success rate = 100%).

With a two sided t-test over subject means we found that VOID ($M = 13.29s, SD = 4.81$) was significantly faster ($T_{26} = -3.76, p < 0.01$) compared to HAND ($M = 23.61s, SD = 9.07$).

### Discussion

Both experiments in our formal study have shown that users were able to perform positioning tasks much more precisely with our *Void Shadows* technique than with the in-air interaction technique, while they needed comparable (DOCKING) or even shorter time for task completion (PUZZLE and TABLE). Surprisingly, the precision of the in-air technique was relatively high, with a mean position error below 1cm in the docking task, indicating that our in-air technique implementation provided sufficient compensation for the noise of the

Kinect sensor. In the synthetic docking task users were at mean 28% more precise with *Void Shadows*. Although the task completion time in the first experiment did not show a significant difference between the techniques, the results indicate a trend that *Void Shadows* performs faster (10.5%). This was confirmed in the more complex puzzle and the table task, that more closely resemble what a real-world task could be like. During this experiment, *Void Shadows* performed 2.8 and 1.78 times faster then in-air interaction for the puzzle and table task, respectively. Therefore, the question arises why the task completion times are different for both experiments.

Observation of participants during the user study showed that *Void Shadows* was primarily fast for object selection, since users could directly select the intended object on the surface. Furthermore, one participant reported issues with friction of the dragged finger on the tabletop, indicating a possible slowdown of object movement across longer distances. However, we also observed that most users separated the positioning task into a 2DOF task in the first phase to move the object close to the target position and then switched to a 1DOF task to adjust to the correct height, although all participants were aware of the fact that *Void Shadows* supports 3DOF positioning by moving two fingers simultaneously. In contrast, observation of participants during the experiments revealed that the in-air interaction technique performed slower during the object selection and target correction phase, since the participants had to adjust to the indirect hand shadow proxy. Furthermore, we observed that the in-air technique was maintaining a fast speed between start and end for object movement, since the participants usually moved the object to the approximate height of the target during positioning and therefore made frequent use of the 3DOF of the in-air technique in the ballistic phase of the motion. Nevertheless, the participants then reduced the motion again to a sequence of 1 or 2DOF tasks during the correction phase. Since task distances were different in both experiments, i.e., on average larger in the DOCKING task than in the PUZZLE and TABLE task, the differences between the selection and the movement times for VOID and HAND might have affected the performance time, especially since multiple objects had to be moved in the second experiment. Nevertheless, more investigation with special focus on object selection and movement times is needed to properly attribute the difference in the performance times between the two experiments. At the current state, *Void Shadows* seems to be particularly appropriate for applications where many relatively short and precise object translations are required.

During the experiments participants reported that the jitter, which was caused by noise in the depth-sensing camera, and sudden displacements of the objects during opening of the hand was disturbing in several cases. However, after training and instruction to open the hand quicker and to use a short amount of time to dwell before releasing the hand, participants were able to leverage the technique that compensated for sudden jumps, and objects were released at the correct locations. Although observation of participants revealed that this dwell time was intuitively applied to correct for the target position, e.g., due to trembling hands or jitter, it cannot be

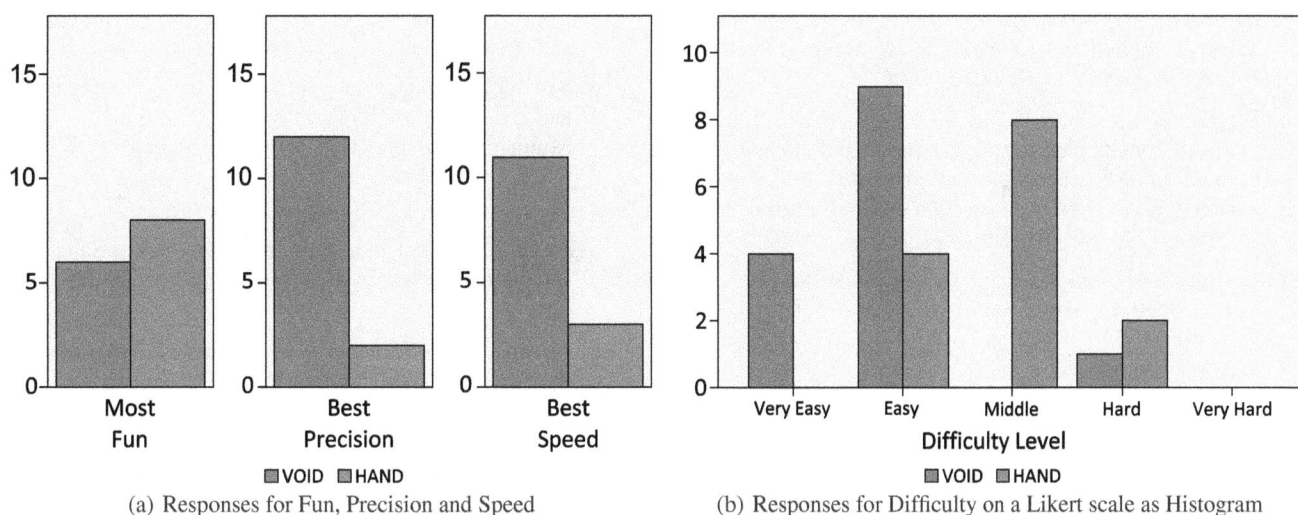

(a) Responses for Fun, Precision and Speed

(b) Responses for Difficulty on a Likert scale as Histogram

**Figure 6. Responses for all participants comparing both techniques against each other for pleasure, precision and speed (a) in the questionnaire, as well as a histogram that shows the perceived difficulty for both techniques (b) on a 5-point-Likert scale.**

excluded that the different sensor technologies (30Hz hand detection vs. 200Hz touch detection) might have influenced the results for task completion time.

In the questionnaire, we asked participants to report which of both techniques was felt more pleasant, more precise and faster. Furthermore, we asked the participants to rate the difficulty of both techniques on a 5-point-Likert scale, ranging from very easy to very hard. Debriefing and evaluation of the questionnaires revealed interesting insights into the users' attitude towards both techniques. For instance, most participants found it appealing to interact with the shadow casting in-air technique (cf. Figure 6(a)), although they stated that they had issues to mentally connect the shadow to a specific light source. Furthermore, the questionnaire results showed (cf. Figure 6(a)) that most participants preferred *Void Shadows* over in-air interaction in terms of speed and precision, but the in-air technique in terms of pleasure. However, although some participants reported the subjective feeling that the in-air technique was faster (3 participants) and more precise (2 participants), their individual results showed that *Void Shadows* was significantly better in terms of precision and the task completion time was not significantly different between both techniques for these subjects. Although both techniques were rated to most extent as easy or medium in terms of difficulty (cf. Figure 6(b)), *Void Shadows* outperformed the in-air technique by a small margin.

## CONCLUSIONS AND FUTURE WORK

In this paper we have introduced *Void Shadows*, a new 3D interaction paradigm that allows users to operate in the space below a tabletop display surface by interacting with virtual shadows cast onto the display surface. We have tested our technique in a formal user study against an in-air technique that casts the user's hand shadow onto objects for interaction and found that *Void Shadows* performs significantly better in terms of precision and significantly faster for complex tasks such as assembly and arrangement of multiple objects. Fur-

thermore, the conducted user study indicates that our technique is primarily fast for object selection and movement across shorter distances, which could be further investigated in future work.

Overall, despite the inspiring early results, there is room for improvement and extension of the technique, e.g., to support precise 6DOF manipulation of 3D stereoscopic objects. For instance, the user could fixate the shadow with two fingers and drag a third finger above the shadow for arcball rotation. Furthermore, as *Void Shadows* uses shadow projections on the display surface, it is possible to operate with objects both below and above the display surface by mirroring the imaginary shadow plane around the display surface. However, this approach also mirrors the stretch and pinch gesture used to adjust an object's height. Therefore, it would be interesting to improve the interaction with objects above the surface and to evaluate the technique's suitability and performance for 3D interaction above the display surface. Furthermore, for many objects the metaphor suffers from obstruction of the scene, since each object casts an individual shadow onto the surface. Therefore, we plan to extend the metaphor in order to hide shadows during a non-interactive user state.

## ACKNOWLEDGMENTS

We would like to thank all participants of the user study for their time and effort.

## REFERENCES

1. Immersion SAS. http://www.immersion.fr/.

2. iMUTS - Interscopic Multi-Touch Surfaces.
   http://imuts.uni-muenster.de/.

3. InSTInCT - Touch-based interfaces for Interaction with
   3D Content. http://anr-instinct.cap-sciences.net/.

4. Benko, H., and Feiner, S. Balloon Selection: A
   Multi-Finger Technique for Accurate Low-Fatigue 3D
   Selection. In *Proceedings of 3DUI'07*, IEEE (2007),
   79–86.

**111**

5. Benko, H., Wilson, A. D., and Baudisch, P. Precise Selection Techniques for Multi-Touch Screens. In *Proceedings of CHI '06*, ACM (2006), 1263–1272.

6. Bruder, G., Steinicke, F., and Sturzlinger, W. To Touch or not to Touch? Comparing 2D Touch and 3D Mid-Air Interaction on Stereoscopic Tabletop Surfaces. In *Proceedings of the 1st symposium on Spatial user interaction*, ACM (2013), 9–16.

7. Coffey, D. M., and Keefe, D. F. Shadow WIM: A Multi-Touch, Dynamic World-In-Miniature Interface for Exploring Biomedical Data. In *SIGGRAPH '10 Posters*, ACM (2010), 96.

8. Cohé, A., Dècle, F., and Hachet, M. tBox: A 3D Transformation Widget designed for Touch-screens. In *Proceedings of CHI '11*, ACM (2011), 3005–3008.

9. Daiber, F., Falk, E., and Krüger, A. Balloon Selection revisited: Multi-Touch Selection Techniques for Stereoscopic Data. In *Proceedings of the International Working Conference on Advanced Visual Interfaces*, ACM (2012), 441–444.

10. Grossman, T., and Wigdor, D. Going Deeper: a Taxonomy of 3D on the Tabletop. In *Proceedings of TABLETOP '07*, IEEE (2007), 137–144.

11. Hachet, M., Bossavit, B., Cohé, A., and de la Rivière, J.-B. Toucheo: Multitouch and Stereo Combined in a Seamless Workspace. In *Proceedings of the 24th annual ACM symposium on User interface software and technology*, ACM (2011), 587–592.

12. Hancock, M., Carpendale, S., and Cockburn, A. Shallow-Depth 3D Interaction: Design and Evaluation of One-, Two- and Three-Touch Techniques. In *Proceedings of CHI '07*, ACM (2007), 1147–1156.

13. Hancock, M., Ten Cate, T., and Carpendale, S. Sticky Tools: Full 6DOF Force-Based Interaction for Multi-Touch Tables. In *Proceedings of the ACM International Conference on Interactive Tabletops and Surfaces*, ACM (2009), 133–140.

14. Herndon, K. P., Zeleznik, R. C., Robbins, D. C., Conner, D. B., Snibbe, S. S., and Van Dam, A. Interactive Shadows. In *Proceedings of the 5th annual ACM symposium on User interface software and technology*, ACM (1992), 1–6.

15. Hilliges, O., Izadi, S., Wilson, A. D., Hodges, S., Garcia-Mendoza, A., and Butz, A. Interactions in the Air: Adding Further Depth to Interactive Tabletops. In *Proceedings of UIST '09*, ACM (2009), 139–148.

16. Hinckley, K., Pausch, R., Goble, J. C., and Kassell, N. F. A Survey of Design Issues in Spatial Input. In *Proceedings of UIST '94*, ACM (1994), 213–222.

17. Ishii, H., and Ullmer, B. Tangible Bits: Towards Seamless Interfaces between People, Bits and Atoms. In *Proceedings of CHI '97*, ACM (1997), 234–241.

18. Kooi, F. L., and Toet, A. Visual Comfort of Binocular and 3D Displays. *Displays 25*, 2-3 (2004), 99 – 108.

19. Martinet, A., Casiez, G., and Grisoni, G. The Design and Evaluation of 3D Positioning Techniques for Multi-touch Displays. In *3D User Interfaces (3DUI)*, IEEE (2010), 115–118.

20. Mendes, D., Fonseca, F., Araujo, B., Ferreira, A., and Jorge, J. Mid-Air Interactions Above Stereoscopic Interactive Tables. In *3D User Interfaces (3DUI)*, IEEE (2014), 3–10.

21. Mizobuchi, S., Terasaki, S., Häkkinen, J., Heinonen, E., Bergquist, J., and Chignell, M. The effect of stereoscopic viewing in a word-search task with a layered background. *Journal of the Society for Information Display 16*, 11 (2008), 1105–1113.

22. Möllers, M., Zimmer, P., and Borchers, J. Direct Manipulation and the Third Dimension: Co-Planar Dragging on 3D Displays. In *Proceedings of the 2012 ACM international conference on Interactive tabletops and surfaces*, ACM (2012), 11–20.

23. Nacenta, M. A., Baudisch, P., Benko, H., and Wilson, A. Separability of Spatial Manipulations in Multi-Touch Interfaces. In *Proceedings of Graphics interface 2009*, Canadian Information Processing Society (2009), 175–182.

24. Schöning, J., Steinicke, F., Valkov, D., Krüger, A., and Hinrichs, K. Bimanual Interaction with Interscopic Multi-Touch Surfaces. In *Proceedings of INTERACT '09* (2009), 40–53.

25. Shibata, T., Kurihara, S., Kawai, T., Takahashi, T., Shimizu, T., Kawada, R., Ito, A., Häkkinen, J., Takatalo, J., and Nyman, G. Evaluation of stereoscopic image quality for mobile devices using Interpretation Based Quality methodology. In *SPIE 7237, 72371E* (2009).

26. Strothoff, S., Valkov, D., and Hinrichs, K. Triangle Cursor: Interactions With Objects Above the Tabletop. In *Proceedings of the ACM International Conference on Interactive Tabletops and Surfaces*, ACM (2011), 111–119.

27. Valkov, D., Giesler, A., and Hinrichs, K. Imperceptible Depth Shifts for Touch Interaction with Stereoscopic Objects. In *Proceedings of the 32nd annual ACM conference on Human factors in computing systems*, ACM (2014), 227–236.

28. Valkov, D., Steinicke, F., Bruder, G., and Hinrichs, K. 2D Touching of 3D Stereoscopic Objects. In *ACM CHI* (2011), 1353–1362.

29. Wilson, A. D., and Benko, H. Combining Multiple Depth Cameras and Projectors for Interactions On, Above, and Between Surfaces. In *Proceedings of UIST '10* (2010), 273–282.

# Object-Based Touch Manipulation for Remote Guidance of Physical Tasks

**Matt Adcock** [*†‡]

*CSIRO
Canberra, Australia

**Dulitha Ranatunga** [*†]

†Australian National University
Canberra, Australia

**Ross Smith, Bruce H. Thomas** [‡]

‡University of South Australia
Mawson Lakes, Australia

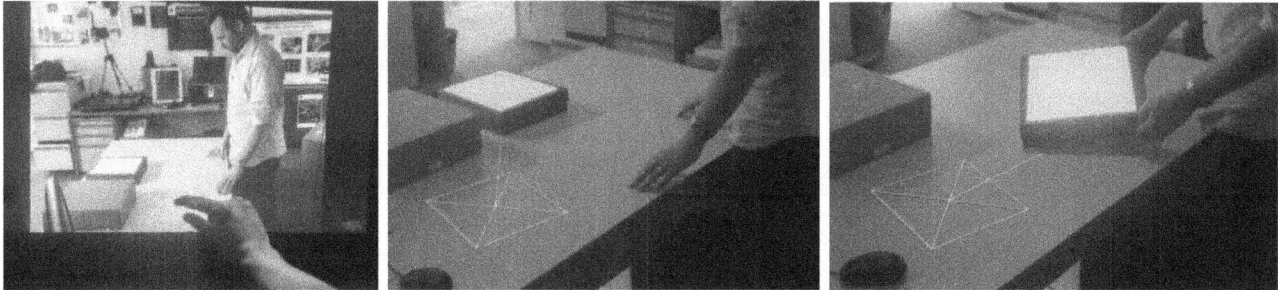

Figure 1. (left) An expert directly specifies a rotation and translation of the box using multi-touch. (center) Rotated and translated visual cue from workers' perspective. (right) As the worker moves the box, the SAR cue is updated.

## ABSTRACT

This paper presents a spatial multi-touch system for the remote guidance of physical tasks that uses semantic information about the physical properties of the environment. It enables a remote expert to observe a video feed of the local worker's environment and directly specify object movements via a touch display. Visual feedback for the gestures is displayed directly in the local worker's physical environment with Spatial Augmented Reality and observed by the remote expert through the video feed. A virtual representation of the physical environment is captured with a Kinect that facilitates the context-based interactions. We evaluate two methods of remote worker interaction, object-based and sketch-based, and also investigate the impact of two camera positions, top and side, for task performance. Our results indicate translation and aggregate tasks could be more accurately performed via the object based technique when the top-down camera feed was used. While, in the case of the side on camera view, sketching was faster and rotations were more accurate. We also found that for object-based interactions the top view was better on all four of our measured criteria, while for sketching no significant difference was found between camera views.

## Categories and Subject Descriptors

H.5.1. [Information interfaces and presentation] Artificial, augmented and virtual realities; H.5.2. [Information interfaces and presentation] Input devices and strategies.

## General Terms

Human Factors, Design, Experimentation.

## Keywords

Spatially Augmented Reality; Remote Guidance; Object Manipulation; Multi touch interaction; 3D CHI.

## INTRODUCTION

Remote guidance takes place when multiple participants in different locations work together to perform a task involving physical objects. Typically the scenario involves an 'expert' with specialized knowledge in the task situated remotely from the physical task environment. They collaborate, using available communication tools, with a 'worker' who is co-located and able to physically interact with the task environment.

In our research, one of the task scenarios we aim to support is a science laboratory technician (worker) at a lab-bench, receiving guidance from a remote supervising scientist (expert). Sometimes that scientist can be remote due to geography, and other times there might be a quarantine barrier in place that is costly to cross[1]. We are therefore motivated to develop systems that support remote guidance of part-tasks such as spatial arrangement (of equipment and specimens) on the research bench top.

There are many different approaches to improving the communication tools and capabilities of the remote helper to enable efficient guiding techniques. These include video-conference situations [16], view sharing based head mounted display (HMD) systems [15] and through the use of spatial augmented reality. Unfortunately, in video-conference based systems, the expert is only able to provide verbal cues in response to the visual feed. HMD systems are a form of augmented reality, however they suffer from being encumbering wearable devices that can limit the helpers' freedom to move or operate.

Spatial Augmented Reality (SAR) systems use projectors to display computer generated graphics directly onto the physical environment [3]. SAR provides the benefit of augmentation without wearable or hand-held devices. Furthermore, since the workspace is augmented spatially, the same graphics can potentially be seen by multiple workers using naked-eye stereo affordances (i.e. simply looking at real-world objects).

Some SAR based remote guidance systems have superimposed the expert's sketches or hand gestures into the worker's

---

[1] This example is inspired though working on the CSIRO's collaboration platform for the Australian Animal Health Laboratory to facilitate the management of exotic diseases.

environment, but they have typically not used any semantic information about the 3D properties of the physical objects.

We propose a method that encompasses the benefits of SAR and incorporates interaction techniques previously developed for 2D manipulation of virtual 3D objects [18]. As shown in Figure 1 and Figure 2, users are able to touch objects on a video feed and manipulate a hidden virtual representation of the physical work environment. Changes made in the virtual scene are used to generate augmentations in the real world that act as spatially aligned guidance for the worker. As objects are moved within the physical scene, the virtual model is updated and the augmentations can also be updated accordingly.

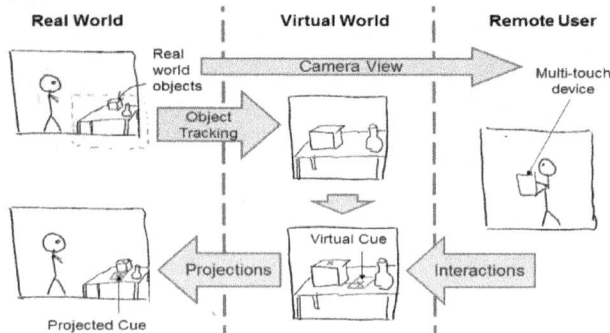

**Figure 2. A workflow of how a virtual scene can be used to mediate in SAR-based remote guidance**

The main contributions of this paper are as follows:

- We extend the concept of object based touch manipulation originally introduced in a works-in-progress paper by Ranatunga et al. [25]
- We have implemented a prototype system that allows an expert to use multi-touch gestures to translate, rotate and annotate an object on a video feed, via a proxy target, causing meaningful projections onto the real world.
- A user study showed that object manipulation is able to improve upon sketching based SAR remote guidance from a view point perpendicular to the work surface.

In the following sections we review some related work. We then review the concept of object-based touch manipulation, including a focus on how some interaction techniques can be employed. We then present an evaluation of two such techniques using our prototype system under two possible camera configurations.

**RELATED WORK**

Our approach draws from a variety of fields, including remote guidance, SAR guidance, 3D multi-touch and proxy-based 2D image manipulation.

Many previous remote guidance systems involve a shared video feed of the worker's environment, composited together with the expert's hands [16], pinpoints [7], or sketch annotations [6,23]. A comparison of existing remote gesture technologies was conducted by Kirk and Stanton Fraser [14]. In particular, they evaluated two SAR-like methods: projected hands, and projected sketches. In the first setup, the helper's hands were recorded from a top down camera and the video feed was directly projected onto the surface of the worker's location. The second approach extended the first by including a digital whiteboard that allowed for the combination of sketching as well as the hands. In both systems, visual feedback to the expert was via a camera feed of the augmented physical world shared with the worker. There was no model of the scene within the system so it was up to the

experts to orient themselves, define reference points, and use relative movements.

In some non-collaborative scenarios, SAR has been shown to benefit guidance of physical tasks. LightGuide is a system that projected guidance cues onto a moving hand to follow a particular path [29]. Rosenthal et al. used micro-projectors to complement on-screen instructions for manual task guidance and determined situations in which guidance improved and decreased performance tasks [28]. Marner et al. [19] showed that, for a procedural button pushing task, SAR overlays led to faster task completion speeds and fewer errors.

Tsimeris explored a variety of projected cues that could assist in the arrangement of physical objects [33]. While the system did incorporate a 2D GUI authoring tool, capable of real-time manipulation, it did not facilitate a collaborative remote guidance scenario, nor any video feedback to a remote expert.

Henderson has shown that dynamic instructions overlaid on or near objects is preferred for psychomotor tasks and is significantly more efficient when compared to a nearby LCD display [11]. That study was specific to HMD based augmented reality and the guidance was entirely pre-authored.

Tecchia et al. employed depth cameras to stream real time virtual representations of the workspace for remote guidance [32]. The system required the expert to wear an HMD showing a depth camera feed from the workspace, while the worker watched a combination of that feed and a depth camera feed taken of the expert's hands. The BeThere system [30] used a similar techniques but required the depth camera and feedback display to be held in the non-dominant hand.

The RemoteFusion system [1] also used depth cameras to capture a 3D scene for a remote expert. The expert could draw on the 3D model and the sketches were projected using SAR onto the physical workspace. Again, unlike the system we present in this paper, RemoteFusion did not perform any segmentation or tracking of the individual objects that made up the scene.

TeleAdvisor [9] was a SAR based remote guidance system that projected a green square into the scene and used it to estimate the location of roughly planar surfaces. The Sticky Light system [8] similarly tracked planar surfaces (or almost any other object) using fiducial markers. Although the expert's annotations 'stuck' to the tracked objects, the input method was still just 'sketching'.

Suenaga et al. [31] implemented a tele-instruction system which used a shared AR space. The expert would manipulate a single ultrasonic probe via a visualization named a 'Web-Mark' which was projected onto the body of a patient. Hiura [12] developed a tele-direction system that creates a virtual model of objects to allow for projected annotations. That system operated somewhat like a 3D version of the copy/paste feature of Wellner and Freeman's Double Digital Desk [34]. We extend these ideas by allowing the expert to manipulate multiple object targets using direct and indirect touch input. Furthermore, our system does not require the expert to first trace the outline of the object(s).

A number of research efforts have explored the ways 2D multi-touch can be used to interact with 3D virtual environments and Liu et al. [18] provide a good comparison of current methods. This is a relatively new field, but already we are seeing useful abstractions emerge which permit different ways of interacting, depending on the required task.

In terms of interaction with captured 2D scenes, there is also related work in video and photo manipulation. Dragicevic et al. [5] described a system for direct manipulation of video playback using inter-frame optical flow. Proxy-based manipulation of photographed objects has been presented by Zheng et al. [35] and Chen et al. [4] using, respectively, cuboid and cylinder proxies. More recently, this idea was extended by Kholgade et al. [13] with more complex 3D proxies sourced from online libraries. In our new system we take inspiration from these approaches, and use proxies to facilitate a remote expert's touch interaction with a live video stream.

## OBJECT BASED REMOTE GUIDANCE

We extended the concept of object based touch manipulation for remote guidance from Ranatunga et al. [25] with spatial direct and indirect touch capability and a sketching feature. Object based touch manipulation for remote guidance applies 3D spatial knowledge of a physical workspace to allow a remote expert to denote understandable guidance via a multi-touch interface.

Interacting with 3D information through a 2D interface is an inherently difficult problem [26]. Object based touch manipulation for remote guidance constrains the expert's interactions to actions that make sense in the physical 3D environment, such as laboratory equipment remaining in contact with a workbench, and aims to make the presented information easier to specify and more understandable. To enable a mapping from the remote expert's interaction with a 2D multi-touch screen into the 3D physical workspace, a virtual world is constructed and maintained to mirror the real world (see Figure 3). Proxy objects in the virtual world can then be interacted with through the use of multi-touch gestures. As soon as the location or orientation of a proxy differs from its respective physical object, SAR visual cues are generated to assist the worker in manipulating the physical object to match the according target pose. The proxy is effectively used by the remote expert to specify the 'end goal' of a physical manipulation for the worker. A more detailed description of object based touch manipulation for remote guidance is presented in Ranatunga et al. [25].

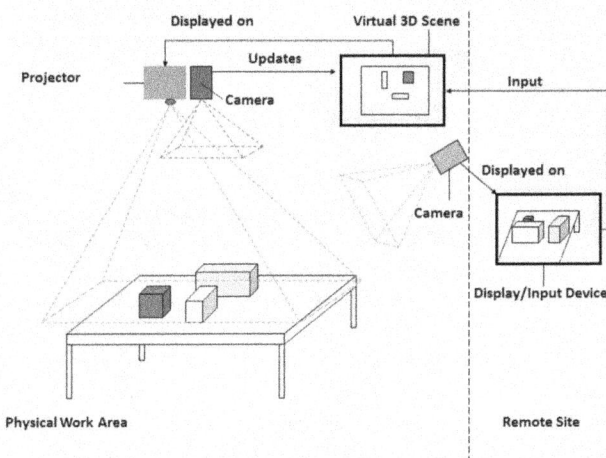

**Figure 3. An overview of our system concept**

SAR systems typically only permit projection of graphics onto the surfaces of physical objects. In sketching based SAR systems, it may be hard for the helper to visualize a meaningful 2D projection for some manipulations (such as rotations) and from some viewing angles (such as anything other than directly

overhead). The proposed system deals with this issue by automatically generating the visualizations.

### Spatial Direct and Indirect Touch

Our system allows 2D gestures performed on a multi-touch display to select and translate based on the constraints of the physical environment. Used by the remote expert, only gestures and a video feed are shown on the display (as shown in Figure 4). The visual cues are presented to the local worker through SAR in the 3D physical space (which are fed back to the remote expert automatically in the captured video). We describe this translation as "spatial direct touch" manipulation [20] as the projected target remains under the user's finger no matter where it moves.

A second finger allows for indirect rotation by moving up and down the vertical axis of the screen (see Figure 5). The rotation finger can be used to rotate the object from anywhere on the screen and both fingers can be moved independently, allowing for simultaneous rotation and translation.

An alternative to the direct-translation/indirect-rotation technique could have been to aim for entirely direct manipulation. However, as we are essentially manipulating real physical objects (albeit via virtual proxy), there are physical constraints to consider.

One technique, now widespread in photo viewing apps on multi-touch tablets and phones, is drag to translate, pinch to scale and twist to rotate [27]. In this case, there is no useful analogue to 'scale' in the physical context, especially when we assume that boxes cannot float in mid air above the table. Attempting to use this technique therefore results in inconsistencies such as can be seen in Figure 6.

We note here that Liu et al. [18] have previously demonstrated that a non-direct manipulation method can out-perform a direct manipulation method in some contexts. Others have also reported that separating the degrees of freedom in the interface can improve the accuracy because they do not require the user to modify one aspect in order to refine another [21,22].

**Figure 4. (Left) Selecting an object, such as one of the boxes, by touching it with one finger on the touch screen, selects it and creates a virtual target. The target is projected directly onto the physical table. (Right) Moving the finger on the touch screen causes the projected target to move accordingly and appear to stay directly under the user's finger.**

**Figure 5. Using a second finger to swipe up and down anywhere on the touch screen will cause the projected target to rotate around the first finger's current position.**

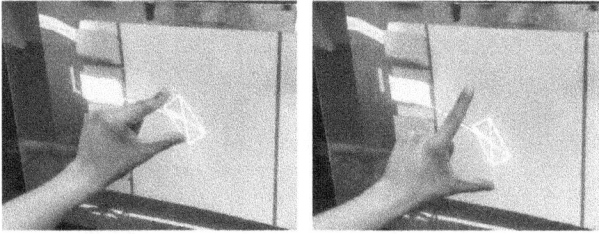

**Figure 6. An alternative interaction technique that uses two fingers to drag/pinch/rotate can experience inconsistencies due to the inability of physical objects to scale up or down in the real world.**

## Sketching

We expect that, for some tasks, sketch based remote guidance will still be useful and therefore we have aimed for our object-based implementation to be compatible with sketching. In our prototype, sketching is implemented in a similar way to the Sticky Light system described by Gunn and Adcock [8], in which geometric knowledge of the physical scene is used to ensure sketched annotations are projected in the correct locations.

When the sketching mode is active, users can use a single finger as input. To avoid finger occlusion issues, a screen-space offset is applied (in a similar way to the *take-off* technique by Potter et al. [24]), giving the impression that the 'digital ink' is flowing from the very tip of the user's finger. Their touch points are sensed and sent to the hidden virtual environment clone of the workspace. There, the touch points are ray-cast onto the respective virtual object and a glowing virtual line is created. This results in the glowing lines being displayed by the projector in the correct location on the respective physical objects.

**Figure 7. Sketching with a finger on the remote expert's touch screen results in glowing lines projected onto the physical objects in the workspace.**

## Prototype Implementation

A prototype system was constructed to demonstrate and evaluate the concept of object based touch manipulation for remote guidance, and the design of this system was inspired by a lab workbench context. The system was implemented with an overhead Kinect depth camera, a projector and an external 'side-on' camera (Lanir et al. [17] found an optimal camera viewpoint can vary with the task). The remote expert interacts with a multi-touch screen. Since the virtual world is hidden from the expert, the visual feedback to the expert is, in fact, the same as the augmented environment provided to the worker. This enforces a strict shared view of the workplace. An example of this can be seen in Figure 1. This overall system arrangement can be seen in Figure 3 and Figure 8 and is described further in [25].

## EVALUATION

We designed and conducted a user study to investigate the performance of this new remote guidance system. The user study was conducted as a counterbalanced 2x2 within-subjects design, with the independent variables being two camera angles that could be practically installed in a science lab (**top**-down or from-the-**side**) and type of SAR interaction (our new **object**-based manipulation or 'traditional' **sketch**ing). There were 12 pairs of participants with each pair working together to complete tasks from each of the 4 conditions:

**top_object** – object based input on the top camera view
**top_sketch** – sketch based input on the top camera view
**side_object** – object based input on the side camera view
**side_sketch** – sketch based input on the side camera view

This study consisted 19 males and 5 females. Participants reported they were generally not familiar with augmented reality, SAR or remote guidance, but most were very familiar with touch screens.

## Setup

Within each pair, participants were randomly assigned a role (either worker or expert), which they kept for the entire duration of the trial i.e. the worker and expert did not swap roles. Both the worker and expert were situated in the same room and could talk naturally with each other. During each trial, the worker was unable to see the expert due to the erection of a physical barrier to block visibility. The room was internal to the building and lighting was kept consistent through the use of indoor lighting. The experimenter was situated with visibility to both environments, giving the ability to take notes without moving around in a distracting manner. The expert had two main displays; the touch screen with which they interacted and a goal screen which displayed instructions.

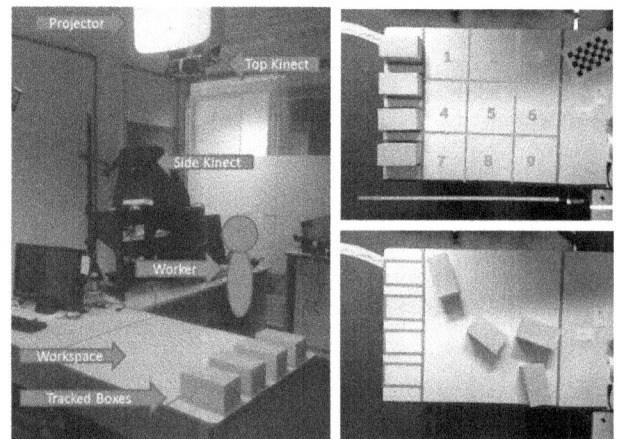

**Figure 8. (Left) The workspace used in the evaluation (Top Right) The grid pattern used to design the arrangement task instructions. (Bottom Right) An example arrangement for the remote expert - using grid squares 1, 5, 6 and 9.**

## Tasks

Each pair of participants would carry out 20 trials in total. Within each trial, participants were tasked with spatially arranging the four identical boxes shown in Figure 8 into positions on a table. It did not matter which box went where, but the worker would not previously know where any of the boxes were supposed to go. Instead, the expert was shown an image such as Figure 8 (bottom right) on an auxiliary computer monitor, and was told to convey the positions to the worker with the aid of object manipulation or sketching. This task is designed to be similar to the spatial arrangement of equipment on a lab-bench. In order to control order effects, a 4x4 balanced Latin Square was used to determine the order that the four conditions were administered.

To maintain a roughly consistent difficulty across each trial, 20 task goal images were generated according to a specific grid location as highlighted in Figure 8 (top right). The angular rotation of each of the 4 boxes was randomly generated such that the total sum of all the rotation would be 180° so as to maintain roughly equal rotational difficulty. The 20 task goals were *clustered* according to their use of similar grid positions such that they could be mapped in structured random order to the 20 trials of each pair. This structured mapping meant that the practice run of each condition would be from Cluster A, the second trial from B, and so on until the last trial, which was always from Cluster E.

### Experimental Procedure
The study was conducted with one pair of participants at a time. The participants were first informed of their randomly assigned role (worker or expert). The experimenter then provided a demonstration of the system from both the expert's perspective and the worker's perspective, with both participants seeing both demonstrations. The demonstration also introduced a user study management application including how to stop and start each trial.

Then, for each condition in the experiment:

(a) The experimenter would demonstrate how to interact with the respective particular condition.

(b) There would be one practice trial

(c) There would be 4 recorded trials

(d) In each trial the following procedure took place:

- The user study management application would light up the starting positions for boxes and wait for the worker to confirm they are reset.
- When both the worker and expert were ready, the expert could press a key to start the timer and the trial.
- The new task goal picture would appear on the experts' second screen.
- The pair would communicate to perform the task, while the experimenter took down any notes and observations.
- The expert would press a keyboard key to stop the timer and end the trial, causing the system to record their box arrangement.

After all the trials were over, participants were then asked to complete a survey to gather their opinions of the tasks they had undertaken.

### Data Collection
The quantities measured during each trial are detailed in Table 1. *Time* is used as the proxy for task efficiency, and *Cost* is inversely proportional to task accuracy.

In addition to these measurements, we also kept the pose (position and orientation) of each box at the start and end of each trial such that scores based off new metrics could be calculated. A screen shot from both cameras was also taken at the end of each trial. These screen shots were used in the case of outliers during the results analysis to visually verify whether any errors occurred in the systems' gathering of data. All of the data was written to a few different files, tagged by a unique identifier associated with the participant ID and time. After all of the trials were complete, a separate python script was written that allowed for easy compilation of data into a single .csv file for statistical analysis.

Upon inspection of the data collected by the system, there were a total of 7 values that had incorrect data recorded. These values had unusually high costs for the translation, rotation and aggregate cost measures. Each value was compared with the screen shots that were taken at the end of each trial. By visual analysis and comparison of the pose matrices of each box, it was determined that the expert had ended the trial while the worker was occluding a box from the tracking camera's view point. Since this invalidated the data from those trials, those 7 values were removed and replaced with 'missing' values in the statistics software tool which, in turn, compensated for this in the analysis.

| Measure | Recording/Calculation Method |
|---|---|
| Total Time (ms) | The difference between the time of the trial starting and the time of the touch screen application being told the trial was over. (Error: 1ms) |
| Translation Cost per box (mm) | The tracking system reported the 4x4 pose matrix of each box. The target pose was saved when the tests were generated, and we record the Euclidean distance between the center of the target and the result box. |
| Rotation Cost per box (radians) | Given a target pose matrix A, and end pose matrix B, we calculate the transformation: C = inverse(A)*B. C represents the transformation to get from one box to the other. We then decompose the rotation part of C into a vector and angle component. The cost is the angle in radians. |
| Aggregate Cost per box (mm) | The Euclidean distance between the top four corners of the target box (defined by depth values closest to the tracking camera) and the top four corners of the result box. |
| Total Translation Cost (mm) | The sum total of the translation cost per box. (Error: <11mm) |
| Total Rotation Cost (radians) | The sum total of the rotation cost per box. (Error: <0.1) |
| Total Aggregate Cost (mm) | The sum total of the aggregate cost per box. (Error: 68mm) |

**Table 1. Quantitative Data Recorded**

*Measurement Error*
The 3D tracking system was used for measuring the translation cost, rotation cost and aggregate cost. The tracking system data; however, had a certain level of noise in its accuracy. To calculate the magnitude of this error before conducting the user study, we captured the tracking data of 4 stationary boxes multiple times and measured the range of values. The maximum error of the total translation cost was found to be 10.4mm (mean of 2.6mm per box). The maximum error of the total rotation cost was found to be 0.06 radians (< 1 degree per box). The maximum error of the total aggregate cost was 67.1mm (mean of 16.8mm per box). The time measurement was meant to be accurate to the nanosecond level; however, the signal to start and stop the timer is also affected by network latency. In either case, this (<1ms, estimated) error would be consistent between all trials and is not formally tested. These values are included in Table 1.

## RESULTS

In this section, we report the results and analysis of each of the four main quantitative measures: Task Time, Translation Cost, Rotation Cost and Aggregate Cost. Note that these are summarized in Table 2 at the start of the next section. We also report on some results from the user questionnaire.

### Time

**Side_object** had the longest trial time with a mean of 117.7 seconds and a standard error of 6.90 seconds. The condition with the shortest average completion time was **top_object** with a mean of 91.2 seconds and a standard error of 5.42 seconds. The overall mean was 106.27 seconds.

A split plot analysis of variance was conducted on the data after a natural log transform was applied. This transform was used to satisfy the assumption of homogeneity in the data.

The spit plot used the four conditions as the main variable and the split on the test cluster whilst adjusting for the effects of different pairs and orders. When tested for differences in completion time, this analysis found a statistical difference between the four conditions ($F(3,24)=3.79$, $p<0.05$). The analysis also showed there was no significant difference in time between test clusters ($F(3,132)=1.60$, $p>0.05$) and even less significance between the different conditions within test clusters ($F(9,132)=0.87$, $p>0.05$).

Performing the Fishers least significant difference (LSD) post-hoc test revealed that **side_object** took significantly longer (at the 5% level) than the other conditions, but the time difference between the other conditions did not differ significantly.

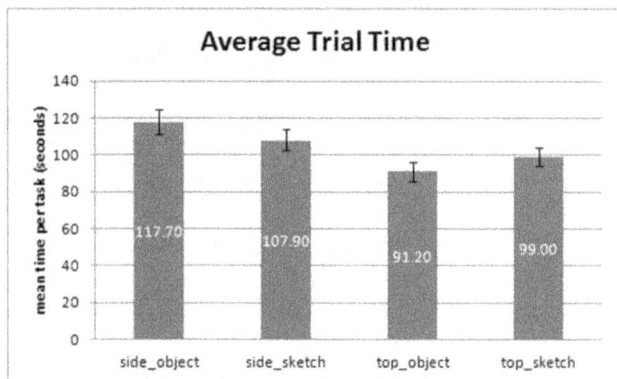

**Figure 9. The average completion of each trial by condition. Error bars represent the standard error of the mean, back-transformed from the log transformation.**

### Cost

*Translation Cost*

**Top_object** had the lowest translation cost mean of 122.9mm (SE=7.7mm). The two side conditions had comparable means: **side_object** had 188.4m (SE=11.6mm) and **side_sketch** had 190.2mm (SE=11.7mm).

A split plot analysis of variance was conducted on the (also log transformed) data to test for differences in translation cost between the four conditions. It was found that a significant difference exists ($F(3,24)=8.56$, $p<0.001$) at the condition level, but not between the test clusters ($F(3,125)=0.96$, $p>0.05$).

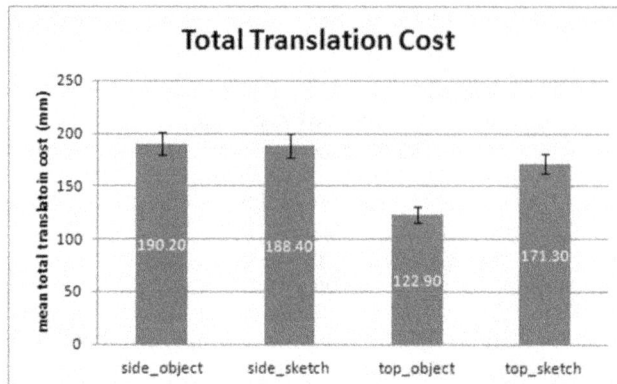

**Figure 10. The average total translation error of each trial by condition. Error bars represent the standard error of the mean, back-transformed after a log transformation.**

Analysis using Fishers LSD post-hoc test showed that **top_object** performed with a significantly lower cost than the other three conditions. Sketching from the top view is not significantly different under the LSD test at the 5% level in comparison with the side conditions.

*Rotation Cost*

The total rotation cost is the sum of the angular error in the four boxes of each trial. As an indication of the range of values, **side_object** had highest mean total rotation cost of 1.727 radians (SE = 0.1112 radians) and **side_sketch** had lowest total rotation cost mean of 1.244 radians (SE=0.1112 radians).

A split plot ANOVA was conducted on the untransformed rotation data with the four conditions as the main variable and the split on the test cluster. The ANOVA adjusted for order effects and the differences between pairs. When tested for differences in rotation cost, the analysis found a statistical difference between the four conditions ($F(3,24)=3.58$, $p=0.028$). The same analysis did not show a significant difference between test clusters ($F(3,125)=1.19$, $p=0.315$), however it did reveal a significance difference in the interactions between test cluster and condition ($F(9,125)=2.59$, $p=0.009$).

The Fishers LSD post-hoc test was applied to the conditions to determine that **side_object** had a significantly higher rotation cost compared to the other three conditions. The difference between **side_sketch** and **top_sketch** is not significant at the 5% level.

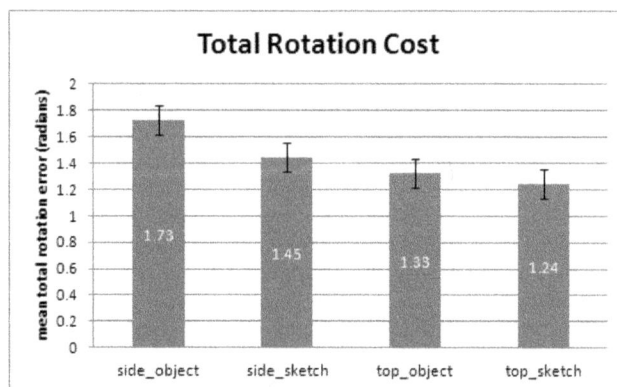

**Figure 11. The average total rotation error of each trial by condition for each test cluster . The error bars represent the standard error of the mean.**

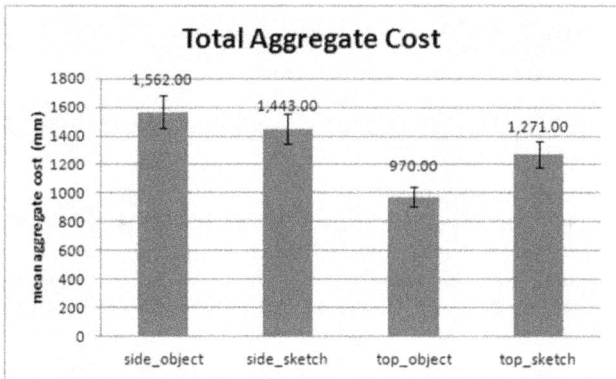

**Figure 12. The average total aggregate cost of each trial by condition. Error bars represent the standard error of the mean, back-transformed after a log transformation.**

*Aggregate Cost*
To test for differences in cost among the four conditions a split plot ANOVA was used on the (log transformed) data with adjustments for pair and order effects, and test clusters as the split. This analysis found significant differences between the four conditions ($F(3,24)=7.48, p<0.01$). It also found significant variation at the test cluster level ($F(3,125)=2.83, p<0.05$) as well as the interactions between test cluster and condition ($F(9,125)=1.97, p<0.05$).

**Top_object** had the smallest aggregate cost with a mean of 970mm (SE=72.44mm). **Top_sketch** had a mean of 1,443mm (SE=92.45mm), while the **side_object** condition performed with the greatest cost (mean=1,562mm, SE=118.84mm). Fishers' post-hoc LSD test was used to determine the significance of these interactions. It was found that the aggregate cost of **top_object** was significantly lower than the cost of all three other conditions. It was also shown at the 5% level, **top_sketch** had a lesser cost than the aggregate cost of **side_object**, but not a significant enough difference from **side_sketch**.

**Qualitative**
The participants in the role of 'Expert' were each presented with a series of statements and asked to rate them on a Likert scale. Figure 14(a) shows that **side_sketch** was not considered as "easy to get the hang of", as the other three conditions. All experts agree that **top_object** was "easy to get the hang of". When asked about ease of communication (Figure 14(b)), we see a positive result in **top_sketch**, **top_object** and **side_object**. However, there was no clear indication as to whether or not it is easy to communicate when sketching from the side. The majority of those with an opinion disagreed with the statement. Participants also felt that by the end of the trial, they were proficient at both systems from both angles (Figure 14(c)).

**Observations**
In general there were key differences in the usage of object and sketch. Each of the pairs independently developed and agreed upon their own strategy for interaction. Many of these strategies repeated themselves between pairs, and this section aims to highlight the different approaches used. Overall, sketching involved a lot less interaction with the system, with a lot of emphasis on the spoken conversation. Generally, the object based trials were conducted with minimal conversation and mostly in silence. This seemed to result in the worker feeling more involved and valuable during sketching.

The interaction graphs in Figure 13 show an example of when the screen was being touched in two corresponding trials, and are indicative of the interaction graphs across most trials. Object manipulation typically involved continual adjustment using the system while the sketching systems tended to be used for initial placements and then verbal adjustments.

Some box layouts were more 'recognizable' than others. For example, three of the boxes in one configuration were in a row, and participants sometimes named this shape. One expert noted "this looks like a conga line" while another called it a "snake". In these cases, participants defaulted to using mostly verbal communication.

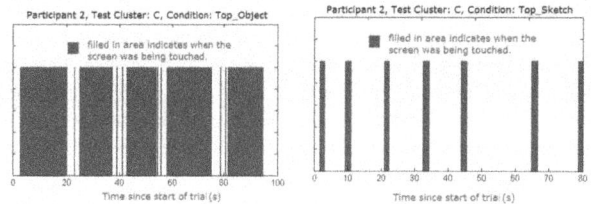

**Figure 13. Typical examples of screen contact timings for two similar tasks (Left) using object based interaction (Right) using sketch based interaction.**

*Strategies for Object based Manipulation*
Typically object manipulation only saw the use of two strategies. Either the expert would position one box and ask the worker to move it, or position all four boxes and then have the worker place them all. The one-at-a-time approach seemed to have benefits and weaknesses. On one hand, it allowed for boxes to be placed and used as a reference point for the placement of the other boxes; however, often this would also become a source of occlusion depending on how the worker moved around the scene. In a few cases, the expert would be distracted by the worker and then ask them to wait until the cues were all positioned. This meant that most pairs of participants ended up on the all-at-once and then adjust strategy. One particular pair had a different strategy to the others though. Instead of being mostly silent in the object mode, this pair was very verbally collaborative; the expert used the

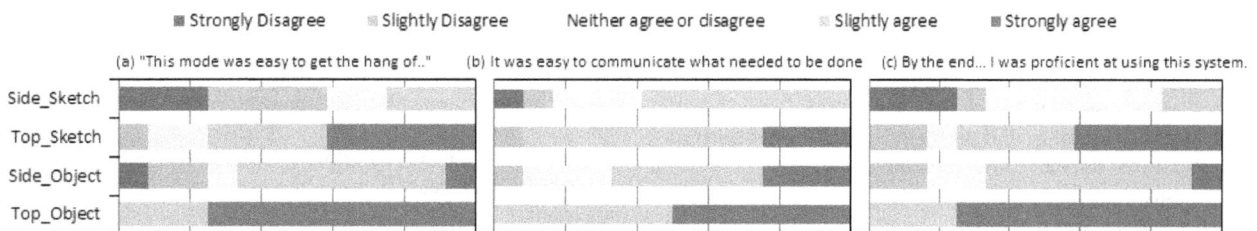

**Figure 14. Participant Responses to Qualitative Survey.**

worker to guide the position of the cue. A typical example was the following:

> Expert: "Okay, now this needs to be closer to the gray line"
> Worker: "Follow my finger and I'll lead you to the gray line".

### Sketching Strategies
The sketching condition saw a multitude of strategies for drawing and specifying the boxes. In this case, one-at-a-time was more common than all-at-once, but the method in which these were specified took the form of either one, two or four lines per box. Figure 15 shows the most common strategies in order of popularity, while the one line method (informally) appeared to be the most efficient. Each of these strategies also seemed to have benefits and limitations.

In the 'Four Lines' approach, the expert could not easily replicate the dimensions of the box- especially from the angled view point, with one participant exclaiming "let me draw that again, that's not supposed to be a diamond, I can't draw rectangles properly". In the 'One Line' approach the worker would align the center of the box with the line. However, the length of the line was often longer than the box, thus verbal adjustments along the line needed to be made. The two lines approach took two forms; either they would draw a 'T' as pictured in Figure 15, or they would draw an 'L' to specify a corner. These were effective methods, though the lines were often not perpendicular, and the correct meaning of the sketch needed confirmation in each case. Other notable strategies that lead to long trial completion times included drawing pairs of vertical and horizontal lines whose intersection points indicated the corners. Several pairs used the markings in the environment to align the positions with the boxes e.g. "between these two gray lines".

**Figure 15. Example Sketching Strategies**
**(left) Four Lines, (center) Two Lines, and (right) One Line**

## DISCUSSION
A summary of the quantitative user study results can be seen in Table 2. It is apparent that the object manipulation technique was able to improve upon sketching, but not in all circumstances.

| Condition | Measure | Object Only | Sketch Only | | Condition | Measure | Top View | Side View |
|-----------|---------|-------------|-------------|---|-----------|---------|----------|-----------|
| Top View | Total Time | = | | | Object Only | Total Time | ✓ | |
| | Translation | ✓ | | | | Translation | ✓ | |
| | Rotation | = | | | | Rotation | ✓ | |
| | Aggregate | ✓ | | | | Aggregate | ✓ | |
| Side View | Total Time | | ✓ | | Sketch Only | Total Time | | = |
| | Translation | = | | | | Translation | | = |
| | Rotation | | ✓ | | | Rotation | | = |
| | Aggregate | = | | | | Aggregate | | = |

**Table 2. Summary of Quantitative Results (Left) Object vs.**
**Sketch, keeping View constant (Right) Top vs. Side Camera**
**View, for each Interaction Technique.**
**'✓' indicates the condition that performed significantly better,**
**while '=' indicates no significant difference.**

When using the top camera view, object manipulation provided a significant benefit to translation accuracy whilst taking the same amount of time as sketching. However, in the side angled camera, we see that the object manipulation method was significantly less effective in terms of time and rotation. The right hand side of

Table 2 highlights that the change of view point has an effect on the performance of the object manipulation technique whereas sketching was not shown to vary in the same way. Many of these quantitative results differed from the participant self evaluations which highlighted a distinct preference for the object manipulation technique.

### Effect of Viewpoint
We originally expected sketching to be hindered by the angled view point, and thus would perform significantly worse than sketching from the top camera. This was based on the assumption of a higher cognitive load making it difficult for the expert to compensate for the perspective change. The difference in difficulty was reported in the questionnaire with many participants stating **side_sketch** was hard to get the hang of and that it was difficult to communicate what needed to be done. In the experimenter observations, it was also noted that many participants verbally exclaimed during the trial 'oh this is hard' or 'hold on, I'm trying to figure out how to adjust'. However, in the quantitative results, despite the perceived difficulty, there was no significant difference in total time spent nor accuracy between **side_sketch** and **top_sketch**. The difference between quantitative and qualitative results can perhaps be explained by the 'learnability' of the system; despite initially having a hard time processing the perspective change, participants also reported that, by the end of the trial, they felt more proficient at sketching from the side.

In the self assessment of the participants, and unlike **side_sketch**, **side_object** was reported as being easy to get the hang of and easy to communicate. Thus, qualitatively speaking, there was no significant disadvantage in using the side view camera.

The quantitative results showed that **side_object** performed worse than **top_object** on all four measures. Firstly, the task time was significantly higher from the side, and this was informally observed to be because the expert would spend a lot of time making minor rotational adjustments to the cue. However, despite all the rotational adjustments, **side_object** was still significantly less accurate than **top_object**. The inference from these results is that object manipulation does not overcome the issues arising from a perspective change.

### Effect of Interaction Technique
The experimenter noted that often when object manipulation took more time than sketching it may have been due to the expert spending more time adjusting for minor rotational differences using the system. Rather, while in the sketching mode, most adjustment requests occurred verbally. The measured data agrees with this, and we can surmise that the time spent adjusting rotations was not particularly efficient.

Qualitatively, most participants preferred object manipulation over sketching, which indicates that despite **side_object** performing differently to **side_sketch**, the expert did not perceive this difference.

### Factors of High Cost
There were several factors that were not quantified but may have had an effect on the cost measurements within these experiments. One of these is the latency inherent in any networked collaborative system. The crux of the issue is there always exists some noticeable delay between the user touching the screen and appropriate feedback appearing in the form of a projection through the video feed. In our system, this issue is noticeable by the expert but not the worker. The majority of experts in our user study explicitly stated that this latency affected the usability of the

system. However, the effect of this latency was disproportionately noticeable between conditions. Specifically, the majority of participants reported that the latency impaired the use of object manipulation while only some reported an effect on the sketching mode. This may be explained by previous familiarity and confidence with sketching.

Another factor is the effect of occlusion. From the side viewpoint, the positions of the boxes would often occlude the visibility (for the expert) of the cues being projected on the table, but this was not much of an issue in the top view. Additionally, the worker's body and movement would also be a source of occlusion that affected the ability of the expert in both views. As a strategy to deal with this, in the object conditions, many pairs resorted to positioning all four box targets before the worker moved any of them. This strategy essentially made the remote guidance very sequential and could almost be described as a form of asynchronous collaboration. In that form of collaboration, the worker and the expert do not need to work together simultaneously, and instead could collaborate with a significant time separation. This could be useful for certain industrial applications; consider for example, the scenario where a manager connects to the remote site at the start of the day, assigns orders (such as highlighting the places to drill) and moves onto other work without needing to supervise the entire time. Later, the manager could reconnect to assign new orders or make adjustments.

## CONCLUSIONS AND FUTURE WORK
We have extended the concept of object-proxy based manipulation for spatially augmented remote guidance. We have implemented a prototype system that allows an expert to use multi-touch gestures to translate, rotate and annotate an object on a video feed causing meaningful projections into the real world.

A user study showed that object manipulation is able to improve upon sketching based SAR remote guidance from a view point perpendicular to the work surface. The study also found that the object based method was less efficient in rotational tasks from an angled viewpoint.

We now suggest some practical improvements to the prototype system, and finish by identifying a new range of research questions to be explored.

The prototype we designed presents a method of SAR remote guidance for spatial arrangement tasks. The primary limitation of this system was the effect of latency on the usability of the system. In any practical implementation, the latency of communication will have a significant impact on the expert. One way of dealing with this could be to provide some immediate local feedback to the expert, realizing that this could potentially cause synchronization issues between the verbal and projected guidance. The idea of dual feedback in collaborative environments has been shown to be effective by Gutwin et al. [10] and insights of that research could be brought into the SAR domain.

Future research may explore the range of tasks that object based methods are suitable for. In the user study we conducted, the tasks were limited to the spatial arrangement of boxes constrained to a plane. There is future work to be undertaken that looks at spatial arrangement in three dimensions, for example, allowing for boxes to be stacked on each other. As a starting point, work conducted by Adcock et al. [2] looks at SAR visual cues for 3D positions of viewpoints (which is, in itself, a challenge for SAR). These cues could be mapped to objects instead. Alternatively, object

manipulation based SAR remote guidance could be applied to procedural and psychomotor tasks of the kind described by Henderson and Feiner [11].

Finally, the potential for future work exists in bringing more real-world constraints into the virtual scene. Greater semantic knowledge of objects within the scene could be used to impose further real-world constraints on the virtual targets. The appropriate constraints to use for various task contexts is now an open question for exploration and research.

## ACKNOWLEDGMENTS
We sincerely thank: the user study participants, Warren Muller for his expert statistics advice, Henry Gardner and Chris Gunn for their support, and the SUI'14 anonymous reviewers for their helpful comments and feedback.

## REFERENCES
1. Adcock, M., Anderson, S., and Thomas, B. RemoteFusion: real time depth camera fusion for remote collaboration on physical tasks. *Proceedings of the 12th ACM SIGGRAPH International Conference on Virtual-Reality Continuum and Its Applications in Industry - VRCAI '13*, ACM Press (2013), 235–242.

2. Adcock, M., Feng, D., and Thomas, B. Visualization of off-surface 3D viewpoint locations in spatial augmented reality. *Proceedings of the 1st symposium on Spatial user interaction - SUI '13*, ACM Press (2013), 1.

3. Bimber, O. and Raskar, R. *Spatial augmented reality: Merging real and virtual worlds*. AK Peters Ltd, 2005.

4. Chen, T., Zhu, Z., Shamir, A., Hu, S.-M., and Cohen-Or, D. 3-Sweep. *ACM Transactions on Graphics 32*, 6 (2013), 1–10.

5. Dragicevic, P., Ramos, G., Bibliowitcz, J., Nowrouzezahrai, D., Balakrishnan, R., and Singh, K. Video browsing by direct manipulation. *Proceeding of the twenty-sixth annual CHI conference on Human factors in computing systems - CHI '08*, ACM Press (2008), 237.

6. Fussell, S., Setlock, L., Yang, J., Ou, J., Mauer, E., and Kramer, A. Gestures Over Video Streams to Support Remote Collaboration on Physical Tasks. *Human-Computer Interaction 19*, 3 (2004), 273–309.

7. Gauglitz, S., Lee, C., Turk, M., and Höllerer, T. Integrating the physical environment into mobile remote collaboration. *Proceedings of the 14th international conference on Human-computer interaction with mobile devices and services - MobileHCI '12*, ACM Press (2012), 241.

8. Gunn, C. and Adcock, M. Using Sticky Light Technology for Projected Guidance. *OzCHI*, (2011), 131–134.

9. Gurevich, P., Lanir, J., Cohen, B., and Stone, R. TeleAdvisor: a versatile augmented reality tool for remote assistance. *Proceedings of the 2012 ACM annual conference on Human Factors in Computing Systems - CHI '12*, ACM Press (2012), 619.

10. Gutwin, C., Benford, S., Dyck, J., Fraser, M., Vaghi, I., and Greenhalgh, C. Revealing delay in collaborative environments. *Proceedings of the 2004 conference on Human factors in computing systems - CHI '04*, ACM Press (2004), 503–510.

11. Henderson, S.J. and Feiner, S.K. Augmented reality in the psychomotor phase of a procedural task. *2011 10th IEEE*

*International Symposium on Mixed and Augmented Reality*, IEEE (2011), 191–200.

12. Hiura, S., Tojo, K., and Inokuchi, S. 3-D tele-direction interface using video projector. *Proceedings of the SIGGRAPH 2003 conference on Sketches & applications in conjunction with the 30th annual conference on Computer graphics and interactive techniques - SIGGRAPH '03*, ACM Press (2003), 1.

13. Kholgade, N., Simon, T., Efros, A., and Sheikh, Y. 3D object manipulation in a single photograph using stock 3D models. *ACM Transactions on Graphics 33*, 4 (2014), 1–12.

14. Kirk, D. and Stanton Fraser, D. Comparing remote gesture technologies for supporting collaborative physical tasks. *Proceedings of the SIGCHI conference on Human Factors in computing systems - CHI '06*, (2006), 1191.

15. Kondo, D., Kurosaki, K., Iizuka, H., Ando, H., and Maeda, T. View sharing system for motion transmission. *Proceedings of the 2nd Augmented Human International Conference on - AH '11*, ACM Press (2011), 1–4.

16. Kuzuoka, H. Spatial workspace collaboration: A sharedview video support system for remote collaboration capability. *Proceedings of the SIGCHI conference on Human factors in computing systems - CHI '92*, ACM Press (1992), 533–540.

17. Lanir, J., Stone, R., Cohen, B., and Gurevich, P. Ownership and control of point of view in remote assistance. *Proceedings of the SIGCHI Conference on Human Factors in Computing Systems - CHI '13*, ACM Press (2013), 2243.

18. Liu, J., Au, O.K.-C., Fu, H., and Tai, C.-L. Two-Finger Gestures for 6DOF Manipulation of 3D Objects. *Computer Graphics Forum 31*, 7 (2012), 2047–2055.

19. Marner, M.R., Irlitti, A., and Thomas, B.H. Improving procedural task performance with Augmented Reality annotations. *2013 IEEE International Symposium on Mixed and Augmented Reality (ISMAR)*, IEEE (2013), 39–48.

20. Martinet, A., Casiez, G., and Grisoni, L. The effect of DOF separation in 3D manipulation tasks with multi-touch displays. *Proceedings of the 17th ACM Symposium on Virtual Reality Software and Technology - VRST '10*, ACM Press (2010), 111.

21. Martinet, A., Casiez, G., and Grisoni, L. Integrality and separability of multitouch interaction techniques in 3D manipulation tasks. *IEEE transactions on visualization and computer graphics 18*, 3 (2012), 369–80.

22. Nacenta, M.A., Baudisch, P., Benko, H., and Wilson, A. Separability of spatial manipulations in multi-touch interfaces. *Proceedings of Graphics Interface 2009*, Canadian Information Processing Society (2009), 175–182.

23. Ou, J., Chen, X., Fussell, S.R., and Yang, J. DOVE : Drawing over Video Environment. .

24. Potter, R.L., Weldon, L.J., and Shneiderman, B. Improving the accuracy of touch screens: an experimental evaluation of three strategies. *Proceedings of the SIGCHI conference on Human factors in computing systems - CHI '88*, ACM Press (1988), 27–32.

25. Ranatunga, D., Feng, D., Adcock, M., and Thomas, B. Towards object based manipulation in remote guidance. *2013 IEEE International Symposium on Mixed and Augmented Reality (ISMAR)*, IEEE (2013), 1–6.

26. Reisman, J.L., Davidson, P.L., and Han, J.Y. A screen-space formulation for 2D and 3D direct manipulation. *Proceedings of the 22nd annual ACM symposium on User interface software and technology - UIST '09*, ACM Press (2009), 69.

27. Rekimoto, J. SmartSkin: An Infrastructure for Freehand Manipulation on Interactive Surfaces. *Proceedings of the SIGCHI conference on Human factors in computing systems Changing our world, changing ourselves - CHI '02*, ACM Press (2002), 113.

28. Rosenthal, S., Kane, S.K., Wobbrock, J.O., and Avrahami, D. Augmenting on-screen instructions with micro-projected guides: When it Works, and When it Fails. *Proceedings of the 12th ACM international conference on Ubiquitous computing - Ubicomp '10*, ACM Press (2010), 203.

29. Sodhi, R., Benko, H., and Wilson, A. LightGuide: projected visualizations for hand movement guidance. *Proceedings of the 2012 ACM annual conference on Human Factors in Computing Systems - CHI '12*, ACM Press (2012), 179.

30. Sodhi, R.S., Jones, B.R., Forsyth, D., Bailey, B.P., and Maciocci, G. BeThere: 3D mobile collaboration with spatial input. *Proceedings of the SIGCHI Conference on Human Factors in Computing Systems - CHI '13*, ACM Press (2013), 179.

31. Suenaga, T., Umeda, T., and Kuroda, T. A Tele-Instruction System for Ultrasound Tele-diagnosis. *ICAT ' 99*, (1999), 84–91.

32. Tecchia, F., Alem, L., and Huang, W. 3D helping hands: a gesture based MR system for remote collaboration. *Proceedings of the 11th ACM SIGGRAPH International Conference on Virtual-Reality Continuum and its Applications in Industry - VRCAI '12*, ACM Press (2012), 323.

33. Tsimeris, J.A. Visual Cues for the Instructed Arrangement of Physical Objects Using Spatial Augmented Reality (SAR). 2010, 1–145. https://www.cis.unisa.edu.au/wiki/Tsimeris-minorthesis.

34. Wellner, P. and Freeman, S. *The Double Digital Desk: Shared Editing of Paper Documents (Technical Report EPC-93-108)*. Cambridge UK, 1993.

35. Zheng, Y., Chen, X., Cheng, M.-M., Zhou, K., Hu, S.-M., and Mitra, N.J. Interactive images: cuboid proxies for smart image manipulation. *ACM Transactions on Graphics 31*, 4 (2012), 1–11.

# Are Four Hands better than Two?
# Bimanual Interaction for Quadmanual User Interfaces

**Paul Lubos**
Department of Informatics
University of Hamburg
paul.lubos@uni-hamburg.de

**Gerd Bruder**
Department of Informatics
University of Hamburg
gerd.bruder@uni-hamburg.de

**Frank Steinicke**
Department of Informatics
University of Hamburg
frank.steinicke@uni-
hamburg.de

## ABSTRACT

The design of spatial user interaction for immersive virtual environments (IVEs) is an inherently difficult task. Missing haptic feedback and spatial misperception hinder an efficient direct interaction with virtual objects. Moreover, interaction performance depends on a variety of ergonomics factors, such as the user's endurance, muscular strength, as well as fitness. However, the potential benefits of direct and natural interaction offered by IVEs encourage research to create more efficient interaction methods.

We suggest a novel way of 3D interaction by utilizing the fact that for many tasks, bimanual interaction shows benefits over one-handed interaction in a confined interaction space. In this paper we push this idea even further and introduce *quadmanual user interfaces (QUIs)* with two additional, virtual hands. These magic hands allow the user to keep their arms in a comfortable position yet still interact with multiple virtual interaction spaces. To analyze our approach we conducted a performance experiment inspired by a Fitts' Law selection task, investigating the feasibility of our approach for the natural interaction with 3D objects in virtual space.

## ACM Classification Keywords

H.5.2 Information Interfaces and Presentation: User Interfaces – Input Devices and Strategies, Evaluation / Methodology.

## Author Keywords

Spatial user interfaces; virtual environments; 3D interaction.

## INTRODUCTION

The advent of affordable head-mounted displays (HMDs) and new interaction devices, such as the Microsoft Kinect or Leap Motion, renewed the interest in immersive virtual environments (IVEs). Such IVEs have the potential to offer natural and direct interaction with objects displayed in the virtual world. In particular, the workspace within the user's arm reach provides a volume, in which the user can grab virtual 3D objects similar to the real world. Spatial interacting via natural gestures in IVEs allows interaction designers to exploit the richness and expressiveness of the interaction.

However, interaction in 3D mid-air is physically demanding and, therefore, often hinders user satisfaction and performance [4]. The increase in the degrees-of-freedom (DoFs) that have to be controlled simultaneously as well as the absence of passive haptic feedback and resulting interpenetration and occlusion issues when "touching the void" [3, 4] are often responsible for reduced performance. Hence, although significant improvements have been made in 3D input technologies, using tracked human gestures and postures in "mid-air" still introduce challenges to the design of high-performance 3D interaction techniques [4].

In this context, *virtual hand techniques* are often considered to be the most natural way of directly interacting with virtual objects as they map identically virtual tasks with real tasks. However, direct interaction with a virtual object in an HMD setup significantly differs from a similar task in the real world [1]. In particular, users often cannot see their real body, but at most a virtual representation in form of a virtual hand, marker or 3D point in space. Furthermore, even small inaccuracies and latency of the used tracking system may cause slight mismatches between visual appearance of the virtual hand and the user's proprioceptive and kinesthetic feedback [3, 4]. Such a decoupling of motor and visual space may degrade performance due to the kinematics of point and grasp gestures in 3D space and the underlying cognitive functions [11].

Despite the well known problems, a large body of literature has shown the benefits of virtual hand interaction, in particular, bimanual interaction, and several promising two-handed interaction techniques have been described [5]. In this paper we propose a novel way of bimanual interaction, which evolves around simulating additional virtual hands for a user resulting in *quadmanual user interfaces (QUIs)*. Using this approach, homing movements of the hands can be effectively reduced by dividing the interaction space into interaction volumes. With this approach we transfer a solution previously devised for large display environments to IVEs, aiming for similar benefits (cf. [8]).

## RELATED WORK

Direct interaction arguably provides the most natural type of interaction with virtual objects, but it is often not possible to use direct interaction for objects that are not located within arm's reach. Performance of constant translational (less so rotational) decoupling of visual and motor

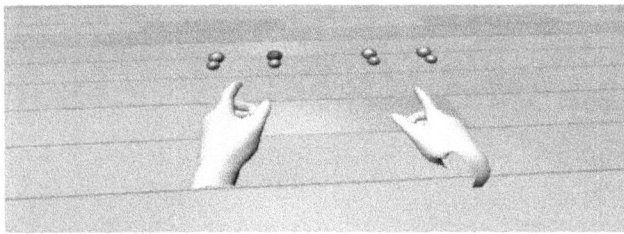

(a) Regular Bimanual User Interface

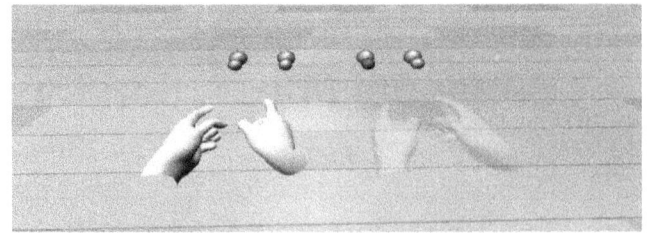

(b) Quadmanual User Interface

**Figure 1. Illustrations of (a) bimanual user interaction and (b) a quadmanual user interface (The active hands are shown opaquely while the inactive hands are shown semi-transparently).**

spaces has been found subject to adaptation [7], i. e., performance increased over time, while optimal performance may be achieved when visual and motor spaces are superimposed or coupled closely [9, 14]. A large body of literature has shown the benefits of bimanual interaction and several promising two-handed interaction techniques have been described [5], e. g., for symmetric interaction tasks [2] or touch interaction [13]. However, it is still an open research question, how the position of virtual objects may affect interaction performance. Direct interaction is subject to perceptual limitations, e. g., the vergence-accommodation mismatch, ghosting or double vision, which can result in strong misperception effects [3, 4]. Depending on the location of virtual objects, users may be unable to discriminate interrelations or perceive distances to objects to be smaller or larger than they are displayed [3]. Such distortions do not appear in the real world and may be related to limitations of current technology to correctly reproduce natural cues from the real world [3]. Moreover, due to varying energy expenditure between users and differences in strength and endurance of arm muscles, interaction performance in mid-air within arm's reach in IVEs may be affected by different factors related to the ergonomics of direct interaction. In particular, contributing factors may include interaction duration, hand and arm postures, frequency of movements, and comfort [1].

### QUI: A QUADMANUAL USER INTERFACE

Figure 1(a) shows a regular *bimanual* user interface in which movements of a user's tracked real-world hands are mapped one-to-one to virtual hands. The *quadmanual* user interface is illustrated in Figure 1(b). With QUIs the user is able to control two pairs of hands. One pair of hands is active, whereas the other pair is inactive and displayed semi-transparently. Using these two virtual hands it is possible to reduce homing movements of the hands as well as the distance between them and target locations by dividing the interaction space into smaller volumes of interaction.

### Controlling Four Hands

Since the user has only two real hands available, a mapping strategy is required to map movements of the user's two real hands to four virtual hands. Two straightforward approaches are possible:

- *simultaneous control*: The user controls both virtual left hands with their real left hand, and both virtual right hands with their real right hand. Although this approach is easy to implement, it has the drawback that all virtual hands are active, even if the user is not focusing on them. Hence, it becomes possible that the hands outside the view interact with the VE, even if not intended to.

- *selective control*: The user controls the virtual left pair of hands with their real left and right hand or they control the virtual right pair accordingly. This approach appears to be more feasible, requiring focus only on the active hands while the inactive hands do not affect the virtual space.

### Activating Hands

To determine which two of the virtual four hands should be active, we decided to exploit the gaze direction of the user, approximated by the head position and orientation. Thus, if the user looks to one pair of hands, this pair is activated, which is visually indicated by an opaque, textured rendering, whereas the inactive pair of hands is shown semi-transparently. The active hands stay active until the user focuses on the other hands. In this case, the former active pair of hands is visualized semi-transparently and all virtual hand movements freeze for this pair.

In theory, users should be more efficient using four than two hands, e. g., if we only consider movement distances to spatial targets for selections as predicted by Fitts' Law [6]. However, it is a challenging task to control four virtual hands with only two tracked hands. Hence, the question arises how much additional perceptual, cognitive and motor effort is required for such an unnatural–or in other words *supernatural*–way of spatial bimanual user interaction.

### EXPERIMENT

In this section we describe a Fitts' Law inspired experiment, in which we explore how much learning is required until QUIs have the potential to outperform bimanual user interfaces. We analyzed direct 3D selection in the user's arm reach in an HMD environment using two-handed interaction to control bimanual and QUIs. We evaluate the following two hypotheses:

**H1:** 3D selection performance is initially higher with bimanual compared to quadmanual user interfaces.

**H2:** With training, the performance difference between bimanual and quadmanual user interfaces decreases.

### Participants

We recruited 11 participants for our experiment. Nine of them were male and two were female (ages 19 - 45, $M = 27.27$). One participant was left-handed, the others were right-handed. All of them had normal or corrected vision. We measured the interpupillary distance (IPD) before the experiment ($M = 6.54$ cm, $SD = 0.32$ cm), and determined their sighting dominant eye (2 left). All participants were naïve to the experimental conditions. The duration of the experiment was one hour.

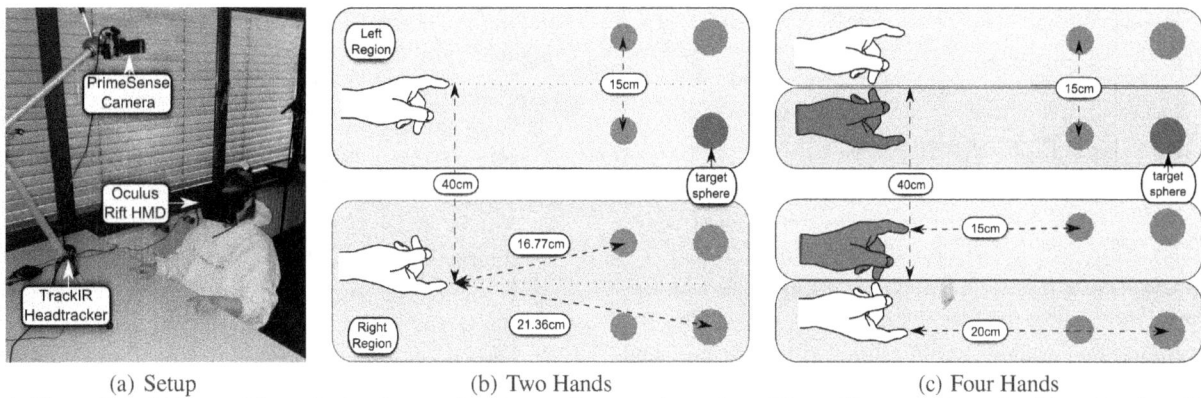

Figure 2. Illustration of (a) a participant during the experiment, as well as experimental conditions with target spheres for (b) two hands and (c) four hands. The virtual, duplicated hands are dark blue.

## Materials

As illustrated in Figure 2(a), users wore an Oculus Rift DK1 HMD tracked in 6 DoF a Naturalpoint TrackIR 5 camera. We used a PrimeSense Carmine sensor and the 3Gear NimbleSDK for skeletal tracking and hand reconstruction. The visual stimulus consisted of a 3D scene (see Figure 1), which was rendered with Unity3D on an Intel computer with a Core i7 3.4GHz CPU and Nvidia GeForce GTX780TI.

Selection targets in the experiment were represented by spheres and colored grey. The current target was colored blue when the user's finger was outside the target, and green when the user's finger was inside. Each trial consisted of 8 spheres on a plane in front of the starting positions, four of which were at a close distance and the others at a far distance (see Figure 2). For the two hand condition the targets were divided into a left region for the left hand and the right region for the right hand. The close targets were at a distance of 16.77cm, the others at 21.36cm. In the four hand condition two targets in a region, at distances 15cm and 20cm and IDs of 2 and 3, were assigned to each of the four hands. Taking the different distances into account, we scaled the targets in the two hands condition up to IDs of 2 and 3 to be able to compare the movement time between the two and the four hands conditions. According to Fitts' Law [6], adapting the target size with respect to the distance between selections results in larger targets for longer selection distances, thus resulting in the same task difficulty between the different interaction volumes.

## Methods

To counterbalance, we used a within-subject $2\times2\times8\times8$ design. The two conditions (bimanual vs. quadmanual), two indices of difficulty (IDs) and eight target positions, were uniformly and randomly distributed among each repetition. We repeated all conditions eight times to measure learning effects. Each trial consisted of a single selection of a single target, where participants had to keep one finger within the target sphere for one second. To account for perceptual limitations, we implemented an ellipsoid selection volume as suggested by Lubos et al. [10]. To make sure all virtual hands were used, we only accepted selections by the correct finger in the correct sphere. Before each trial, participants held both index fingertips within spheres at the starting position, i.e., the initial positions were the same for each trial.

## Results

We analyzed the results with a repeated measure ANOVA and Tukey multiple comparisons at the 5% significance level. Degrees of freedom were corrected using Greenhouse-Geisser estimates of sphericity when Mauchly's test indicated that the assumption of sphericity had been violated.

The results for movement time, including the selection time of one second, are shown in Figure 3. We found a significant difference between the conditions on movement time ($F(1, 10)=26.88$, $p<.001$, $\eta_p^2=.73$). The mean movement time for the four hands was M=3.338, SD=.464 and for the two hands M=2.870, SD=.400. We also found a significant main effect of repetition on movement time ($F(1.79, 17.85)=13.65$, $p<.001$, $\eta_p^2=.58$). We found a significant effect of hand dominance on movement time ($t(10)=-3.96$, $p<.01$). The mean movement time for the dominant hand was M=2.97, SD=.330 and M=3.13, SD=.411 for the non-dominant hand.

We analyzed differences in movement time between the co-located hands and the shifted, virtual hands. The mean movement time for the co-located hands was M=3.046, SD=.375 and M=3.509, SD=.633 for the non-co-located hands. We found a significant difference ($t(10)=-3.57$, $p<.01$). We didn't find significant interaction effects.

Additionally, participants answered subjective questions on a scale of 1=yes, 5=no. We asked whether having four hands made the task easier (M=3.55, SD=1.21), whether seeing the transparent hands helped (M=2.55, SD=1.64), whether it was hard to control four hands (M=3.82, SD=1.25), and whether they wanted four hands (M=2.18, SD=1.47).

## Discussion

The results show that for four hands the movement time is initially higher than for two hands. Since we adjusted the targets to the same IDs, the main difference between these selections was the time necessary to process the input, which can be explained by the human action cycle [12]. Compared to simple bimanual selections, an additional step is needed to turn the head towards the target if the corresponding virtual hands are not activated. Nevertheless, this result confirms our hypothesis H1.

125

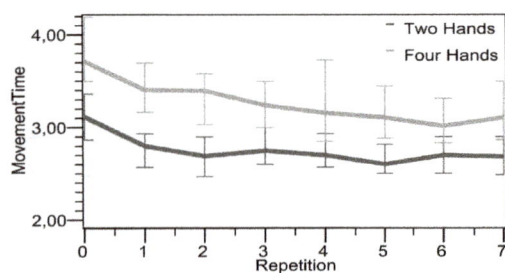

**Figure 3. Results of the experiment: The *y*-axis shows the measured movement time and the *x*-axis shows the repetitions.**

Furthermore, our results show a training effect, as the mean selection times decrease per repetition, which confirms our hypothesis H2. As the experiment was designed to ensure there was no difference in task difficulty between two and four hands, meaning that the target size was artificially increased for the two hands conditions, the difference would be even smaller with targets of the same size, i. e., selections with four hands appear to be feasible. For time critical tasks, bimanual or single hand interaction might be more feasible, but as a training effect is evident in our results, and since it offers reduced homing times, future studies might show that a quadmanual approach is faster for certain time critical tasks. Furthermore, by reducing the need for long homing motions to switch from one interactive element to another in a virtual scene, QUIs reduce the tracking space necessary to properly track the user's hands. Current hand tracking sensors, such as the Leap Motion, have a very limited tracking volume; this drawback may be overcome with QUIs.

## CONCLUSION

In this paper we introduced quadmanual user interfaces, which allow users in IVEs to comfortably interact with a wide virtual interaction volume from a smaller real-world hand tracking volume. Our study investigated the cognitive demand of controlling four hands and compared it to bimanual interaction by measuring the movement time in a Fitts' Law inspired experiment. While the task is more difficult to complete at first, the result showed that the difference is decreasing in time and, while statistically significant, is negligible. With our approach it is possible to solve tasks where just two hands are not enough, yet by deactivating two hands at a time, we limit the potential. Future research could investigate, whether moving the currently inactive hands might increase the usability of our technique, making it feel more natural. However ways to prevent involuntary manipulation of the virtual world with hands which are not in focus at the time, have to be considered. In our experiment, we used the user's head direction to determine which set of virtual hands they wanted to control.

Future research could investigate alternative forms of activating the hands, e. g., eye tracking devices could improve the detection of the user's focus point to better control QUIs. Furthermore, as most user interfaces have a number of specific regions of interest, such as a taskbar, it is possible to define those regions, either through heuristics or manually, and then allow users to place their virtual hands in these regions, eliminating the need to stretch the arms into uncomfortable positions and enabling them to solve tasks quicker due to reduced

homing times. Potentially, even more than two sets of hands might be feasible for 3D interaction.

## REFERENCES

1. Argelaguet, F., and Andujar, C. A survey of 3D object selection techniques for virtual environments. *Computers & Graphics 37*, 3 (2013), 121–136.

2. Balakrishnan, R., and Hinckley, K. Symmetric bimanual interaction. In *Proc. of ACM CHI* (2000), 33–40.

3. Bruder, G., Steinicke, F., and Stuerzlinger, W. Effects of visual conflicts on 3D selection task performance in stereoscopic display environments. In *Proc. of ACM 3DUI* (2013), 115–118.

4. Bruder, G., Steinicke, F., and Stuerzlinger, W. Touching the Void Revisited: Analyses of Touch Behavior On and Above Tabletop Surfaces. *Lecture Notes in Computer Science: Human-Computer Interaction - INTERACT 2013 8117* (2013), 278–296.

5. Buxton, W., and Myers, B. A Study in Two-Handed Input. In *Human Factors in Computing Systems* (1986), 321–326.

6. Fitts, P. The Information Capacity of the Human Motor System in Controlling the Amplitude of Movement. *Journal of Experimental Psychology 47*, 6 (1954), 381–391.

7. Groen, J., and Werkhoven, P. Visuomotor adaptation to virtual hand position in interactive virtual environments. *Presence 7*, 5 (1998), 429–446.

8. Kobayashi, M., and Igarashi, T. Ninja cursors: using multiple cursors to assist target acquisition on large screens. In *In Proc. of ACM CHI 08, 949958. ACM* (2008).

9. Lemmerman, D., and LaViola, Jr., J. Effects of interaction-display offset on user performance in surround screen virtual environments. In *Proc. of IEEE Virtual Reality* (2007), 303–304.

10. Lubos, P., Bruder, G., and Steinicke, F. Analysis of Direct Selection in Head-Mounted Display Environments. In *Proc. of IEEE 3DUI* (2014), 11–18.

11. MacKenzie, C. L., Marteniuka, R. G., Dugasa, C., Liskea, D., and Eickmeiera, B. Three-dimensional movement trajectories in fitts' task: Implications for control. *Q.J. Exp. Psychology-A 39*, 4 (1987), 629–647.

12. Norman, D. *The Design of Every-Day Things*. PhD thesis, MIT, 1998.

13. Ohnishi, T., Lindeman, R., and Kiyokawa, K. Multiple Multi-touch Touchpads for 3D Selection. In *Proc. of 3DUI* (2011), 115–116.

14. Teather, R., Allison, R., and Stuerzlinger, W. Evaluating visual/motor co-location in fish-tank virtual reality. In *Proc. of Toronto International Conference* (2009), 624–629.

# Visual Aids in 3D Point Selection Experiments

**Robert J. Teather**
McMaster University
1280 Main Street West
Hamilton, Ontario, Canada
teather@mcmaster.ca

**Wolfgang Stuerzlinger**
York University
4700 Keele Street
Toronto, Ontario, Canada
wolfgang@cse.yorku.ca

## ABSTRACT

We present a study investigating the influence of visual aids on 3D point selection tasks. In a Fitts' law pointing experiment, we compared the effects of texturing, highlighting targets upon being touched, and the presence of support cylinders intended to eliminate floating targets. Results of the study indicate that texturing and support cylinders did not significantly influence performance. Enabling target highlighting increased movement speed, while decreasing error rate. Pointing throughput was unaffected by this speed-accuracy tradeoff. Highlighting also eliminated significant differences between selection coordinate depth deviation and the deviation in the two orthogonal axes.

## Author Keywords

3D pointing; selection; cursors; stereo display; depth cues.

## ACM Classification Keywords

H.5.1 [Information Interfaces and Presentation]: Multimedia Information Systems – virtual reality. H.5.2 [Information Interfaces and Presentation]: User Interfaces – input devices, interaction styles.

## General Terms

Performance, Human Factors.

## INTRODUCTION

Target selection is a fundamental task in 3D user interfaces, as in the 2D desktop paradigm. However, 3D selection is considerably more complicated and comparatively less well-understood, despite considerable research on the topic [3, 4, 14]. Perhaps the largest difference is that selecting a point in a 3D volume requires control of at least three degrees of freedom (3DOF). Virtual hand techniques, for example, require movement in each of the $x$, $y$, and $z$ axes. In contrast, 2D selection requires only 2DOFs, which is readily handled by the mouse. To date, no standard 3D input device or selection technique exists.

Systems that employ 3D selection typically also use 3D display technologies, which introduce additional

complexities. Targets farther from the viewer appear visually smaller due to the perspective transformation. Yet, it is well-known that target size affects selection difficulty [15, 23]. The influence of perspective-scaled target size largely depends on the selection technique [37]. Current stereo displays also introduce the well-known conflict between vergence and accommodation [17]. Consequently, selection of targets in 3D space (e.g., via direct touch) is difficult [11, 36], even with the additional depth cues afforded by stereo.

Researchers investigating 3D selection often add additional visual aids to improve performance. Extra depth cues such as head motion parallax [20], texturing [34], or shadows [18] enhance perception of depth, and may thus improve selection performance. Other forms of feedback may also be helpful. Haptic feedback, for example, helps participants "feel" target depths, which may improve performance [12]. Its absence, however, may impair one's ability to find the true depth of targets [36].

Recent work [11, 36] employed specific visual aids for 3D touch-based selection experiments. Aside from stereo and head-tracking, these aids include texture, avoiding floating targets, and "highlighting" for extra visual feedback – i.e., changing target colour when touched/intersected by the tracker/finger. These studies used a 3D extension of the ISO 9241-9 standardized methodology, which improves comparability between studies [19]. However, it is unclear if such visual aids influence the consistency of results. For example, is it valid to compare results of a 3D selection study using texturing to one that does not?

We address this methodological concern by evaluating the impact of each factor on 3D point selection. We present a study quantifying the effects of texturing, target highlighting, and "support cylinders" that eliminate floating objects. The rationale behind avoiding floating objects is that such objects are rare in the real world. Humans may have a hard time with such an atypical task. Our experiment uses the same 3D variant of the ISO 9241-9 method employed by others [11, 36] . We exclusively used touch-based interaction: a tracked stylus that required participants to touch the tip to targets in 3D to select them.

## RELATED WORK

Most direct 3D selection techniques fall roughly into two broad paradigms: ray-based techniques (including occlusion) and virtual hand techniques [1, 7, 14, 28]. Virtual hands use intersection of the hand/cursor with the target and thus require depth precision. Since our current work focuses on evaluating visual aids in depth motions, we exclusively study virtual hands. Our virtual "hand" uses a tracked stylus to approximate the actual hand position.

Virtual hand (and ray-based) selection techniques are largely equivalent to pointing tasks, i.e., they specify a unique position (of an object) in the environment. Numerous 3D pointing studies have been conducted [4, 12, 21, 27, 35], yet 3D pointing is still not as well understood as its 2D equivalent [31]. Research comparing pointing in the real world vs. virtual reality indicates that VR performance is substantially worse [21, 26, 32]. Several factors contribute to this difference, notably including input latency and noise [35], tracker registration [32] and tactile feedback [12]. However, visual cues seem critical as the largest differences occur during the correction phase of motion, where visual feedback is used in a tight feedback loop [21, 26].

Due to the direct correspondence between input and display spaces, target selection is affected by several visual cues and feedback mechanisms. Early work [4, 5] focused on stereo and head-tracking and found that target position significantly affected task completion time and accuracy. Depth movements were slower and less accurate than screen-parallel movements. Participants were better able to judge depth with stereo enabled. These results were later confirmed in a docking task [5] – stereo significantly reduced movement error in depth.

Other visual aids are important in 3D pointing. Partial target occlusion improves selection with volumetric cursors, especially when combined with stereo [39]. Visual feedback also improves object position memorization [13]. Color change is a commonly used visual feedback mechanisms. The recent Virtual Mitten technique [1], for example, uses colour changes to indicate pressure applied to a handheld grip device. Other recent work focused on visual feedback for hand-based grasp techniques [29]. The authors report that changing the selected object colour was preferred by participants, even though it did not necessarily offer the best performance. Similar approaches improved participant speed and accuracy of 2D pointing in sub-optimal viewing conditions [16]. However, highlighting selected targets in a 2D pursuit tracking task did not improve performance [25].

### Pointing and Fitts' Law
We use a 3D extension of the ISO 9241-9 standard [19] based on Fitts' law [15]. This paradigm has been previously employed in 3D pointing studies [10, 11, 36, 37].

Fitts' law states that the difficulty in selecting an object is based on the distance to and size of the target. Increasing distance or decreasing size increases selection time and vice versa. The predictive form of the model is thus given by:

$$MT = a + b \cdot ID, \quad \text{where} \quad ID = \log_2\left(\frac{A}{W} + 1\right) \quad (1)$$

$MT$ is movement time, and $a$ and $b$ are empirically determined via linear regression for a given condition. $ID$ is the index of difficulty (in bits), which indicates overall task difficulty. $A$ is distance to the target (amplitude), and $W$ is the target width.

ISO 9241-9 [19] employs a standardized pointing task (Figure 1) based on Fitts' law. The standard uses throughput as a primary measure [6]. Throughput (TP) is defined in bits per second as:

$$TP = \frac{\log_2\left(\frac{A_e}{W_e} + 1\right)}{MT}, \quad \text{where} \quad W_e = 4.133 \cdot SD_x \quad (2)$$

The log term is the *effective* index of difficulty, $ID_e$, and $MT$ is the average movement time for a given condition. Effective amplitude, $A_e$, is the average *actual* movement distance for a given condition. Effective width ($W_e$) is computed using $SD_x$, the standard deviation of the distances between the selection coordinates and the target along the task axis (the line between adjacent targets). By multiplying $SD_x$ by 4.133 (±2.066) standard deviations, the experiment accuracy rate is adjusted to 96%, i.e., to a 4% miss rate. This accuracy adjustment enables the comparison between studies with differing error rates [23].

By "normalizing" experimental accuracy, throughput incorporates speed and accuracy into a single measure. It has been shown to be unaffected by speed-accuracy trade-offs [24]. Effective measures better account for user behavior, and thus enhance comparison.

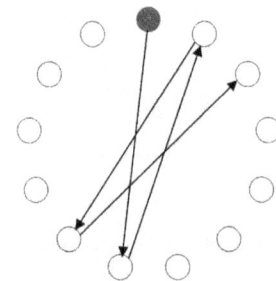

**Figure 1. ISO 9241-9 reciprocal selection task with thirteen targets. Participants click the blue target, starting with the top-most one. Targets advance in the pattern indicated by the arrows. Arrows show the ordering for the first four targets.**

### ISSUES IN 3D POINTING STUDIES
Several issues arise in extending the ISO standard to 3D pointing studies. It is unclear how important each is in ensuring consistent results. While some issues have been identified before [33], we review the most important ones here. Note that additional issues may arise in general 3D point selection studies.

### Stereo Viewing
A major concern is cue conflicts inherent to stereo displays. The human visual system unable to focus simultaneously at

objects at different depths (e.g., a finger and a target), and most stereo systems suffer from the vergence-accomodation conflict. Consequently, when focusing on a 3D target displayed on the screen, viewers see a blurred finger or when focusing on the finger, they see a blurred target [9]. Systems using stereo touchscreens also suffer from diplopia [38]. This likely impacts both the initial ballistic phase of pointing, as the motor program may target the wrong location in space, and also the correction phase, where visual cues are very important [21, 26].

Cursor/ray-based selection avoids full 3D pointing, as they only select objects visible from the viewer or along a ray. Thus, stereo may be less important with such techniques than virtual hands, but likely still improves scene perception. A 2D performance model describes such techniques quite well [37]. Displaying the cursor in mono eliminates (at least some of) the negative effects of stereo conflicts, yet may cause greater eye strain [30]. We exclusively investigate stylus-based touch in our experiment; pilot testing revealed that stereo is necessary for such techniques.

### Selection Distribution

Another concern is that the distribution of selection coordinates in a 3D pointing experiment may not be spherical [22, 40]. This may be due to depth perception inaccuracies. This is illustrated by a recent analysis of 3D touch on a tabletop [11, Fig. 6]. The definition of throughput in ISO9241-9 relies on a (roughly) symmetrical and normal hit distribution [19]. Large deviations may invalidate the underlying assumption(s) of the accuracy adjustment. Thus, part of our work focuses on investigating the distribution of selection coordinates in a 3D pointing task.

### Floating Targets

Objects floating in space correspond poorly to real world pointing tasks. Fitts' original pointing experiments, for example, involved selecting physical objects in the real world with a pen [15]. Consequently, to enhance realism in pointing experiments, some researchers [21, 36] have used objects (e.g., cylinders) as "support pedestals" for targets. This helps visually "anchor" the targets in space. However, it is unclear if this is necessary; the effect of such cylinders has not been previously evaluated.

### Target Shapes

Another question concerns the shape of the target area or volume participants must select. The two most obvious choices are discs and spheres. Discs are equivalent to 2D targets. This enables direct comparisons between 2D and 3D pointing [36]. However, the visual profile of discs depends on the viewing angle. Consequently, they make the most sense when oriented "flat" toward the viewer. Their extremely small depth extent also makes them difficult to select with touch-based techniques; it is unlikely that participants are able to reliably intersect a flat disc target. For discs, a crossing paradigm [2] is likely more

appropriate, but would prevent comparison with other pointing studies.

Spherical targets, on the other hand, are the natural 3D extension of the circular targets recommended by ISO9241-9. Like circles, they have a single "size" parameter, i.e., diameter. A disadvantage is that positioning spheres on top of "support pedestals" may be visually strange. An alternative option is to use a hemisphere, which effectively centers the sphere at the top of the cylinder. This option may distort the computation of effective target width, though. In our experiment, we opt to use (full) spherical targets.

### Selection Feedback

Several cues indicate when we have touched a target in reality, including tactile feedback and stereo viewing with correct vergence and accommodation. However, most VR systems do not present these correctly, if at all. Consider, for example, selecting a 3D target using a tracked finger. Due to the absence of tactile feedback, the finger will pass *through* the target. Stereo cues now indicate that the target is in front of the finger, while occlusion cues indicate the opposite – the finger *always* occludes the screen. Consequently, another means of selection feedback is required.

Recent work [11, 36] used target highlighting for this very reason. When the target is touched, it changes colour. This provides feedback that selection (e.g., via a button) will be successful, and helps the user choose between multiple targets. Our current work addresses the question of how important this feedback really is.

## METHODOLOGY
### Participants

Sixteen participants took part in the study (aged 19 to 39, mean age of 23.4, $SD = 4.5$ years). Eight were female. All had normal stereo vision. Stereo vision was assessed by showing a stereo stimulus 10 cm in front of the screen and asking them to touch its perceived position. Participants were disqualified if they could not (roughly) find the object's 3D position.

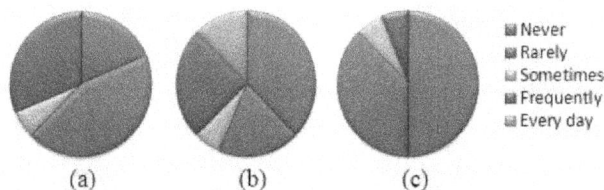

**Figure 2. Participant gaming with (a) mouse and keyboard games, game controllers, and spatial devices (Wiimotes, Kinects, etc.). Rarely: once or twice per month. Sometimes: several times per month. Frequently: several times per week.**

Participants were asked about their gaming experience. Results are summarized in Figure 2 for mouse/keyboard games (Figure 2a), console controller games (Figure 2b), and spatial input games, e.g., using Wiimotes, Kinects, or similar devices (Figure 2c).

## Apparatus
*Hardware*

The experiment was conducted using a PC running Windows 7. The PC had an Intel *i5* quad-core 3.4 GHz processor, 16 GB of RAM. An NVidia Quadro 4400 graphics card that supports quad-buffered stereo graphics was used, with NVidia 3DVision Pro glasses for stereo. The setup is depicted in Figure 3.

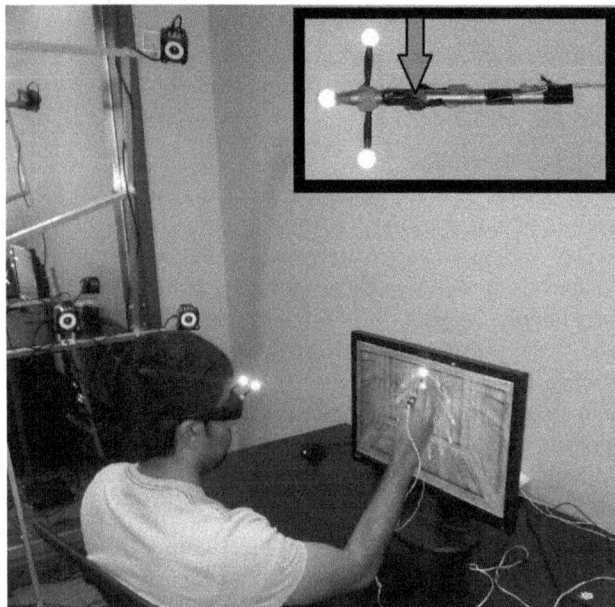

**Figure 3. A participant performing the task in our fish-tank VR setup. Top right inset: Stylus used in the experiment with tracker markers. The stylus button is indicated by an arrow.**

A tracked stylus was used as the input device. The marker positioned at the tip of the stylus was treated as the "hot spot". The stylus used a re-engineered USB mouse to provide button click events. The button was positioned where the thumb would naturally grip the stylus, i.e., opposite to the fingers. See Figure 3 inset. This was intended to reduce or eliminate the so-called "Heisenberg effect" [8] – that pressing a button on a tracked input device can cause the tip to move slightly upon selection.

The glasses and stylus were tracked using five NaturalPoint *Optitrack S250e* cameras calibrated to ~0.5 mm precision with NaturalPoint's software. We did not use smoothing, as the increased latency may outweigh the benefits [35].

*Software*

Software was developed in C++ and OpenGL and depicted the inside of a box. See Figure 4. The scene was always presented in stereo with head-tracking as the task was impossible without these cues. Targets were presented as spheres. Depending on the condition, targets either floated at or in front of the display, or were positioned at the tops of support cylinders, see Figure 4. Targets were always presented in a circle parallel to the display surface, like (most) previous work. The software logged selection times, error rates, selection coordinates, and stylus motion trails.

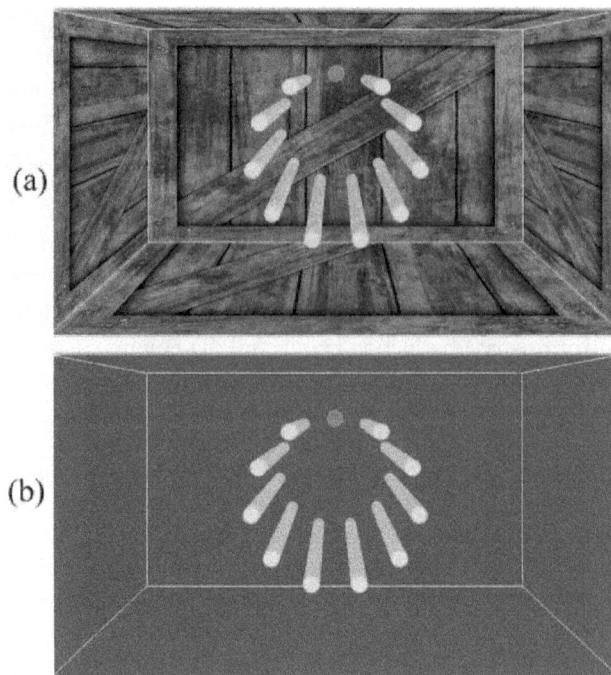

**Figure 4. The scene presented by the software (a) Texture-on view. (b) Texture-off view. The "wooden" cylinders supporting the target spheres were excluded in the "cylinders-off" conditions. This figure shows targets at the screen surface.**

Similarly, depending on the condition the entire scene was either presented with or without textures. A wood-grain texture with strong texture gradient was used on the cylinders, while a wooden crate texture was used on the box (Figure 4a). In the texture-off conditions (Figure 4b), the cylinder and box were set to the average colour of their respective texture to maintain the same average luminance. The target spheres were never textured to improve comparability with previous work. White lines were drawn along the edges of the box to help facilitate perception of its structure in the texture-off conditions. The lines were also shown in the texture-on conditions for consistency.

The default sphere colour was bright gray. The active target, i.e., the sphere participants were to select, was red (the top-most target in Figure 4). In the highlighting-on conditions, spheres changed blue when intersected by the stylus tip. In the highlighting-off conditions, spheres did not change colour when touched.

Head and stylus tracking used NaturalPoint's SDK. Since the stylus tip marker would make selection with a single point cursor difficult – it would occlude targets – we treated the stylus tip as a 0.25 cm radius sphere cursor instead. This cursor was not actually displayed. A hit was recorded if the participant pressed the button while the cursor sphere intersected the target sphere. In highlight-on conditions, the target sphere changed colour upon being intersected by the cursor sphere. Note that this made selection somewhat easier: targets were effectively 0.25 cm larger.

**Procedure**

Participants were first greeted by the experimenter who then demonstrated all conditions. After providing informed consent, participants briefly practiced (~20 to 30 selection trials) each condition. This introduction took less than five minutes. Subsequently, participants began the experiment. Participants were instructed to select the red target sphere as quickly and accurately as possible, maintaining a consistent speed/accuracy tradeoff. Selection involved intersecting the 0.25 cm "cursor" with the target sphere. This necessitated depth movement, unlike previous work, which focused on screen-space selection [37]. Hence we report the 3D size and distance of targets below, rather than adjusting these for perspective.

After each selection trial, the active target advanced according to the pattern shown in Figure 1, regardless if the trial ended in a hit or a miss. Per ISO 9241-9, the same ordering was always used to avoid influencing the task with visual search or other cognitive tasks. Upon completing all trials in a circle of targets, the next circle of targets appeared with different target size, distance, and depth values. Participants could take breaks when the top target was active (as in Figure 4), as timing began after selecting it.

At the end of the experiment, participants completed a brief questionnaire that recorded their demographic information and preferences for the conditions.

**Design**

The experiment used the following independent variables with the specified levels:

*Texture*: on or off

*Highlighting*: on or off

*Cylinders*: on or off

*Target Size*: 1.0 cm, 1.5 cm, 2.0 cm

*Target Distance*: 3.5 cm, 7.5 cm, 9.5 cm

*Target Depth*: 0 cm, 5 cm, 10 cm

The $2 \times 2 \times 2 = 8$ combinations of texture, highlighting, and cylinders were counterbalanced by a balanced Latin square. Target size, target distance, and target depth were selected randomly (without replacement) for each circle of 11 targets. All combinations of these factors appeared (only once) for each texture-highlight-cylinder condition. Note that target size and distance were used only to provide a range of task difficulties, and were not analyzed explicitly. Target depth is measured from the screen surface. Each circle of targets consisted of eleven targets, 10 of which were recorded. In total, participants completed $2 \times 2 \times 2 \times 3 \times 3 \times 3 \times 10 = 2160$ recorded trials. Hence, over all 16 participants, our analysis is based on 34560 selection trials.

The dependent variables were movement time (milliseconds), error rate (missed target percentage), and throughput (bits per second). We also analyzed selection deviation in the z-axis (cm).

**RESULTS AND DISCUSSION**

Results were analyzed with repeated measures ANOVA.

**Movement Time**

Movement time was measured as the time to select the target. The grand mean movement time was 972 ms ($SD = 319$ ms). In general, participants were able to do the task quickly at slightly under 1 second per selection. Movement times across the 8 primary conditions are summarized in Figure 5.

There was a significant main effect for highlighting on movement time ($F_{1,15} = 5.9$, $p < .05$). Highlighting actually *increased* movement time – i.e., participants were slower when highlighting was enabled. Neither texture ($F_{1,15} = 0.04$, ns) nor cylinders ($F_{1,15} = 0.07$, ns) significantly affected movement time.

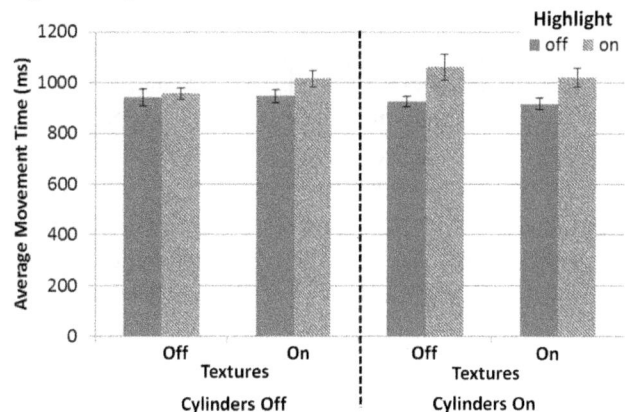

**Figure 5. Movement time by textures, cylinders, and highlight. Higher scores are worse. Error bars show ±1 *SE*.**

Target depth significantly affected movement time ($F_{2,15} = 8.9$, $p < .001$). The 10 cm depth condition (1151 ms) was slower than the 0 cm (863 ms) or 5 cm (904 ms) depth conditions. The interaction between highlighting and target depth was also significant ($F_{2,30}$ 6.1, $p < .01$). The slowest condition was 10 cm with highlighting-on. No other interactions were significant.

**Error Rate**

Error rate was the average number of selection trials that ended with a miss, expressed as a percentage of all trials for a condition. The error rates were generally high, with the best conditions hovering around 15%. Error rates are depicted in Figure 6.

There was a significant main effect for highlighting ($F_{1,15} = 29.5$, $p < .0001$). Like movement time, target depth significantly affected error rate ($F_{2,15} = 57.0$, $p < .0001$). The farther the targets were from the screen, the higher the error rate. The interaction effect between highlighting and target depth was also significant ($F_{2,30} = 15.5$, $p < .0001$). Globally, highlighting reduced the error rate by almost half – the highlighting-on conditions had 55% the error rate of the highlighting-off conditions. This was most pronounced with 10 cm targets, where error rates were as high as 42.6% with highlighting-off. This was approximately twice as high as the error rate with highlighting-on at 10 cm target depth. The lowest error rate was 11.6% for targets displayed at the screen surface (0 cm) with highlighting-on. Neither texture ($F_{1,15} = 0.38$, ns) nor cylinders ($F_{1,15} = 0.21$, ns) significantly influenced error rate. Their interactions were not significant.

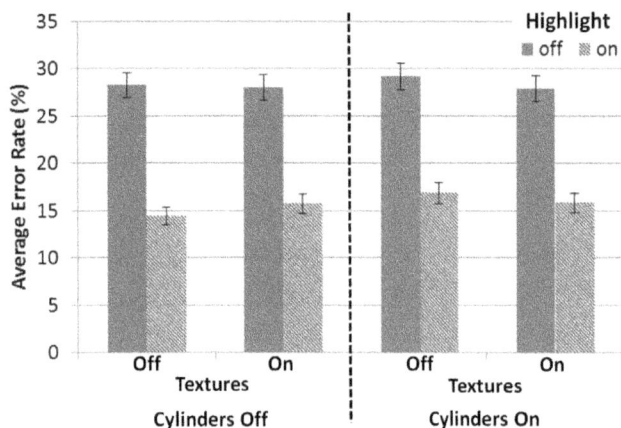

Figure 6. Error rate by textures, cylinders, and highlight. Higher scores are worse. Error bars show ±1 SE.

## Throughput

Throughput was calculated with a variation we previously suggested [36] and which other researchers use [22, 36]]. The standard (2D) calculation projects the task into 1D motions along the task axis, and does not consider depth. Rather than projecting selection coordinates onto the task axis, we used the Euclidean distance between the selection coordinate and the target. The standard deviation of these distances replaced $SD_x$ in Equation 2. Effective width and amplitude were then computed normally. This modified approach "penalizes" selections that may be visually aligned with the target, but far from it in the depth dimension. We argue that this is better suited to 3D selection. See Figure 7.

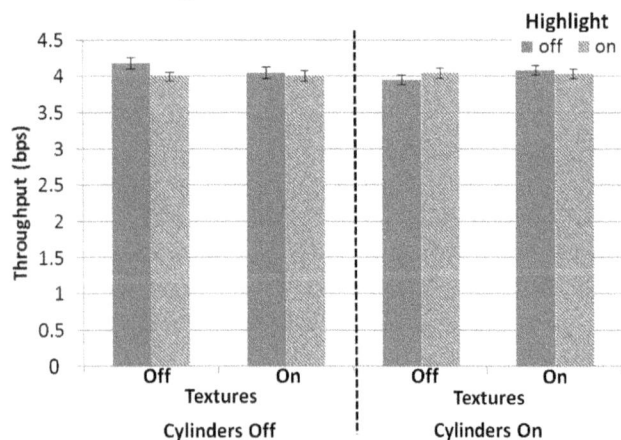

Figure 7. Throughput by textures, cylinders, and highlight. Higher scores are better. Error bars show ±1 SE.

Only target depth significantly affected throughput ($F_{2,15} = 31.4$, $p < .0001$) – both 0 cm and 5 cm targets had significantly higher throughput than 10 cm. Unlike

movement time and error rate, highlighting was not significant ($F_{1,15} = 0.42$, ns). Texture ($F_{1,15} = 0.04$, ns) and cylinders ($F_{1,15} = 0.03$, ns) were not significant, nor were any interaction effects.

## Depth Deviation

We analyzed depth deviation to address our concerns about the selection coordinate distribution. This metric was calculated as the standard deviation of selection coordinate $z$ values, i.e., the "in-out" axis. Depth deviation scores are summarized in Figure 8.

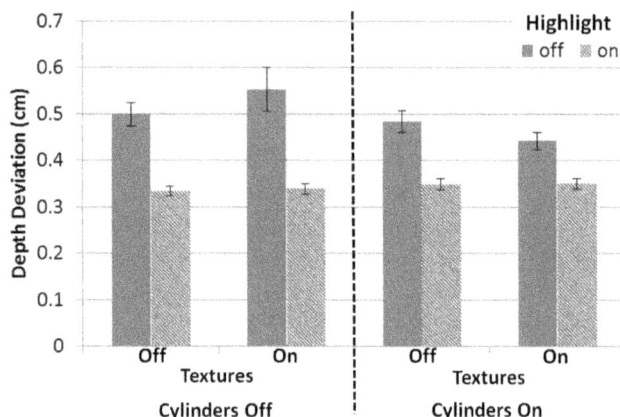

Figure 8. Depth deviation by textures, cylinders, and highlight. Higher scores are worse. Error bars show ±1 SE.

Like movement time and error rate, highlighting had a significant main effect on depth deviation ($F_{1,15} = 9.1$, $p < .01$). Depth deviation was significantly lower with highlighting-on, which had a mean score of 0.34 cm compared to 0.49 cm depth deviation for highlighting-off. Like the other independent variables, cylinders ($F_{1,15} = 0.56$, ns) and texture ($F_{1,15} = 0.05$, ns) had little effect, nor were their interactions significant. No interaction effects with these factors were significant either.

Target depth significantly affected depth deviation ($F_{2,15} = 23.5$, $p < .0001$). Depth deviation was lowest with 0 cm targets (0.25 cm), and was significantly higher with both 5 cm targets (0.40 cm) and 10 cm targets (0.59 cm). The interaction between highlighting and depth was significant ($F_{2,30} = 8.1$, $p < .005$). Like error rate, highlighting had a stronger effect on depth deviation for targets farther from the screen, and little effect on targets at 0 cm. This is likely due to the tactile presence of the screen, which "flattened" the selection distribution in the 0 cm condition. This makes it difficult to compare the 0 cm condition to the 5 and 10 cm conditions. Hence we primarily focus on the differences due to highlighting *within* the same depth. The effect of highlighting was strongest with the 10 cm targets: an average error of 0.73 cm with highlighting-off, vs. 0.45 cm with highlighting-on.

To facilitate comparison with previous work [9, 22], we visualized selection coordinates as scatter plots in Figure 9. The figure depicts the selection coordinates as a "side-view" for *all* cylinder-on, texture-on trials. Since this includes all 11 target locations, each coordinate has been adjusted by first transforming the target to the origin. In terms of the tracker coordinate system, the participant would sit at the left side of the plot facing right.

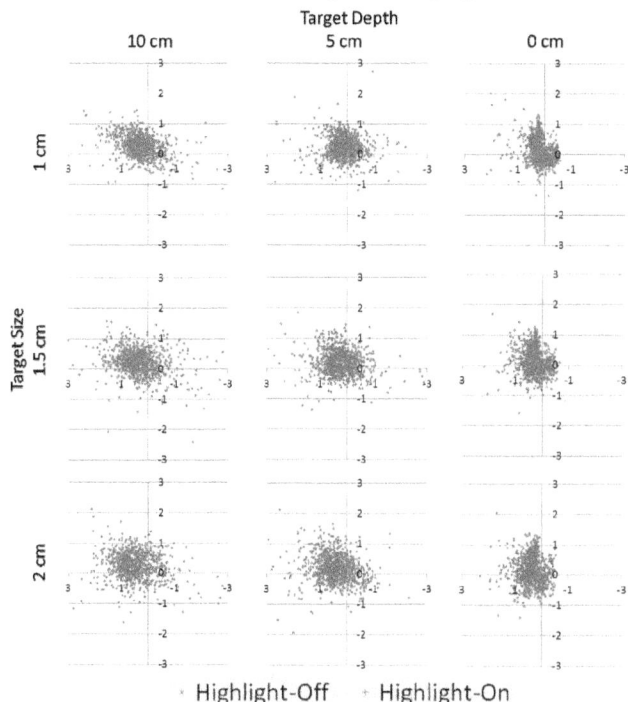

**Figure 9. Selection distributions for all cylinder-on, texture-on trials, separated by target depth and target size. Highlighting-on is shown in red, and highlighting-off is shown in blue. The horizontal axis of each plot is the *z*-axis of selection coordinates, while the vertical axis shows the *y*-axis (in cm).**

As seen in Figure 9, and supporting our depth deviation analysis, selection coordinates are generally more variable with greater target depths. The presence of the screen surface is visible at the 0 cm depth conditions (the right-most column), as these are relatively "flat" compared to the 5 cm and 10 cm target depths. After all, touching the screen surface stopped the stylus. Any values below 0 cm are tracking noise at the screen surface due to reflections.

The effect of highlighting is notable. The coordinates for the highlighting-off conditions are more variable, especially in the depth direction (the horizontal axis). In contrast, the highlighting-on coordinates are more circular, better approximating the target shape, as indicated by the significant effect for highlighting.

Finally, depth deviation was about 25% greater than coordinate deviation in both the *x* and *y* axes. This difference was significant ($F_{2,15} = 11.5$, $p < .0001$). However, there was significant interaction effect between the deviation axis and highlighting ($F_{2,30} = 7.2$, $p < .005$). Interestingly, this indicates that in highlighting-on conditions, depth deviation was not significantly worse than *x* or *y* axis deviation. This is reflected in the more circular patterns in Figure 9 for this condition.

**Subjective Results**

We asked participants about the perceived effect of each of the main independent variables. Figure 10 summarizes these results.

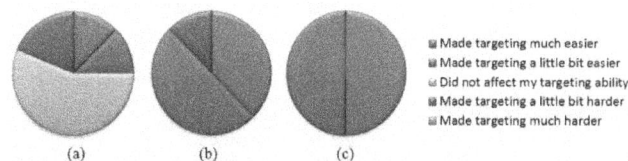

**Figure 10. Participant subjective responses for (a) texturing, (b) cylinders, and (c) highlighting.**

Notably, no participant reported that any of the visual aids "made targeting much harder" for any independent variable. Participants were largely ambivalent toward texture (Figure 10a) and the majority did not feel texture affected their performance. Most reported that they found cylinders (Figure 10b), and especially highlighting helpful (Figure 10c). Interestingly, the participants seemed to be aware of the relatively small effect of texturing. In contrast, they found the presence of cylinders helpful, despite the absence of quantitative results to support this.

**DISCUSSION**

Our results indicate that for all dependent variables investigated, texturing and the cylinders mattered very little. This is somewhat surprising, as the texture gradient on the cylinders should provide a strong depth cue [34]. Nevertheless, these factors were not significant in our analysis. While it is not in the nature of the statistical tests used to explicitly *prove* that these factors have no effect, we currently cannot reject the null hypothesis. Any effects of texturing and highlighting are certainly smaller than target depth and highlighting. Hence, we cautiously recommend that other researchers conducting 3D pointing experiments could use or ignore texturing at their discretion. However, since participants reported that they found cylinders helpful, we still recommend the use of such a "support" object for targets.

Target highlighting, on the other hand, had a significant effect on *all* dependent variables except throughput. This is in line with 2D results investigating similar effects with visually sub-optimal conditions [16]. In our case, the vergence-accommodation conflict common to stereo displays is a likely cause for the effect. This is further supported by the fact that performance (in terms of movement time, error rate, and depth deviation) was generally worse the farther targets were from the screen – stereo conflicts become more pronounced at greater depths. This is also consistent with previous work [35].

Interestingly, highlighting-on increased movement time, but decreased error rate substantially. Pointing is a classic speed-accuracy tradeoff task. Clearly, highlighting strongly influences the speed-accuracy tradeoff: participants were slower and more precise with highlighting-on. The difference in movement time was quite small, approximately 100 ms. The effect on error rate was much stronger – error rates were roughly cut in half with highlighting-on. It is likely that in the highlighting-on conditions, participants slowed down in anticipation of the appearance of the highlight. This suggests that they relied heavily on highlighting to accurately detect the 3D position of the target. On the other hand, stereo display and head-tracking alone seem to be insufficient for users to achieve the same accuracy with highlighting-off.

The high error rates (~15% in the best conditions) indicate the participants had some difficulty in the task. This is likely due to fatigue. Although the task was somewhat similar to stylus use on a tablet, our display was upright and required holding the arm up to the display. After numerous trials, this becomes fatiguing, and several participants complained of this during the experiment. It is also possible that participants of our experiment were simply inherently fast and thus inaccurate. The movement times reported here are roughly 25% lower than those in previous work [35] and error rates are roughly double. While the previous work used a similar stylus-based technique, the display was tipped on its back (instead of upright), which is likely less fatiguing. We thus believe these two factors together largely explain the high error rates.

That throughput was not influenced by highlighting reveals an important quality of the metric. Previous work pointing indicated that throughput is constant despite speed-accuracy tradeoffs [24]. Unlike MacKenzie and Isokoski, we did not explicitly ask participants to focus on speed or accuracy. Highlighting seemed to implicitly provide these emphases, however. Consequently, our work appears to be the first (indirect) confirmation of the immunity of throughput to speed-accuracy tradeoffs in 3D selection tasks. The throughput scores were also roughly consistent with previous work [35], further supporting use of the metric.

Finally, it is notable that participants were able to perform the task so well as to create a roughly spherical selection distribution (see Figure 9). Consistent with previous work [22, 40], depth deviation was higher than either the $x$ or $y$ axes. However, the magnitude of our depth deviations is smaller than in other recent work using head-mounted displays [22]. Perhaps most surprising is how strong the effect of highlighting was. In our experiment, highlighting substantially reduced depth deviation, yielding roughly spherical selection distributions. Lubos et al. [22] also used similar feedback, yet had substantially more ellipsoid shaped selection distributions (in the depth direction). This may be due to differences in the display technology used.

## CONCLUSIONS

We presented a study investigating several issues in the visual presentation of 3D point-selection experiments. The study used the ISO 9241-9 method, and compared the effects of texturing, target "support" cylinders, and target highlighting as visual feedback. Highlighting had the strongest effect overall. With highlighting, selection time significantly increased while accuracy improved, cutting error rates almost in half. Participants also strongly preferred highlighting. Consequently, we recommend researchers consider the use of target highlighting in 3D pointing experiments. At the very least, its presence or absence should be reported to ensure comparability with other work.

Notably, throughput was largely unaffected by the influence of highlighting. As previously demonstrated [24], this is likely because throughput is largely immune to speed-accuracy tradeoffs. The effect of highlighting "skewed" this tradeoff in favour of accuracy in our experiment, yet throughput compensated for this skew. This further emphasizes the utility of the throughput measure.

Finally, in terms of recommendations to system designers, it is evident that some form of visual feedback, such as highlighting, is important in improving the usability of 3D selection interfaces. We argue that the small cost in terms of movement time is acceptable considering the large improvement in error rates. Highlighting may be somewhat distracting in cluttered environments, but this is a topic for future work. Our other visual aids, texturing, and using cylinders to prevent objects from floating had relatively little effect. Nevertheless, we suggest that researchers conducting 3D pointing experiments should be clear to report these design decisions as they may affect the comparability of their results.

While we focused exclusively on touch-based 3D point selection, in future work, we will investigate highlighting, cylinders, and texture on remote pointing techniques.

### Acknowledgements
Thanks to Eduardo Soto for assistance running the experiment. This work was supported by NSERC.

## REFERENCES

1. Achibet, M., Marchal, M., Argelaguet, F., and Lécuyer, A., The Virtual Mitten: A novel interaction paradigm for visuo-haptic manipulation of objects using grip force, *Proc. of the IEEE Symposium on 3D User Interfaces - 3DUI 2014*, (New York: IEEE, 2014), 59-66.

2. Apitz, G., Guimbretière, F., and Zhai, S., Foundations for designing and evaluating user interfaces based on the crossing paradigm, *ACM Transactions on Computer-Human Interaction*, 17, 2010, 9.

3. Argelaguet, F. and Andujar, C., A survey of 3D object selection techniques for virtual environments, *Computers & Graphics*, 37, 2013, 121-136.

4. Boritz, J. and Booth, K. S., A study of interactive 3D point location in a computer simulated virtual environment, *Proc. of the ACM Symposium on Virtual*

*Reality Software and Technology - VRST '97*, (New York: ACM, 1997), 181-187.

5. Boritz, J. and Booth, K. S., A Study of Interactive 6 DOF Docking in a Computerized Virtual Environment, *Proc. of the Virtual Reality Annual International Symposium*, (New York: IEEE, 1998), 139-146.

6. Bowman, D. A, Johnson, D. B., and Hodges, L. F., Testbed evaluation of virtual environment interaction techniques, *Proc. of the ACM Symposium on Virtual Reality Software and Technology - VRST '99*, (New York: ACM, 1999), 26-33.

7. Bowman, D. A. , Kruijff, E., LaViola, J. J. , and Poupyrev, I., 3D User Interfaces: Theory and Practice. Addison Wesley Longman Publishing Co., Inc., 2004.

8. Bowman, D. A., Wingrave, C. A., Campbell, J. M., Ly, V. Q., and Rhoton, C. J., Novel uses of pinch gloves for virtual environment interaction techniques, *Virtual Reality*, 6, 2002, 122 - 129.

9. Bruder, G., Steinicke, F., and Stuerzlinger, W., Touching the void revisited: Analyses of touch behavior on and above tabletop surfaces, *Proc. Human-Computer Interaction–INTERACT 2013*. Springer, 2013, 278-296.

10. Bruder, G., Steinicke, F., and Sturzlinger, W., Effects of visual conflicts on 3D selection task performance in stereoscopic display environments, *Proc. of the IEEE Symposium on 3D User Interfaces - 3DUI 2013*, (New York: IEEE, 2013), 115-118.

11. Bruder, G., Steinicke, F., and Sturzlinger, W., To touch or not to touch? Comparing 2D touch and 3D mid-air interaction on stereoscopic tabletop surfaces, *Proc. of ACM Symposium on Spatial User Interaction - SUI 2013*, (New York: ACM, 2013), 9-16.

12. Chun, K., Verplank, B., Barbagli, F., and Salisbury, K., Evaluating haptics and 3D stereo displays using Fitts' law, *Proc. of the IEEE International Workshop on Haptic, Audio and Visual Environments and Their Applications*, (New York: IEEE, 2004), 53-58.

13. Cockburn, A., Quinn, P., Gutwin, C., Ramos, G., and Looser, J., Air pointing: Design and evaluation of spatial target acquisition with and without visual feedback, *International Journal of Human-Computer Studies*, 69, 2011, 401-414.

14. Dang, N.-T., A survey and classification of 3D pointing techniques, *Proc. of the IEEE International Conference on Research, Innovation and Vision for the Future*, (New York: IEEE, 2007), 71 - 80.

15. Fitts, P. M., The information capacity of the human motor system in controlling the amplitude of movement, *Journal of Experimental Psychology*, 47, 1954, 381-391.

16. Fraser, J. and Gutwin, C., The effects of feedback on targeting performance in visually stressed conditions, *Proc. of Graphics Interface*, (Toronto: Canadian Human-Computer Communication Society, 2000).

17. Hoffman, D. M., Girshick, A. R., Akeley, K., and Banks, M. S., Vergence-accommodation conflicts hinder visual performance and cause visual fatigue, *Journal of Vision*, 8(3), 2008, 1-30.

18. Hubona, G. S., Wheeler, P. N., Shirah, G. W., and Brandt, M., The relative contributions of stereo, lighting, and background scenes in promoting 3D depth visualization, *ACM Transactions on Computer-Human Interaction*, 6, 1999, 214-242.

19. ISO 9241-9 Ergonomic requirements for office work with visual display terminals (VDTs) - Part 9: Requirements for non-keyboard input devices: *International Standard*, International Organization for Standardization, 2000.

20. Kulshreshth, A. and LaViola Jr, J. J., Evaluating performance benefits of head tracking in modern video games, *Proc. of the ACM Symposium on Spatial User Interaction - SUI 2013*, (New York: ACM, 2013), 53-60.

21. Liu, L., Liere, R. v., Nieuwenhuizen, C., and Martens, J.-B., Comparing aimed movements in the real world and in virtual reality, *Proc. of the IEEE Virtual Reality Conference - VR 2009*, (New York: IEEE, 2009), 219-222.

22. Lubos, P., Bruder, G., and Steinicke, F., Analysis of direct selection in head-mounted display environments, *Proc. of the IEEE Symposium on 3D User Interfaces - 3DUI 2014*, (New York: IEEE, 2014), 11-18.

23. MacKenzie, I. S., Fitts' law as a research and design tool in human-computer interaction, *Human-Computer Interaction*, 7, 1992, 91-139.

24. MacKenzie, I. S. and Isokoski, P., Fitts' throughput and the speed-accuracy tradeoff, *Proc. of the ACM SIGCHI Conference on Human Factors in Computing Systems - CHI 2008*, (New York: ACM, 2008), 1633-1636.

25. Mould, D. and Gutwin, C., The effects of feedback on targeting with multiple moving targets, *Proc. of Graphics Interface 2004*, (Toronto: Canadian Human-Computer Communications Society, 2004), 25-32.

26. Nieuwenhuizen, K., Liu, L., Liere, R. v., and Martens, J.-B., Insights from Dividing 3D Goal-Directed Movements into Meaningful Phases, *IEEE Computer Graphics and Applications*, 29, 2009, 44 - 53.

27. Pawar, V. M. and Steed, A., Profiling the behaviour of 3D selection tasks on movement time when using natural haptic pointing gestures, *Proc. of the ACM Symposium on Virtual Reality Software and Technology - VRST 2009*, (New York: ACM, 2009), 79-82.

28. Poupyrev, I., Ichikawa T., Weghorst, S., and Billinghurst, M., Egocentric object manipulation in virtual environments: Empirical evaluation of interaction techniques, *Proc. of Eurographics '98*, (New York: ACM, 1998), 41-52.

29. Prachyabrued, M. and Borst, C. W., Visual feedback for virtual grasping, *Proc. of the IEEE Symposium on 3D User Interfaces - 3DUI 2014*, (New York: IEEE, 2014), 19-26.

30. Schemali, L. and Eisemann, E., Design and evaluation of mouse cursors in a stereoscopic desktop environment, *Proc. of the IEEE Symposium on 3D User Interfaces - 3DUI 2014*, (New York: IEEE, 2014), 67-70.

31. Soukoreff, R. W. and MacKenzie, I. S., Towards a standard for pointing device evaluation: Perspectives on 27 years of Fitts' law research in HCI, *International Journal of Human-Computer Studies*, 61, 2004, 751-789.

32. Sprague, D. W., Po, B. A., and Booth, K. S., The importance of accurate VR head registration on skilled motor performance, *Proc. of Graphics Interface 2006*, (Toronto: Canadian Information Processing Society, 2006), 131-137.

33. Stuerzlinger, W., Considerations for targets in 3D pointing experiments, *Workshop on Interactive Surfaces for Interaction with Stereoscopic 3D - ISIS3D 2013*.

34. Surdick, R. T., Davis, E. T., King, R. A., Corso, G. M., Shapiro, A., Hodges, L., and Elliot, K., Relevant cues for the visual perception of depth: is where you see it where it is?, *Proc. of the Human Factors and*

*Ergonomics Society Annual Meeting*, (SAGE Publications, 1994), 1305-1309.

35. Teather, R. J., Pavlovych, A., Stuerzlinger, W., and MacKenzie, I. S., Effects of tracking technology, latency, and spatial jitter on object movement, *Proc. of the IEEE Symposium on 3D User Interfaces - 3DUI 2009*, (New York: IEEE, 2009), 43-50.

36. Teather, R. J. and Stuerzlinger, W., Pointing at 3D targets in a stereo head-tracked virtual environment, *Proc. of the IEEE Symposium on 3D User Interfaces - 3DUI 2011*, (New York: IEEE, 2011), 87-94.

37. Teather, R. J. and Stuerzlinger, W., Pointing at 3D target projections using one-eyed and stereo cursors, *Proc. of the ACM Conference on Human Factors in Computing Systems - CHI 2013*, (New York: ACM, 2013), 159 - 168.

38. Valkov, D., Steinicke, F., Bruder, G., and Hinrichs, K., 2D touching of 3D stereoscopic objects, *Proc. of the ACM Conference on Human factors in Computing Systems - CHI 2011*, (New York: ACM, 2011), 1353-1362.

39. Zhai, S., Buxton, W., and Milgram, P., The "Silk Cursor": Investigating transparency for 3D target acquisition, *Proc. of the ACM Conference on Human Factors in Computing Systems - CHI '94*, (New York: ACM, 1994), 459 - 464.

40. Zhai, S., Milgram, P., and Rastogi, A., Anisotropic human performance in six degree-of-freedom tracking: An evaluation of three-dimensional display and control interfaces, *IEEE Transactions on Systems, Man and Cybernetics, Part A: Systems and Humans*, 27, 1997, 518-528.

# Designing the User in User Interfaces

**Mark Bolas**

Director for Mixed Reality Research

Institute for Creative Technologies

Associate Professor

USC School of Cinematic Arts Interactive Media Division

## ABSTRACT

In the good old days, the human was here, the computer there, and a good living was to be made by designing ways to interface between the two. Now we find ourselves unthinkingly pinching to zoom in on a picture in a paper magazine. User interfaces are changing instinctual human behavior and instinctual human behavior is changing user interfaces. We point or look left in the "virtual" world just as we point or look left in the physical.

It is clear that nothing is clear anymore: the need for "interface" vanishes when the boundaries between the physical and the virtual disappear. We are at a watershed moment when to experience being human means to experience being machine. When there is not a user interface - it is just what you do. When instinct supplants mice and menus and the interface insinuates itself into the human psyche.

We are redefining and creating what it means to be human in this new physical/virtual integrated reality - we are not just designing user interfaces, we are designing users.

## Author Keywords

user interace; virtual reality; posthuman factors; transhumanism; mixed reality

## ACM Classification Keywords

H.5.2 User Interfaces (D.2.2, H.1.2, I.3.6): Prototyping

## BIO

Mark Bolas is the Director of the Mixed Reality Lab at the USC Institute of Creative Technologies and an Associate Professor in the Interactive Media & Games division of the School of Cinematic Arts, where he directs the Mixed Reality Studio. His work focuses on researching perception, agency, and intelligence - creating virtual environments and transducers that fully engage one's perception and cognition to create a visceral memory of the experience.

Bolas leads research projects for the Army Research Office, the Office of Naval Research, and DARPA, as well as a variety of other clients, including content for the entertainment industry. He has led the development of a number of influential products including the open-source FOV2GO, which informed the design of the Oculus Rift; the Wide-5 HMD; Pinch interface gloves; and the Boom and Molly telepresence system. Bolas' 1988-89 thesis work "Design and Virtual Environments" was the first effort to map the breadth of virtual reality as a new medium.

In addition to USC, he has taught at Stanford University and Keio University, exploring tangible interfaces, augmented reality, and computational illumination. These projects have explored context-sensitive audio interfaces, socially interactive toys, augmented reality, confocal illumination, and mobile phone web logging.

Bolas co-founded Fakespace Labs, Inc. in 1988 and developed and sold VR hardware and systems for dozens of major research labs over the decades. He holds more than twenty patents and has been recognized with awards from the Consumer Electronics Association, Popular Science, SIGGRAPH Best Emerging Technology, IEEE's Industry Excellence, and IEEE's Virtual Reality Technical Achievement Award.

# Getting Yourself Superimposed on a Presentation Screen

**Kenji Funahashi**
Nagoya Institute of Technology
Gokiso-cho, Showa-ku, Nagoya, Japan
kenji@nitech.ac.jp

**Yusuke Nakae**
Nagoya Institute of Technology
(present: System Research Co.,Ltd.)
ynakae@center.nitech.ac.jp

## ABSTRACT
We propose using intuitive interface presentation support software. A presenter is superimposed on a screen.

## Author Keywords
Presentation support; Augmented reality; 3D interface.

## ACM Classification Keywords
H.5.1 Information Interfaces and Presentation: Multimedia Information Systems—*Artificial, augmented, and virtual realities*

## INTRODUCTION
When attending a conference some audiences lose attention following points on the screen. Although presenters usually use a pointer rod or a laser pointer, they are not convenient or easily visible on a large screen. A camera and another screen are also needed to show gestures. In this paper we propose using intuitive interface presentation support software [1]. A presenter is superimposed onto a screen, and the person can draw there interactively. Realizing presenter movement on screen by recognizing natural and small actions, the person can move within a limited stage space. Presenters can point to any important areas and draw supplementary items with their own hand through our software, and of course show gestures on a large screen. It is expected that audiences will be better able to understand and focus.

## MOVEMENT AND DRAWING
It is necessary to move within a limited area. First the presenters knee angles are obtained. When one of them is less than the pre-defined threshold value, the person on the screen is moved exaggeratedly in all directions according to their actual movement and the angle. It is needed to change position vertically on the screen while superimposed smaller. When both of the knee angles are less than the other threshold, the person moves down at a speed depending on the angles. When lifting one arm to stretch out, the person moves up according to the extent that the arm is lifted. The locus of the hand is also drawn on the screen while the hand position is higher than the waist and at the back of the head.

## RESULTS AND CONCLUSIONS
We used Microsoft Kinect and Windows SDK Ver. 1.8 API to build a pilot system on a Windows PC. It also has a horizontal inversion mode to use this system while watching laptop monitor (Figure 1 and 2). We got positive evaluations through an experiment; i.e. it is easy to move, and it is helpful for presenting slide shows. Despite some favorable results, bugs remain. We can not erase notes yet, meaning that we should implement an erase function, and we would also like to recognize a page feeding action, leaving them for future work.

Figure 1. System appearance.

Figure 2. Movement and drawing.

## ACKNOWLEDGMENTS
This work was supported in part by JSPS KAKENHI Grant Number 24501186.

## REFERENCES
1. Uchiyama, K., Nakae, Y., and Funahashi, K. Presentation support software superimposing presenter. In *Proc. 19th Annual Conference of the Virtual Reality Society of Japan* (2014, in Japanese).

# Measurements of Operating Time in First and Third Person Views using Video See-through HMD

**Takafumi Koike**
Hosei University
Koganei-shi, Tokyo
Japan
takafumi@hosei.ac.jp

## ABSTRACT

We measured the operation times of two tasks using video a transparent video head mounted display (HMD) in first and third person views.

## Author Keywords

HMD; First Person View; Third Person View

## ACM Classification Keywords

D.2.2 Design Tools and Techniques: User Interactions

## INTRODUCTION

An HMD with a third person view has previously been proposed by Higuchi et al.[1], and this view is already quite common for changing between different viewpoints in video games. We need to clarify user operations in various views for future free-viewpoint systems using HMDs. In this study, we performed experiments in three different views (Fig. 1) and measured the operating times for each.

## EXPERIMENTS

We used PlayStation Eye as the camera and Oculus Rift as the HMD. Two tasks were performed in the experiments: 1) walking in a maze and 2) placing blocks into a target configuration (Fig 2). These two tasks were chosen because the display resolution of the HMD is not so high. The first operation was to measure sensing user position and the second operation was to measure sensing the depth of objects.

Table 1 shows experimental results of each views. We have got clear differences between each views.

**Table 1. Results of operation times (sec). These values are averages of the times of six participants.**

|       | FPV  | TPFV | FTPV  |
|-------|------|------|-------|
| maze  | 37.8 | 61.3 | 84.2  |
| block | 62.2 | 72.3 | 101.2 |

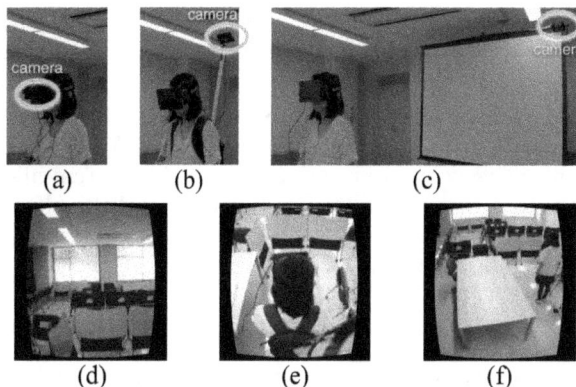

Figure 1. (a) First person view (FPV), (b) tracking third person view (TTPV), which views user's head from behind, (c) fixed third person view (FTPV), which views from a fixed position in a room, (d) images from FPV, (e) images from TTPV, and (f) images from FTPV.

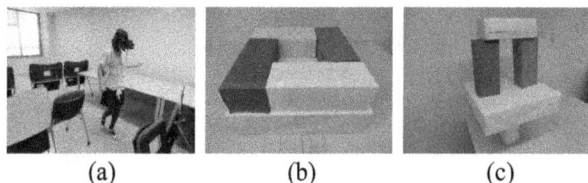

Figure 2. Experimental set-up and objects used: (a) walking in a maze, (b) initial layout of blocks, (c) target layout of blocks.

## DISCUSSION AND CONCLUSION

All operation times had significant differences, as expected. However, the time differences for placing blocks were relatively small. The distance between the camera position and the eye position was 150 mm, and so the first person viewpoint led to visually induced motion sickness. Motion sickness was also caused by low camera resolution, long latency, and low display resolution of the HMD. This indicates that we need a higher-quality transparent video HMD and that we should control the experiments more carefully.

## REFERENCES

1. K. Higuchi, Y. Ishiguro, and J. Rekimoto. Flying eyes: Free-space content creation using autonomous aerial vehicles. In *CHI '11 Extended Abstracts on Human Factors in Computing Systems*, pages 561–570, 2011.

# Re:Form — Rapid Designing System based on Fusion and Illusion of Digital/Physical Models

**Keiko Yamamoto**
Kyoto Institute of Technology
Kyoto, Japan
kei@kit.ac.jp

**Ichiroh Kanaya**
Osaka University
Osaka, Japan
kanaya@pineapple.cc

**Monica Bordegoni**
Politecnico di Milano
Milan, Italy
monica.bordegoni@polimi.it

**Umberto Cugini**
Politecnico di Milano
Milan, Italy
umberto.cugini@polimi.it

## ABSTRACT

Our goal is to allow the creators to focus on their creative activity, developing their ideas for physical products in an intuitive way. We propose a new CAD system allows users to draw virtual lines on the surface of the physical object using see-through AR, and also allows users to import 3D data and make its real object through 3D printing.

## Author Keywords

CAD; AR/MR; 3D printing; collaboration.

## ACM Classification Keywords

H.5.2 Information Interfaces and Presentation (e.g., HCI): User Interfaces

## PROPOSED SYSTEM

"Creativity" is the most important ability for human-beings. Creative activity is a repeat of imagination and externalization. If creators could follow this process smoothly, they could create their products more effectively.

There have been many sketch-based interaction systems using TUIs (Tangible User Interfaces) and/or AR/MR technologies for computer-aided designing of physical products. However, the users cannot evaluate 3D actuality and realistic touches of the object while designing because the virtual models made by these systems do not have that actuality. Recent development of 3D printing technologies, on the other hand, helps us making physical models from CAD data quickly. However, the users cannot interact with the object in realtime.

Figure 1 illustrates outline of our proposed system. Users can (1) draw on a 3D surface, which is the surface of a

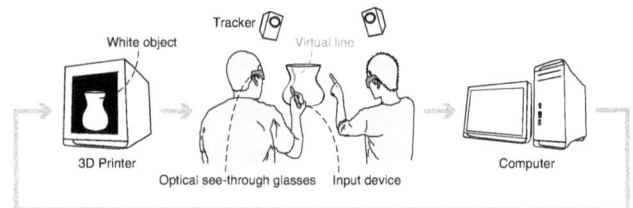

Figure 1. Outline of our system

white object printed using a 3D printer, (2) change line attributes (thickness, colors, etc.), (3) map some textures and/or virtual shade on the surface by applying HYPERREAL technology[1], (4) import physical and digital data, and (5) multiple users can manipulate the object using hands and/or input devices like [2].

Proposed system can control the virtual shape of physical objects with shading-pattern projection on the real object. The input device is a pen like device equipped with sensors for detecting user's finger pressure and position. Users can directly draw on the surface of a physical object by changing its stroke attributes, by changing how to grasp the device without selecting and searching a tool or icon.

We embed an image marker to a white object of which we track the position using Vuforia[1]. We also embed a different image marker to an input device. Users can create and modify physical objects over and over by the proposed system. Furthermore, the system can be run on a distributed environment so that users can collaborate on their design work from a distance.

## REFERENCES

1. K. Yamamoto *et al.*, "The HYPEREAL Design System — An MR-Based Shape Design Environment —," in *Proc. 11th International Conference on Virtual Systems and Multimedia*, 2005, pp.201–206.

2. K. Yamamoto *et al.*, "Grasping Interface for 3-D Model Designing System," *Journal of the Society for Art and Science*, 2008, Vol.7, No.3, pp.102–112. (in Japanese)

*SUI'14*, October 4–5, 2014, Honolulu, HI, USA.
ACM 978-1-4503-2820-3/14/10.
http://dx.doi.org/10.1145/2659766.2661205

[1]https://www.vuforia.com

# Supporting Remote Guidance through 3D Annotations

**Philipp Tiefenbacher**
Technische Universität
München
philipp.tiefenbacher@tum.de

**Tobias Gehrlich**
Technische Universität
München
tobias.gehrlich@tum.de

**Gerhard Rigoll**
Technische Universität
München
rigoll@tum.de

## ABSTRACT

Remote guidance enables untrained users to solve complex tasks with the help of experts. These tasks often include the positioning of physical objects to certain poses. The expert indicates the final pose to the user. Therefore, the quality of annotations majorly influences the success of the remote collaboration.

This work compares two kinds of annotation methods (2D and 3D) in two scenarios of different complexity. A pilot study indicates that 3D annotations reduce the execution time of the user in the complex scenario.

## Author Keywords

augmented reality; 3D annotation; collaboration.

## ACM Classification Keywords

H.5.2 Information Interfaces and Presentation: User Interfaces—*Interaction styles*;

## INTRODUCTION

Possible annotation types for remote guidance can be characterized by pointers, 2D annotations and 3D annotations. Currently, no work compares the effectiveness of 2D versus 3D annotations. We created two different scenarios: The first scenario includes planar positioning tasks, whereas the second scenario is in 3D. Both scenarios have to be solved by a novice, who receives either 2D or 3D annotations from a remote expert.

**Annotation Concepts**: The differences of the two annotation concepts can be classified according to [1].

*Dimensionality*: The main difference between the two annotation types: 2D and 3D.

*View-point reference frame*: In case of 2D sketches, the expert's view matches the egocentric viewpoint of the mobile user. For the 3D annotations, the mobile user keeps the egocentric viewpoint. However, the expert is able to move an additional, independent virtual camera. This way, the expert has an egocentric viewpoint, too.

*Mounting and registration*: Only the expert is authorized to create annotations. The 2D sketches are human-mounted since the positions depend on the mobile device, which is grasped by the novice. The 3D annotations are fixed to the 3D world. The expert manipulates the predefined, virtual 3D models through keyboard.

*SUI'14*, October 4–5, 2014, Honolulu, HI, USA.
ACM 978-1-4503-2820-3/14/10.
http://dx.doi.org/10.1145/2659766.2661206

## STUDY & RESULTS

The novices hold a 11.6" mobile PC. The expert works on a stationary 22.8" touch monitor. The subjects communicate only by voice and the selected annotation type. Each subject performs the study with one annotation type.

**Scenarios**: Each participant has to place six physical objects per scenario.

*Simple scenario*: Subjects of the 2D placement scenario arrange objects to a connected geometrical shape. This scenario is constrained by the assumption that all objects reside on a common surface. Translation and rotation each only have 2 DoF, leading to a total of 4 DoF.

*Complex scenario*: This scenario has no limitations regarding translation and rotation. The physical objects can be freely rotated and translated.

**Results**: We conducted a pilot study with one expert and six subjects. Important times for this kind of task are the execution time of the worker $T^w$ and the interaction time of the expert $T^e$. Both times are visible in Figure 1. $T^e$ of the 2D

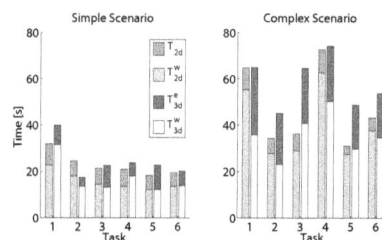

Figure 1. The times for the simple (left) and complex (right) scenarios.

sketches is almost the same in both scenarios. The 3D annotations need more time ($T_{3d}^e$) in the complex scenario than in the simple scenario. In the simple scenario, $T_{2d}^e$ and $T_{3d}^e$ do not vary much.

In the complex setting, 4 of 6 execution times $T_{3d}^w$ are shorter than $T_{2d}^w$. This indicates that 3D annotations are beneficial for complex tasks and similar to 2D sketches for easier tasks.

## ACKNOWLEDGMENTS

The research leading to these inventions has received funding from the European Union Seventh Framework Programm (FP7/2007-2013) under grant agreement n° 284573.

## ADDITIONAL AUTHORS

Takashi Nagamatsu (Kobe University, email: nagamatu@kobe-u.ac.jp)

## REFERENCES

1. Tönnis, M., Plecher, D. A., and Klinker, G. Survey Representing Information - Classifying the Augmented Reality Presentation Space. *Comput. Graph. 37*, 8 (2013), 997–1011.

# Simulator for Developing Gaze Sensitive Environment Using Corneal Reflection-based Remote Gaze Tracker

**Takashi Nagamatsu**
Technical University of Munich
Kobe University
nagamatu@kobe-u.ac.jp

**Michiya Yamamoto**
Kwansei Gakuin University
michiya.yamamoto@kwansei.ac
.jp

**Gerhard Rigoll**
Technical University of Munich
rigoll@tum.de

## ABSTRACT

We describe a simulator for developing a gaze sensitive environment using a corneal reflection-based remote gaze tracker. The simulator can arrange cameras and IR-LEDs in 3D to check the measuring range to suit the target volume prior to implementation. We applied it to a museum showcase and a car.

## INTRODUCTION

Gaze tracking is appropriate for spatial user interaction, such as direction of remote objects. By using a gaze tracking system, we can interact with remote objects by just gazing at objects. Directing by gaze can be more accurate than directing by a finger. Since a head mounted type gaze tracker is bothersome to wear, a remote type gaze tracker is suitable for some applications. Corneal reflection based remote gaze trackers are accurate but have a limitation of the tracking range, which are mostly designed for measuring gaze on a computer display. For example, the Tobii eye trackers work best when the angle between the eye tracker and the user's gaze point is below 35° [1]. In order to achieve gaze tracking in various real environments beyond the measuring range of commercially available gaze trackers, we must design a gaze tracking system to suit the target volume. Our approach to achieve this is to simulate the gaze tracking range in 3D prior to setting cameras and IR-LEDs (hereinafter referred to as LEDs). In this paper, we describe a developed simulator.

## SIMULATOR FOR GAZE SENSITIVE ENVIRONMENT

In order to measure the wide range of gaze (i.e. various positions and directions of the eye), we must use many LEDs to reflect on the corneal surface, and we must also consider where we should put cameras and LEDs and which LEDs should be switched on. We developed a simulator based on the mathematical model [2] proposed by Nagamatsu et al, which is a common model for corneal reflection-based gaze trackers. According to the model, the measuring range of gaze direction forms a cone (we call it a gaze cone), which is calculated from the relation between a

camera, eye, and LED. The necessary number of cones is different between gaze calculation methods, and the gaze can be calculated inside of a cone or a common range of several cones. As an example, we simulated a gaze measuring range for a gaze tracker for a museum showcase developed by Nagamatsu et al. [3] (Fig. 1). As another example, we simulated a gaze measurable range for a gaze tracker for a car. Figures 2 and 3 show simulation results for the museum showcase and car, respectively. In the Figures 2 and 3, gaze cones (transparent blue), cameras (blue), and LEDs (yellow) are shown. The simulator can move the positions of cameras, eyes, and LEDs, and change the status of LEDs: ON or OFF. We can adjust the settings to check the measuring range.

**Figure 1. Gaze tracker for a museum showcase**

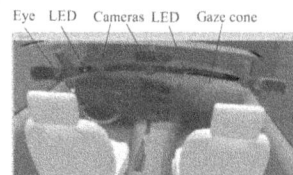

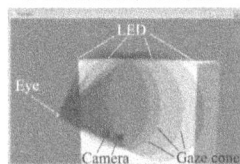

**Figure 2. Simulation for a museum showcase**

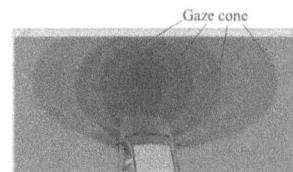

**Figure 3. Simulation for a car**

## CONCLUSION

We presented a simulator for developing a gaze sensitive environment. We can design various gaze controlled environments by using the simulator. This leads to a considerable enrichment of the spatial user interaction.

## REFERENCES

1. http://www.tobii.com/

2. Nagamatsu,T.,Yamamoto,M.,Sugano,R.,and Kamahara,J. Mathematical model for wide range gaze tracking system based on corneal reflections and pupil using stereo cameras. In *Proc. ETRA2012*, ACM (2012), 257-260.

3. Nagamatsu, T., Fukuda, K., and Yamamoto, M. Development of Corneal Reflection-Based Gaze Tracking System for Public Use. In *Proc. PerDis2014*, ACM (2014), 194-195.

*SUI'14*, October 4–5, 2014, Honolulu, HI, USA.
ACM 978-1-4503-2820-3/14/10.
http://dx.doi.org/10.1145/2659766.2661207

# Emotional Space: Understanding Affective Spatial Dimensions of Constructed Embodied Shapes

**Edward Melcer**
NYU Polytechnic School of
Engineering
Brooklyn, NY 11201
eddie.melcer@nyu.edu

**Katherine Isbister**
NYU Polytechnic School of
Engineering
Brooklyn, NY 11201
katherine.isbister@nyu.edu

## ABSTRACT

We build upon recent research designing a constructive, multi-touch emotional assessment tool and present preliminary qualitative results from a Wizard of Oz study simulating the tool with clay. Our results showed the importance of emotionally contextualized spatial orientations, manipulations, and interactions of real world objects in the constructive process, and led to the identification of two new affective dimensions for the tool.

## Author Keywords

Emotional assessment; Affect; Embodiment; Wizard of Oz.

## ACM Classification Keywords

H.5.m. Information interfaces and presentation (e.g., HCI): Miscellaneous.

## INTRODUCTION

In recent years, HCI researchers and practitioners have recognized the importance of emotion and pleasure in user experience [1]. Unfortunately, traditional emotional assessment tools encounter difficulty with more nuanced aspects of emotion in an interactive experience. Our recent work on emotional assessment [2] has identified two causes for these issues: (1) current emotional assessment tools provide a limited taxonomy to select emotions from, and (2) emotional assessment tools only provide snapshots of emotion and are unable to capture the temporal aspects of changing emotions over time. This led to the design of a new emotional assessment tool, the Constructive Sensual Evaluation Instrument (CSEI). The CSEI utilizes affective dimensions of shape to provide a multi-touch gestural interface for constructing affective embodied shapes.

We propose that the use of affective dimensions of shape creates a larger, constructive emotional space where users

*SUI'14*, Oct 04-05 2014, Honolulu, HI, USA
ACM 978-1-4503-2820-3/14/10.
http://dx.doi.org/10.1145/2659766.2661208.

can express a wider range of emotions and capture temporal aspects through recorded changes in shape over time.

## EXPERIMENT

We conducted a Wizard of Oz study to simulate individual and collaborative use of the CSEI system with clay. For the study, we created a protocol that combined clay shape creation with a think-aloud method and semi-structured interviews. A total of 6 male and 8 female subjects (ages 22-51, M=36.5) participated. Each test was conducted with two participants and contained two individual and two collaborative embodied shape construction phases.

## OBSERVATIONS AND RESULTS

The study revealed repetition to be a key dimension in the construction of embodied shapes. Participants used repetition to embody low arousal emotions in two distinctly different ways: (1) repetition of a single shape manipulation during the construction process (e.g. repeatedly rolling), and (2) repetition of salient visual features.

The orientation of a shape and its extrusions was another key dimension found in the study. Participants more commonly associated an emotion with shapes utilizing orientations that matched spatial orientations of real world objects or actions. For instance, several participants commented on orienting extrusions upwards and away from the center in order to match the look of an explosion.

## CONCLUSION

We found embodiment of emotion through shape relies on spatial orientations, manipulations, and interactions of real world objects that are viewed as emotionally similar. For our study results, this manifested in the affective dimensions of repetition and orientation. Our results suggest re-evaluation of the CSEI's affective dimensions to consider (1) patterns in spatial manipulation and (2) the spatial orientation of shapes and extrusions.

## REFERENCES

1. Höök, Kia, et al. "Evaluation of Affective Interactive Applications." Emotion-Oriented Systems. Springer Berlin Heidelberg (2011), 687-703.

2. Melcer, E., Isbister, K. "CSEI: The Constructive Sensual Evaluation Instrument."*Workshop on Tactile User Experience Evaluation Methods*. CHI 2014, N.p.

# Augmented Reality Paper Clay making based on hand gesture recognition

**Pei-Ying Chiang**
National Taipei University of
Technology
Taipei, Taiwan
peiyingc@csie.ntut.edu.tw

**Wei-Yu Li**
National Taipei University of
Technology
Taipei, Taiwan
t101598058@ntut.edu.tw

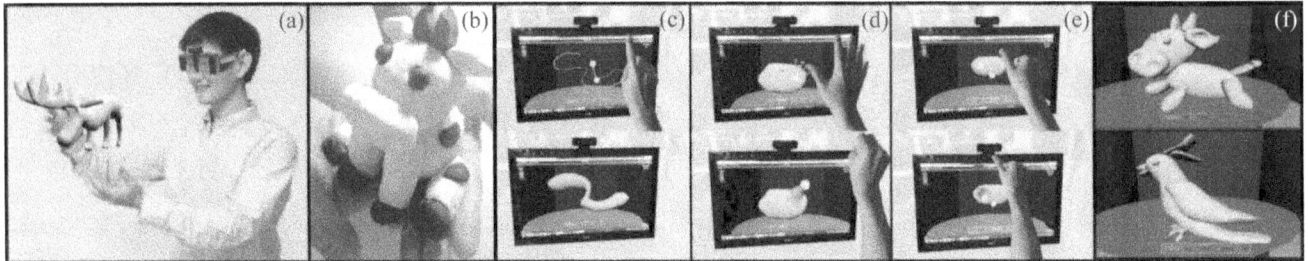

Figure 1. (a) Concept illustration of augmented reality paper clay making. (b) Real paper clay making. (c)The draw-to-create tool.
(d) The grab-to-extrude tool. (e) The press-to-dent tool. (f) The 3D models created using our 3D modeling system.

## ABSTRACT

We propose a gesture-based 3D modeling system, which allows the user to create and sculpt a 3D model with hand-gestures. The goal of our system is to provide a more intuitive 3D user interface than the traditional 2D ones such as mouse or touch pad. Inspired by how people make paper clay, a series of hand gestures are designed for interacting with the 3D object and their corresponding mesh processing functions are developed. Thus, the user can create a desired virtual 3D object just like paper clay making.

## INTRODUCTION

3D modeling is one of the most fundamental and important topics in computer graphics and other related fields. It has attracted intensive research interest ever since the birth of the field of computer graphics. As a result, many 3D modeling systems such as Maya have been developed. While their capabilities of producing complex models are increasing, it may take a long time for users to get familiar with those creation tools. Casual users may easily get frustrated. Furthermore, with the development of 3D graphics-based applications, users demand more flexibility in quick creation and sharing of their own 3D contents. In light of these observations, we investigate in this work of simplified modeling techniques that enable the users to create 3D models easily and flexibly. Therefore, we extend the sketch-based 3D modeling system [1] from 2D input to

*SUI'14*, October 4–5, 2014, Honolulu, HI, USA.
ACM 978-1-4503-2820-3/14/10.
http://dx.doi.org/10.1145/2659766.2661209

3D input. Our main goal is to develop an Augmented Reality (AR) 3D modeling system user interface. As Figure 1(a), the user wearing AR glasses can mold the 3D model with hand gestures just as if they were touching and molding clay in Figure 1(b).

## SYSTEMS AND GESTURE DESIGN

Our hand-gesture recognition function is developed based on Intel Gesture Camera Developer Kit [2]. We design easy-to-learn gestures so the user can make a 3D model without long leaning process. A delicate 3D model can be easily created as follows: The user first draws a 2D contour of a desired 3D shape. The system then automatically inflates [1] this contour to generate an initial rotund 3D model as Figure 1(c). The user can then sculpt it with various gestures as shown in Figure 1(d)(e), which simplified the sculpting process. The experimental result is shown in Figure 1(f).

## CONCLUSION AND FUTURE WORK

The main contribution of our system is providing an intuitive 3D user interface that allows the user create a desired 3D object as modeling paper clay. Due to the limitation of [2], the motion tracking is not yet very precise. We are currently improving the accuracy and developing more advanced mesh-processing functions.

## REFERENCES

1. Igarashi, T., et al. 1999. Teddy: a sketching interface for 3D freeform design. In Proc. SIGGRAPH '99, July. ACM Press, New York, NY, USA, 409-416.

2. Intel perceptual computing. https://software.intel.com

# Projection Augmented Physical Visualizations

**Simon Stusak**
University of Munich (LMU)
simon.stusak@ifi.lmu.de

**Markus Teufel**
University of Munich (LMU)
teufel@cip.ifi.lmu.de

## ABSTRACT

Physical visualizations are an emergent area of research and appear in increasingly diverse forms. While they provide an engaging way of data exploration, they are often limited by a fixed representation and lack interactivity. In this work we discuss our early approaches and experiences in combining physical visualizations with spatial augmented reality and present an initial prototype.

## Author Keywords

physical visualizations; information visualization; projection augmentation; spatial augmented reality

## ACM Classification Keywords

H.5.m INFORMATION INTERFACES AND PRESENTATION (e.g., HCI): Miscellaneous

## INTRODUCTION

Physical Visualizations (PV) are visualizations in which data is mapped to physical form instead of pixels [1]. Vande Moere [3] writes that PVs have the potential of sparking curiosity and turning data exploration into a fascinating experience. Spatial Augmented Reality is used to extend arbitrary physical objects with a digital layer. *Shader Lamps* by Raskar et al. [2] is a popular example in which a projector is used to augment real world objects with a texture. As most PVs are limited by fixed visual appearance, a digital augmentation seems a promising approach to minimize this constraint and provide an additional layer for interaction.

## CONCEPT PHASE

The design of projection augmented physical visualizations can be split into several dimensions. The physical visualization itself is the characteristic element and its material (e.g. plastic, wood), fabrication (e.g. 3D printer, laser cutter), size and space for the projection should be taken into account. The projection can differ on the basis of its position (e.g. direct projection on the PV, projection near the PV) and its purpose (e.g. showing additional information, enabling interaction with the data). Furthermore the input modality should be considered (e.g. touching the PV, disassembling and reassembling the PV, remote input device).

*SUI'14*, October 4–5, 2014, Honolulu, HI, USA.
ACM 978-1-4503-2820-3/14/10.
http://dx.doi.org/10.1145/2659766.2661210

## PROTOYPE

For our initial prototype (see figure 1) an area chart as type of visualization was chosen because it offers much space for augmentation. It was built out of birch wood, as this type of wood is easily processed with a laser cutter and its bright tint is well-suited for projection augmentation. Based on web technologies 3D models for the projection and 2D vector shapes for the laser cutter were generated. The calibration process was done using mapamok[1]. The PV visualizes the export of small arms and light weapons of different countries. The projection was used to display labels and legends, to show additional data in form of stacked area charts and to provide vertical and horizontal guides to simplify comparison of different data items. Interaction, e.g. moving the guides or changing the data for the stacked area chart was done with a remote tablet device.

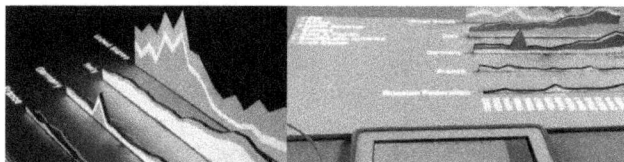

**Figure 1. Projection Augmented Area Chart**

## CONCLUSION AND FUTURE WORK

Our exploration reveals that projection augmentation can enhance PVs. Guides for example help to overcome problems arising from perspective distortion. The augmentation of the PVs surface with additional information can compensate its static nature without losing the advantages of physical objects, which can be touched and explored with all senses [3]. As our early prototype only supports interaction using a remote tablet device the next step is to implement direct touch interaction on the PV itself. Another promising approach would be to integrate the position of the user and adapt the projection depending on their movements.

## REFERENCES

1. Jansen, Y., Dragicevic, P., and Fekete, J.-D. Evaluating the efficiency of physical visualizations. In *Proceedings of CHI '13*, ACM (2013), 2593–2602.

2. Raskar, R., Welch, G., Low, K.-L., and Bandyopadhyay, D. Shader lamps: Animating real objects with image-based illumination. In *Proceedings of the 12th Eurographics Workshop on Rendering Techniques.*, Springer (2001).

3. Vande Moere, A. Beyond the tyranny of the pixel: Exploring the physicality of information visualization. In *Information Visualisation, 2008. IV'08*, IEEE (2008), 469–474.

[1]https://github.com/YCAMInterlab/mapamok

# Using LEGO to Model 3D Tactile Picture Books by Sighted Children for Blind Children

**Jeeeun Kim**            **Abigale Stangl**            **Tom Yeh**

Sikuli Lab, University of Colorado Boulder

430 UCB, Boulder, CO 80309, USA

{jeeeun.kim, abigale.stangl, tom.yeh}@colorado.edu

## ABSTRACT

3D printing has shown great potential in creating tactile picture books for blind children to develop emergent literacy. Sighted children can be motivated to contribute to the modeling of more tactile picture books. But current 3D design tools are too difficult to use. Can sighted children model a tactile book by LEGO pieces instead? Can a LEGO be converted to a digital model that can be then printed?

## Author Keywords

Children, Blind, Tactile Pictures, Design Space

## ACM Classification Keywords

H.5.m. Information interfaces and presentation

## INTRODUCTION

3D printed tactile picture books help children with visual impairments cultivate emergent literacy and emotion [1]. One promising approach to expanding the catalog of 3D-printed tactile picture books is to involve children with sight to contribute to creation of 3D tactile model elements in a storybook, such fruits or animals. However, for this young group, current 3D design tools are not intuitive. It requires children to understand mouse interaction on 2D screen, such as scrolling to pan or rotate. For children, it is difficult to become familiar with spatial concepts underlying a design software tool, but they may be familiar with physical construction tasks, such as making LEGO models. We are studying how we let children model a children book's content using LEGO blocks, and how we map the physical model constructed by children to a digital 3D model, which can be in turn printed by a 3D printer.

## APPROACH

First, a group of children choose a children book to model. They use LEGO pieces to construct physical interpretation of them from book contents. The resulting physical models are scanned via a 3D scanner. From the scanned, we extract its key features through projections in three most principal perspectives: top, front, and side. We match these features to retrieve a visually similar 3D model from large repositories [2][3]. Finally, the best match is sent to design space, MakerWare, for future customization and refining.

*SUI'14*, October 4–5, 2014, Honolulu, HI, USA.
ACM 978-1-4503-2820-3/14/10.
http://dx.doi.org/10.1145/2659766.2661211

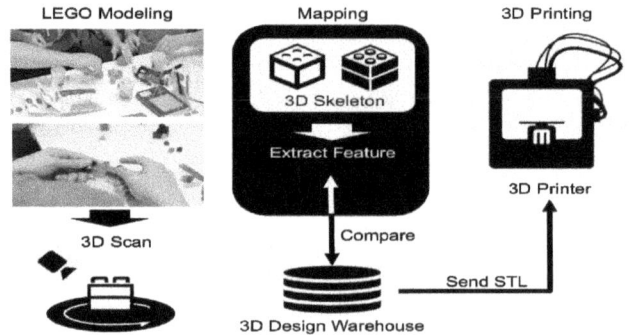

**Figure 1. Physical LEGO blocks are recognized as skeleton, and STL files are searched from 3Dwarehouse by comparison.**

## PILOT RESULTS

We conducted a design workshop with 8 children (ages 14-16, top left of Figure 1). We first introduced them to the idea of 3D-printed tactile picture books. Then, we presented to them several children's books and gave them the freedom to choose which one to model. They spent the next 15 minutes to construct models using LEGO. Figure 2 (column 1) shows examples of the models constructed.

Each LEGO model was scanned. For instance, a LEGO camel is characterized by the two bumps on the back. The model is mapped to a camel model from Thingiverse (thing:182086) by projected images onto 2D planes of it. Salient features of the camel enabled the system to differentiate it from other animals. Figure 2 (columns 2 and 3) shows how scans can be turned into ready-to-print models in STL formats.

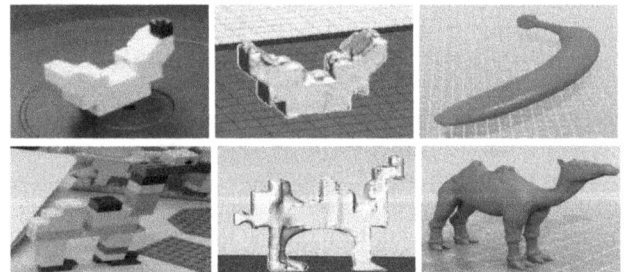

**Figure 2. Banana and Camel of original blocks (left), scanned (middle), and mapped design from 3Dwarehouse, (right)**

## REFERENCES

1. Stangl, A., Kim, J., and Yeh T. 3D Printed Tactile Picture Books for Children with Visual Impairments: A Design Probe *In Proc. IDC '14* ACM Press (2014)
2. Thingiverse http://thingiverse.com
3. 3D Warehouse https://3dwarehouse.sketchup.com

# Evaluating a SLAM-based Handheld Augmented Reality Guidance System

Jarkko Polvi[1], Takafumi Taketomi[1], Goshiro Yamamoto[1], Mark Billinghurst[2],
Christian Sandor[1], Hirokazu Kato[1]

[1]Nara Institute of Science and Technology, Japan      [2]University of Canterbury, New Zealand
{jarkko-p, takafumi-t, goshiro, sandor, kato}@is.naist.jp      mark.billinghurst@canterbury.ac.nz

## ABSTRACT
In this poster we present the design and evaluation of a Handheld Augmented Reality (HAR) prototype system for guidance.

## Author Keywords
Handheld augmented reality; guidance; user study.

## ACM Classification Keywords
H.5.2 [User Interface]: Graphic user interface (GUI), Screen design, user-centered design.

## INTRODUCTION
HAR has a huge potential to introduce Augmented Reality (AR) to the mass consumer market due to widespread use of suitable handheld devices. Compared to other mobile AR mediums, HAR also offers benefits like superior information input methods and a possibility for easier collaboration. However as Grubert et al. [1] and Olsson et al. [2] point out, HAR is not currently considered useful due to, for example, insufficient utility and irrelevant content. Thus, it is important to evaluate how HAR performs in different kinds of practical use scenarios.

In this poster, we focus on the usefulness of HAR in two generic guidance scenarios. We describe the design and evaluation of our prototype HAR guidance system and address its usefulness and usability related issues. The contribution of our work is the lessons learned from the user studies of the prototype system.

## PROTOTYPE SYSTEM
Our prototype system was developed for the iPad and it uses Simultaneous Localization And Mapping (SLAM) for tracking. SLAM tracking allows the system to be used more freely in different kinds of unknown environments. The task flow in our system is as follows: First the desired area of interest (a correct SLAM map) must be selected from an overview image of the real environment. After the area is selected the SLAM map tracking needs to be initialized by choosing the correct viewpoint. Finally, the annotations can be seen overlaid onto the real world.

Figure 1: The evaluation scenarios: the device set-up scenario (left) and the object assembly scenario (right).

## USER STUDIES
We have performed two user studies on our prototype system. A small-scale study (6 participants) was conducted on the initial prototype in a device set-up scenario (Fig. 1, left) in order to identify usability issues. We improved the system and then conducted a within-group comparative study (27 participants) against two conventional iPad guides: a picture and a video guide. This study was done in an object assembly scenario (Fig. 1, right) where we measured performance and subjective feedback.

We derived five guidelines based on the results of our evaluations: location of the AR environment, the information about the off-screen AR content, navigational shortcuts, view pausing, and feedback. We were unable to find performance benefits from the use of AR compared to conventional multimedia guides. Main reasons for this was the overall complexity of the AR compared to the two other guides and the simplicity of the assembly scenario.

## CONCLUSION
We have described the design and evaluation of our HAR guidance prototype. Even though we did not able to prove the superiority of our system, we gained information about the possible improvement areas of HAR in guidance. The use of HAR in generic guidance could be justified if other benefits of HAR are also made use of. Future work will see more improvements based on the results of the comparative user study. We will then expand our system to more complex practical use scenarios that require inputting information and authoring AR content.

## REFERENCES
1. Grubert, J., Langlotz, T. and Grasset, R. Augmented reality browser survey. *Graz University of Technology 2011*, (2011).

2. Olsson, T. and Salo. M. Online user survey on current mobile augmented reality applications. In *Proc. ISMAR 2011*, IEEE Press (2011), 75-84.

# Natural Pointing Posture in Distal Pointing Tasks

**Heejin Kim**
Pohang University of
Science and Technology
gimigimi@postech.ac.kr

**Seungjae Oh**
Pohang University of
Science and Technology
oreo329@postech.ac.kr

**Sung H. Han**
Pohang University of
Science and Technology
shan@postech.ac.kr

**Min K. Chung**
National Research
Foundation of Korea
deermin@nrf.re.kr

## ABSTRACT
In this poster, we present an experiment to capture user's natural pointing posture in distal pointing tasks at large displays and to examine the effect of pointing posture on the performance of distal pointing tasks. There were two types of pointing posture: stretched (69%) and bended arm posture (31%). The types did not affect movement angle, but affected angular error, task completion time and mean angular velocity.

## Author Keywords
Distal pointing task; natural pointing posture; large display

## ACM Classification Keywords
H.1.2 [**User/Machine Systems**]: Human factors; H.5.2 [**User Interfaces**]: Ergonomics, Input devices and strategies.

## 1. INTRODUCTION
3D interaction such as distal pointing is becoming more common [1] as large displays are becoming more prevalent [2]. The first step for designing effective 3D interaction is to understand natural human behavior because 3D interaction is natural and intuitive way to interact. In this study, we investigated natural human posture during distal pointing and the effect of the posture on the performance of distal pointing.

## 2. EXPERIMENT
Thirty people (ten females) who are right-handed voluntarily participated in the experiment for distal pointing. Their ages were between nineteen and thirty (mean: 26.6 years and standard deviation: 3.4 years). Targets were presented in a large screen (94 inch), and the participants were instructed to move their dominant hand from starting point to the target as naturally as possible. A pointing task was started when the participants pressed a button held in their non-dominant hand and was ended when they pressed the button again. To get natural motion and the perceived position of the target, any visual cue (display cursor) was not provided. Each participant performed a total of 408 pointing tasks for various target locations and distances to display. During the tasks, task completion time and the location of the fingertip was automatically saved in each participant's log-file. To capture the location of the hand, motion capture system (Motion analysis HAWK) was used.

## 3. RESULTS
There were two types of natural pointing posture: stretched arm posture and bended arm posture (Figure 1). One person who

changed her arm posture from bended to stretched as distance from display increased was excluded from the analysis. Twenty out of twenty-nine (69%) stretched their arm and nine bended their arm during the tasks. An ANOVA was performed to see whether the types of pointing posture affect the performance in terms of task completion time, mean angular velocity, movement angle (the angle between lines drawn from the participant's eye to the fingertip for starting point and the target) and angular error (the difference in angle between lines drawn from the participant's eye to the target, and from the eye to the fingertip). There were no significant effects of pointing posture for movement angle ($F_{(1,27)}=2.43$, $p=0.1308$), but angular error ($F_{(1.27)}=12.7$, $p=0.0014$), task completion time ($F_{(1,27)}=6.81$, $p=0.0146$) and mean angular velocity ($F_{(1,27)}=9.3$, $p=0.0051$) were significantly affected by pointing posture. Time for stretched arm (1420.57 ms) was longer than that for bended arm (1069.20 ms), and mean angular velocity for bended arm (9.28 °/s) was faster than that for stretched arm (6.83 °/s). Angular error for bended arm (5.19°) was bigger than that for stretched arm (2.46°).

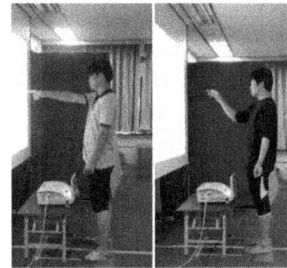

**Figure 1. Pointing posture in distal pointing: stretched arm posture (left) and bended arm posture (right).**

## 4. CONCLUSION
There were two types of natural pointing posture which are stretched and bended arm posture, and most of the participants posed stretched arm posture during distal pointing tasks. Although velocity was different, the location of participants' hand for a target was the same for both type of pointing posture. This could be an interesting characteristic and can be used as a basic resource to understand user's natural behavior for 3D interaction.

## 5. REFERENCES
1. Jauregui, D.A.G., Argelaguet, F., and Lecuyer, A.2012. Design and evaluation of 3D cursors and motion parallax for the exploration of desktop virtual environments. 3D User Interfaces (March 2012), 69-76.

2. Kaviani, N., Finke, M., Fels, S., Lea, R. and Wang, H. 2009. What goes where? Designing interactive large public display applications for mobile device interaction. In Proceedings of the ACM ICIMCS'09 (Kunming, Yunnan, China, November 23–25, 2009)

# Real-time Sign Language Recognition using RGBD Stream: Spatial-Temporal Feature Exploration

**Fuyang Huang, Zelong Sun, Qiang Xu**
The Chinese University of
Hong Kong, Shatin, HK
{fyhuang,zlsun,qxu}
@cse.cuhk.edu.hk

**Yim Binh Sze, Wai Lan Tang**
The Chinese University of
Hong Kong, Shatin, HK
{felix_cslds,gtang}@cuhk.edu.hk

**Xiaogang Wang**
The Chinese University of
Hong Kong, Shatin, HK
xgwang@ee.cuhk.edu.hk

## ABSTRACT
We propose a novel spatial-temporal feature set for sign language recognition, wherein we construct explicit spatial and temporal features that capture both hand movement and hand shape. Experimental results show that the proposed solution outperforms existing one in terms of accuracy.

## Author Keywords
Sign language recognition; human-computer interaction

## ACM Classification Keywords
H.5.2 Information interfaces and presentation (e.g., HCI): User Interfaces (H.1.2)

## INTRODUCTION
In this work, we use Microsoft Kinect as input device to record RGBD stream, from which skeleton positions and hand shape are extracted as spatial features. Temporal features are then constructed by building a temporal pyramid of these spatial features. A simple support vector machine (SVM) is then used to classify the concatenated spatial-temporal feature. Our experimental data set includes 100 Hong Kong sign words. Each word is performed 3 times by 3 people each. The result shows that our system achieves higher accuracy than existing solution and that less training samples are required compared to the method using time-variant model such as Hidden Markov Models (HMMs).

## FEATURE DESIGN
To ensure informativeness and discrimination of the proposed features, we abstract the sign language features into two parts: joint positions and hand shapes, both spatially and temporally. With the help of Kinect, joint positions are provided and hand contour can be segmented simply by thresholding the depth image. Histograms of Oriented Gradients(HOG) is then adopted to describe the shape of segmented hand part.

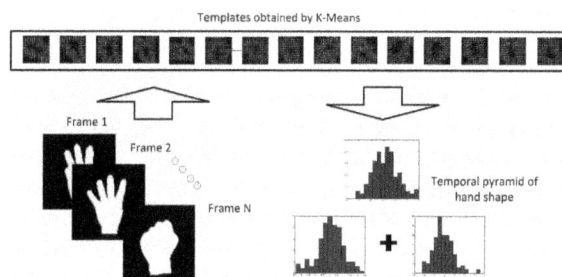

Figure 1. Hand shape descriptor

| Data set | 1 | 2 | 3 |
|---|---|---|---|
| SVM-linear | **89.9%** | 79.7% | 80.8% |
| SVM-sigmoid | 89.6% | **80.8%** | **81.4%** |
| SVM-radial basis | 89.7% | 79.7% | 80.5% |
| HMMs [1] | 75.6% | 70.2% | 71.5% |

Table 1. Comparison for different methods

To improve the robustness, we build a set of hand shape templates for matching with the segmented hands. Finally, these matching similarities of each frame accumulate to form a histogram of hand shapes. To capture the temporal feature, we employ Histogram of Oriented Displacements (HOD) to describe hand movement and hand shape transformation. In total, two three-levels temporal pyramids are built for movement and transformation separately.

## EXPERIMENT AND CONCLUSION
We compared our result against a popular HMM-based method proposed by Zafraulla et al.[1]. Three different SVM kernels were applied to our work as shown in table 1. Cross-validation test presented that our method achieved maximum accuracies of 89.9%, 80.8% and 81.4% for data set 1, 2 and 3 respectively, which outperformed its counterpart [1]. The reason was that the HMM models had too many implicit temporal parameters to be fitted, however we explicitly involved the temporal information in the features.

## REFERENCES
1. Zafrulla, Z., Brashear, H., Starner, T., Hamilton, H., and Presti, P. American sign language recognition with the kinect. In *Proceedings of the 13th international conference on multimodal interfaces*, ACM (2011), 279–286.

*SUI'14*, October 4–5, 2014, Honolulu, HI, USA.
ACM 978-1-4503-2820-3/14/10.
http://dx.doi.org/10.1145/2659766.2661214

# Exploring Tablet Surrounding Interaction Spaces For Medical Imaging

**Hanae Rateau**
University Lille 1
CNRS (LIFL/IRCICA)
INRIA (Lille)
hanae.rateau@inria.fr

**Laurent Grisoni**
University Lille 1
CNRS (LIFL/IRCICA)
INRIA (Lille)
laurent.grisoni@lifl.fr

**Bruno De Araujo**
DGP lab, University of
Toronto
brar@dgp.toronto.edu

## ABSTRACT

Medical imaging is essential to support most diagnosis. It often requires visualizing individual 2D slices from 3D volumetric datasets and switching between both representations. Combining an overview with a detailed view of the data [1] enables to keep the user in context when looking in detail at a slice. Given both their mobility and their adequacy to support direct manipulation, tablets are attractive devices to ease imaging analysis tasks. They have been successfully combined with tabletops [3], allowing new ways to explore volumetric data. However, while touch allows for a more direct manipulation, it suffers from the well-known fat finger problem which can interfere with the display, making it hard to understand subtle visual changes. To overcome this problem, we propose to explore the space around tablet devices. Such approach has been used for displays [2] to separate several workspaces of the desktop. Here, we use such space to *invoke commands* that are not required to be performed on the tablet, thus maximizing the visualization space during manipulations.

## ACM Classification Keywords

H.5.2 User Interfaces: Input devices and strategies, Interaction Styles

## Author Keywords

tactile interaction;spatialized interaction;mid-air gestures

## INTERACTING AROUND THE TABLET

The core concept is to broaden the interaction with the tablet by using the space around it. We cut out this space into 8 areas denominated as slabs (see Figure 1). These 8 slabs can then be used as spaces for gestural interaction close to the device. Since the user is not required to use the tablet to interact with the displayed data, it opens new possible options to use these new inputs and control image attributes. For example, the

*SUI'14*, October 4–5, 2014, Honolulu, HI, USA.
ACM 978-1-4503-2820-3/14/10.
http://dx.doi.org/10.1145/2659766.2661215

**Figure 1. Slabs arrangement around the tablet and prototype setup.**

right slab can be devoted to manipulating the detailed view on the tablet. The top slab could be used to interact with the distant overview. And the top right slab could be used as a view filter selector.

To illustrate such concept, we developed a simple prototype that uses the right slab of the tablet to allow the arbitrary slicing of a volume. The user sees the whole volume on a distant display and the tablet displays the slice. Here, we use the right slab of the tablet to determine the slice position and the tablet orientation gives the slice orientation.

## FUTURE WORK

As future work, we would like to explore further functionalities to support medical imaging and assess the benefits of tablet surrounding interaction spaces through user studies. We think that using the surrounding space of the tablet would help the mental representation construction.

## REFERENCES

1. D. Coffey, N. Malbraaten, T. B. Le, I. Borazjani, F. Sotiropoulos, A. Erdman, and D. F. Keefe. Interactive slice wim: Navigating and interrogating volume data sets using a multisurface, multitouch vr interface. *IEEE TVCG*, 18(10):1614–1626, Oct 2012.

2. D. Hausen, S. Boring, and S. Greenberg. The unadorned desk: Exploiting the physical space around a display as an input canvas. In *Proc. of Interact 2013*, Cape Town, South Africa, Sep 2013.

3. M. Spindler, W. Büschel, C. Winkler, and R. Dachselt. Tangible displays for the masses: spatial interaction with handheld displays by using consumer depth cameras. *Personal and Ubiquitous Computing*, 18 (5):1213–1225, Jun 2014.

# Proposing a Classification Model for Perceptual Target Selection on Large Displays

| Seungjae Oh | Heejin Kim | Hyo-Jeong So |
|---|---|---|
| POSTECH | POSTECH | POSTECH |
| oreo329@postech.ac.kr | gimigimi@postech.ac.kr | hyojeongso@postech.ac.kr |

## ABSTRACT

In this research, we propose a linear SVM classification model for perceptual distal target selection on large displays. The model is based on two simple features of users' finger movements reflecting users' visual perception of targets. The model shows the accuracy of 92.78% for predicting an intended target at end point.

## Author Keywords

Large Displays; Distal Freehand Pointing; Spatial Perception

## ACM Classification Keywords

H.5.2 [**User Interfaces**]: Input devices and strategies

## INTRODUCTION

When investigating large public display interaction, wall-sized displays are frequently installed at public spaces [1], and direct touch interaction is inappropriate to handle large visual spaces beyond arm's reach [2]. To design more natural and intuitive distant interaction with large displays, we explore the relationship between users' visual perception of targets on grid-like configuration of the display surface and corresponding pointing location of user's finger over the motor space volume. Our approach is to predict an intended target among 35 targets on a large display using the linear Support Vector Machine (SVM).

## EXPERIMENT

We recruited thirty right-handed participants (20 males, 10 females) for the experiment. The ratio aspect of the 94-inch visual projection is 16:10 (2.01m x 1.26m) with a resolution of 1280 x 800. Four Motion Analysis Hawk cameras were installed to capture right-finger locations at 60Hz, which is considered to be fast enough to cover natural hand tremor and hand acceleration. The participants were holding a clickable switching device on their secondary hand to activate the tracking. During the experiment, two targets in black and red were presented to the participants (see Figure 1). The fixed black target was located at the center of the target configuration. A red target was randomly presented among the 7 x 5 grid positions (Figure 1a). The participants were instructed to activate the tracking system after pointing the black target, and then, to move their index finger to aim a red target along with deactivating the tracking (Figure 1b). Each participant performed total 420 trials (35 targets x 3 repetitions x 4 distances) at four different distances from the display (1m-4m).

## RESULTS

From the tracking data of each trial, we extracted two spatial locations of users' fingertip where users perpetually associated to the starting target and ending target, respectively. Since the aim of this research is to predict a target from users' forefinger movement around the display area, we calculated two factors that can be simply calculated when users face toward the display: (a) a position vector (MotorDir), which refers to subtraction between an ending location and a starting location, and (b) an angle between the users' main eye and the two spatial locations (MotorAng). Thirty-five targets were numbered from bottom-left to top-right (TarOrder, see Figure 1a). A linear SVM was applied to classify and predict an intended target (TarOrder). We used the libSVM library of Weka 3.6.11. 218 out of 12,600 samples (1.73%) were excluded because of tracking errors. Among 12,382 samples, two-thirds were used as a training set, and the rest as a test set. Among the 4,210 test samples, the linear SVM correctly classified 92.78% of the test set (Average F-Measure = 0.927). To improve classification performance, we used MotorDir, which minimizes personal variance among different users when pointing the starting target. Target grid intervals were nonlinear distances because we considered linear angle increments inside the tangent, which preserves perceived visual angles of users regardless of the experimental distances.

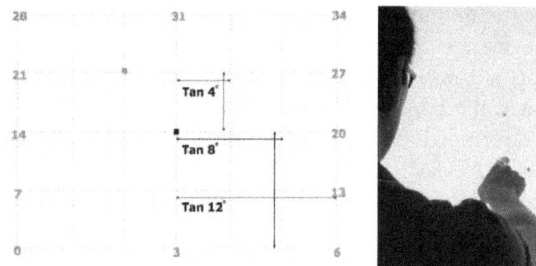

**Figure 1. a) Grid-like target configuration with TarOrder and nonlinear grid interval. b) Participant pointing targets**

## CONCLUSION

We applied machine learning for the target selection on large displays. Most of the classification errors took place at targets on the four edges. Our future works are to improve the classification model and to conduct a user study with the improved model.

## REFERENCES

1. Jota, R., Nacenta, M.A., Jorge, J.A., Carpendale, S., and Greenberg, S. A comparison of ray pointing techniques for very large displays. *In Proc. Graphic Interface 2010*, ACM Press (2010), 269–276.

2. Vogel, D. and Balakrishnan, R. Distant freehand pointing and clicking on very large, high resolution displays. *In Proc. UIST 2005*, ACM Press (2005), 33–42.

# Investigating Inertial Measurement Units for Spatial Awareness in Multi-Surface Environments

**Alaa Azazi, Teddy Seyed, Frank Maurer**

University of Calgary, Department of Computer Science

2500 University Dr. NW

{alaa.azazi, teddy.seyed, frank.maurer}@ucalgary.ca

## ABSTRACT

In this work, we present an initial user study that explores the use of a dedicated inertial measurement unit (IMU) to achieve spatial awareness in Multi-surface Environments (MSE's). Our initial results suggest that measurements provided by an IMU may not provide value over sensor fusion techniques for spatially-aware MSE's, but warrant further exploration.

## Author Keywords

Inertial tracking systems; indoor navigation systems; gestures and interactions; HCI; multi-surface applications.

## ACM Classification Keywords

H.5.2 [Information interfaces and presentation]: User Interfaces, Input devices and strategies.

## INTRODUCTION

We present a user study that examines the challenges with sensor-fusion based approaches [1], by evaluating an IMU to determine its accuracy for location and orientation tracking within spatially-aware MSE's. In MSE's, this type of information is important in using gestures to transfer content, a common task in MSEs [1][3] Specifically, we evaluated the applicability and usability of the SmartCube IMU, developed at the Alberta Center for Advanced MNT Products (ACAMP). Our initial work explores two major questions: How accurate are the position and orientation measurements returned by the SmartCube? And whether it is a feasible alternative to sensor fusion techniques?

## EXPERIMENT

Ten volunteers participated in our study. We developed a specialized application to display a set of targets on a large wall-display connected to a PC. A Microsoft Surface tablet application was created to communicate spatial data from the SmartCube, and act as a device to send content.

Users were instructed to stand at certain locations in the room (fixed and randomized), and send content [2] from the tablet, to a number of visual targets that were shown on the display - one target at a time, by rotating the device in the 3D space.

## RESULTS

Sending content from a fixed location, without visual feedback, showed a success rate of 7%, deviating 21.4 cm from the target on average. Performing the same task with visual feedback of the position on the large wall-display had a higher success rate 21%, with target deviation averaging at 20.6 cm. Tasks that depended on location measurements showed negative results, with a success rate of 0%, deviating from the target by 1 to 3 meters. Feedback received from the study participants indicated that attaching an external module to the tablet reduced the tablet's mobility. Participants, also, thought that the visual feedback was crucial to understand the system's perspective and understanding of the room.

## CONCLUSION

Our limited initial study highlighted the inaccuracy of the SmartCube for providing spatial-awareness in a MSE. An interesting observation revealed from the study and comments from participants was the use of visual feedback to offset sensor inaccuracy. This may suggest that providing visual feedback for multi-surface interactions is valuable and will allow users to compensate for inaccurate tracking technologies or MSE's that require constant calibration.

## REFERENCES

1. Seyed, T., Sousa, M. C., Maurer, F., and Tang, A. SkyHunter: a Multi-Surface Environment for Supporting Oil and Gas Exploration. *Proc. ITS 2013*.

2. Voida, S., Podlaseck, M., Kjeldsen, R., and Pinhanez, C. A Study on the Manipulation of 2D Objects in a Projector/Camera-based Augmented Reality Environment. *Proc. CHI 2005*, ACM Press (2005), 611-620.

3. Yatani, K., Tamura, K., Hiroki, K., Sugimoto, M., and Hashizume, H. 2006. Toss-It: Intuitive Information Transfer Techniques for Mobile Devices Using Toss and Swing Actions. *IEICE-Trans*. Inf. Syst., 89 (1): 150–15.

# LeapLook: A Free-Hand Gestural Travel Technique using the Leap Motion Finger Tracker

**Robert Codd-Downey**
Electrical Engineering and Computer Science,
York University
robert@cse.yorku.ca

**Wolfgang Stuerzlinger**
Electrical Engineering and Computer Science,
York University
wolfgang@cse.yorku.ca

## ABSTRACT

Contactless motion sensing devices enable a new form of input that does not encumber the user with wearable tracking equipment. We present a novel travel technique using the Leap Motion finger tracker which adopts a 2DOF steering metaphor used in traditional mouse and keyboard navigation in many 3D computer games.

## Author Keywords

LeapMotion, interaction, gestures, travel

## INTRODUCTION

Travel refers to the non-cognitive subset of navigation which is the act of changing one's position and orientation to reach a goal. In a virtual environment, travel is accomplished by manipulating the virtual viewpoint through an interaction technique. Intuitively and empirically, physical walking and walking-in-place are the most natural means of travel from an egocentric viewpoint, however, limitations of space and tracking equipment in standard desktop applications, prevent practical use. The Leap Motion is a small peripheral device utilizing similar technology to that of the Xbox Kinect but instead targets high fidelity finger tracking in a smaller desktop setting.

## LEAPLOOK TECHNIQUE

Our technique adopts a traditional 2DOF steering metaphor found in many FPS video games to facilitate 3DOF motion within a cartesian plane. Pointing gestures were chosen due to their simplicity and demonstrated effectiveness in other techniques [1]. Using this approach only four motions are needed to provide the necessary control; forward, reverse, left/right turn. These motions can be mapped to three hand poses/gestures shown in Figure 1a-c. The overlap between forward and turn gestures requires that a fourth gesture shown in Figure 1d to provide the ability to stop and indirectly turn-in-place. This gesture was chosen as it combines both forward and reverse gestures, intuitively negating each other. These gestures do not provide a way for the user to turn while

reversing. This is acceptable as most video games do not provide a mechanism for a user to see behind them, furthermore it has been suggested [2] that a user only reverses to make minor corrections during navigation.

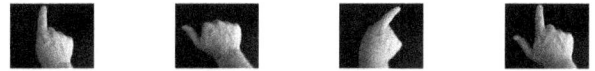

(a) Forward    (b) Reverse    (c) Turn    (d) Stop

**Figure 1: Gestural Mappings**

We define relative control over an angle of rotation as the rate of change of said target angle proportionate to the amount of absolute measure in the source angle. Turning is implemented as relative yaw control which implies a yaw of $5°$ results in a $\alpha 5°$ per second change in yaw. A direct mapping was not used because it would make turning around and other actions needlessly difficult. Additionally a damping factor was added to the user's velocity, which increased linearly with the yaw of the user's index finger.

## DISCUSSION

FPSs provide users with additional capabilities such as strafing and jumping, these can be incorporated into the gesture set without modification of the original gestures. Strafing and jumping could be implemented via left/right horizontal translation and up-down vertical translation of the hand, respectively. Furthermore speed adjustments could be affected by the amount of curl in the user's index finger. Extending this technique to 3D (i.e., flying) requires care as explicit 6DOF control can be cognitively detrimental. The addition of relative pitch control via pitch of the index finger while only adding one additional controllable degree of freedom would indirectly give altitude control. Caution must be taken when extending this technique as some gestures may prevent the full time use of an armrest causing fatigue, a common problem with free-hand gestural interactions.

## REFERENCES

1. Bowman, D., Koller, D., and Hodges, L. Travel in immersive virtual environments: an evaluation of viewpoint motion control techniques. In *Virtual Reality Annual International Symposium, 1997., IEEE 1997* (1997), 45–52, 215.

2. Tan, D. S., Robertson, G. G., and Czerwinski, M. Exploring 3d navigation: Combining speed-coupled flying with orbiting. In *Proc. SIGCHI Conference on Human Factors in Computing Systems*, CHI '01, ACM (New York, NY, USA, 2001), 418–425.

# Safe-&-Round: Bringing Redirected Walking to Small Virtual Reality Laboratories

**Paul Lubos**
Department of Informatics
University of Hamburg
paul.lubos@uni-hamburg.de

**Gerd Bruder**
Department of Informatics
University of Hamburg
gerd.bruder@uni-hamburg.de

**Frank Steinicke**
Department of Informatics
University of Hamburg
frank.steinicke@uni-hamburg.de

## ABSTRACT

Walking is usually considered the most natural form for self-motion in a virtual environment (VE). However, the confined physical workspace of typical virtual reality (VR) labs often prevents natural exploration of larger VEs. Redirected walking has been introduced as a potential solution to this restriction, but corresponding techniques often induce enormous manipulations if the workspace is considerably small and lacks natural experiences therefore.

In this poster we propose the *Safe-&-Round* user interface, which supports natural walking in a potentially infinite virtual scene while confined to a considerably restricted physical workspace. This virtual locomotion technique relies on a safety volume, which is displayed as a semi-transparent half-capsule, inside which the user can walk without manipulations caused by redirected walking.

## Author Keywords

Spatial user interfaces; locomotion; virtual environments

## ACM Classification Keywords

H.5.m. Information Interfaces and Presentation (e. g. HCI): Miscellaneous

## SAFE-&-ROUND USER INTERFACE

When walking through a VE we distinguish between three stages in the Safe-&-Round user interface (see Figure 1): (i) walking in the safe inner region, (ii) redirected walking around the outer path, and (iii) a transition between these two stages.

A user can freely walk within the safe inner region where movements match between the real and virtual space. The boundaries of the workspace are represented by a semi-transparent half-capsule. When approaching the boundaries of the safe inner region, the opacity of the barrier increases to inform users that they are about to enter the redirected walking path. Once the user walks through the semi-transparent barrier, we compute the minimum angle necessary to reorient

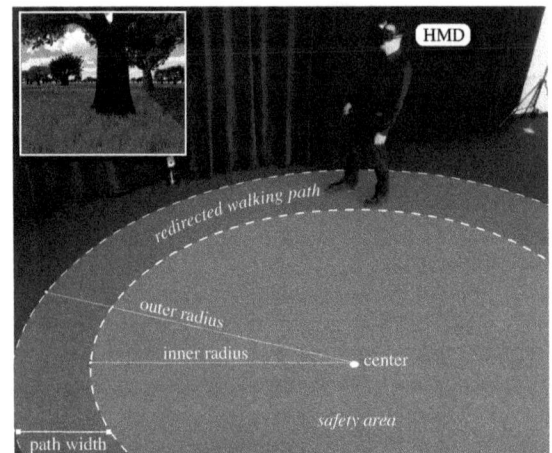

Figure 1. User exploring a VE using the Safe-&-Round interface. Illustrations show the safety area and the redirected walking path. The inset shows the user's view with a visual barrier to his right side preventing him from physical collisions.

them and start to apply camera rotations to guide them on the path that leads around the inner safety area (see Figure 1).

After users transitioned onto the redirected walking path, visual cues in the form of a virtual barrier [1] are used to inform users that this path is located close to the boundaries of the workspace, which prevents collisions with physical obstacles in the real world. The redirected walking path leads around the circular safety area, creating a circular path with the maximum possible radius in the physical workspace [2], thus providing a near-constant and predictable magnitude of manipulations.

Once users come close to an object of interest in the VE, we determine the remaining visual distance during walking and slowly start reorienting the user such that the region of interest falls into the safety region once the user reaches the target. The user then can perform tasks within the virtual workspace at the new location.

## REFERENCES

1. Cirio, G., Marchal, M., Regia-Corte, T., and Lécuyer, A. The magic barrier tape: A novel metaphor for infinite navigation in virtual worlds with a restricted walking workspace. In *Proc. of ACM VRST*, ACM Press (2009), 155–162.

2. Steinicke, F., Bruder, G., Jerald, J., Fenz, H., and Lappe, M. Estimation of Detection Thresholds for Redirected Walking Techniques. *IEEE Transactions on Visualization and Computer Graphics (TVCG) 16*, 1 (2010), 17–27.

# The Significance of Stereopsis and Motion Parallax in Mobile Head Tracking Environments

### Paul Lubos
Department of Computer Science
University of Hamburg
paul.lubos@uni-hamburg.de

### Dimitar Valkov
Department of Computer Science
University of Münster
dimitar.valkov@uni-muenster.de

## ABSTRACT
Despite 3D TVs and applications gaining popularity in recent years, 3D displays on mobile devices are rare. With low-cost head tracking solutions and first user interfaces available on smartphones [1], the question arises how effective the 3D impression through motion-parallax is and whether it is possible to achieve viable depth perception without binocular stereo cues. As motion parallax and stereopsis may be considered the most important depth cues [3], we developed an experiment comparing the user's depth perception utilizing head tracking with and without stereopsis.

## Author Keywords
Perception, virtual environments, spatial user interfaces

## ACM Classification Keywords
I.3.7. Computer Graphics: Three-Dimensional Graphics and Realism

## EXPERIMENT
Since currently no mobile device allows both frame sequential stereo and motion parallax, a PC Display was occluded to a size of a 10inch tablet and used to render frame sequential stereo at 120Hz viewed through NVIDIA's 3D Vision 2 shutter glasses. The subject's head was tracked using a WorldViz PPT setup with 8 cameras and a infrared (IR) marker hat. The experiment was conducted with 11 participants who were tasked to use a mouse, for high precision, to position a marker in 2DOF beneath spheres of varying depths from 10cm behind the screen to 5cm in front of the screen in 2.5cm intervals.

The results from the experiment show that subjects are more accurate when stereo is enabled, which corresponds to the results of other studies in the field [4]. As illustrated in Figure 1, there was a significant difference between the active and inactive stereoscopic depth cues on the depth error distance ($F_{10}^1 = 8.897$, $p < .05$), however the participants were still able to estimate the depth of the target within 5mm 98.12% of the time without stereoscopic cues, whereas 99.93% of the guesses with enabled stereo were within 5mm. Additionally, the scenes used were fairly simple to allow precise control

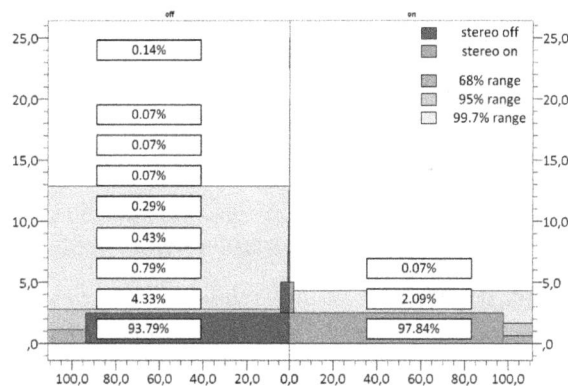

Figure 1. Results of the experiment: The x-axis shows the frequencies of the error distances measured in percent, the y-axis shows the measured error distances in mm. Frequencies are binned in 2.5mm intervals. The left side shows the results with disabled stereo, the right side with enabled stereo. Colored backgrounds indicate the deviation ranges.

of the experiment environment and avoid distraction by other depth cues. As shown by Hubona et al. [2], other depth cues like shadows could improve the accuracy further, potentially reducing the differences between the conditions.

Our results show that if the precision in 95% of the cases has to be below 1.54mm, stereoscopic cues are useful. However, if a precision below 2.56mm is enough, then monocular depth cues are viable. The results lead to the conclusion, that the depth perception gained from motion cues appears viable, especially for mobile applications.

## REFERENCES
1. Francone, J., and Nigay, L. Using the user's point of view for interaction on mobile devices. In *ACM IHM* (2011), 4:1–4:8.

2. Hubona, G. S., Shirah, G. W., and Fout, D. G. The relative contributions of stereo, lighting, and background scenes in promoting 3D depth visualization. *ACM TOCHI* 6, 3 (1999), 214–242.

3. Reinhart, W. F., Beaton, R. J., and Snyder, H. L. Comparison of depth cues for relative depth judgments. In *SC-DL tentative*, International Society for Optics and Photonics (1990), 12–21.

4. Willemsen, P., Gooch, A. A., Thompson, W. B., and Creem-Regehr, S. H. Effects of stereo viewing conditions on distance perception in virtual environments. *Presence: Teleoperators and Virtual Environments 17* (2005), 91–101.

# Depth Cues and Mouse-Based 3D Target Selection

**Robert J. Teather**
McMaster University
teather@mcmaster.ca

**Wolfgang Stuerzlinger**
York University
wolfgang@cse.yorku.ca

## ABSTRACT
We investigated mouse-based 3D selection using one-eyed cursors, evaluating stereo and head-tracking. Stereo cursors significantly reduced performance for targets at different depths, but the one-eyed cursor yielded some discomfort.

## Author Keywords
Mouse, stereo display, head-tracking, one-eyed cursor.

## ACM Classification Keywords
H.5.2 [Information Interfaces and Presentation]: User Interfaces – input devices, interaction styles.

## INTRODUCTION
Recent work on screen-space 3D selection [2] reinforced the benefits of the "one-eyed" cursor [3] to eliminate stereo conflicts. Other research indicates that one-eyed cursors may cause eye fatigue [1] and hinder performance relative to stereo cursors. We re-evaluate the one-eyed cursor in situations where depth is irrelevant to assess its negative effects in isolation from its benefits, (e.g., remote targets).

## EXPERIMENT
We used a 3D version of ISO 9241-9 [2] with 16 participants and NVidia *3DVision Pro* for stereo. Five OptiTrack S250e cameras were used for head tracking.

The software depicted the inside of a wooden crate with target spheres on wooden cylinders (Figure 1), in either stereo or mono, with or without head tracking, and with a stereo 3D or one-eyed cursor. In mono view, the same image (0 disparity) was presented to both eyes. The one-eyed cursor was only displayed to the dominant eye.

**Figure 1. Experimental software depicting 11 targets. Arrows added to illustrate the ordering of the first four targets.**

Participants clicked the red target with the mouse. Each click advanced the target by the pattern shown in Figure 1.

The experiment used the following within-subjects factors:

*Stereo Display*: Stereo-On, Stereo-Off (i.e., mono)
*Head-Tracking*: HT-On, HT-Off
*Cursor*: STC (stereo cursor), OEC (one-eyed cursor)
*Target Size*: 0.5, 0.75, 1.0 cm
*Target Distance*: 3.5, 7.5, 9.5 cm
*Target Depth*: -10, 0, +10 cm

Stereo, head-tracking, and cursor were counterbalanced by a Latin square. Target size, distance, and depth were random for each target circle. There were 12 recorded selection trials per circle. Thus there were $2 \times 2 \times 2 \times 3 \times 3 \times 3 \times 12 = 2592$ trials per participant. We only report "screen-projected" throughput [2] due to space constraints.

## RESULTS
There was a significant interaction between stereo, depth, and cursor ($F_{2,30} = 12.4$, $p < .001$), see Figure 2: the STC 0 cm conditions are better than the STC +10 cm or -10 cm conditions, but not the OEC conditions. The best stereo-off conditions (both STC at +10 cm) were higher than the stereo-on at both -10 and +10 cm target depths. There was no difference in the stereo-off conditions.

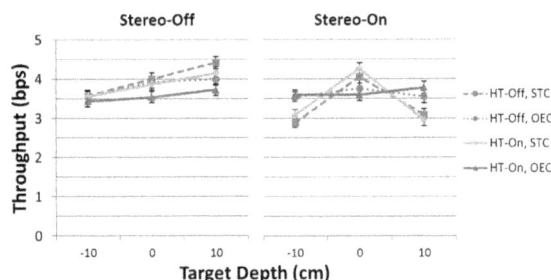

**Figure 2. Throughput by condition. Error bars show ±1 *SE*.**

## CONCLUSION
The stereo cursor significantly hurt performance for targets at different depths. The one-eyed cursor eliminated this effect, but had a small negative effect in mono view.

## REFERENCES
1. Schemali, L. and Eisemann, E., Design and evaluation of mouse cursors in a stereoscopic desktop environment, *Proc. IEEE 3DUI 2014*, 67-70.
2. Teather, R. J. and Stuerzlinger, W., Pointing at 3D target projections using one-eyed and stereo cursors, *Proc. ACM CHI 2013*, 159 - 168.
3. Ware, C. and Lowther, K., Selection using a one-eyed cursor in a fish tank VR environment, *ACM TOCHI*, 4, 1997, 309-322.

# An In-Depth Look at the Benefits of Immersion Cues on Spatial 3D Problem Solving

**Cassandra Hoef, Jasmine Davis, Orit Shaer**
Wellesley College
Wellesley, MA 02481
{choef, jdavis4, oshaer}@wellesley.edu

**Erin T. Solovey**
Drexel University
Philadelphia, PA, USA
erin.solovey@drexel.edu

## ABSTRACT

We present a user study that takes an in-depth look at the effect of immersion cues on 3D spatial problem solving by combining traditional performance and experience measures with brain data.

## INTRODUCTION

Interactive stereoscopic 3D displays offer the promise to enhance 3D spatial problems solving by leveraging three different immersion cues: binocular parallax, motion parallax, and haptic feedback. However, this potential has not yet been proven empirically. Our goal is to understand which immersion cues contribute to improve 3D spatial problem solving.

Our pilot studies utilized traditional performance and user experience measures including: time, task workload and spatial presence to explore the benefits of various immersion cues on 3D spatial problem solving. While we found no significant differences in terms of time-on-task and subjective workload, there were significant differences in the ways users perceived their presence in the virtual environment. Our preliminary findings also indicated that despite no apparent performance gains, users expressed preference for haptic feedback.

These intriguing results led us to extend prior explorations by looking at brain activity using functional near-infrared spectroscopy (fNIRS) as a supplemental measurement to more traditional performance metrics, along with tests to assess overall spatial reasoning skill of the participants. By looking at brain activity as well as overall spatial reasoning ability, we can examine whether there are immersive features that lead to lower mental load during spatial problem solving. Here, we present preliminary results.

## USER STUDY

We have designed a 2x2 mixed factorial study. The between-subject factor is the *combination of immersive cues* used by the interaction device, which has four settings: non-stereo, stereo (i.e. binocular parallax and motion parallax), non-stereo with haptic feedback, and stereo with haptic feedback. The within-subject factor is *difficulty level* of the puzzle.

### Procedure and Apparatus

Data was collected from 28 users, all right-handed females, randomly assigned one of four experimental conditions. Each participant completes 11 puzzles at 5 levels of difficulty. The dependent variables are *completion time, subjective workload rating* (NASA-TLX), *subjective presence rating* (MEC-Spatial Presence Questionnaire), and *fNIRS brain measurements*. All participants com-

*SUI '14*, Oct 04-05 2014, Honolulu, HI, USA
ACM 978-1-4503-2820-3/14/10.
http://dx.doi.org/10.1145/2659766.2661222

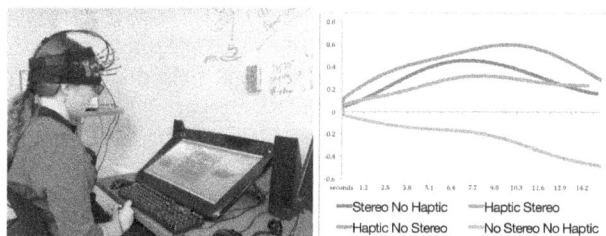

**Figure 1. Left: zSpace 3D stereoscopic display and fNIRS brain sensors. Right: Average change in oxy-hemoglobin in Level 5.**

plete two pencil and paper tests to assess spatial reasoning ability and a demographic questionnaire.

We use zSpace, a passive polarized 3D system with circularly polarized glasses that provides head-tracking and stylus-tracking at 6-DOF (Figure 1). The fNIRS machine, an ISS, Inc. Imagent, is a non-invasive device that detects blood oxygen levels in the brain. The device has shown promise in the field of HCI [1, 2, 3].

### Spatial Reasoning Task - zPuzzle

Our experimental task is based on the online game, Interlocked. We implemented a version for zSpace using Unity3D, which supports stereo, 6-DOF stylus and haptic feedback.

### Preliminary Results

Preliminary results indicate significant effect of immersion cues on task workload (physical demand and frustration), on perceived spatial presence (attention allocation, spatial situation, spatial presence self location, and cognitive involvement) as well as in fNIRS brain data. In addition, we found a significant effect on time-on-task in difficulty levels three, four, and five. Participants working in condition 1 (no stereo, no haptic) tend to perform worse than participants in condition 2 (stereo, no haptic). Also, in some cases participants in condition 3 (no stereo, haptic) performed significantly worse than participants in condition 4 (stereo, haptic). Figure 1, right, shows that in the most challenging level, we observed significantly lower levels of oxy-hemoglobin in Condition 1 (no stereo, no haptic) than in other conditions.

## ACKNOWLEDGMENTS

This work is partially funded by a Brachman-Hoffman Award.

## REFERENCES

1. Afergan, D., et al. Dynamic difficulty using brain metrics of workload. *Proc. CHI'14.* 3797–3806.
2. Hirshfield, et al. Brain Measurement for Usability Testing and Adaptive Interfaces: An Example of Uncovering Syntactic Workload with Functional Near Infrared Spectroscopy. *Proc. CHI'09.*
3. Solovey, E.T., et al. Using fNIRS brain sensing in realistic HCI settings: experiments and guidelines. *Proc. UIST '09*

# HoloLeap: Towards Efficient 3D Object Manipulation on Light Field Displays

**Vamsi Kiran Adikharla**
Holografika Kft.
Budapest, Hungary

**Paweł Woźniak**
t2i lab, Chalmers University of
Technology
pawelw@chalmers.se

**Robert J. Teather**
McMaster University
Hamilton, ON, Canada
teather@mcmaster.ca

## ABSTRACT

We present HoloLeap, which uses a Leap Motion controller for 3D model manipulation on a light field display (LFD). Like autostereo displays, LFDs support glasses-free 3D viewing. Unlike autostereo displays, LFDs automatically accommodate multiple viewpoints without the need of additional tracking equipment. We describe a gesture-based object manipulation that enables manipulation of 3D objects with 7DOFs by leveraging natural and familiar gestures. We provide an overview of research questions aimed at optimizing gestural input on light field displays.

## Author Keywords

Light field displays; 3d interaction; object manipulation.

## ACM Classification Keywords

H.5.m. Information interfaces and presentation (e.g., HCI): Miscellaneous.

## HOLOLEAP

We propose HoloLeap – a system for interacting with light field displays (LFDs) using hand gestures. LFDs [1] offer several advantages over volumetric or autostereo displays including adjacent view isolation, increased field of view, enhanced depth perception and horizontal motion parallax.

For our initial investigation, we designed manipulation gestures for translation, rotation, and scaling. We also included continuous rotation ("spinning"). After reviewing previous work [2], we designed a custom gesture set, as the increased depth perception of a LFD may affect object manipulation. Our goal was to enhance the ad-hoc qualities of mid-air gestures. Compared to handheld devices (e.g., a mouse) gestural interaction allows one to simply walk up and immediately begin manipulating 3D objects.

Rotation uses a single hand. The user rotates their wrist in the desired direction to rotate the object. It allows for fast

correction for each rotational degree of freedom and multiple axes of rotation in a single gesture. Moving two hands at once without increasing the distance between them translates the object. Scaling is activated by increasing and decreasing the distance between palms. HoloLeap does not use zooming as LFDs have a limited depth range. Scaling is provided as an alternative to facilitate model inspection and to easily provide an overview. Continuous rotation (spin) is activated with a double-hand rotation gesture. Rotation and translation gestures are shown in Figure 1.

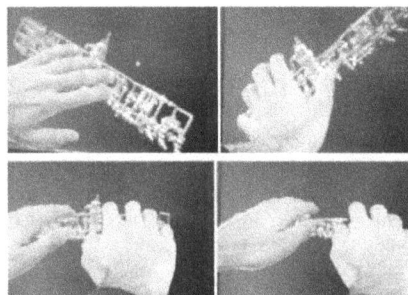

**Figure 1. Top: Z-axis rotation. Bottom: Z-axis translation.**

HoloLeap uses a Holografika HoloVizio HV640RC large-scale light field display (http://www.holografika.com/). It offers continuous motion parallax. The installation covers an area of 3050mm x 2150mm x 2700mm.

## OPEN QUESTIONS

Firstly, transformation speed, especially in relation to large sized displays, requires more study. Different mappings between the gesture speed and transformation are as yet untested. While this is a known challenge, the increased depth perception of a LFD complicates it, as viewing an object from different angles by different users creates relative differences in perception. We see a need for additional user studies addressing this problem in greater detail.

Broadly, we aim to start discussion on the appropriateness of gestural input for light field displays and investigate how users can capitalize on the unique features of these devices.

## REFERENCES

1. Balogh, T., Kovacs, P. T., and Barsi, A., Holovizio 3D display system, IEEE 3DTV Conference 2007, 1-4.

2. Malik, S., Ranjan, A., and Balakrishnan, R., Interacting with large displays from a distance with vision-tracked multi-finger gestural input, Proc. of UIST 2005, 43-52.

# Real-time and Robust Grasping Detection

**Chih-Fan Chen, Ryan Spicer, Rhys Yahata, Mark Bolas and Evan Suma**
USC Institute for Creative Technologies
{cfchen, spicer, ryahata, bolas, suma }@ict.usc.edu

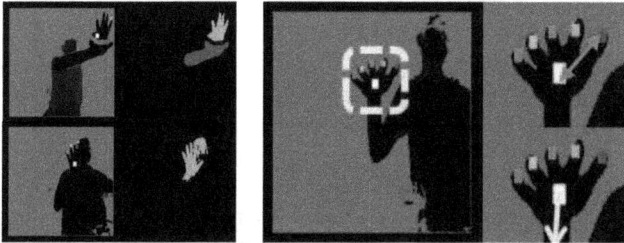

Figure 1. (left) Noise caused by background/sensing (right) The features used for training

## Author Keywords
Hand Tracking, 3D user interface

## ACM Classification Keywords
H.5.2 User Interfaces: Interaction styles; I.3.7 Three-Dimensional Graphics and Realism: Virtual reality

## INTRODUCTION
Depth-based gesture cameras provide a promising and novel way to interface with computers. Nevertheless, this type of interaction remains challenging due to the complexity of finger interactions and the under large viewpoint variations. Existing middleware such as Intel Perceptual Computing SDK (PCSDK) or SoftKinetic IISU can provide abundant hand tracking and gesture information. However, the data is too noisy (Fig. 1, *left*) for consistent and reliable use in our application. In this work, we present a filtering approach that combines several features from PCSDK to achieve more stable hand openness and supports grasping interactions in virtual environments. Support vector machine (SVM), a machine learning method, is used to achieve better accuracy in a single frame, and Markov Random Field (MRF), a probability theory, is used to stabilize and smooth the sequential output. Our experimental results verify the effectiveness and the robustness of our method.

## METHOD
We use a Creative Interactive Gesture Camera and the PCSDK [2] to acquire the hand openness, the number of detected fingertips, the average distance from fingertips to the palm, the position of the hand and the normal direction of the palm (Fig.1, *right*). As the system cannot differentiate between the left and right hand, we use data from a PhaseSpace motion capture system to match data from the PCSDK with the left and right hand. However, adding markers to the hands introduces more noise which causes imperfection of hand segmentation and poor tracking (Fig. 1, *left*).

To increase the accuracy of hand openness, we use the features acquired from PCSDK to train a model by SVM [1]. Although SVM can improve the accuracy of hand openness in single frame, the output label will oscillate and become unusable because it lacks the temporal property. MRF is applied to refine the sequential labels by optimizing the state transition from the confidence of hand openness and previous label. Matching with the hand position from Phasespace, we can use the hand openness of both hands to interact with the virtual environment.

We compared the proposed method with the result from PCSDK and only SVM. The model is trained by using 11918 frames and is tested on 3 video clips with total of 5215 frames. The accuracy is the percentage of frames that have the same state with the ground truth and the transition error is the percentage of the frames with an incorrect state change. In Table 1, although the accuracy of the proposed method will be slightly lower than SVM, it has lower state transition error.

Table 1. Comparison of proposed and other methods

| Method | Proposed Method | SVM | Intel SDK |
|---|---|---|---|
| Accuracy | 92.02% (4800/5215) | 93.90% | 73.75 % |
| Transition error | 1.25 % (65/5215) | 5.66% | 2.07% |

## CONCLUSION
We presented a method for filtering and fusing data from depth-based gesture camera and motion tracking. Our experiments confirmed the proposed method is more robust and reliable user interface than the compared methods. Its speed for our application and performance make it suitable for many applications such as 3D user interfaces and virtual reality control.

## ACKNOWLEDGMENTS
This work is supported by the Office of Naval Research through grant no. W911NF-04-D-0005-0041. The content does not necessarily reflect the position or the policy of the Government, and no official endorsement should be inferred.

## REFERENCES
1. Chang, C.-C., and Lin, C.-J. LIBSVM: A library for support vector machines. *ACM Transactions on Intelligent Systems and Technology 2* (2011), 27:1–27:27.

2. Intel Computing SDK. https://software.intel.com/en-us/vcsource/tools/perceptual-computing-sdk/home.

# A Raycast Approach to Hybrid Touch / Motion Capture Virtual Reality User Experience

**Ryan P. Spicer, Rhys Yahata, Mark Bolas and Evan Suma**

USC Institute for Creative Technologies

{spicer, ryahata, bolas, suma}@ict.usc.edu

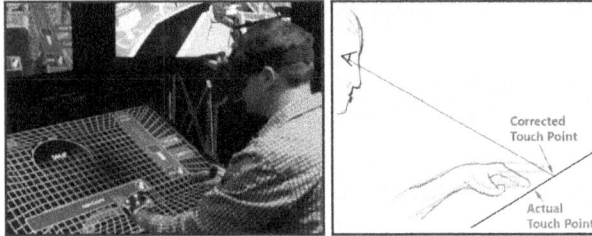

Figure 1: *Left:* Our virtual environment uses a tracked HMD and a touch screen. *Right:* Our approach, illustrated in a one-dimensional case. The physical user is indicated in green; the self-avatar as seen in the HMD in blue.

## Author Keywords

Virtual Reality; 3D User Interfaces; Touch Screens

## ACM Classification Keywords

H.5.2 User Interfaces: Interaction Styles; I.3.7 Three-Dimensional Graphics and Realism: Virtual Reality

## INTRODUCTION

We present a novel approach to integrating a touch screen device into the experience of a user wearing a Head Mounted Display (HMD) in an immersive virtual reality (VR) environment with tracked head and hands. In our system, the user's hands are tracked by a plastic rigid body with motion capture markers. This rigid body straps to the back of the user's hand. This design is convenient, but lacks fingertip tracking.

Our interaction uses an infrared multitouch overlay on a LCD display. This overlay is used for user input both inside and outside of the HMD experience (Figure 1, *left*).

Since the user's fingertips are not tracked, they may not align with the self-avatar's fingertips. This error is amplified because users may have different length fingertips, and the hand rigid bodies may not be placed identically on all users.

As a result of these errors, the user's self-avatar fingertip, as viewed through the HMD, does not consistently align with the real-world user's fingertip as sensed by the touch surface. This causes the user to perceive frustrating, inaccurate responses from the user interface.

## APPROACH

We developed a raycast-based approach to determine corrected touch locations accurate to the user's perspective in the virtual environment. When the a touch event is reported, we determine the closest self-avatar pointer finger to the touch point, based on the rigid body attached to each hand. We then check if the touchpoint is within some threshold distance, experimentally set at 10cm, of the self-avatar fingertip.

If the fingertip is within the threshold, we raycast from the user's eye point through the index finger of the user's self avatar hand. We use the intersection of this ray with the virtual screen to compute a perspective-correct touch point.

If neither self-avatar finger is nearby, we assume that the user is interacting without the HMD and hand trackers, and use the original touch point. These corrected touch points are positioned relative to the self-avatar fingertip as seen by the HMD user. Differences in hand size or finger length do not impact the results because the corrected touch point is computed relative to the self-avatar fingertip as viewed through the HMD. Likewise, differences in hand tracker position are reflected in the position and orientation of the self-avatar fingertip (Figure 1, *right*).

This approach does not require an active touch screen. We have used the system to create interactive surfaces in midair, or on blank wood and glass surfaces for haptic feedback. In this use case, we detect a touch based on the self-avatar fingertip colliding with an object in the virtual environment that represents the screen.

## LIMITATIONS AND FUTURE WORK

This approach has several limitations that may be addressed in the future. The system does not afford multi-touch gestures. Since the fingertips are fixed in the user's self-avatar, the same approach is not useful for multi-finger gestures. This challenge could be addressed by e.g. determining the transforms of other touchpoints relative to the index finger touchpoint, as determined based on the orientation of the hand.

## ACKNOWLEDGEMENTS

This work was supported by the Office of Naval Research through Award No. W911NF-04-D-0005-0041. The content does not necessarily reflect the position or the policy of the Government, and no official endorsement should be inferred.

*SUI'14*, October 4–5, 2014, Honolulu, HI, USA.
ACM 978-1-4503-2820-3/14/10.
http://dx.doi.org/10.1145/2659766.2661226

# Augmenting Views on Large Format Displays with Tablets

**Phil Lindner[1], Adolfo Rodriguez[1], Thomas D. Uram[2], Michael E. Papka[1,2]**
[1]Department of Computer Science, Northern Illinois University, DeKalb IL 60115
[2]Argonne National Laboratory, Argonne IL 60439

## ABSTRACT

Large format displays are commonplace for viewing large scientific datasets. These displays often find their way into collaborative spaces, allowing for multiple individuals to be collocated with the display, though multi-modal interaction with the displayed content remains a challenge. We have begun development of a tablet-based interaction mode for use with large format displays to augment these workspaces.

## INTRODUCTION

While large-format displays are commonly used for displaying scientific visualizations, interaction with them remains a challenge. We seek to improve this interaction using a tablet PC as a lens through which additional data about the visualization can be presented.

Large high-resolution displays make it possible to view a dataset at its native resolution. This allows for all the fine details within the data to be shown in the correct positional context, and avoids the need to pan and zoom. For example, the entire dataset of a climate visualization can be viewed in full fidelity on a large format display. That same dataset displayed on a desktop would require a user to zoom in to see the full fidelity and potentially lose track of his position in the global state. We are now interested in the next evolution of the large-scale display space: how to add additional information without spoiling the space for others. Using the climate visualization example, a user may be interested to see additional detail about the underlying data, such as numeric representations of the temperature for a particular region or some lightweight statistical data.

We will describe an environment that we have been prototyping using a pair of applications—one is tablet-based and the other runs on the large format display system—that cooperate to display an image with embedded location coding, and interprets these location codes to show additional or alternate data at that location (which could be an image or region-specific data).

## DESCRIPTION

Our test scenario includes a 2x2 tiled display for displaying visualization images, and an iPad for interpreting the location on the screen and displaying a related visualization image. To achieve this, we decorate the image on the

display with QR codes which encode their horizontal and vertical location. With a distance range of one foot to five feet, we determine the required number and separation distance of QR codes on the tiled display to ensure that one code is always visible to the camera. When the iPad is held vertically in front of the display, images are read continually from the camera and the QR codes within the images are decoded to obtain the location. From the location and size of the codes, the iPad application computes the region of the image that is visible to the camera, and zooms and pans its image to the corresponding location. The display application indicates the viewing rectangle by drawing it on-screen to aid user orientation within the image when it is not immediately obvious from the image context.

In our test scenario (Figure 1), we produced visualizations of multiple variables of a cosmology simulation. The visualization image, displaying matter density, is presented on the large format display. The second image, a visualization of dark matter density, is loaded by the iPad application. When the iPad is held in front of the screen, it determines the portion of the matter density image that is visible to the camera, and displays the corresponding region of the image of the dark matter density. In this mode, the tablet acts as a lens, revealing related information within the context of the initial visualization source.

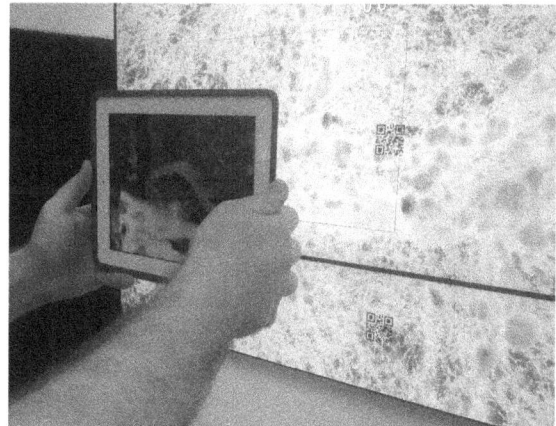

**Figure 1. Using a tablet as a "lens" to view dark matter density data corresponding to the visible region of a matter density image.**

## FUTURE WORK

This initial work has been done as a proof-of-concept. We plan to extend it by improving the tracking performance, further obscuring or completely concealing the QR codes, and using the tablet to display additional data about the visible region.

# Hidden UI: Projection-based Augmented Reality for Map Navigation on Multi-touch Tabletop

**Seungjae Oh**
POSTECH
oreo329@postech.ac.kr

**Hee-seung Kwon**
POSTECH
aruno@postech.ac.kr

**Hyo-Jeong So**
POSTECH
hyojeongso@postech.ac.kr

## ABSTRACT

We present the development of the interactive system integrating multi-touch tabletop and projection-based Augmented Reality (AR). The integrated system supports the flexible presentation of multiple UI components, which is suitable for multi-touch tabletop environments displaying complex information at different layers.

## Author Keywords

Projection-based AR; Multi-touch Tabletop Interaction

## ACM Classification Keywords

H.5.1 [**Multimedia Information Systems**]: Artificial, augmented, and virtual realities; H.5.2 [**User Interfaces**]: Interaction style, Graphical user interface (GUI).

## INTRODUCTION

Recently, projecting visual information on various physical objects and human body has gained its popularity as a new interaction approach, and has been applied to various fields such as medical imaging, education, and computer interface [1, 2]. In this research, we combine multi-touch tabletop and projection-based AR to support clear visualization of tabletop information and interaction. Projection AR serves as UI overlaid to a user's hand. Simultaneously, the projection system can provide ambient information to users. By doing so, it is possible to solve interaction problems in multi-touch tabletop contexts, such as hand occlusion, ambiguity of gestures, and interference of multiple UI elements. We developed a map navigation system, as a prototype of the suggested interactive system to demonstrate its core functionalities.

## INTERACTION STYLE AND SYSTEMS

Our hardware system consists of two primary components. The first component is a 10-point multi-touch tabletop with a 46-inch IR touchscreen and a PC. The screen resolution is 1920x1080 with touch resolution of 4096x4096. The second component is a Panasonic PT-CW330, hyper short focus projector (1280x800). The short focal length simplifies the hardware set-up compared to previous systems. Rendering surface of the projector was aligned to the tabletop display precisely. On the software side, our application was implemented with

Processing. We used the simple multi-touch toolkit (SMT) of Processing for multi-touch implementation and Unfolding map library for map navigation.

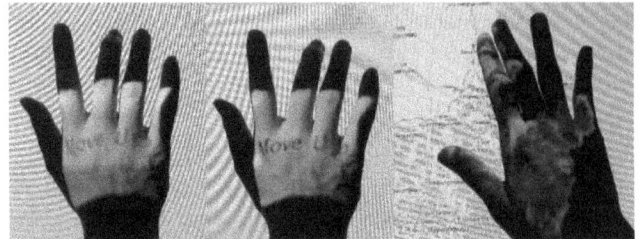

Figure1. a) UI button interaction and color feedback (left) b) Display of contextual information. Users can select to see a duplicated map or overlaid information (right).

Several UI elements like buttons, taps, and markers are presented through the projector, which is an efficient way to maximize the usage of the display surface due to less interference of UIs. Projected Hidden UIs are visible only when a user hand appears over a specific surface area. Since our system provides a drag-and-drop functionality of UI positions, there is no restriction on the positioning of the Hidden UIs. Users can handle UI elements more easily and intuitively because presenting the expected action of UI elements on their hand moderates potential occlusion problems (Figure 1a). Our projection-based AR system is particularly effective when it offers users with contextual information at multiple layers. For instance, when using the map application, users can seamlessly explore different types of projected maps (Figure 1b) or can easily switch across different types of location-based services and information (e.g., restaurants, friends, weather, etc.).

## CONCLUSION

In this research, we demonstrate the user scenario of the interactive information surface with hidden UIs implemented with projection-based AR. Further work involves the verification of efficiency and effectiveness of the suggested tabletop environment.

## REFERENCES

1. Harrison, C., Benko, H., Wilson, A.D. OmniTouch: wearable multitouch interaction everywhere. In *Proc.* UIST 2011, ACM Press (2011), 441-450.

2. Sodhi, R., Benko, H., Wilson, A.D. LightGuide: projected visualizations for hand movement guidance. In *Proc.* CHI 2012, ACM Press (2012), 179-188.

# Author Index

www.ingramcontent.com/pod-product-compliance
Lightning Source LLC
Chambersburg PA
CBHW081533220326
41598CB00036B/6424